My People's
Passover Haggadah

My People's Passover Haggadah
Volume 1

TRADITIONAL TEXTS,
MODERN COMMENTARIES

EDITED BY
RABBI LAWRENCE A. HOFFMAN, PhD
AND DAVID ARNOW, PhD

CONTRIBUTORS

DAVID ARNOW, PhD

RABBI CAROLE B. BALIN, PhD

MARC BRETTLER, PhD

RABBI NEIL GILLMAN, PhD

ALYSSA GRAY, PhD

RABBI ARTHUR GREEN, PhD

JOEL M. HOFFMAN, PhD

RABBI LAWRENCE A. HOFFMAN, PhD

RABBI LAWRENCE KUSHNER

RABBI DANIEL LANDES

RABBI NEHEMIA POLEN, PhD

WENDY I. ZIERLER, PhD

Jewish Lights Publishing
Woodstock, Vermont

My People's Passover Haggadah, Volume 1:
Traditional Texts, Modern Commentaries

2008 First Printing
© 2008 by Lawrence A. Hoffman and David Arnow

Library of Congress Cataloging-in-Publication Data
Haggadah. English & Hebrew.
My people's Passover Haggadah : traditional texts, modern commentaries / edited by Lawrence A. Hoffman and David Arnow.—1st ed.
v. cm.
Text of Haggadah in Hebrew with English translation; commentaries in English.
Includes bibliographical references and index.
ISBN-13: 978-1-58023-354-5 (hardcover : v. 1)
ISBN-10: 1-58023-354-6 (hardcover : v. 1)
ISBN-13: 978-1-58023-346-0 (hardcover : v. 2)
ISBN-10: 1-58023-346-5 (hardcover : v. 2)
1. Haggadot—Texts. 2. Seder—Liturgy—Texts. 3. Judaism—Liturgy—Texts. 4. Haggadah.
I. Hoffman, Lawrence A., 1942– II. Arnow, David. III. Title.
BM674.643.H64 2008
296.4'5371—dc22
2007048984

First Edition
10 9 8 7 6 5 4 3 2 1
Manufactured in the United States of America
♲ Printed on recycled paper.

Published by Jewish Lights Publishing
A Division of LongHill Partners, Inc.
Sunset Farm Offices, Route 4, P.O. Box 237
Woodstock, VT 05091
Tel: (802) 457-4000   Fax: (802) 457-4004
www.jewishlights.com

Contents: Volume 1

CONTENTS

PART II THE PASSOVER HAGGADAH

A. SETTING THE STAGE

Here's What You'll Find in Volume 2

Acknowledgments

We wanted regularly to credit scholarly sources, but given the need to limit footnotes, we were unable to do so. The nature of this work, a commentary, would have required our listing several names of prominent authors over and over again, on virtually every page, making it impossible for readers to negotiate the text. We want here, therefore, to thank those who provided comprehensive scholarly treatments that we drew upon with regularity:

Baruch M. Bokser. *The Origins of the Seder.* Berkeley: University of California Press, 1984.

E. Daniel Goldschmidt. *Haggadah shel Pesach V'toldoteha.* Jerusalem: Bialik Press, 1960.

Heinrich Guggenheimer. *The Scholar's Haggadah.* Northvale, NJ: Jason Aronson, 1998.

Menachem Kasher. *Haggadah Sh'lemah.* Jerusalem: Torah Sh'lemah, 1967.

Joshua Kulp. *The Historical Haggadah*, rev. ed. (Jerusalem: Schecter Institute of Jewish Studies, forthcoming).

Shmuel and Ze'ev Safrai. *Haggadat Chazal.* Jerusalem: Karta, 1998.

Joseph Tabori, The *Passover Haggadah.* Philadelphia: Jewish Publication Society, 2008 (forthcoming).

_____. *Pesach Dorot.* Israel: Hakibbutz Hameuchad, 1996.

To learn more about their works, please see our annotated bibliography.

The authors of the commentaries represent a panoply of contemporary scholars, all students of the Haggadah text, and all committed to a life of prayer, but representative of left, right, and center in the Jewish world. As editors, we could not ask for a more scholarly and helpful group of colleagues; we are indebted to every one of them, who, together, have made the editing of this Haggadah a joy.

These wonderful colleagues are matched by the many others who have been of help. Stephen P. Durchslag opened up his massive private collection of Haggadot to us, providing many of the illustrations in these pages; more, he shared his knowledge of and love for them. We hope we have conveyed both in these pages. Laurel Wolfson, at the Hebrew Union College–Jewish Institute of Religion (HUC-JIR) Klau Library provided Haggadah illustrations from the library holdings. We are grateful to her and to the Klau Library for sharing these resources, especially during a period of library transition when time to help anyone was indeed scarce. Thanks also to Avner Moriah, illuminator of *The Moriah Haggadah;* Rabbi Marc D. Angel and KTAV Publishing House, who graciously permitted use of Rabbi Angel's rendering of *Bendigamos* that was published in *A Sephardic Passover Haggadah* (Hoboken, NJ: KTAV Publishing House, 1988); and Ruth

ACKNOWLEDGMENTS

Weisberg, illustrator of *The Open Door: A Passover Haggadah*, for generously permitting us to reproduce some of their work. We also appreciate the help of Dr. Jay Rovner, manuscript bibliographer at The Jewish Theological Seminary of America, in understanding a fascinating but complex caption in an illuminated manuscript we've reproduced as an illustration. Student rabbis Jill Cozen Harel and Rachel Kort were superb and reliable research assistants. Tamara Arnow, Zevik Zehavi, and Rabbi Reena Spicehandler provided invaluable assistance in proofreading the Hebrew text of the Haggadah. Rabbi Miles B. Cohen helped refine the text with his careful eye and profound understanding of Hebrew grammar and typographical conventions.

Some of the contributors to *My People's Passover Haggadah* would like to acknowledge assistance they received from particular individuals.

Carole B. Balin acknowledges: Drs. David Ellenson, Eric Friedland and Wendy Zierler for their guidance and suggestions; Tina Weiss at the New York Campus and Daniel J. Rettberg at the Cincinnati Campus of the Klau Library HUC-JIR; Dean Ruth Weisberg for her willingness to let us reproduce her image of the "Four Children" from Sue Levi Elwell, ed., *The Open Door: A Passover Haggadah* (New York: Central Conference of American Rabbis, 2002), and for giving generously of her time. Thanks to the "mighty staff" at Joseph Jacobs Advertising Co., especially Elie Rosenfeld and David Koch; and to Stephen P. Durchslag, for use of his first rate Haggadah collection.

Daniel Landes acknowledges: Aaron Katchen, member of the Pardes Kollel, and Trudy Greener.

Wendy Zierler acknowledges: Marcie Lenk, who as a study partner explored a variety of sources that appear in this work; Debra Griboff, research assistant; Dan Rettberg and Tina Weiss of the HUC-JIR libraries; and the students of her seminar on Exodus and the Haggadah, HUC-JIR, Spring 2007.

Lawrence Hoffman thanks Dr. Blake Leyerle for insights on the Greek symposium; Drs. Paul F. Bradshaw, Frank Henderson, and Gordon Lathrop, who provided generous help regarding the relationship, historical and theological, between the Passover Seder and early Christian liturgy; and his teachers who introduced him to the *Haggadah* while he was a student: Drs. Leon Liebreich, Eugene Mihaly, and Jakob Petuchowski, *zikhronam liv'rakhah*.

David Arnow acknowledges the invaluable assistance of Rabbis Elie Kaunfer, Jeffrey Hoffman, Burton L. Visotzky, and of Gloria Jackel, Barry R. Mark and Elliott Malki, student rabbi Noah Arnow, Adam Arnow, the encouragement of Joan and Robert Arnow, and above all, of Madeleine Arnow, whose support was unending!

How fortunate we were to depend on the wonderful people at Jewish Lights who supported this volume energetically. Emily Wichland handles all publication details with the kind of love and care that is rare. Stuart M. Matlins, founder of Jewish Lights Publishing, takes personal pride in the entire *My People's Prayer Book* series—as well he should. He helped conceptualize it from the start, and remains its most ardent supporter. It was with his urging that we undertook this Haggadah, a much larger project than any of the prayer-book volumes. We are grateful for the privilege of working with a publisher as astute and spiritually committed as Stuart. Finally, our thanks are due to Debra Corman, who so arduously and lovingly read and corrected the final manuscript.

Introduction

How to Get the Most Out of This Book

Lawrence A. Hoffman and David Arnow

THE ART OF JEWISH READING

I remember the day I looked at a manuscript of a prayer book that no one could identify. It had been smuggled out of Russia (then the Soviet Union), and was obviously the liturgy for Rosh Hashanah, but who had written it? And when? It was handwritten, so the style told us much, but in addition, someone had written marginal notes in another handwriting, and yet a third person had written comments to the comments—a third unknown scholar of years gone by whose name we wanted to rescue from oblivion.

Standing before the massive volume, I reflected on the sheer joy of studying a traditional Jewish text. I had seen printed versions before, but never a handwritten instance. What a wonderful habit we Jews developed once upon a time: writing a text in the middle of the page and then filling up the margins with commentaries. Every page becomes a crosscut through Jewish history. Jewish Bibles come that way; so do the Talmud, the Mishnah, and the codes. We never read just the text. We always read it through the prism of the way other people have read it.

To be a Jewish reader, then, is to join the ranks of the millions of readers who came before us, leaving their comments in the margins, the way animals leave tracks in the woods. Go deep into the forest, and you will come across deer runs, for example: paths to water sources, carved out by hundreds of thousands of deer over time. The deer do not just inhabit the forest; they are part of the forest; they change the forest's contours as they live there, just as the forest changes them, by offering shelter, food, and water. There is no virgin forest, really; it is an ecosystem, a balance between the vegetation and the animals who live there.

So, too, there are no virgin texts. They too are ecosystems, sustaining millions of readers over time. When we read our classic texts, we tread the paths of prior readers, in search of spiritual nourishment.

This analogy has served as the introduction to all ten volumes of *My People's Prayer Book*. As the series that gave birth to *My People's Passover Haggadah*, its opening metaphor on reading text fits here too—and especially here, for the Haggadah is a book not just of the Jewish *People*, but of ordinary Jewish *people*. It is a book we all own, handle, store at home, and spill wine upon! Even more than the Siddur, then, it has attracted commentary—and not just words, but songs, illuminations, new prayers, and oral traditions built up around our various tables. Pick up a Siddur and you have the history of our People writ large; pick up a Haggadah and you have the same—but also the chronicle of Jewish life writ small: the story of families and friends whose Seders have become their very own local cultural legacy.

My People's Passover Haggadah is for each and every one of these family groups looking to enrich their annual experience of Passover in their own unique way. Toward that end, we have assembled a remarkable set of contemporary voices, all of them in love with the book they comment on, anxious to share the insights that have moved them most. You are invited to share their path, and to the extent you wish, make it part of your own—while breaking new ground yourself, passing on your marginal notes to their marginal notes as well, should you wish.

THE LITURGICAL TEXT WE USE

There is no shortage of Haggadah texts, so we had to decide which one to use as our point of reference. For many reasons, we elected the version compiled by E. D. Goldschmidt (1895–1972), of blessed memory.

Until 1935 Goldschmidt served as librarian at the Prussian state library in Berlin. With the rise of Hitler, he fled to Israel, where he applied his prodigious mastery of text to preserving the Jewish People's heritage of prayer by publishing scientific editions of one liturgical text after another. They were "scientific" in that he painstakingly waded through hundreds (if not thousands) of manuscripts at the Hebrew University to compile the most authentic wording, purged of errors that had crept into the various versions of the text. Much as he mastered our entire liturgical heritage, publishing articles on the most arcane practices of this or that Jewish community, now or in the past, he remained partial to the Haggadah, completing his analysis of it in 1960. In many ways, the 1960 edition has not been surpassed. That is the text we use here.

Goldschmidt's work symbolizes also the largest Jewish project of our time: to make available the entire cultural heritage of the Jewish People. From its inception, the State of Israel has been committed, above all, to providing a safe haven for the ingathering of Jews worldwide. It was, and still is, in that regard, a Zionist state, Zionism being the historic movement, now over a hundred years old, dedicated to rebuilding and restoring a Jewish homeland, a refuge for Jews being persecuted anywhere in the world. But Zionism has always had its cultural side as well—the commitment to the restoration of Hebrew, the Jewish People's historic language; and the furthering of Jewish arts and learning. This latter goal lay behind the decision of the Hebrew University to become the official repository of every Jewish manuscript ever written—in the original, if possible, but at least in microfilm copy, if necessary. As every Jew, from anywhere in the world, could find a home in Israel, so every instance of every Jewish community's cultural creativity would find a place in Israel's national library of the Jewish People.

Goldschmidt committed his life to the ingathering of Jewish liturgy. *My People's Passover Haggadah* continues his pioneering effort at restoring the Jewish People's worldwide and centuries-old life of prayer and celebration.

We have supplemented Goldschmidt's Hebrew text with two marks—the *meteg* and the *kamats katan*. Ordinarily, the stress falls on the last syllable of each Hebrew word. The *meteg* (אַ) marks the stress when it falls on a syllable other than the last. In the Sefardi pronunciation of Hebrew, the *kamats* (אָ) has two sounds. The usual one is "a" as in father. The second one is "o" as in store. The latter is the *kamats katan*, which we have marked with a longer stem (אׇ).

The Goldschmidt text was translated by Joel M. Hoffman. The translation strives to reproduce not only the content of the original Hebrew but also its tone, register, and style, so as to bring to modern readers the same experience (to the greatest extent possible) that the original authors would have conveyed with their words. In terms of content, we assume that, by and large, words have meaning only to the extent that they contribute to sentences and concepts—as, for example, "by and large," which has nothing to do with "by" or "large."

Our dilemma is that there are two kinds of translations: word-for-word and concept-for-concept. Take the title of the Spanish book (and movie) *Como agua para chocolate*, which was translated into English literally as "Like Water for Chocolate." Unfortunately that English phrase means almost nothing, while the original Spanish reflects the belief that hot chocolate is best made with water that is almost but not quite boiling. "Water for chocolate," then, is water about to boil, and a colloquial translation of the title might run along the lines of "at the boiling point." The word-for-word translation, in this case, fails to convey the meaning of the text.

In the current volume we note similar translation difficulties in the translation notes. When a literal translation into English conveys the sense of the Hebrew, we use it. When a better concept-for-concept translation exists, we use that, frequently providing a literal translation in the notes.

Sometimes we can find no good translation. English and Hebrew may differ too greatly, our modern culture may diverge too much from the ancient one in which the Haggadah was written, or we may simply lack enough knowledge to properly understand the Hebrew. In all of these cases, we do the best we can, advising the reader of our limited success in the translation notes.

We try to reproduce a tone and register similar to the original text: formal, but not archaic; prose or poetry, depending on the Hebrew. Where the Hebrew uses obscure words, we try to do the same, and where it uses common idiom, we try to use equally common idiom. Parallel structure and other similar literary devices found in the Hebrew are replicated as much as possible in the English translation. Our translations are best appreciated if they are read in conjunction with the running commentary by Joel Hoffman that describes why one set of words was chosen rather than another.

We have not doctored the translation of the text to make it more palatable to modern consciousness. Blatant sexisms are retained, for instance, wherever we think the author intended them. And because Hebrew is not a gender-neutral language, neither is this translation. We depend upon our commentaries to bridge the gap between the translation of the original and our modern sensitivities.

It is important to realize that readers of the Haggadah often know it so well that they read into it their own ingrained understanding of what the prayer lines mean. That understanding may be informed by centuries of midrash, oral traditions passed down to us, and prior translations that make implicit judgments on what the Hebrew "really" means, rather than what it simply says. Sometimes what it "simply says" is anything but simple. It may be ambiguous or even opaque. Our translation strives to be a pure translation, devoid of secondary interpretive influences. It may at times be deliberately as ambiguous and as opaque as the Hebrew, inviting readers all the more to read the comments that explain why the translation reads the way it does.

For the Aramaic, we consulted yet another classic Haggadah—the work of yet another master liturgist, Philip Birnbaum. Back in 1949, here in America, Birnbaum labored over a Siddur that would contain the traditional liturgy in a modern scientific format. By 1953, he had published a Haggadah as well. The Aramaic sections are few and relatively straightforward; except for a few words and lines here and there that are our own, rather than create an altogether new translation, we simply borrowed his.

The variety of new Haggadot over the course of the last century astounds! Some poked not so innocent fun at Jewish power brokers; others bore pictures of immigrant families struggling with the new world. Even atheists who despised religious ritual used the ritual of the Seder to express that revulsion. Hundreds were typed during World War II, by Jewish soldiers in England's Palestine Brigade, taking time out for a Seder that celebrated the possibility of their Zionist dream. Every modern Jewish denomination has produced several. These and others are also our topic here.

Essays, Commentaries, and Their Sources

My People's Passover Haggadah begins with a collection of essays that reflect on the Seder from diverse points of view. The first presents the favorite metaphors of our contributors to answer a deceptively simple question: "What is the Haggadah, anyway?" Others explore the Seder from a historical perspective, examining its ancient origins and character, its relationship to Christianity, the laws and lore of the Seder plate, the role of the Seder in the context of changing Jewish identity, the evolution of feminist critiques of the Haggadah, modern Haggadot published by our official denominations, and the history of the all time most widely distributed Haggadah—The Maxwell House Haggadah.

The heart and soul of *My People's Passover Haggadah* is its choice of commentaries that surround the text. Translator Joel M. Hoffman explains his choice of words, provides alternatives, and compares his own translation with others. Carole B. Balin surveys a selection of the modern Haggadot to which we referred above, looking at the last two hundred years to see how their writers agonized over attempts to update this book of Jewish books for modern times. Marc Brettler comments on the way the Bible is embedded in the Haggadah. Neil Gillman and Wendy I. Zierler provide theological reflections on what the Haggadah might mean, should mean, could mean, cannot mean, or must mean—even if we wish it didn't. Gillman confronts the many tough theological questions raised by the Haggadah. Zierler's feminist commentary is an especially important breakthrough in that it surveys Haggadot created over the decades since feminism emerged in the 1960s. Alyssa Gray presents a snapshot of a world rarely available to English readers, the *Rishonim*, our medieval commentators up to the sixteenth century, and Daniel Landes gives us the Halakhah of the Seder, both the rules by which this sacred liturgical drama has traditionally been carried out and the reasoning behind them. Lawrence Kushner and Nehemia Polen offer a kabbalistic commentary, adding wisdom from the world of Chasidic masters, as does Arthur Green, whose commentary we have labeled "Personal Spirituality" for reasons that we think will readily become apparent to the reader. David Arnow surveys the world of classical midrash. Lawrence Hoffman presents a history of the Haggadah, with some theological reflection as well. Our commentators thus present an enormously broad spectrum of Jewish thought. This is indeed our entire People's Passover Haggadah.

The historical commentary had to deal with the fact that the Goldschmidt text we use was intended only for Ashkenazi Jews—more specifically, the Ashkenazi version common in eastern Europe, often under the influence of Elijah ben Solomon of Vilna, known as the *Gra*, or Vilna Gaon (1720–1797). To balance the picture, this commentary sometimes cites Sefardi practice also. But the word "Sefardi" has two distinct meanings.

Nowadays it usually describes Jews whose liturgy was influenced by Chasidism and the specific brand of Kabbalah initiated mostly by Isaac Luria (the *Ari*) in sixteenth-century Palestine. But "Sefardi" can also mean the old Spanish-Portuguese custom carried by Jews from Spain in 1492 and then brought to the Netherlands, from where it moved to England (among other places) and eventually to America as well. Whenever necessary, the commentary on the history of the *Haggadah* differentiates the two, "Sefardi" for the first and "Spanish-Portuguese" for the second.

A WORD ABOUT JEWISH LAW

Our commentators refer regularly to Halakhah (Jewish law), a topic that deserves its own introduction here since it is so essential to Judaism, but is not easily accessible to western readers. Frequently misunderstood as mere legalism, it is actually more akin to Jewish poetry in that it can approach the height of Jewish writing, the pinnacle of Jewish concern. It describes, explains, and debates Jewish responsibility, yet it is saturated with spiritual importance. Jewish movements may be differentiated by their approach to Halakhah, but Halakhah matters deeply to them all.

Halakhah addresses the proper performance of the commandments, said to number 613 and divided into positive and negative ones, numbering 248 and 365 respectively. Strictly speaking, commandments derived directly from Torah (*mid'ora'ita*) are of a higher order than those rooted only in rabbinic ordinance (called *mid'rabbanan*), but all are binding.

The earliest stratum of Halakhah is found primarily in the Mishnah, a code of Jewish practice promulgated about 200 CE, and the Tosefta, a parallel volume usually dated slightly later but containing early material as well—in the view of some, perhaps earlier sometimes than what we find in the Mishnah. The earliest accounts of the Seder are found in these two books, and we have provided original texts and translations of them as appendices. They are presented in columns, side by side, to allow readers to see the differences for themselves. The Mishnah version we include is especially interesting, since it is the most reliable medieval manuscript, rather than the standard printed edition, which actually includes material that "seeped" into it from the Haggadah. Because other books normally cite the printed edition, we do so throughout our volume too, but at least in the appendix, readers can see what the Mishnah probably looked like before additions, some large and some small, crept into the text that printers eventually canonized as normative.

The Mishnah is the foundation for further rabbinic discussion in the Land of Israel and Babylonia, which culminated in the two Talmuds, one from each center, called the Palestinian Talmud (the Yerushalmi) and the Babylonian Talmud (the Bavli). While dates for both are uncertain, the former is customarily dated to about 400 CE, and the latter between 550 and 650.

With the canonization of the Bavli, Jewish law developed largely by means of commentary to the Talmuds and by responsa, applications of talmudic and other precedents to actual cases. These are still the norm today, but they were initiated by authorities in Babylonia called Geonim (sing., Gaon) from about 750 to shortly after 1000 (we use the concluding date of 1038, the death of the last great Gaon, by the name of Hai). In that same era, Palestinian practice was recorded in what we now call Genizah fragments, bits and pieces of Haggadot preserved in the old synagogue of Cairo and unearthed at the turn of the twentieth century. The oldest complete extant Haggadah manuscript was found there, and we provide it also (in Hebrew and translation) as an appendix. As far as we know, ours is the first complete translation of this Haggadah.

By the tenth century, other schools of Jewish thought and practice had developed in North Africa and western Europe. Authorities in these centers are usually called *Rishonim* ("first" or "early" [ones]) until the sixteenth century, when they become known as Acharonim ("last" or "later" [ones]). The first law code is geonic (from about 750), but it was the *Rishonim* who really inaugurated the trend toward codifying, giving us many works, including three major ones that are widely cited here: the *Mishneh Torah*, by Maimonides (Moses ben Maimon, 1135–1204), born in Spain, but active most of his life in Egypt; the *Tur*, by Jacob ben Asher (1275–1340), son of another giant, Asher ben Yechiel, who had moved to Spain from Germany, allowing Ashkenazi and Sefardi practices to intertwine in his son's magnum opus; and the *Shulchan Arukh*, by Joseph Caro (1488–1575), who also wrote influential commentaries on both the *Mishneh Torah* and the *Tur* before composing what would become the most widely used Jewish legal corpus ever.

Several commentaries here draw centrally on these sources, and not just for halakhic guidance but for historical information as well. Most of what Jews have written through the ages has been halakhic in nature, so reconstructions of Jewish ritual at any stage of its development, and even the theological assumptions that underlay Jewish practice, must often be reconstructed from legal sources that purport only to tell us what to do, but end up telling us why as well.

There is no way to convey the richness of even a single one of these works, let alone the legion of other sources in Jewish tradition on which *My People's Passover Haggadah* draws: the long list of *midrashim*, the library of mystical and philosophical works, biblical and talmudic commentaries, and then commentaries on those commentaries. Most are literary, but as of the fifteenth century, more subtle commentary in the form of art became common; so within our pages, we supply a handful of classic images—from handwritten manuscripts and from printed texts, early and late. Suffice it to say that the commentaries of *My People's Passover Haggadah* access many of the greatest works of our people. To facilitate reading, we have supplied selective endnotes to many of the commentaries, and an index and glossary that defines most of the sources cited as well as the technical terms employed throughout the book.

The commentators who contributed to *My People's Passover Haggadah* represent all of us, all of *Am Yisrael,* all of those God had in mind when God said to Ezekiel (34:30), "They shall know that I, Adonai their God, am with them, and they, the House of Israel, are My people." Unabashedly scholarly and religious at one and the same time, this effort will be deemed a success if it provides the spiritual insight required to help those at Seders everywhere fulfill the Haggadah's goal—to truly experience a taste of redemption:

In each and every generation people must regard themselves as though they personally left Egypt!

Part I

Celebrating Passover

Contextual Reflections

Four Faces of the Haggadah
Top Right: Palestine, Kibbutz Na'an, 1940, Bringing in the Spring Grain Harvest.
Top Left: Cologne, Germany, 1838. Bottom Right: Chicago, Illinois, Lazar's Kosher Sausage Factory, 1940s. Bottom Left: New York, The Central Conference of American Rabbis (Reform), 1923.

What Is the Haggadah Anyway?

Lawrence A. Hoffman

Sometimes things are so familiar that we take for granted what they are. The Haggadah is the book of prayer we use for the Passover Seder, isn't it? That is its definition. But sometimes definitions are not enough. The dictionary defines "home" as "dwelling place; a fixed residence of family or household." But that hardly helps us make sense of such Americanisms as "Home, home on the range," "home-free" in a game of tag, college "homecoming," a baseball player who "steals home," and Robert Frost's assurance that "Home is the place where, when you have to go there, / They have to take you in." More than we need definitions, we need metaphoric ways of thinking. Definitions are semantic technicalities. The most important parts of life are not lived technically. It turns out to be very useful to ask what, other than by definition, a Haggadah is.

If we make the mistake of thinking it is just a book for the Seder, we are likely to make the mistake of leading a Seder as if it is the act of serial reading out loud—and unless the book is written poetically and the readers practiced in dramatic delivery, we all know how boring that can be. Many Seders are aborted because they are on their way to an early death by boredom anyway.

The Haggadah is indeed a guide to the Seder, but there are all kinds of guides. Military guides measure the terrain with battles in mind. Historical guides review battles of the past but a whole lot more as well. Religious guides rehearse sacred memories, whether or not they led to battles. Moral guides apply lessons of conduct to the terrain of human behavior, not to physical space at all. So what kind of guidance does the Haggadah provide? The answer to that question determines how we think about and celebrate the Seder. But an answer is impossible without thinking metaphorically.

Seders are meant to be lived experiences, not historical treatises, and metaphors are things we live by.[1] So we asked contributors if there was a metaphor for the Haggadah that defines how they "live" their Seder. The rest of this essay presents the ones we received. But metaphors (or similes—I lump them together here) are slippery things. Both "love" and "hot water" are things you metaphorically can be in, and even though they sometime overlap, they are meant very differently. Drawing the right lesson from a friend's observation that you are in love depends on your not confusing the two.

I provide no comment to the authors' own words. To some extent they explain what they mean. To some extent they leave that open to readers' speculation.

Those of us who offer our favorite metaphors hope they will be useful as guides. We hope they animate your Seder by determining how you lead or participate in it and by opening up conversations during it.

Here (in alphabetical order by contributor's last name) are metaphors that some of us find helpful in understanding what the Haggadah is.

"The Haggadah Is a Cubist Composition": David Arnow

Imagine what we'd see if Pablo Picasso had painted the saga of Exodus about a hundred years ago, just when he was helping to create cubism.

He'd break apart his subject into planes, rotate them, then reassemble them so that we could see the whole from multiple points of view. Individual facets, sometimes jarringly juxtaposed, would generally contain a recognizable feature, but we'd see the Exodus in a new way, albeit somewhat confusing. And if we gazed at such a work in the early twentieth century, we might marvel at the artist's creative freedom.

The Haggadah is not so different. Rejecting standard narrative, it presents us with an ensemble of interlocking facet-like passages and ritual acts. Each one refers to an important aspect of the story but relates to adjacent sections in a seemingly disjointed fashion. In part, that's because eighteen hundred years ago the Mishnah instructed us to recount the Exodus at the Seder by making a midrash on several verses from the Book of Deuteronomy that contain an especially succinct version of the Passover story. The root of this word, *d.r.sh*, means to expound or to search out new meanings from ancient Scripture, and the midrashic spirit infuses the Haggadah. One rabbinic sage described the midrashic process this way: "Turn it [Scripture] and turn it, for all is contained within it" (M. Avot 5:22). This is exactly what the Haggadah does to the biblical Exodus. And the process has continued for almost a millennium as the Haggadah's evolution superimposed newer facets onto old ones.

"Turn it and turn it …" That's what the cubists did. So did each generation of compilers and readers of the Haggadah—a liberating experience, to be sure, and a fitting one for a text that celebrates the journey from slavery to freedom!

"The Haggadah Is a Filter": Marc Brettler

The Haggadah is, of course, by and large a retelling of the biblical story of the Exodus from Egypt. It quotes and paraphrases many biblical passages, yet, it is far from a representative summary of the biblical stories; instead, it is a particular selection of these texts. It is much like looking at an image using a filter that highlights particular features while making others disappear. The bulk of the Haggadah is from the classical rabbinic period, so it uses a classical rabbinic filter.

This explains, for example, why, in narrating the plagues against the Egyptians, the Haggadah uses the version found in Exodus, with ten plagues, rather than the different retellings in Psalms 78 or 105—in this filter, Torah texts were made more visible than those from Psalms. Filtering is also seen in the insistence that the first-born were killed by God rather than an angel. Exodus 12:23 makes it very clear that beside God, there was some agent called "the Destroyer" involved: "Adonai will protect the door and not let the Destroyer enter and smite your home." But that perspective is filtered out, perhaps in a desire to give God more power or to conform to rabbinic notions of monotheism. Similarly, two divergent traditions about when Passover begins, on the New Moon (e.g., Exod. 23:15) or midmonth (e.g., Lev. 23:5), are known from the Bible, and the former is filtered out, leaving only the latter.

The most famous filtering, of course, concerns the protagonist of the story. In the Bible, God and Moses often work in tandem; this is seen, for example, in the very striking verse after the parting of the sea in Exodus 14:31, "they had faith in Adonai and His servant Moses." Except for his presence once in a biblical quote, however, Moses is absent from the Haggadah—he is filtered out. The Haggadah is, therefore, not so much a retelling of the Exodus story as it is a reworking of the biblical texts as seen through a classical rabbinic filter.

"THE HAGGADAH IS A TEXTBOOK": NEIL GILLMAN

The Passover Seder is a class, with the Haggadah as textbook and the Seder leader as primary instructor. This metaphor stems from the notion that the *mitzvah* to be fulfilled at the Seder is to tell the story of our people's redemption from bondage. The method of instruction is thoroughly up-to-date in that it uses not only words but also choreography (sitting and standing, opening and closing doors, holding up different symbolic foods, searching for the *afikoman*) and other forms of experiential learning (consuming different foods, dripping the wine with our fingers, and music). Also unusual is that the participants can be both students and teachers; the learning is thoroughly democratic, as befits the experience of freedom.

The Haggadah textbook, moreover, is never complete; it is always in the process of formation. The printed text is simply the point of departure, and every class is encouraged to edit the book as the class progresses, to omit and/or to add to the received text. Though each Seder is roughly the same, no two are identical, and even the same family's Seder may change from year to year as the participants change.

"THE HAGGADAH IS THE SCRIPT FOR A SACRED DRAMA": LAWRENCE A. HOFFMAN

Liturgy in general is sacred drama—sacred because of the way it is "performed" and the personal stake the performers have in performing it. It is clearly "theater": people play roles (getting an *aliyah*, opening the ark), they wear costumes *(tallit* and *kippah)*, and they have assigned lines to chant or read out loud. Unlike ordinary drama, however, it is not performed for an audience. The performers and the audience are one and the same. They do not just "play" the roles; they *are* the roles, and they take the roles so seriously that they internalize them as their identities. When the actress playing Lady Macbeth leaves the theater, she is not expected to murder someone on the way home; when Jews put down their Haggadah, they *are* expected to have a heightened Jewish identity and to be more attuned to their Jewish responsibilities. People, that is, who leave the Seder and ignore the plight of the homeless have missed the point.

The Haggadah is the Seder's dramatic script. But scripts come relatively open or closed. In closed scripts, the playwright determines everything; director and actors get almost no leeway at all. Open scripts give over the play to the interpretive capacity of those who plan and play it. The Haggadah changes through time, and its enactment varies from year to year. The printed text looks fixed but its performance is open.

Dramas have shape and direction; they are stories that establish a problem and then solve it in the end. The Haggadah presents the foundational story of how we got here, and as its problem, it asks, implicitly, why it matters if the Jewish People continues. Each year demands its own compelling solution. That is why its script remains open and why, also, we have to reenact it year after year. If it comes out exactly the same as the year before, we have failed our dramatic duty. If we finish the Seder knowing for certain why the age-old tale of Israel's origins informs the people we are and the lives we pledge to lead, then, and only then, can we conclude *Dayyenu*—that, and only that, is enough.

"THE HAGGADAH IS A RIDDLE": LAWRENCE KUSHNER

The Haggadah is obviously not the story of how we got out of Egypt. It's a feature-length riddle. As anyone can see, it's a centuries-long hodgepodge of midrashim, songs, customs, laws, and stories—some of which even contradict one another. (Questions come before the events they question. Matzah was slaves' bread; no, it was first baked in haste. Except for a single biblical quotation, Moses' name is never mentioned. Why is Deuteronomy 26:9–10 omitted from the interpretative sequence?) The real question (and therefore the core pedagogic experience) is how on earth can one make a coherent and linear story out of such a haphazard mess? To which I would respectfully reply: sort of like real life.

"THE HAGGADAH IS TRANSFORMATION": NEHEMIA POLEN

In the Bible, the central focus is the paschal lamb, its slaughter and consumption in a sacred, precisely regulated meal. In the Haggadah, the central act is text study—the fluid, creative, transformative text study known as midrash, which freely juxtaposes and rearranges biblical verses to disclose and provoke new layers of meaning. Engagement in this midrashic process links the generations even as it beckons for new voices to emerge. At the first Passover, Moses told the children of Israel, "You shall not go out [*lo tets'u*] of the entrance to your house until morning" (Exod. 12:22). By contrast, the Haggadah tells us, "Go out [*tsei ul'mad*] and learn"—that is, "go out" from conventional ways of seeing the sacred text. Aspire to new ways of seeing, of learning, of teaching. You will thereby be freed to see your life in new ways as well. This freedom will invite your children to ask, to answer, to join the endless chain of voices. Welcome to the Seder.

Passover in the Bible and Before

David Arnow

More than half a century ago an article on the origins of Passover began as follows: "As is well known to all Old Testament scholars the Hebrew *Pesach* offers not only one of the most central problems but also one of the most debated within the field of O.T. research. Worked through over and over again it has not yet found its definite solution—and it probably never will, owing to its complicated nature given already in the sources themselves."[1] Some fifty years later, the scholarly language of that assessment seems stilted. But its content remains as true as ever. Scholars have made great progress in unraveling the history of Passover's origins, but whether we have a final and definitive solution remains to be seen. The complications are far from trivial.

When (for example) was the original festival celebrated? Exodus 12:17–18 prescribes a Feast of Unleavened Bread for the evening of the fourteenth of the month, "for on this very day I brought your ranks out of the Land of Egypt." A bit further we read, "You go free on this day, in the month of Aviv [*b'chodesh ha'aviv*]" (Exod. 13:4). But in biblical Hebrew, *b'chodesh ha'aviv* can mean the "month" of Aviv; the "new moon" of Aviv, that is, the beginning of the month; or possibly "the season of ears," that is, the season when barley begins to ripen, not a specific date.[2]

Where was the paschal offering to take place? Passages from Exodus describe a family-based ritual. "Each of them shall take a lamb to a family, a lamb to a household" (Exod. 12:3). Later, Moses instructs the heads of the clans, "Go, pick out lambs for your families, and slaughter the passover offering" (Exod. 12:21). By contrast, Deuteronomy (16:2) mandates that the offering be made "in the place where Adonai will choose to establish His name," that is, the Temple in Jerusalem.

One or two festivals? Leviticus (23:5–6) describes what sound like two distinct holidays: "In the first month, on the fourteenth day of the month, at twilight, there shall be a passover offering [*pesach*] to Adonai, and on the fifteenth day of that month Adonai's Feast of Unleavened Bread [*chag hamatzot*]." But Deuteronomy (16:2–3) instructs us, "Slaughter the Passover sacrifice [*pesach*].... Eat nothing leavened with it." Deuteronomy seems to have combined the Passover sacrifice *(pesach)* and the Feast of Unleavened Bread *(chag hamatzot)* into one and the same event.

Traditional commentators harmonize the differences between texts to produce a picture of unchanging continuity. Most scholars, however, argue that the Bible represents an amalgam of originally separate sources, each one reflecting practices from different locations and historical periods. First we'll consider the biblical Passover as a fusion of two ancient festivals and then we will explore its possible origins in light of New Year's festivals in the ancient Near East.

THE FUSION OF TWO ANCIENT FESTIVALS?

Julius Wellhausen (1844–1918), the great German Protestant Bible scholar, is best known for his contribution to what is called the Documentary Hypothesis—the view that the Torah is a finely edited version of what were once several diverse documents composed over time. This once (and still, in some circles) heretical perspective actually originated among traditionalist Jewish commentators who had trouble harmonizing differences in reports and who noticed internal inconsistencies in the biblical text. Very few scholarly hypotheses have proved as durable as this one. Though still undergoing constant scrutiny and fine-tuning, it remains the dominant paradigm governing almost all academic study of the Bible. Wellhausen was the genius who brought the theory to maturity. He was also the person who most shaped scholarly opinion on the origins of Passover.

He argued that sacrifice found its roots in the need for secure access to "fruitful soil ... the basis at once of life and religion."[3] The biblical Passover must have evolved from the fusion of two ancient types of sacrifice: *pesach*, exemplifying pastoral bounty, and *matzot*, representing agrarian abundance. Abel's sacrifice of firstlings from his flock illustrates the first. Cain's offering "from the fruit of the soil" embodies the second.

Nomadic families slaughtered their *pesach* offering, a firstling from the flock, at sunset in the spring when the lambing season had ended and shepherds were about to set off to summer pastures. To ward off evil spirits, blood from the animal was smeared on the entrance of shepherds' dwellings. A Muslim ritual called *fidya*, "redemption" or "ransom," shares some of the same elements: sacrificing and eating an animal at a time of transition and smearing thresholds with blood. (*Fidya* is cognate with פדה, a Hebrew verb that appears in the Exodus legislation demanding redemption of the first-born [Exod. 13:13].) In this context, *pesach*, the meaning of which scholars have debated, can reasonably be defined as "protection."[4]

Following Kings David and Solomon, the Land of Israel was divided into the north (Israel) and the south (Judah). *Pesach* may originally have been more widely practiced in the south, where seminomadic animal breeders were more prevalent than in the agriculturally richer north. In the north, greater emphasis fell upon a spring grain festival, *matzot*, celebrated near the full moon before the harvest. The biblical injunction to celebrate Passover in the month of Aviv is important. In modern Hebrew, *aviv* means "spring." But in the Bible, *aviv* refers to the stage of a grain's ripening when it remains tender and produces a white milky substance when squeezed.[5]

Just when barley had begun to ripen, farmers held a sacred feast to ensure a rich harvest—of the nearly ripe barley and of wheat, still some weeks from maturity. For farmers there could scarcely be a more vulnerable moment. Passover marks the beginning of the dry season in Israel, liturgically noted in later times by the change from the prayer for rain to the prayer for dew. But with the weather turning warm, too much heavy rain brought various types of fungal disease that could devastate the crop. 1 Samuel (12:16–18) calls on God to punish sinful Israel by sending thunder and rain in "the season of the wheat harvest."

Celebrated at local sanctuaries with grain from the previous year's harvest, the festival of *matzot* marked the time after which the community could begin to consume the new crop, probably toasting it, because it remained green. Leaven, or sourdough, was avoided to prevent symbolic contamination of the still vulnerable new crop.

Over time, these agrarian rituals were given new interpretations, linking them to pivotal events in Israel's sacred history narrative. Wellhausen believed that the Pilgrims' Prayer (Deut. 26:5–10), a declaration recited by farmers when they brought offerings of first fruits to the Temple in Jerusalem—and now the basis of the Haggadah's midrash on the Passover story (see *My People's Passover Haggadah*, Volume 1, p. 1)— represents a good example of this process. Tersely recounting the wandering Aramean's descent into Egypt, enslavement, and eventual redemption, the prayer concludes: "He brought us to this place and gave us this land, a land flowing with milk and honey. Wherefore I now bring the first fruits of the soil which You, O Adonai, have given me" (Deut. 26:9–10). Wellhausen concludes, "Observe here, how the act of salvation whereby Israel was founded issues in the gift of a fruitful land."[6] As the offering of first fruits was linked to the Exodus, so too what had formerly been a sacrifice to safeguard the flock was connected with the story of God's striking the Egyptian first-born and sparing those of the Israelites. Smearing blood on doorways—once a protective device against demons—came to signify the blood of the paschal sacrifice that the Israelites daubed on their doorposts so "Adonai will pass over [*pasach*] the door and not let the Destroyer enter and smite your home" (Exod. 12:23).[7] Unleavened bread acquired a new historical identity: "bread of distress" (Deut. 16:3).

Many scholars agree that these two spring rites were combined, transformed, and historicized under Josiah, who ruled the Southern Kingdom of Judah from 640 to 609 BCE.[8] Judah had become home to many northerners, who had fled the Assyrian armies that destroyed their country in 722 BCE. Josiah had even briefly reconquered the Northern Kingdom, which still remained home to a significant portion of his population.[9] Both of these factors supported the creation of a festival that unified northern and southern ritual practice.

Most important, however, Josiah initiated a far-reaching religious reform that included centralizing all forms of sacrifice within the Temple in Jerusalem and eliminating rival local sanctuaries. The language of Deuteronomy, a book thought to reflect Josiah's era, proclaims a new order: "You are not permitted to slaughter the passover sacrifice in any of the settlements that Adonai your God is giving you; but at the place where Adonai your God will choose to establish His name, there alone shall you slaughter the passover sacrifice …" (Deut. 16:5–6).

Biblical accounts of Josiah's Passover underscore its novelty. Josiah "commanded all the people, 'Offer the Passover sacrifice to Adonai your God as prescribed in this scroll of the covenant.' Now the Passover sacrifice had not been offered in that manner in the days of the chieftains who ruled Israel, or during the days of the kings of Israel and the kings of Judah" (2 Kings 23:21–22). Bernard Levinson highlights the revolutionary nature of the new approach:

> The insistence that the Passover should be a sacrifice performed at the central sanctuary—of all places—completely annuls its original identity as a slaughter that took place at the threshold of the family domicile. The authors of Deuteronomy remove the rite's original clan focus to make it instead the constitutive national holiday, with each family observing it simultaneously at the central sanctuary. Passover, as the holiday in which the family members were originally forbidden from leaving their residence (Exod. 22), under pain of death, now becomes an observance which the citizens are forbidden to celebrate at home.[10]

Deuteronomy also embodies another noteworthy development. Whereas Exodus (23:17 and 34:23) and Deuteronomy (16:16) both specify that "all your males" are to participate in the three annual Pilgrimage Festivals, the latter also speaks more inclusively: "You shall rejoice before Adonai your God with your son and daughter…. Bear in mind that you were slaves in Egypt, and take care to obey these laws." (Deut. 16:11–12). As the historicization of the festival took hold, it is not difficult to imagine children asking questions about the meaning of the Passover pilgrimage and parents telling them the story of the Exodus.[11]

2 Chronicles (35:1–19), a later source that reveals a clear priestly interest, illustrates another phase in the centralization of Passover. Here, as in Ezra (6:20), another source that highlights priestly concerns, it is the Levitical Priests who slaughter the paschal sacrifice. What Exodus describes as an offering to have been sacrificed by the heads of families had become an act performed on their behalf by officials of the Temple. Blood from the offering, once smeared on the Israelite's doorposts, was now dashed on the altar. These innovations continued to influence practice, but only up to a point. The Mishnah (Pes. 5:5–6) vividly describes rows of priests rapidly passing basins containing the blood from the paschal sacrifice from hand to hand until it reached the altar, where it was sprinkled against its base. But the Mishnah is equally clear that these offerings were slaughtered not by Levitical Priests, but by the people *themselves*, as had been the case in earlier days of the ancient rite.

AN ANCIENT NEW YEAR'S FESTIVAL?

Now that we've considered Passover's origins from the perspective of the fusion of two ancient festivals, we can turn to the position that views the festival's roots in the New Year's rituals common in the ancient Near East.[12] Although they differed from one another, these celebrations shared many of the following characteristics: they fell near the vernal equinox, banned leaven, featured animal sacrifices, and often involved various blood rites. This theory maintains that the paschal offering and the Festival of Matzot were always elements of a single ritual. Indeed, these ancient festivals regularly combined elements reflecting pastoral and agrarian traditions.[13] For example, the New Year festival held in Phrygia, an ancient kingdom in what is now central Turkey, mourned the death and celebrated the resurrection of Attis, the god of vegetation, who was also known as a shepherd.

The parallels between Passover and these ancient New Year's festivals include a remarkable "coincidence" of timing. Rather than linking Passover to the somewhat movable time of the harvest, many passages in the Bible specifically tie it to the month of Aviv, when the spring equinox occurs.[14] The Bible calls it the *first* month of the year. Ancient New Year's rituals extended over a week or more. The Babylonians, for example, celebrated *Akitu*, an eleven-day festival held in early *Nisannu* (whence the Hebrew *Nisan*). The duration of this festival corresponds precisely to the interval from God's instruction that the Israelite household's select a lamb for the paschal sacrifice on the tenth of Nisan to the completion of the Festival of Unleavened Bread on the twenty-first of the month.[15]

In order to ensure health and good fortune, it was essential to carry out New Year's rites in a state of extreme ritual purity. Leaven, associated not just with bread's rising, but, more importantly, with its rot and decay, had to be stringently avoided lest it contaminate the New Year's sacrificial offering and the ripening cereal crops. The biblical injunction (Exod. 12:10) to eat the offering in a single evening and to burn any remains may likewise reflect the fear of decay and ritual impurity.

Ancient New Year's rituals included several other practices that may have left their imprint on the development of Passover. These included recitation of the community's version of the creation story, a tale that often involved the victory of its god over various rivals. Passover's recounting of the creation of the Israelite people and the triumph of its God over Pharaoh reflects a variation on that motif. These ancient rituals also included a journey from the city to the desert in which participants dressed in costumes. This expressed the desire to flee from the evil spirits and contamination that remained behind in the cities, as well as a wish to search out the gods associated with bountiful harvest. Although this ritual finds more concrete expression in Sukkot (another harvest time), it obviously remains present in Passover as we recall the flight from Egypt to the desert. The Book of Exodus (12:11) describes the appropriate costume for the journey: "This is how you shall eat it: your loins girded, your sandals on your feet, and your staff in your hand...."[16]

These, then, are some of Passover's origins. But sacred times, like sacred spaces, do not arrive ex nihilo. Sacred places often enjoy a spiritual authority that precedes that of their current occupants. Saint Peter's Basilica in Rome stands upon the site of an ancient temple dedicated to Cybele, mother of the Phrygian gods.[17] Holy seasons are no different. It is not accidental that Passover falls near the full moon of the vernal equinox, a sacred moment throughout the ancient Near East. Call it the lure of tradition or the pragmatics of marketing, the hoariest of our religious rituals stand on even older footings. Those foundations still inform the contour of the rituals built upon them, although their underlying contributions only become apparent when we dig beneath the surface.

The importance of Passover lies not in the purity of its ancient origins, but in its capacity to adapt, and thereby to remain an unending source of hope for the prospect of redemption—regardless of the obstacles that beset us.

Passover for the Early Rabbis

Fixed and Free

David Arnow

Eighteen or nineteen hundred years ago, celebrations on the night of Passover had evolved to the point that if you happened upon one, you'd say, "Okay! It must be Passover. And this must be a Seder!" But you would hardly have encountered a traditional Seder as we know it today. To get a sense of what those early Seders were like, we can turn to the Mishnah, a law code or teaching manual compiled around the year 200 CE in the Land of Israel. The Mishnah contains a sketch of what we can definitely recognize as a forerunner of our Seders—some of the rituals it prescribes and the words it contains are identical to those found in the Haggadah. Here we'll explore the Mishnah's vision of the Seder, highlighting the brilliant balance it struck between elements that were fixed versus those that were left open for spontaneous creativity. But before we can truly appreciate the Mishnah's approach, we must briefly consider what the celebration of Passover involved in earlier times, particularly with regard to one of the signal elements of the Seder as we know it, the requirement to recount the story of the Exodus.

The Seder is largely a post-Temple phenomenon. Jews did keep Passover before that, of course, but earlier sources describing the festival dwell on the sacrifices and make no reference to telling the Passover story. If such a "telling" did occur, it must have been highly spontaneous, as far as we know following no rules—just the opposite of our Seder, a Hebrew word meaning "order."

For example, writing in the first century CE, Philo described the celebration: "And each house is at that time invested with the character and dignity of a temple, the victim being sacrificed so as to make a suitable feast for the man who has provided it and of those who are collected to share in the feast, being all duly purified with holy ablutions. And those who are to share in the feast come together not as they do to other entertainments, to gratify their bellies with wine and meat, but to fulfill their hereditary custom with prayer and songs of praise" (Special Laws II:148).[1] Josephus, writing somewhat later in the same century, describes the sacrifice of vast numbers of offerings, which were later consumed by groups of between ten and twenty pilgrims (The Wars of the Jews 6:9:3). But neither Philo nor Josephus mentions anything about telling the Passover story.

The Seder developed as an adaptation to the inability to offer the paschal sacrifice in the wake of the Temple's destruction.[2] The earliest post-Temple descriptions of the night of Passover therefore depict a relatively new, still evolving ritual. The Tosefta and the Mishnah, both from the late second or early third century, contain two such descriptions. The Tosefta has traditionally been seen as a commentary on the Mishnah, although some modern scholars, Judith Hauptman among others, have argued that the Tosefta actually contains a layer of pre-Mishnaic material that was reworked by the compiler of the Mishnah. Hauptman makes a strong argument that the Toseftan Seder represents an earlier stage in the ritual's development than that found in the Mishnah.[3] Suffice it to say, strong cases can be made for and against this position. I adopt it here because, as I hope will become clear, the Tosefta's Seder lacks an important practice contained in the Mishnah. The Tosefta includes nothing about telling the Passover story, a requirement that appears only in the Mishnah. (For a schematic comparison of the night of Passover in the Mishnah and Tosefta, see *My People's Passover Haggadah*, Volume 2, Appendix I, pp. 225–234.)

The Toseftan Seder prescribes drinking four cups of wine; reclining; eating matzah, bitter herbs, and *charoset*; and reciting the *Hallel* in full—"neither abbreviated nor expanded" (Pes. 10:8). It also mandates an all-night study session concentrating on the laws of the Passover sacrifice. Aside from the references to the Exodus contained in the first two psalms of the *Hallel*, the Toseftan Seder does not mention anything about telling the Passover story. As Hauptman speculates, perhaps the *Hallel*'s allusions to the Exodus embodied the Tosefta's limited attempt to tell the Passover story. The Tosefta also asserts that it is a man's responsibility to make his children and wife happy on a holiday and recommends doing so with wine. This source also seems quite concerned about the possibility of children falling asleep at the Seder and suggests that adults snatch matzah from one another to prevent youngsters from nodding off. Despite its concerns about drowsy children, other than the humorous spectacle of matzah snatching, the Toseftan Seder offers nothing to engage them.

The Mishnaic Seder preserves these core rituals—wine, reclining, matzah, bitter herbs, *charoset*, and *Hallel*—but adds an entirely new dimension: telling the Passover story, at least in part through a question-and-answer format.[4] Three considerations may have inspired this innovation. First, the Torah itself includes four well-known injunctions to explain aspects of the story to one's children, although it is not clear that prior to the rabbinic period these verses inspired telling children the story of the Exodus on the night of Passover.[5] The one place where the Torah does require a short narration of the Exodus involves a recitation by farmers at the Temple before the altar and in the presence of a priest—not an explanation to children. Farmers would recite a specific passage from Deuteronomy (26:5–10) known as the Pilgrims' Prayer upon bringing their first fruits to the Temple. This was not connected with Passover, but with Yom Habikkurim (literally, "the Day of First Fruits"), an entirely different festival than Passover. Nonetheless, this version of the Passover story must have been the most familiar of the Bible's many treatments of the subject. It therefore provided a readily available frame around which to weave the tale.

The second factor that may have contributed to the Mishnah's focus on telling the story of the Exodus is its assertion that "words of Torah" serve as a valid substitute for inaccessible sacrificial rites: "If three have eaten at the same table and have spoken words of Torah, it is as if they have eaten from the table [i.e., the sacrificial altar] of the Omnipresent ..." (M. Avot 3:4). Elsewhere in Jewish liturgy, that same theology explains the recitation of *instructions* on how to carry out sacrifices, which substituted for actually performing them. It thus makes perfect sense that the liturgy for the Seder has become known as the Haggadah, literally, "the telling."

Finally, in contrast to the Toseftan Seder, the Mishnah's interest in story telling reflects greater influence of the Greek symposium, a banquet in which wine—*symposium* means "to drink with"—and conversation played a special role.[6] The symposium included dipped hors d'oeuvres eaten while reclining, praises to the gods, and stylized conversation, sometimes following a question-and-answer format. Discussion focused on subjects of historical or philosophical interest and occasionally even on the significance attributed to particular foods. Plutarch (46–120 CE), a contemporary of some of the rabbis who appear in the Haggadah, cautioned against overly arcane discussion, lest it intimidate participants and reduce participation. "Our discourse should be like our wine, common to all, and of which everyone may equally partake."[7]

But the Mishnah went further than simply mandating that the Passover story be told. It modeled a flexible approach to telling the story in such a way as to engage the younger generation. The following excerpt of the Mishnah's treatment of the night of Passover features many of its innovations.

> *Mishnah Pesachim 10:4* [They] poured for him the second cup—and here the child asks, and if the child lacks understanding, his father instructs him. How is this night different from all [other] nights? For on all the [other] nights we dip once, this night twice. For on all the [other] nights we eat leavened and unleavened bread, this night we eat only unleavened. For on all the [other] nights we eat meat roasted, steamed, or cooked [in a liquid, boiled], this night only roasted. According to the child's understanding, his father instructs him. [He] starts with disgrace and ends with glory; and [he] expounds from, "My father was a wandering Aramean" [Deut. 26:5], until he finishes the entire portion.

A careful reading suggests that originally children were expected to ask their own spontaneous questions, and only if they failed to do so were parents expected to use the *Mah Nishtanah* as a prompt to point out differences between the Seder and all other nights. Indeed, the Talmud (Pes. 115b) relates an instance in which the young Abaye (later to become one of the greatest sages of the fourth century) asked why a traylike table had been removed prior to the meal, and the Seder leader responded, "You have exempted us from saying the *Mah Nishtanah*!" (Here it seems that in the absence of a child's independent query, the Seder leader recited at least the opening *Mah Nishtanah* and possibly the rest of the "questions," a responsibility later given over to youngsters. The cause of this development remains a matter of scholarly debate.)

The Mishnah also mandates that the Seder leader tell the Passover story by expounding (*doresh*, "to make a midrash", "to draw out meaning") from those well-known verses from Deuteronomy 26, the Pilgrims' Prayer. What had been precisely *recited* in the Temple on Yom Habikkurim would serve as the basis for a midrashic elaboration that a father would tell his children at the Passover table in an age when the Temple no longer stood.

Perhaps the architects of this early Seder were familiar with the Toseftan Seder and decided to improve upon it. Aside from the all-night study session on the laws of the Passover sacrifice, the Tosefta leaves us a ritual that is precisely defined, with little explicitly left to the imagination of the Seder leader or children. The Mishnah balances elements that are fixed with those left open for a more spontaneous approach geared to the level of our children's understanding.

Why did the Mishnah require a midrash on these verses as opposed to a recitation of the biblical passage? In one sense, this may reflect parallel concerns in the realm of prayer with respect to maintaining a balance between *keva*, fixed prayer, and *kavvanah*, spontaneous prayer. For instance, Rabbi Eliezer (first and second centuries) states that "one who makes his prayer fixed, has not made a genuine supplication" (M. Ber. 4:4). The Talmud explains that this refers to one who fails to introduce something new into one's prayer. Likewise, Rabbi Shimon bar Yochai, the second-century sage, warned, "Be careful [i.e., precise] when you recite the *Sh'ma* …, but when you pray, do not make your prayers fixed …" (M. Avot 2:18). The Mishnah's instruction to expound within a set biblical framework and to adjust one's exposition in response to the evolving maturity of the audience maintained freshness in a religious milieu that clearly appreciated the dangers of staleness.

It is the nature of ritual to become repetitive, and repetition means fixity. But rituals have different kinds of scripts that range from the relatively open to the relatively closed. Completely closed scripts allow no change. Completely open scripts stop being rituals. Cultures vary with regard to what they prefer. Temple culture was closed. As we saw, the Pilgrims' Prayer was precisely scripted. Rabbinic culture, however, allowed greater openness in some rituals because it was predicated on a belief in the oral Torah side by side with the written Torah. An element of openness was essential for the interpretation of the written Torah in light of how rabbis from different times and places—not to mention different personalities—understood the oral Torah. So the Mishnaic Seder is closed-scripted enough to be ritual, but open-scripted enough to emphasize the whole point of rabbinic Judaism: that Judaism is not a closed book, but an ever evolving enterprise of interpretation mediated by the rabbinic application of oral Torah.

Still, it is possible that the Mishnah's instruction to expound on the Pilgrims' Prayer really intended that the Seder leader recite a preexistent midrash. If so, we can be rather sure that the Mishnah did not have in mind the complex midrash that we now find in our Haggadah. This midrash did not reach its completion until the geonic period many centuries after the Mishnah.[8] Other scholars believe that even though parts of the midrash appear only in relatively late written sources, this material may in fact be very old and was orally preserved until someone finally got around to writing it down.[9]

A sample of a different midrash on the same verses from Deuteronomy prescribed by the Mishnah is helpful. This recently discovered midrash from the tannaitic era includes an elaboration on the words "great, numerous, and powerful" that appear in Deuteronomy 26:5, the second verse of the Pilgrims' Prayer:

> "Great"—this teaches that they were all tall in stature. "Numerous"—this teaches that they were many in population. "And powerful"—this teaches that they did not die.[10]

Assuming that there were a variety of midrashim in oral circulation, we can readily imagine a father eighteen hundred years ago or so borrowing this midrash, and maybe spicing it up with others, along with one of his own, in the hopes that his tale would catch the interest of his children and keep them awake!

In requiring the Seder leader to create or collect material for a midrash, I think the Mishnah may also have understood that "the medium is the message," as Marshall McLuhan used to say. Egypt was about productivity, not creativity. The freedom with which we tell the Passover story mirrors our liberation from Egypt. In the creativity we bring to this task, we imitate God, the ultimate free creator, who, according to tradition, fashioned the world through ten utterances (M. Avot 5:1).

Alas, as the Haggadah developed, we lost the Mishnah's delicate balance: *keva* (fixity) completely overwhelmed *kavvanah* (spontaneity). The Four Questions, beloved as they are, became a prescribed recitation, as did the midrash on "My father was a wandering Aramean." The myriad commentaries on the Passover Haggadah, spanning more than a thousand years and still going strong, as these volumes indicate, have all sought to provide Seder participants with ever new insights to help restore at least a measure of the Mishnah's sense of freshness, balance, and spirit of creativity.

Lifting the Matzah
Southern Germany, 1480–1490
HUC Manuscript 444, The First Cincinnati Haggadah
Klau Library, Cincinnati, Hebrew Union College–Jewish Institute of Religion

This Bread

Christianity and the Seder

Lawrence A. Hoffman

Judaism and Christianity are like a double helix, swirling around each other through time. History, however, has not been kind to our relationship. It may not be universally true that power corrupts and absolute power corrupts absolutely, but that has often been the case with religion, so it is no surprise to find that the all-powerful medieval Church sometimes used Jews as tools to further other ambitions. And even when power came without corruption, Jews did not generally fare well, since Christian theology explicitly condemned them for denying, and even killing, the savior. His coming, in any case, had voided the Jewish covenant with God. These were annual lessons in medieval Europe, sometimes played out in murder and mayhem as part and parcel of Holy Week and the Easter season.

This was by no means the case always and everywhere. In many eras, Jews and Christians lived side by side, working, trading, and conversing together in harmony. But when they did not or, perhaps better put, whenever powerful Christian rulers or prelates preferred that they did not, it was particularly at Easter that Jews learned to fear for their lives. Nothing could be more ironic. Easter had arisen as a Christian Passover, intended only to announce the "good news."

TWO MIDRASHIC JUDAISMS

The negative side of Christian-Jewish relations has overshadowed the positive side of our history together, preventing us from seeing the opportunities available to us just because we have so much in common. It is important not to paper over our differences. But the very vitriol of our mutual distrust was possible in the first place only because we at least share things on which to differ, not the least of which being Western history itself. As I say, we are a virtual double helix, joined at the hip by circumstances that brought rabbinic Judaism and Christianity into the world together.

My thanks go to friends and colleagues Paul Bradshaw, Frank Henderson, and Gordon Lathrop for their enormous help reading and offering critiques of this chapter.

Both of us are midrashic expositions of the same holy Scriptures, what Christians have historically called the Old Testament and what Jews call the *TaNaKH* (a Hebrew acronym for *Torah, N'vi'im, K[H]'tuvim*, "Torah, Prophets, and [sacred] Writings," the threefold Jewish organization of what is also called [among Christians] the Hebrew Bible). There were many "Judaisms" in the several centuries surrounding the year of Jesus' birth, most of them historical dead ends—the Sadducees (a Jewish sect identified by Josephus) and Dead Sea Scroll Judaism, for example—and any number of takes on Christianity that were eventually labeled heresies, relegated, similarly, to be victims rather than victors of history. The Sadducees are a particularly instructive case, because they insisted on treating the Torah literally, a strategy doomed long-term to failure in the face of inevitable historical change. The survivors of that remarkable era of religious creativity and intensity are rabbinic Judaism and Christianity, both of which avoided literalism by adopting a midrashic approach to Scripture.

The Rabbis conceived of it as the application of an oral law given side by side with the written one on Sinai, a parallel source of revelation that arrives at new truths buried in old words. Christians used the life of Jesus as their touchstone. Perhaps the most pertinent example for this book derives from the instructions in Exodus 12:46 and Numbers 9:12 to eat the *pesach* whole: "Do not break any bone of it." The Gospel of John 19:32–36 therefore insists that the two men who were crucified alongside Jesus had their legs broken, while Jesus was removed from the cross intact, so that "Scripture might be fulfilled: 'None of his bones shall be broken.'" The Rabbis would have used these verses to prove an interpretation of another one—as in the Haggadah itself, where they interpret one verse (Deut. 26:8), "Adonai brought us out of Egypt," to mean "not by an angel and not by a seraph and not by a messenger, but rather the Holy One of Blessing himself," and then prove it with a second verse (Exod. 12:12), "As it says, 'I will pass through the Land of Egypt.'" John does not do that. Instead of juxtaposing two verses, he compares the Bible with the life of Jesus. In this case, John cites the verses demanding that the paschal lamb be whole to prove that Jesus is the new paschal lamb.

The years following the Temple's destruction in 70 CE thus saw two parallel developments, one that became Judaism, the other Christianity. Only then do we find Jewish authorities who bear the name "rabbi" and who redefine Judaism by arriving at the rabbinic categories of thought that we now take for granted. And only then do we get Christians writing Gospel accounts of Jesus' life, arriving at similar categories that would forever define Christianity. The Rabbis remind us regularly of the prior scriptural basis for what they say; so do the Gospels. Neither "take" is more "authentic" than the other. They are equally sincere efforts to go beyond pure literalism and arrive at a creative solution to the issue that faces all religions, always: how to apply ancient lessons in a changing environment that challenges the age in which the original revelation occurred and to do so by retaining religion's essence—its ability to address ultimate human problems that never go away no matter how times vary. A magnificent case in point is the way both Judaism and Christianity reinterpreted the biblical Passover.

Nowadays the "Christian" year seems centered around Christmas. But that is not so much the *Christian* year as it is Madison Avenue's idea of what the Christian year ought to be. It is Easter, not Christmas, that defines Christian faith. That is because it was Jesus' death, not his birth, that came to matter. His birth became only retroactively important.

For Jews, too, calendrical priorities have shifted. Nowadays we put greater emphasis on Rosh Hashanah and Yom Kippur, the High Holy Days, which we consider the beginning of our year. The biblical new year, however, was the month of Passover, from which everything important followed. "At this time we were saved from Egypt, and at this time we will ultimately be delivered again," said Rabbi Joshua. His younger contemporary, the church father Origen agreed, "We were saved at this time in Egypt, so are saved at this time now." They differed only on whether that deliverance had begun or not.

So both Christians and Jews intensified their effort to understand the Exodus from Egypt as the basis for all that followed. The result for Jews was the Seder. The result for Christians was, first of all, the Eucharist; and then the development of Easter itself, with its Seder-like vigil the night before. Our two religions are defined by these two parallel ritual events, especially (for our purposes) the Seder meal and the Eucharist.

JESUS' LAST SUPPER

The New Testament begins with four accounts of Jesus' life called gospels. The first three, Matthew, Mark, and Luke, are similar and are called, together, "the synoptic Gospels." Mark is the earliest, composed shortly after 70; Luke and Matthew were written about twenty years later. The fourth Gospel, John, is quite different. It is a later creation, from about 120, and it expressly revolves around theology. Theology is important to the other three Gospels too. But they can be described as theology through history; the Gospel of John is frequently history through theology.

All four Gospels relate Jesus' last supper to a Seder. For the synoptics, it *was* a Seder, and Jesus was the new lamb of God. Jesus' most ardent evangelist in those years, the apostle Paul, who wrote from about the 40s to the 60s, announces, "Our paschal lamb, Christ, has been sacrificed" (1 Corinthians 5:7).

The Book of Exodus details the Israelites' preparation for the night when the first-born Egyptians were to be killed. On the tenth of the month, they chose a lamb and held it in wait until the night of the fourteenth; they then slaughtered it, smeared its blood on the doorways of their homes, and roasted and ate the carcass. That lamb was the original paschal sacrifice, in Hebrew, the *pesach*, from which we get the Hebrew name of the holiday (interpreted as being from the Hebrew root *p.s.ch*, meaning "pass over," since God "passed over" [*pasach*] the homes with lamb blood on the doorways). Christianity called Jesus the second *pesach*. That is why Jesus' death was so important;

he too had been slaughtered. As Israel was saved by the blood of the Passover lamb, so Christians (as the new Israel) were saved by the blood of the second. The first Jewish Christians, therefore, kept a Seder at its regularly appointed time, the fourteenth of the month of Nisan; but for them, it marked the death of Jesus, their new lamb. (As the lamb that comes directly from God, he is also called explicitly, "the lamb of God" [John 1:29, 30]).

Eventually that date was seen to pose a difficulty for the theology that saw Jesus as the paschal lamb. The Gospels agree that Jesus was resurrected on a Sunday, the third day after the crucifixion. Counting back from Sunday (as day one) meant that Jesus was killed on a Friday, and the last supper had to be the Thursday night before that. The Gospel of John therefore concluded (correctly) that if Jesus was the second paschal lamb, his last supper could not have been a Seder, since the paschal lamb had to be slaughtered the day *of* the Seder, not the day *after*. If it had been killed on crucifixion day (Friday), then whatever Seder Jews kept that year would also have been on Friday, the night *after* Jesus and his disciples had dined together.

Some Christians kept a Seder (as all Jews did) on the fourteenth anyway, linking their celebration (like the Jewish one) to the death of the original lamb that had taken place that day. For them, it was the *death* of Jesus (as the second lamb) that mattered.

Other Christians began to celebrate the *pascha* (as they called it, the Aramaic word for *pesach*) on the Sunday after Passover, because Sunday was their usual weekly day of worship. But since Sunday had been resurrection day, emphasis began to fall not on Jesus' death but on his resurrection. Since this practice was in the central city of Rome, it had powerful influence elsewhere. What Christians seem to have originally meant by "keeping pascha" was an all-night fast and vigil at which the great stories of salvation were told, centering in the story of the Exodus and the story of the death and resurrection of Jesus, followed by the Eucharist held at dawn, as the breaking of the fast. The original Jewish date of Nisan 14 remained the practice for a shrinking minority, however, who were called Quartodecimans, after the Latin word for "fourteen."

Practice varied until 325. Emperors before Constantine had treated Christianity as an upstart and, therefore, by Roman standards, an illicit religion. His predecessor, Diocletian, is especially remembered for persecuting the new faith. Constantine changed all that and was even reported by the contemporary church historian Eusebius to have converted to Christianity on his deathbed. Whatever the historical facts about Constantine, his death in 321 spurred Christianity forward to become a world religion. Four years thereafter, the church held its famous Council of Nicea, where, among other things, it declared the Quartodeciman practice heretical. The Jewish calendar has lunar months but a solar year, so any monthly date (the rotation of the moon around the earth) falls at different yearly times (the earth's rotation around the sun). Passover eve (the fourteenth day of Nisan) is almost always the fourteenth day of the first month after the spring equinox. Easter Sunday was therefore set as the first Sunday after the fourteenth day of the first month after the equinox, a deliberate effort to eliminate "Judaizing" among the faithful, and the night vigil was moved to Saturday night through Sunday morning.

THE EUCHARIST

Historically speaking, the background for the Eucharist, the defining Christian ritual, is "the Lord's Supper." With relatively minor differences regarding detail, all three synoptic Gospels agree with an earlier letter sent by Paul to the Christians in Corinth:

> The Lord Jesus on the night he was betrayed took a loaf of bread, and when he had given thanks, he broke it and said, "This is my body that is for you. Do this in remembrance of me." In the same way he took the cup after supper, saying, "This cup is the new covenant in my blood. Do this, as often as you drink it, in remembrance of me." (1 Corinthians 11:23–25)

The parallel accounts of the Gospels and of Paul differ somewhat, but if the order of events given here is accurate, we can regard it as a proper Jewish meal. "Taking bread" would coincide to the *Motsi*; the cup after dinner is the cup drunk at the Seder as part of the *Birkat Hamazon*, the Grace after Meals (originally, wine was drunk then at all meals). The interpretation, by contrast, is strikingly novel. We will see later why the disciples (who were Jewish) were not as puzzled by it as Jews today generally are. For now, however, all we need to know is that Jesus' last words (classically known as "the Institution Narrative") are the focus of Church ritual. Its history is enormously complex, with as much written on it as any other topic in the history of scholarship. But the general idea is easily conveyed.

Jews in the first century divided their worship between synagogue and home. Early Christians did likewise. Home ritual frequently, back then, took place in more or less formal eating groups called *chavurot* (singular: *chavurah*), and included wider circles than simply those who happened to live together. Following Greco-Roman custom, people met in such fellowship groups to celebrate festive occasions, including holidays and life-cycle events. The meals were called *symposia* (singular: *symposium*). Jesus' last supper with his disciples was a symposium. So too were rabbinic Seders. Christians held celebratory symposia on Saturday nights, recollecting Jesus' last words and continuing the important meal fellowship of the movement around Jesus before he was killed. Such a meal was sometimes called *agape*, best translated as "love-feast." Very early on, it came to be accompanied by the ritual prescribed by Jesus at his last supper, called a *eucharist*, from the Greek word meaning "to give thanks."

By the fourth century, Christians had also developed a set of daily prayers, not just a *eucharist*. As Jews have formal services three time daily, so too did some Christians. By the late fourth century (when monasticism first appeared), they were encouraged to pray five times a day. These daily prayers have gone by many names, depending on what church we are talking about. Episcopalians call them "the Daily Offices." Roman Catholics call it "Liturgy of the Hours." Meanwhile, a regularized schedule of biblical readings with accompanying prayers, the whole thing called "Liturgy of the Word," became part of worship as well. Some Protestants (Baptists, for example) have infrequent Eucharist. Others (Quakers and the Salvation Army) hold no Eucharist, although they make much use of it metaphorically, for example, calling every meal the "Lord's Supper." But for those who hold it regularly in church, a full Sunday morning worship is likely to have a Liturgy of the Word followed by the Liturgy of the Eucharist. The topic relevant to Passover is the Eucharist.

The Eucharist had not always been a Sunday morning thing. It began quite naturally as part of the *agape* meal, in which diners did what Jesus had asked them to. Over time it was set free from the meal, and but for a few monastic references in the early Middle Ages, the meal itself died out. The Eucharist was retained independently but moved to Sunday mornings, along with the developing Liturgy of the Word. Sunday is not the only day when these are found; but it is the most significant day, since it represents the Church's equivalent of the Jewish Sabbath, the day of Jesus' resurrection, known as "the Lord's Day."

Slowly but surely, prayers were attached to the Eucharist too. Jews would recognize some: the Lord's Prayer, for example, and the Christian version of the Jewish *K'dushah* ("Holy, holy, holy …"), called the *Sanctus*, both of which found their way there by the late fourth century. The main prayer invoked Jesus' words from the last supper (the Institution Narrative), providing the intent of what is otherwise just action: sharing bread and wine. For centuries, the "bread" was exactly that: bread. Nowadays, for Roman Catholics and some Episcopalians, it is a waferlike substance— unleavened bread, in the belief that this is what Jesus would have used at the Passover. Exactly what happens to that wafer (or bread) at the time of its being eaten is the subject of debate that separated western Christians into warring factions—the Roman Catholic Church on one hand, the various branches of Protestantism on the other. But our tale of the Eucharist vis-à-vis Judaism antedates the Protestant Reformation, so except for the discussion of current issues facing Jews and Christians at Easter time, all we have to worry about are developments in the pre-Reformation Church—prior, that is, to the great divide into Roman Catholicism and the various Protestant alternatives. (It is commonplace to think of today's Roman Catholic Church as the proper historical continuation of the past, and to see Protestants as break-off groups, but it would be more accurate to say that both Roman Catholicism and Protestantism derive from the same historical circumstances of the sixteenth century—just as we ought to think of contemporary Orthodox and Reform Judaism as parallel attempts to mold a common medieval past into responses to the nineteenth century.) For convenience sake, we are omitting the history of Orthodox Churches, not because they are unimportant in their own right, nor because Jews in the Mediterranean and eastern Europe were not affected by them, but because the focus of this book is the European experience that most Jews in the West take as their heritage.

It all goes back to what Jesus meant when he said, "This is my body," and its relationship to things said and done at the Seder.

"THIS IS MY BODY"

No one can claim to know the fullness of what those words mean. As we have them in the Christian Scriptures, they are reasonably opaque. Theologians wax eloquent in explaining them, not necessarily with historical exactitude in mind, but for purposes of determining the religious intent that is inherent in celebrating the Eucharist. Historians too have offered several "takes" on the subject, some of them patently wrong, many others probably correct—in part. The part for us to consider is the connection between Jesus' words and the way the Seder is conducted. Even if Jesus' last supper was not a Seder, it was a symposium meal, and it followed the basic ritual of ancient Jewish meals, the Seder being the one we know most about.

If we keep in mind the Jewish culture in which Jesus and his disciples lived, it is hard to imagine anyone listening to Jesus' words without reacting with surprise, befuddlement, and even shock. Why didn't the disciples ask for a clarification? How is it that they seem to have understood him? What did they think Jesus meant?

It is possible, of course, that Jesus never said the words in question; they may have been falsely attributed to him by people who composed the Gospels some forty years and more after Jesus died. That is unlikely, however, and in any event, we have a record of the words in Paul's letter to the Corinthians only twenty to thirty years afterward. Since Paul too does not seem surprised that Jesus could have said such a thing, we must assume that his words made sense to Jews in Jesus' time, who passed them along with some understanding of the context in which they were uttered. The problem is that we cannot comprehend what Jesus could have meant without that context, and context is never explained by people who just live it and assume that everyone else knows it as well as they do. We have a record, then, of what Jesus said, but not the context that made it credible. It is that context that we have to reconstruct.

The main point is the identification of bread with Jesus' body and wine with his blood. The latter is relatively easy to understand, since red wine is a natural symbol for blood. Remembering that Jesus was considered the new Passover offering that saved through its blood, we can well understand why Jesus, expecting to die the next day, might have pointed to the lesson his followers should learn from his blood shed on the cross. "I am the way to salvation," he was inferring. "That means my death is like the death of the ancient Passover offering. My blood is spilled to save you."

Though Jews today may not recognize it, this is a clear parallel with Passover. The rabbinic Seder of antiquity also uses wine as a symbol for blood. The sweet dip called *charoset* is typically made from red wine, which the Bible calls "blood of grapes." The Yerushalmi (Jerusalem Talmud, codified c. 400 CE) calls *charoset* "a remembrance of the blood," meaning the blood of the lamb that saved Jews in Egypt. Jesus may have known that interpretation, which is probably not novel to the Talmud, but much older.

Charoset was already important in the time of the Mishnah (c. 200 CE), which debates its status as a commandment (a *mitzvah*). Three foods are commanded by the Bible: the paschal lamb *(pesach)*, unleavened bread *(matzah)*, and bitter herbs *(maror)*; since *charoset* is not among them, there is no reason why that question should even have been raised. *Charoset* had begun as a simple and unimportant condiment to go with the leaf of bitter romaine lettuce that served as *maror* ("bitter herbs"). But once it was there, it attracted symbolic significance. The blood of sacrificed animals was an important symbolic element in the sacrificial system generally. If *charoset* was "in remembrance of the blood" of the original *pesach*, it might well have been considered a *mitzvah* by some. When Jesus identified the wine as his blood, he was attaching a meaning that would have sounded perfectly compatible with the way Jews already thought of wine.

More challenging is the identification of bread as "my body." We might understand Jesus saying this about the Passover lamb, and indeed, if the last supper had been a Seder, he might have. But he pointed to bread. Why? The answer must be that by Jesus' time, bread was identified with the lamb; bread too had become a symbol of salvation.

As the "staff of life," bread was an obvious choice as an item to be used symbolically. Indeed we use it that way all the time, as when we say "to earn our daily bread" (by which we mean more than bread, certainly); or when we say "bread" or even "dough" (from which bread is made) to mean "money"—as in, "Give me some bread, man!" The amazing thing about bread is that it is both the most basic staple and the most difficult food to come by. Most of us just buy it from a bakery, without even considering the effort that goes into plowing, sowing, reaping, sorting, threshing, winnowing, grinding, sifting, mixing, kneading—and only then, baking it! Especially in antiquity, when rainfall was unpredictable and there was no mechanized equipment, bread was an apt symbol of the harsh circumstances of life with which human beings have had to contend ever since being expelled from the Garden of Eden. That the Rabbis thought this way is established by a midrashic discussion of the trees that Adam and Eve encountered there (*Gen. Rab.* 15:7). Since the Bible already raises the question of the trees in the Garden of Eden, the Rabbis speculate on the nature of the trees that the garden contained. As paradise, Eden must have had all sorts of unexpected vegetation.

Their interest was not just antiquarian. Eden, they believed, was paradise past, which rabbinic theology thought would be recaptured in the world-to-come, a time when, once again, we would not have to work by the sweat of our brow. So the Rabbis identify the perfect tree as a bread tree. Imagine: bread growing right out of the ground!

The Talmud discusses this very thing, in its conversation over the standard blessing over bread, *Barukh … hamotsi lechem min ha'arets*, "Blessed [is God] … who brings forth bread from the earth." The earth as we know it yields only grain, not ready-made bread—but real bread grows from the ground in paradise. So the Rabbis say, explicitly, that the blessing does not refer to bread growing from the earth *nowadays*; rather, it means that *hu atid l'hotsi lechem min ha'arets*, "In the future"—that is, in the messianic times ahead—"God will bring forth bread from the earth" (*Gen. Rab.* 15:7; Ber. 38a–b).[1] The Passover sacrifice released the Israelites from exile in Egypt, and the bread of each meal looks ahead to freedom from the exile that is intermediate between Eden and the world-to-come. Passover, the time of the first redemption, prompted thoughts of a future era, the second (and final) time when once again bread would grow directly out of the ground.

Christian sources of the time buttress the case made by Jewish ones. In two of the Gospels (Matt. 6:9–15; Luke 11:2–4), Jesus recommends a prayer to his disciples. We know it as "the Lord's [i.e., Jesus'] Prayer." But Jesus was a Jew, so its content is fully Jewish—similar, in fact, to the Jewish *Kaddish*, which had nothing to do with mourning at first, but was instead a messianic prayer for the coming of God's ultimate rule on earth. Unlike the *Kaddish*, the Lord's Prayer contains four petitions: (1) forgive our sins; (2) lead us not into temptation; (3) deliver us from evil; (4) give us our daily bread. The first three requests are clearly on topic: we are not admitted into the messianic "Kingdom of God" if our sins are not forgiven, if we give in to temptation, and if we do evil. Why, however, would a prayer for redemption ask for "daily bread" unless it meant the bread that God will bring forth from the earth *(motsi lechem min ha'arets)* only in the messianic future?

Like the Talmud, the Church fathers say explicitly that "bread of the future" is exactly what is meant here. It is "supernatural bread," says one; more precisely, adds another, "It is bread for the Kingdom ... not the bread that enters the body, but the bread of eternal life."[2]

In the first and second centuries then (and even afterward), bread was like the Passover offering (the *pesach*)—both were symbols of salvation. The current use of *afikoman* still presupposes this meaning. Four halakhic rules govern its use: (1) it cannot be eaten until nightfall; (2) it must be eaten before midnight; (3) it must be consumed while we are full; (4) it must be the last food we eat that night. All four rules were originally applied to the *pesach* and then transferred to the *afikoman*.

In addition, we have the practice of breaking a piece of matzah as the Seder begins and announcing, "This is the bread of affliction." Surely that parallels what Jesus did when, before eating, he "took a loaf of bread ... broke it, and said, 'This is my body.'" The only reason the disciples were not astounded is that they knew how the Passover meal began—with a "This is ..." statement, acknowledging bread as the stand-in for the Passover lamb. To be sure, even if Jesus' supper was not a Seder, it featured bread at the beginning, just as the Seder did. So in a clever play on words, Jesus borrowed the common ritual words, "This is" and followed them with "my body," since he was the new lamb, which everyone knew bread symbolized.

"IN REMEMBRANCE OF ME"

A second problem with understanding Jesus' words is his instructions, "Do this in remembrance of me." It should come as no surprise that remembering in some sense should be associated with Jesus' last meal—not if the meal was being pictured as a Seder, at any rate, since Exodus 12:14 says, explicitly, "This day shall be to you one of remembrance: you shall celebrate it as a festival to Adonai throughout the ages, you shall celebrate it as an institution for all times." But in what sense did Jesus mean it?

He might, perhaps, have meant it superficially, the way a composer might ask her family to listen to a particular piece of music "in remembrance of me." But that meaning of "remember" depends on a historical understanding that the Rabbis did not have. They saw their time on earth as just an interim measure until the messiah arrived. Details of history in the period until then were thoroughly insignificant. With ritual, at least, when they said "remember," they had a deeper meaning in mind.

Jews nowadays have lost that meaning because we did not preserve a theological vocabulary to talk about things. Classical Jewish literature is legal, not theological. By contrast, Christians (under the influence of Hellenistic thought) did explore theology, which became as native to Christianity as law is to Jews. That is the problem with words like "salvation" and "grace." Jews today are apt to find both terms too Christian for comfort. But the ideas for which they stand were original to Judaism. It is just that they survived only in Christian writings, so that we do not think of them that way. The Hebrew words are in our ancient texts, but being uncomfortable with "salvation" and "grace," we usually translate them as "deliverance" and "compassion," words we can handle because they sound more secular. This is a mistake. It robs us of our own theological heritage. The only reason Christians were able to use both "salvation" and "grace" is that they learned the ideas from Jews.

It reminds me of the true story of a woman who went to a funeral of a Christian friend and heard Psalm 23 read aloud. "I wish we Jews had literature like that," she said. If we only hear Psalm 23 in Hebrew that we do not understand and then hear Christians (and Christians alone) say, "The Lord is my shepherd, I shall not want," we are apt to think that beautiful line is indeed Christian. But, of course, it is not. So, too, *chonen* is a perfectly fine Hebrew word that means "grace," just as *y'shu'ah* and *g'ulah* refer to supernatural acts of God that "save" us. Sometimes, then, Jews can learn what our own prayers mean by perusing early years of Christian theology.

When Christians speak of ritualized remembering, they mean the Greek word *anamnesis*, implying the telescoping of time so that past, present, and future come together. That is why the Haggadah tells us to act "as though we ourselves went out of Egypt." It is meant more literally than the subjunctive case in English would imply. By *anamnesis*, our memory projects us truly back into Egyptian slavery, making us and it one.

The Jewish word for "remember" is *zekher* (or sometimes *zikaron*). That too has more precise meaning than the ordinary English suggests. *Zekher* operates not just through time but also across space and even lines of logic (see *My People's Passover Haggadah*, Volume 2, L. Hoffman, "Remembering [*zekher*] the Temple according to Hillel," pp. 126–127). That is why we can ask God to remember us. Could God possibly forget? Of course not. So "remember" is better understood as pointing ourselves out to God—exactly what we do in ritual. We become present to God in such a way that God's attention is directed toward us, as if to say to us, "You are never forgotten; you are in

God's sight; God cares for you." When Jesus asks his disciples to "do this in remembrance of me," he is asking them to act in such a way that they point the way toward him, for he is the way to salvation. In like manner, the Sefardi Seder ends by saying of the *afikoman*, "Remembering the Passover offering that was eaten while full" (*zekher l'pesach hane'echal al hasova*). What is meant is that the final piece of matzah points the way to the original *pesach*, the sacrifice that once saved us. What Jesus is to Christians, the original paschal lamb is to Jews.

TWO PARALLEL SYMBOL SYSTEMS

As two religions arising out of biblical Judaism at the same time and place, and doing so with a similar midrashic mind-set, Christianity and Rabbinic Judaism developed parallel symbol systems:

- *Covenant:* For Jews, a covenant began when we were saved from Egypt, culminating in the giving of Torah at Sinai. For Christians, a second covenant, marked by the coming of Christ, superseded the first covenant made at Sinai. (We will see in a moment that Christians today do not necessarily believe in supersession.)
- *Testament:* For Jews, there exists a single testament, a written record of the covenant. For Christians, a *new* testament, or Scripture, acknowledges the new means of salvation. The two Christian testaments refer to the two covenants—the giving of Torah and the coming of Christ, respectively—both of which are acts of God's grace.
- *Sacrifice:* Jews consider themselves saved from Egyptian servitude by a sacrificed lamb. Christians see Jesus as the second lamb. In both cases, we are saved by the blood of the lamb.
- *Sacrificial ritual:* Jews established a sacrificial cult, intended to save us from our sins—a lesson preached expressly in the Seder at the end of *Dayyenu* (see *My People's Passover Haggadah*, Volume 2, p. 67). Christians developed a Eucharist, which is interpreted as a regularized and ritualized sacrifice celebrating and reiterating the original sacrifice of Jesus on the cross. When the Temple ended, Jews focused less on sacrifice and more on prayer. Sacrifice remained a dominant theme among Christians, however. They already regarded their prayer, and especially their eucharistic praying, as the sacrifice of praise that God really wanted, but they also saw the eucharistic ritual as a celebration of the original sacrifice of Jesus on the cross.
- *Salvation, deliverance, redemption* (parallel English words for the Hebrew *y'shu'ah* and *g'ulah*, and alluding to the point behind the whole religious enterprise): Until the year 70 CE, when the Temple was destroyed, Jews offered sacrifices as stipulated in Torah to effect atonement and deliverance. The blood was splattered on the altar, because as a sacrifice, it was the blood that saved. Christians too seek

y'shu'ah, but from Jesus, the new sacrifice, whose name in Hebrew is indeed that: *Yeshu'ah*, "deliverance."

- *Faith* or *works* (deeds): Jews and Christians differ on the way salvation is achieved. Christianity demands a life of Christian faith; Jews emphasize a life of works *(mitzvot)* that save. This is not to say that Jews had no faith and Christians no rules of conduct. Both had strong views on what to believe and how to live. What they differed on was which of the two brought salvation.
- *Covenantal meal:* At first Christians held a regular meal, the *agape*. It was eventually transformed into a repetitive meal-like ritual involving bread and wine, understood by early Christians as in some sense being Christ's body and blood. The exact status of the bread and wine, however, became the focus of bitter disagreement that caused serious disagreement among Christians. Jews have not generalized the meal into a regularized rite. Instead we have a single annual meal, the Seder. It too uses wine as a reminder of the blood of the lamb—the one slaughtered in Egypt; and bread, the matzah, which reminds us of the *pesach* (Passover lamb) that saved us in Egypt.
- *Annual reiteration of original saving event:* Jews celebrate Passover *(Pesach)*. Christians celebrate Easter (originally called *Pascha* [Aramaic for *Pesach*]). For Jews, says the *Haggadah* (see *My People's Passover Haggadah*, Volume 2, p. 73), it is "In each and every generation people must regard themselves as though they personally left Egypt." Christians believe that through their Eucharist, Jesus is actually present with them.
- *In memory of/pointing:* Jews eat matzah "in memory of the *pesach*." Christians eat eucharistic bread "in memory of Jesus." In both cases, the bread directs attention to the lamb that saves.

The history of the Middle Ages and early modern period erected a virtual chasm between Judaism and Christianity. But ritually and theologically, a remarkable parallelism has joined them together from the very beginning. What matters is how we understand this remarkable relationship.

THEOLOGY OF RELATIONSHIP

What relationship the two religions ought to have with one another is a theological decision. For much of history, Christians had enough power to demand Jewish conversion to the new covenant—or face consequences ranging from economic and social exclusion to outright death. In what is now a post-Christian era of Western history, Christians have become more open to collaboration with Jews. In the 1960s, for example, all but the most conservative Christian churches admitted their past crimes against Jews and denounced supersessionism, the doctrine that God's covenant with Christians abrogates the earlier one made with Jews.

But it was not always this way. If we are to be totally honest about the relationship between Christianity and Passover, we need to record the negative side of the relationship: animosity stirred up particularly at Easter because of the claim that Jews are responsible for killing Christ.

The best example is a homily composed by Melito, a bishop in Sardis, now part of Turkey (died c.180). In turn, this homily, combined with the form of the text in Lamentations 1:12, influenced a tenth-century Christian liturgical text that continues to be used to this day. In form it is a litany, very similar to *Dayyenu*, which some think is related directly to Melito's composition (see L. Hoffman, *My People's Passover Haggadah*, Volume 2, pp. 66–67). The following selected stanzas convey an accurate impression of the whole:

> I led you out of Egypt and you prepared a cross for your savior.
> [Refrain] My people what have I done to you? In what way have I saddened you? Answer me!
> I led you through the desert for forty years and fed you with manna, and introduced you to a very good land, and you prepared a cross for your savior.
> [Refrain] My people …
>
> ....
> I slew the Egyptian through his first-born sons, and you have delivered me to be flogged.
> [Refrain] My people …
> I led you out of Egypt after having drowned Pharaoh in the Red Sea, and you delivered me to the princes of the priests.
> [Refrain] My people …
> I opened the sea before you, and you opened my body with a lance.
> [Refrain] My people …
> I went before you in a column of fiery cloud, and you led me to the tribunal of Pilate.
> [Refrain] My people …
> I fed you manna in the desert, and you fell on me with slaps and whips.
> [Refrain] My people …
>
> ....
> I exalted you with great strength, and you hanged me at the gallows of the cross.
> [Refrain] My people …[3]

This poem is taken as being an early instance of what Christian liturgy calls "Reproaches," a liturgical addition to the Good Friday service. The anti-Jewish sentiment of the texts used in the Reproaches nowadays has been toned down some, especially by interpreting them as having nothing to do with Jews and being, instead, a reproach against Christians who fail their savior. But the object of the poems historically cannot be in doubt. Some churches omit the Reproaches. But those churches that still say them have had to face the fact that however they may be explained nowadays as addressing Christians, they *seem* to be denunciations of Jews, who were regularly charged (especially during Lent and Holy Week leading up to Easter) with denying, denigrating, and even killing Christ. During the Middle Ages, the Reproaches served as justification for Easter-time mayhem against Jewish neighbors.

Overall, we Jews and Christians have entered a third stage of interreligious dialogue. The first stage, typical of medieval days, was not dialogue, but disputation—Jews and Christians debated, but neither party had any interest whatever in learning from the other; and given the power imbalance, it was a foregone conclusion that the Christians would "win." Stage two emerged in the last half of the twentieth century, when disputation became diplomacy. We shared what we had in common and nodded respectfully when we differed, still convinced, however, that we had nothing to learn from one another. Believing that only one of us could be right, wherever we parted ways, it had to be the other party who had strayed.

Only now have we begun true dialogue: honest and open sharing of where we stand, open to the possibility that, without in any way compromising our own position, we can learn from one another, even though we cannot dictate to each other where or even if that learning may occur. Here, we see learning in both directions. Christians learned—and then transformed—an entire set of Jewish symbols. Now Jews have much to learn by recovering the original theological meaning of rituals that Christianity retained and Jews lost.

PASSOVER/EASTER CHALLENGES

That a Jew can even write an essay like this should not be taken for granted. Until relatively recently, no Jew would even want to, let alone be able to, without fear of retaliation. We have come a long way. But Passover/Easter time remains charged with historical and emotional baggage that is not easily overcome.

I have already alluded to the major challenge for Christians: confronting the Reproaches. Some churches also, though not many, still retain vestiges of a prayer for the conversion of the Jews. And during the Easter season, most churches feature the Christian scriptural readings from the Gospel of John, the most vitriolic Gospel with regard to Jews. But here, as a Jew, I reach the limit of what I can say. It is not for Jews to amend Christian practice, for Jews cannot know what this reading or that prayer means within Christian life. As Jews have halakhic boundaries that cannot easily (if at all) be crossed, so Christians too have internal limits that may prevent even the most willing of them to alter the liturgy in ways that Jews (or even Christians themselves) might prefer. I, frankly, am amazed at the extent to which most churches have responded favorably, and even radically, with regard to troublesome Easter liturgy.

A second challenge has arisen with the growing trend for Christians to keep Easter Thursday with a Seder. The week before Easter had been growing in importance for centuries. At first (by the fifth century), Good Friday, Easter Saturday, and Easter Sunday came to be seen as a single unit of three connected days called the *triduum* (Latin for "three days"). In the Middle Ages, ritual expanded bit by bit until the whole week was seen as holy, beginning with Palm Sunday. Various rituals became attached to the Thursday of Holy Week, but none of them involved reproducing an actual Seder. That is, however, exactly what many churches do now, and in good faith, hardly with the intent of co-opting a Jewish event for their own purposes. Yet some Jews see such a co-option anyway, since practices within the Jewish Seder—even those that Jesus could never have known, because they came into being centuries after his death—are given Christological meaning. How to handle this Christian attempt to replicate a last supper as Seder in a way that honors Jewish sensitivities, yet affords Christians their right to expand holy time, will take much discussion and good will.

Jews are hardly free from our own introspection. As much as medieval Christianity had little good to say about Jews, medieval Jewish liturgy experimented with prayers condemning Christians. In the worst of the lot, a *piyyut* (synagogue poem) described Jesus as "bastard son of a harlot." To avoid censorship, the poem was usually printed with convenient lacunae and eventually disappeared. One would like to believe that even had they been in power, Jews would have erased this sort of thing from their liturgical canon, but who knows? Power corrupts no matter who holds it. Still, such poems have long been jettisoned, to the point where Jews are universally shocked to discover that we even had them; the reason for getting rid of them hardly matters by now.

But one offending prayer still remains within the Haggadah. I am thinking of the after-dinner request that God "pour out Your wrath on the nations who do not know You." Most liberal Haggadot now omit it; as prayers go, it is easily scrapped, since it entered the Haggadah late in time, not until after the Crusades—as a response to Jewish deaths occasioned by them. It is hardly canonical the way more ancient prayers might be. But many modern Haggadot still include it, more out of inertia than conviction. Some do not stop to examine it at all—it is Hebrew, after all, a language most do not understand, and (to be honest) many Jews who are not familiar with the Haggadah lose heart after reading through the first half of it, then eat, and never get to it altogether. Others retain it, arguing that it is just a collection of psalm verses after all or that it has contemporary meaning when facing, say, the Holocaust. Speaking just for myself, I find that argument akin to the Christian claim that the Reproaches are really addressed to Christians, not to Jews. "Pour out Your wrath on the nations who do not know You" sounds very much like, "Have mercy for those who know You not as Thou art revealed in the Gospel of Thy son." That is an update made in the Episcopal Church in 1928 to the wording of the Anglican *Book of Common Prayer* since 1549: "Have mercy upon all Jews, Turks, infidels and heretics." In 1979 the Episcopal Church omitted that too as offensive. If dialogue is to continue, both parties have to own up to the fact that liturgy matters; it can be hateful and hurtful.

But at the same time, it can be sublime, and at its best, both the Christian celebration of the resurrection and the Jewish Seder are just that. Christians greet Easter Sunday with the triumphant cry that "Christ has risen," certain that in so doing, all who believe have overcome death themselves. Jews close the Haggadah with "Next year in Jerusalem," a messianic cry for those who take it literally, and a symbol of all that promises peace, life, and a final day of universal deliverance by those who do not. Those who experience either the Christian or the Jewish promise are likely to say, "It does not get any better than that."

The Seder Plate

The World on a Dish

David Arnow

Given the challenges of navigating the Haggadah and the many steps of the Seder, one could hardly be blamed for hoping the Seder plate might provide a refuge of sorts. After all, what could be simpler than matching up the items with the pictures or names now commonly featured on such plates? Alas, the Seder plate—what it may have included in times past, what it contains nowadays, the placement of these items, and their significance—recapitulates the complexity and long evolution of the festival itself.

The plate and its contents are significant not just because of the discussion they have engendered in Jewish legal codes and compendia of Jewish customs over the centuries. In its relationship to the proceedings of the evening, the laden plate functions as a microcosm. In Hebrew, this plate or dish is known as the *k'arah* (קְעָרָה). As we'll see, midrashic sources sometimes compare the oceans of the earth to a *k'arah*. Indeed, a talmudic expression that has found its way into modern Hebrew speaks of "turning the *k'arah* upside down."[1] It means to spoil everything, or to deny the existence of God. With that in mind, it should come as no surprise, for example, that the various arrangements of the plate are associated with some of Judaism's most fertile thinkers.

Here we will explore the origins of the plate, its contents, the traditions associated with each item, contemporary innovations involving the plate, and, finally, customs as to how the plate should be arranged.[2]

ORIGINS

The origins of the plate reach back to the removable traylike table that had been standard equipment in the Greco-Roman symposium and in Jewish formal meals as well. As guests reclined on their left side, a succession of hors d'oeuvres and other dishes were served on trays set upon table legs that were stabilized by inserting them into slots in the floor.[3] Without specifically mentioning such a tray, the Mishnah's description of the night of Passover simply states that unleavened bread, lettuce, and *charoset* are brought before the head of the household (Pes. 10:3). This omission notwithstanding, we can assume that these items were brought out on some sort of plate, platter, or tray.[4] Indeed, the Talmud recounts an incident during the Seder in which a child asks why such a traylike table was being removed before the meal had been served—and this spontaneous query obviated the need for the *Mah Nishtanah* (Pes. 115b). The Babylonian Talmud explains removal of the tray as an act deliberately geared to provoke children's curiosity.[5] A ritualized remnant of the incident reported in the Talmud appears in the directions contained in many traditional Haggadot: the Seder plate is removed before recitation of the Four Questions.

Our current Seder plate usually has six items on it: a roasted shank bone and egg, matzah (on, under, or nearby the plate), bitter herbs, *charoset*, and *karpas*. In theory, they all go back to the Mishnah, but in practice, it is not immediately evident how we got from there to here. The Mishnah (Pes. 10:3) simply says that they bring to the Seder leader "matzah, lettuce [*chazeret*], *charoset* and two cooked dishes."[6]

ROASTED SHANK BONE AND EGG

The roasted shank bone and egg have become what the Mishnah described as "two cooked dishes." Why two cooked dishes? The Bible describes two types of sacrifices in connection with Passover, the paschal offering and the "sacred offerings." With regard to the first, Exodus (12:8) mandates that "they shall eat it [i.e., the Passover offering] roasted over the fire, with unleavened bread and with bitter herbs"—two of the other items found on our Seder plate. According to Exodus, only animals from the flock (sheep or goats) could be used for the paschal sacrifice. The origins of the second sacrifice reach back to Deuteronomy 16:2, which states that the paschal offering could be drawn from either the flock or the herd (i.e., cattle). 2 Chronicles 35:13 tries to harmonize this contradiction by mandating two offerings, the paschal offering and what is called "sacred offerings." The Talmud refers to this second offering as the *chagigah* or festival offering of the fifteenth of Nisan, an obligatory sacrifice preferably offered on the first day of the holiday. But according to the Talmud, there was also an optional offering known as the *chagigah* of the *fourteenth* of Nisan. This sacrifice was a function of whether the group eating the paschal offering was small enough to be sated by it. If not, the *chagigah* would be sacrificed as well. At the festival meal the *chagigah* was consumed first (Pes. 70a), so as to allow celebrants to savor the paschal offering on a fairly full stomach.

The Talmud (Pes. 114b) thus mandated two cooked dishes at the Seder. Rav Yosef, an early fourth-century talmudic sage, provided what has become the most common interpretation of that requirement: one—now generally a roasted shank bone—commemorates the paschal offering; and the second—now a roasted or boiled egg—commemorates the *chagigah* sacrifice (probably the voluntary sacrifice that was offered on the fourteenth of Nisan).[7] But the Talmud allowed considerable leeway for fulfilling the requirement. Rava, an early fourth-century sage, preferred beets and rice;

Chizkiya (mid-fourth century) used fish—an item intermittently mentioned in sources more than a thousand years later—smeared with egg; Ravina (late fourth to early fifth century) stated that a bone with its broth would suffice

Despite Rav Yosef's interpretation of the two cooked dishes, many others arose. A common explanation held that the shank bone, *z'ro'a*, represents God's "outstretched arm," *z'ro'a n'tuyah* (e.g., Exod. 6:6). In Aramaic *beiyah* means "egg," but the word also appears in an old Aramaic expression: "God, be willing [*b'ah*] to take us out" with the outstretched arm. Others saw the egg, traditionally associated with mourning, as a doleful reminder of the lost Temple. A related custom, serving boiled eggs at the Seder, also serves as an expression of mourning for the Temple. Although eggs are a traditional food of mourning, they also symbolize spring and eternal life, all of which helps explain their connection to Passover and Easter.

Sherira Gaon (Gaon of Pumbedita, 986–1006) noted a custom of including a third symbolic cooked food—in addition to the shank bone and egg—"in memory of Miriam, as it says, 'I brought you from the Land of Egypt, I redeemed you from the house of bondage, and I sent before you Moses, Aaron, and Miriam'" (Mic. 6:4). The evocation of human beings in the redemption from Egypt—very much along the lines of the symbolism of *charoset* (see below)—challenges the dominant understanding of the Haggadah as attributing complete responsibility for the Exodus to God alone.

Sherira Gaon also connected the custom of three cooked dishes to the three mythic animals that according to midrashic traditions would be consumed in the banquet ushering in messianic times. Each of them represented one domain in creation: the leviathan (a fish from the sea), the *ziz* (a bird of the air), and *shor habar* (the wild ox). One of the earliest printed Haggadot (Soncino, Italy, 1486) calls specifically for a fish to represent the leviathan.

MATZAH (PLURAL, MATZOT)

Today, many Seder plates contain three matzot either on or beneath them. Others require putting the matzot on a separate plate or bundling them in matzah holders made from cloth. Commentators have associated the three matzot with various triads: Kohen (the ancient priestly tribe), Levi (from the tribe of Levi), and Israel (the remaining tribes); the three measures of choice flour that Abraham requested Sarah to bake for the three visiting angels (Gen. 18:6)—an event that the midrash sets on the night of Passover;[8] Abraham, Isaac, and Jacob, the three patriarchs; or the three types of unleavened bread offered for a thanksgiving offering (Lev. 7:12).

Nonetheless, just how many matzot the plate should contain—two or three—touches on arguments reaching back nearly a thousand years. The Talmud (Ber. 39b) comments, "All admit that on Passover one puts the broken cake in the whole one and breaks [them together]. What is the reason? Scripture speaks of 'bread of poverty' [Deut. 16:3]." In those days, matzah was a pliable, flat bread, like pita or even wraps. The Talmud describes using one and a half matzot, suggesting the initial presence of two in order to end up with one broken and one whole piece. Among many others, Maimonides and the Vilna Gaon followed the tradition of two matzot.[9]

The conflict arose because it had become a custom on festivals, as on Shabbat, to say a blessing over the bread with two loaves in commemoration of the double portion of manna the Israelites gathered prior to Shabbat (Exod. 16:22). For Passover this implied three matzot—two for reciting the blessing over the bread and one to produce a broken piece over which the blessing for the matzah would be recited. The *Shulchan Arukh* affirms this practice, clearly the dominant one these days.[10]

BITTER HERBS

Along with bitter herbs, some Seder plates have a space for lettuce, in ancient times considered a form of bitter vegetable. Why? In describing the night of Passover, the Mishnah (Pes. 10:3) mentions lettuce—using the Hebrew word *chazeret*—twice, first as an hors d'oeuvre and then as a bitter herb. To be precise, the standard Mishnah says: (1) "they [the servants] brought [unnamed food]; he [the Seder participant] dipped in the *chazeret*, until he got to the [main] course where they served bread. [Then] (2) they brought matzah, *chazeret*, and *charoset*.

Nowhere in the account do we even get the word *maror*! Instead, we get (in both instances) *chazeret*, which meant some kind of greens. The Talmud says they used *chasah*, the word for lettuce. So *chazeret* was a generic word for greens, including lettuce, probably romaine lettuce, which served well because it was bitter enough to fulfill the requirement of eating bitter herbs. Also, as a piece of lettuce, it could be dipped in condiments, like sweet *charoset*. The first dipping (1) evolved into the ritual of dunking *karpas* in salt water. The second (2) became what we call *maror*. But, over time, two customs developed in connection with the *maror*: first, *maror* was dipped in *charoset*; second it was eaten on matzah as part of the Hillel sandwich. The Talmud (Pes. 114b–115a) expressed hesitation about using the same vegetable more than once at the Seder and thus created room for three different vegetables. Hence some Seder plates include (1) *karpas*, (2) *maror* (these days, either lettuce or horseradish root), and (3) *chazeret*, while others leave space for only *karpas* and *maror*.

But horseradish is hardly the only acceptable bitter herb. The Mishnah (Pes. 2:6) indicates that any of the following suffice: lettuce *(chazeret)*, endive *(ulshin)*, chervil *(tamkha)*, a kind of vine *(charchavina)*, and *maror*, simply bitters.[11] The *Mekhilta D'rabbi Shimon bar Yochai*, a tannaitic midrash (i.e., pre-200 CE) notes that one sage included "even thorns and wild lettuce," while another said that palm ivy was acceptable, although he could not find anyone to join him in eating it![12]

Opinion divides about whether horseradish should be grated or not. Some held that eating ungrated horseradish could be dangerous to one's health, while others argued that grating the horseradish—changing it from its natural form—rendered it unfit for use at the Seder.[13] Apart from this, when it comes to dipping horseradish in *charoset*, an ungrated, spoonlike slice has clear advantages!

It is noteworthy that the Haggadah describes the "Hillel" sandwich of bitter herbs and matzah—only missing a morsel of the paschal offering—as a remembrance of the Temple rather than of the Exodus itself. The earliest mention of Hillel's practice appears around the end of the second century in the Tosefta (Pischa 2:22). The language of the ritual developed in the Talmud (Pes. 115a), which uses the expression "remembering the Temple according to Hillel." As the ritual functions in the Seder, we witness the extension of the symbols first connected with the Exodus to another redemptive context, the loss and rebuilding of the Temple, and by implication, to the broader stage of history.

The theme of remembering the Temple recurs often in the Haggadah—as one might expect insofar as the Seder developed as a substitute for the no longer available Temple-based paschal offering. However, commentators have pointed to another connection between the Seder and the fall of the Temple. The ninth of Av, on which we mourn the Temple's destruction, always falls on the same day of the week as the first Seder, and albeit to a different degree, both are marked by bitter memories. A fifth-century midrash comments on this, noting that the Bible uses the expression of eating *m'rorim*, "bitters," both in connection with the Exodus and the destruction of the Temple.[14]

CHAROSET

The Mishnah (Pes. 10:3) refers to *charoset* as one of the meal's appetizers but does not specify whether eating it is required or not. Since it is not one of the biblically required foods, it would seem not to be required, but a minority opinion requires it anyway. Nor were the talmudic sages in agreement as to the significance of *charoset* (Pes. 116a). One argued that it should be thick to remind us of "the mud," presumably a reminder of what the Israelites used to fashion bricks. Another held that it should contain spices "as a reminder of the straw," again an ingredient in brick making. (Subsequent commentators would recommend cinnamon or ginger, suggesting that they bore the proper resemblance to straw.)[15] Still another maintained that it should be tart like apples, in remembrance of a talmudic legend connected with the righteous women of the Exodus. These women defied Pharaoh's separation of husbands and wives, arranged to rendezvous with their husbands, then had sex with them under the apple trees, returning nine months later to the orchards to give birth (Sot. 11b). The Jerusalem Talmud mentions only that *charoset* should be murky or soft as a "remembrance of the blood" associated with the first plague or smeared on the doorposts of the Israelite home to protect them from the last plague, the slaying of the Egyptian first-born (Pes. 70a, 10:37d). It is worth noting that all these explanations of *charoset*'s meaning are phrased similarly—*zekher* (remembering, remembrances) mud, *zekher* straw, and *zekher* blood. As one scholar wrote, "The rabbinic practice of calling a set of actions 'remembrances' of the past indicates the ritual process at work"[16] (see *My People's Passover Haggadah*, Volume 2, L. Hoffman, "Remembering [*zekher*] the Temple, according to Hillel," p. 126).

KARPAS

The designation of *karpas*, that is, celery or parsley, as opposed to any other green vegetable, came about relatively late.[17] The Talmud speaks only of *y'rakot*, "vegetables." Amram Gaon (ninth century) mentions *karpas* among many other options, and Saadiah Gaon (tenth century) says that one recites the blessing over "the type [of vegetable] one wishes, so long as it is not bitter."[18] According to one scholar, the ultimate preference for *karpas* only came about through the influence of the circle of *Rashi* (1040–1105), students of the great eleventh-century French commentator. Some scholars believe that this group disseminated a mnemonic enumeration of the Seder's fifteen steps that now appears in virtually all Haggadot. *Karpas* is the third term on that list.[19]

Karpas became the object of fascinating interpretations. Chizkiah ben Manoach (fourteenth century, France) identified it with the laurel wreath worn by victorious warriors after battle, affirming Israel's ultimate victory over its enemies. He also linked *karPAS* with the ornamented tunic, *k'tonet PASim* (Gen. 37:3) that "Jacob gave to Joseph, which led to a chain of events that brought our ancestors into Egypt." The interpretation alludes to a teaching from the Talmud: "A man should never single out one son among his other sons, for on account of the two ounces of silk that Jacob gave Joseph in excess of his other sons, his brothers became jealous of him and the matter resulted in our forefathers' descent into Egypt" (Shab. 10b). Another approach read *karpas* backwards (ספרכ): *samekh*, the first letter, has a numerical value of sixty and alludes to sixty myriad or the six hundred thousand Israelite males (Exod. 12:37) who went forth from hard labor, *farekh*, the last three letters of the word.

ITEMS TO PROVOKE QUESTIONS

The Seder plate also became the repository of early efforts to engage youngsters during the evening. The Talmud reports that Rabbi Akiva used to distribute parched or toasted grain and walnuts to children "so they should not fall asleep and should ask" questions.[20] (There were precautions of course—such toasted grains could not violate the prohibition against *chamets*, for example.) Zedekiah ben Abraham (thirteenth century, Italy) says that on the Seder plate there are "toasted grains, types of sweets and fruits to entice the children and to drive away their sleepiness and so that they will see the change and will ask" questions.[21] One of the earliest printed Haggadot (Soncino, 1486) alludes to a similar custom.

CONTEMPORARY INNOVATIONS

As we have seen, the Seder plate has sometimes served as a stage on which to highlight ideas that the Haggadah itself does not adequately address, such as the role of women in bringing about the Exodus. The custom of three cooked dishes (*My People's Passover*

Haggadah, Volume 1, p. 39) and one of the Talmud's interpretations of *charoset* (*My People's Passover Haggadah*, Volume 2, p. 117) both illustrate this. In recent times the plate has functioned similarly, as extra items have been added to raise consciousness and discussion about a range of issues. During the Soviet Jewry movement of the 1970s and 1980s, many Jews added a fourth matzah, the "Matzah of Hope," to the plate and accompanied it with a reading on oppression and liberation. Following the exodus of so many Jews from the former Soviet Union, some of the organizations working to eliminate the still widespread practice of slavery have adopted the fourth matzah to raise consciousness about this enduring horror.[22]

In the early 1980s Susannah Heschel began adding an orange to the Seder plate, "a symbol of the struggle of people who have been marginalized within the Jewish community; that includes gay and lesbian Jews, and indeed all Jewish women" (see Zierler, *My People's Passover Haggadah*, Volume 2, p. 105).[23] This innovation seems to have inspired another. In 2003 a multimedia performance debuted in Philadelphia: "An Olive on the Seder Plate." In a performance that explores how American Jews struggle with Israeli policy toward the Palestinians, the olive represents the Palestinian people. Regardless of how many oranges or olives find their way onto Seder plates, it is likely that this venerable tray will remain a vehicle confronting ever new issues of concern and relating them—not without controversy!—to the ancient story of liberation from Egypt.

THE ARRANGEMENT OF THE PLATE

Although there are many variations, today the placement of the items on the plate tends to follow the custom of three individuals, each of whom exerted enormous influence on Jewish practice:[24]

- Moses Isserles (the *R'ma*, 1530–1572, Krakow), whose glosses on the *Shulchan Arukh* enabled this law code to gain acceptance among Ashkenazi Jews, making it perhaps *the* most authoritative of the codes.
- Isaac Luria (the *Ari*, 1534–1572, Safed), the renowned kabbalist whose work suffuses Jewish mysticism.
- Elijah ben Solomon (the Gaon of Vilna, the *Gra*, 1720–1797), among the most influential halakhists since Maimonides.[25]

The *R'ma* and the *Gra* differed on the number of items on the plate, but they followed the same organizing principle, namely that, as the Talmud states, one should not "reach over" one commandment to fulfill another.[26] In his gloss on the *Shulchan Arukh* (Orach Chayim, 473:3), the *R'ma* put it this way: "One should arrange the dish in front of him [the leader of the Seder] so that he will not have to reach over a *mitzvah*. That is, the *karpas* [which is eaten as the first "food" *mitzvah*] should be closest, with the vinegar or salt water [in which the *karpas* is dipped] closer than the matzah [which is eaten later], and the matzah closer than the *maror* and the *charoset* [which come only after the matzah]. The latter should be closer to him than the meat and the egg [symbols of the ancient sacrifices]."

The Seder Plate

Moses Isserles
The *R'ma*, 1530–1572

Roasted   Roasted
Egg   Shank Bone

Charoset   *Maror*

Three Matzot

Salt Water   *Karpas*

Isaac Luria
The *Ari*, 1534–1572

Three Matzot

Roasted   Roasted
Egg   Shank Bone

Maror

Karpas   *Charoset*

Lettuce

Elijah ben Solomon
The Vilna Gaon,
The *Gra*, 1720–1797

Charoset   *Maror*

Two Matzot

Roasted   Roasted
Egg   Shank Bone

But positioning the meat and the egg last might create the impression that they too were being reserved to be eaten in fulfillment of a commandment. In fact, the shank bone, at least, is distinctly not allowed to be eaten for fear of giving the impression that we are still offering up a lamb as a sacrifice. To rectify this misimpression, the Vilna Gaon placed the meat and egg at the forefront of the plate, where they would clearly have to be passed over. The *Gra*'s position harks back to the Talmud's concern about whether or not one should lift and display the meat, matzah, and bitter herbs as one explains their significance as mandated by Rabban Gamaliel. The Talmud requires raising and showing the matzah and *maror* but forbids doing so with the meat—"lest he give the appearance of eating consecrated meat" that was slaughtered outside the Temple (Pes. 116b). The *Mishnah Berurah*, a highly influential legal code from the nineteenth century that often follows the *Gra*'s rulings, states: "There are authorities who write that one need not bother about having to skip over the meat and the egg, since they do not serve for a *mitzvah*, but are merely for purposes of commemoration."[27]

Isaac Luria, the *Ari*, took a very different approach.[28] First, instead of just one form of bitter herbs *(maror)*, he used two—adding lettuce, *chazeret*, (for the Hillel sandwich). Including the three matzot and the plate itself, the *Ari* thus counted ten items (see below), each of which corresponds to one of the ten *sefirot*, or divine emanations. The arrangement of the items on the plate conforms to the kabbalistic "tree" that in turn represents a range of concepts including the mystical "body" of God. The *Ari*'s mostly oral teachings were written down by Hayim Vital, one of his principal disciples. Vital's description of the *Ari*'s custom gained wider currency when it was quoted in *Ba'er Hetev*, a popular eighteenth-century commentary on the *Shulchan Arukh*. As we will see, the Lurianic arrangement is not concerned with presenting items on the plate in the order in which they are used during the Seder so as to avoid "passing over a *mitzvah*."[29]

The *Ari* tersely outlines the correspondence between the *sefirot* and the items on the Seder plate[30]:

The upper, middle, and third matzot: the three remaining tribes—Kohen, Levi, and Israel—and the three faculties of divine wisdom—*Chokhmah* (wisdom), *Binah* (understanding), and *Da'at* (knowledge)
Roasted shank bone: *Chesed*—kindness, God's right hand
Roasted egg: *G'vurah*—strength, judgment, God's left hand
Maror: *Tiferet*—glory, which mediates between kindness on the right and judgment on the left
Charoset: *Netsach*—eternity
Karpas: *Hod*—splendor
Lettuce: *Y'sod*—foundation
The Seder plate that holds everything: *Malkhut*—kingdom

While further exploration of Lurianic Kabbalah lies beyond the purview of this discussion, it is worth noting that according to the *Zohar*, *Malkhut* also refers to the sea, the "lower waters."[31] Earlier midrashic traditions lead in the same direction. When the Israelites dedicated the *mishkan*, the portable Tabernacle they traveled with through the desert, each of the twelve tribes donated a set of identical items, the first of which was a silver dish, a *ke'arah*. Nachshon, son of Amminadav, according to legend the first to plunge into the Red Sea, brought the first donation. Why a dish? Because, the midrash answers, it points to God's ultimate sovereignty, even over the unruly sea: "He offered a dish as a symbol of the sea, which encompasses the whole world and resembles a dish."[32]

Peoplehood with Purpose

The American Seder and Changing Jewish Identity

Lawrence A. Hoffman

Surveys regularly record lighting Chanukah candles and keeping a Passover Seder as the two most popular forms of personal American Jewish practice. Of the 5.5 to 6.2 million Jews here (estimates vary somewhat), 4.3 million do both. Chanukah would have surprised almost every Jewish generation before this one; Passover would not. We have stories of even the most unlikely Jews marking Passover eve in some way—like the Union soldiers during the Civil War who received permission from their superiors to take the night off for religious purposes. They owned no Haggadah, but were well fortified with wine. Having heard that *charoset* symbolizes the mortar used in Egypt, but having none at hand, they took an actual brick with them. It is not clear how much praying took place, but they were careful to drink the wine. Two things stand out about their story. First, the soldiers felt emboldened to requisition the Seder requirements; second, the army knew enough about Passover and Jews to think the request reasonable.

In America today, then, Jews who belong to no synagogue, put up no *m'zuzah*, and do not keep Shabbat somehow manage to schedule a Seder.

Many reasons come to mind.[1] The popularity of Easter season, with an annual Easter egg hunt even on the White House lawn, makes some kind of parallel Jewish ceremony desirable. Jews who can afford it like dinner parties and know how to entertain—making a Seder feels comfortable to them. The pediatric part of the Seder—hiding the *afikoman* and asking the Four Questions—appeals to the desire to educate our children Jewishly. The event is a lot of work, but a single annual celebration, labor-intensive as it may be, is easier than the regularized weekly commitment that things like Shabbat observance demand. And finally, there is the Passover message itself, freedom—a match made in heaven between Jewish tradition and American values. By now, we Jews have shaped our Seder into a quintessentially American religious ritual.

Some things mark all Seders: family, friends, and community celebration; storytelling; eating and drinking; and just plain fun. These all go back to very ancient roots in the evolution of human ritual. Long before there was a central Temple of any sort, there were family gatherings around the sacred; the great myths of peoples everywhere were probably told and retold as ritual events; as for fun, even in the Middle Ages Jews enjoyed their Seders—a medieval manuscript shows a man pointing to his wife when he announces *maror* ("bitter herbs"), and another one shows her pointing back.

But Seders do vary, as do the Haggadot on which they depend. These variations are consequential in that they speak more deeply to us than might otherwise seem apparent. Rituals are like that—we may not know how strongly we feel until they are done "wrong" (try changing just a single song in a synagogue service).

Average people usually have little power to affect synagogue prayer—they like it or not, attend or don't. But the Seder is a home event, and the people who arrive are our guests; we feel responsible for their well-being, the way we would at any dinner party we throw, but even more so here because so much is at stake. It is the annual event par excellence that assembles the extended family (with all its baggage). To get there properly, they buy new clothes, leave work early, cajole children to be nice, and get home late. They do it for all the reasons mentioned above, but also because they think they should. A Seder is what Jews do—an American-Jewish obligation. And having fulfilled their responsibility, they leave with a deep sense of satisfaction or the opposite, glad to have experienced Jewish identity again, or just to have the dreaded thing over with for another year.

Once upon a time, most Seders in any Jewish town were pretty much the same. The Haggadah text was set, its usage determined by a common understanding of Halakhah ("law") and *minhag* ("custom"). As medieval villages became towns, and towns became cities, that homogeneity melted away. After the 1492 expulsion from Spain, Sefardim and Ashkenazim lived side by side, each with different practices. Eighteenth-century Poland pitted Chasidim against *Mitnagdim*. In our time, we probably argue less but differ more.

Even the Sefardi/Ashkenazi and Chasidim/*Mitnagdim* splits were never wholly opposites, however. Each camp hosted variations, and many Jews borrowed from them both. The group titles we use are more like ideal types than they are valid descriptions of actual practice. They are useful because they provide guidelines for categorizing different kinds of Judaism that Seder participants espouse; they let us situate people at a more or less particular point on the spectrum of Jewish identity.

We too use labels to mark identity. Since the middle of the nineteenth century, they have been denominational titles, which to some extent are still applicable. But it is more useful to think of a broader typology, somewhat linked to denominational preferences, but not wholly so. By devising Seder types, we can actually isolate alternative models people have of Judaism—what at least thoughtful people mean when they say they are Jews. The Seder becomes a litmus test of Jewish continuity—not whether American Judaism will continue, but what forms it is likely to take as it does so.

Broadly speaking, our Passover Haggadah, the story Americans tell about our past and our present Jewish selves, falls into three broad categories: (1) Haggadah as mitzvah; (2) Haggadah as religion; and (3) Haggadah as ethnicity.

THE HAGGADAH AND JEWISH IDENTITY

Books exist only if people write them, and Seders happen only if people keep them. As an author shapes a book, so Jews who keep a Seder determine the shape that Seder takes. We all know that. What is not so appreciated, however, is that the direction of influence works both ways. As much as Jews shape their Seder, the Seder shapes the Jews who keep it. Religious ritual, generally, does that, since ritual is the way we put our best foot forward to each other and to others. We are suspicious of people who ritualize in secret—a problem for Mormons, who even open their temples, on occasion, deliberately to dispel lingering fears that something sinister takes place there. Think too of the truly negative instances of ritual that get reported from time to time, today or in the past: human sacrifice among the Incas, let us say; or a wife throwing herself onto her husband's funeral pyre in India. What makes us cringe is less what is done than the fact that people whom we otherwise admire actually do it. Theological considerations aside, the whole point of ritual is what it says about the ritualizers. Ritualizers intuit this. That is why rituals have such staying power. Thinking of our identities as relatively unchanging, we find it disturbing to have ritual that blows with every convenient wind.

But the opposite is true too. Change is part of life: we age, move, watch generations come and go, and undergo circumstances of history that cannot be ignored. Any of these things is likely to show up first in our rituals. Something we once loved to do starts looking empty; we find ourselves looking at our watches, not our prayer books. Rituals are like mirrors that way. The more we do them, the more we focus their looking glass upon ourselves. If our identities have altered, our mirror image looks less and less familiar. For minor changes, we add a prayer, change a song, or otherwise fiddle with the ritual until it comes out looking better. In a major identity crisis, the ritual mirror looks cracked beyond repair. Nothing short of an entire ritual overhaul will work. Because of the centrality of Passover in this country, the Haggadah provides particularly good insight into the American Jewish looking glass of who we are.

The history of our Haggadah is simultaneously the history of various waves of Jews coming to these shores, hammering themselves together into a loosely organized Jewish community, and negotiating identity as Jews and Americans simultaneously.

I say "negotiating" because whenever Jews move somewhere, it takes some time to work out the way their Jewish heritage will mesh with their new host culture. During an initial *colonization* stage,[2] they simply move in, usually fleeing from some old country of residence. In this case, Jews arrived in several waves: a small group of Sefardim (Spanish-Portuguese Jews) in the seventeenth century from Brazil; then central European Ashkenazim, often lumped together as the "Germans," in the mid- to late nineteenth century; later still, eastern European Jews (the "Russians"), our largest wave by far, from 1881 to 1924; and the most recent arrivals, refugees from Hitler's Europe and the former Soviet Union. The foundation of American Jewish culture is most impacted by the middle two of these, émigrés from central and eastern Europe.

In the colonization stage, we bring with us the Judaism we knew from somewhere else and then unpack it to see how it goes with the lay of the land. Part of what Jews brought here, for example, was a sacred calendar, which we shaped to fit American values, letting some holidays fall and others rise in prominence; as we saw, Chanukah lights and the Passover Seder were big winners.

But the rise of Chanukah and Passover (as well as the relative fall of, say, Tisha B'av) is already part of the second stage, *consolidation*. This is when Jews build institutions that reflect life in their new home. The Sefardim, for instance (coming as they did in the Colonial period), faced the need to develop a system of "congregationalism," local synagogues that were the Jewish equivalents of village churches. German Jews joined the nineteenth-century American experiment in denominationalism—separation of church and state made Protestants compete for members, and denominationalism proved to be an efficient way to replicate churches as the frontier spread west and south. By the time the Russians arrived, they found German Jews established as the denomination called Reform. Differences in ethnicity and class forged them into their own movement, Conservative Judaism. As an instance of the Haggadah reflecting identity, we will see that the first Reform Haggadah was part of the way the Russians were excluded from the German Jews' Passover celebrations.

The first two stages necessarily occur whenever Jews move anywhere, and we Americans have patently concluded them. It remains a matter of question as to whether the last two occur. Normally, consolidation matures into *creativity*, a distinctive cultural contribution that arises from the particular mix of Judaism and the host culture where it has taken up residence. When, how long, and with what success depend on the difference between *acculturation* and *assimilation*. Acculturation is the perfectly normal process of reshaping our culture to be at home wherever it is that we have moved. Assimilation is what happens when we become so much at home that we lose our Jewish distinctiveness completely. Insofar as Jews have acculturated, American Jewish creativity has already begun—think, for example, of our vast system of Federations, a Jewish version of the American corporate culture established nationally but with international ties to Israel; or the plethora of Haggadot that line the shelves of bookstores every Passover. It is probable, however, that we are just now *fully* entering the stage of American Jewish creativity, and that too is part of our Haggadah story (as we shall see, at the end this survey).

We would rather not think of stage four: *collapse*. If past history is repeated, economic growth, freedom, and opportunity will some day decline here the way it has everywhere else. If so, we can expect Jews (like other Americans) to emigrate and begin the four-stage process all over again somewhere else.

OUR HAGGADAH INHERITANCE

The waves of immigrants arrived with whatever religious heritage they had known back home, including a Haggadah. They surely did not recognize, however, how much the Haggadah they brought with them had been subject to historical change. The Bible knew Passover, but no Seder and no Haggadah to guide it. The earliest Rabbis (prior to 200 CE) laid down the conceptual outline for that: the Haggadah would be a "telling" of Israel's tale of Passover freedom. It would begin with *g'nut*, Israel's enslavement, then build to *shevach*, a crescendo of praise for the God who brought freedom, and conclude with a proud assertion of what freedom entailed: nothing short of *g'ulah*, "redemption," not just in the past, from Egypt, but implicitly in the future too, from the travails of history in general. Every single version of the Haggadah has followed this basic outline of Israel's story.

By the geonic era (c. 750–1038) a more or less official Haggadah had come into being—the product of powerful Jewish authorities in Babylonia (Iraq), who recorded their own practice and dispatched it with expectations of its being followed elsewhere. Palestinian Jews had their own ideas of what to do, but in the end, Babylonians prevailed, so that today Jews everywhere follow Babylonian practice—albeit modified by later ages, faced with the need to reflect their own lives in the Haggadah's ancient tale. The most substantial additions occurred in western Europe in the wake of the Crusades and the troubling centuries thereafter. Along the way, songs were added, some of them only a few centuries old.

All of this became effectively canonized as the book to buy, primarily because printers said so. Before the invention of printing, localism mattered; books were copied by hand, circulated poorly, and used by only the very few. With printing, certain versions became de facto official, some of them Ashkenazi (the "German" custom) and some of them Sefardi (the Spanish-Portuguese alternative). There were numerous versions of each, of course, as well as mixtures, like the Haggadot of Chasidim from Poland, Ashkenazi to their core but influenced by Sefardi Kabbalah. The basic text was pretty much the same everywhere: the old geonic prototype with medieval additions.

By the nineteenth century, printing became inexpensive enough for any enterprising rabbi to write his own Haggadah. Modernity produced an altogether new model: Reform Haggadot that stood out because they translated important prayers into the vernacular and then took things out, instead of just putting new additions in. Jews in all waves of immigration brought the standard Haggadah, but modified—streamlined as in German Reform, perhaps, or outfitted with kabbalistic meditations. And in America, it changed further. Just exactly how is the subject of this essay.

That Jews who arrived here brought some version of the standard Haggadah with them is certain. It is hard to know, however, how many of them actually used it or, if they did use it, how much of it they managed to read at any given Seder before giving up on most of it. I suspect the majority of American Jews came with the assumption that a family Seder ought to continue, but there is no way to know how many did not feel that way—how many, that is, simply dropped out of Judaism, choosing assimilation over acculturation. A pair of forces pushed people in that direction. First, modernity suspected religion, and Jews wanted to be modern. Second, even though America advised religious loyalty, it was ambivalent on the subject. Waves of revivalism kept reminding us of the importance of belonging to some religion or other; "Every American should belong to a religion," President Eisenhower famously said. But intellectual heroes like Ralph Waldo Emerson and Walt Whitman thought true religion to be something internal to the soul, not a matter of denominational display. Jews were therefore free, if not to jettison Judaism, than at least to relegate it to an unimportant corner of their lives. If they had a Seder, it would likely have become mostly a dinner with relatively little Haggadah reading, and for them, any old Haggadah would do—they rarely got through most of it anyway.

What they would have had at first was precisely that: any old Haggadah, either brought here from Europe or published cheaply by some publishing entrepreneur—the venerable Maxwell House Haggadah, for example. Eventually, we devised alternatives, perhaps recognizing, at least unconsciously, that the Haggadah provides the best annual account of what a Jew is and a historical/moral rationale for choosing to remain one. It was the Seder, after all, that children were most likely to remember. Also, the better our relationships with non-Jewish friends and neighbors, the more likely it was that we would have them too as guests around the Seder table, witnessing what we said about ourselves. Eventually, even the media began covering Seders as worthy news events. How we portrayed ourselves at the Seder mattered more and more.

We should be careful not to miss the forest for the trees. Saying or omitting this or that prayer, using English rather than Hebrew, even the specific Haggadah edition that we use—these are just trees in a larger forest of meaning. The bedrock issue (rarely discussed or even recognized) is what we think we are saying when we declare ourselves Jewish. We have traditionally described ourselves as a people; so the Haggadah is, above all, the story of the Jewish People, taken out of Egyptian bondage—isn't it?

HAGGADAH AS *MITZVAH*

Our very title, *My People's Passover Haggadah*, should be suggestive. It is, of course, an extension of the larger series, *My People's Prayer Book*, but there, too, readers ought to pause at the words "*My People's.*" It is hard to imagine a parallel Christian ritual or worship book called "*My People's.*" Peoplehood is a distinctively Jewish idea.

It is, however, entirely out of keeping with modern consciousness, which measures us by almost everything else—nationality, ethnicity, religion, age, and gender—but not "people." If "my people" means anything at all these days, it is a parody on two highly placed executives who conclude a business deal with the guarantee that "my people will talk to your people." That is not what the Bible means when it summons us to become "God's People." So what then did it mean? Until the nineteenth century, no one worried about it. Jews knew they were a people—in Hebrew, an *am*—because what else was there to be?

Identity by peoplehood was challenged when Napoleon's empire-building highlighted, instead, nationalities and religions. On the heels of the French Revolution, Napoleon marched through Europe rationalizing age-old medieval systems that had carved out duchies, independent cities, and private land holdings of all sorts, and hammering them together into the quintessentially modern nation-state of France. Along the way, he encountered Jews, equally quintessential as an anomaly because they had been classified as altogether separate pariahs defying identity. Europe had, as it were, rearranged its inhabitants like so many messy papers on a desk, relegating Jews to a pile of anachronisms belonging nowhere. The rational thing to do was admit them to French citizenship, but that meant ascertaining if they were indeed French, a question Napoleon put to a representative body of Jewish notables known as the Paris Sanhedrin. The ticket to entry into free French status was the acknowledgment that like Catholics and Protestants, Jews too were French by nationality and just Jewish by religion. It took little insight to know the correct answer. Recognizing that Napoleon had no modern concept of "peoplehood," the assembly voted that Jews were Jewish by religion and French by nationality: *Sh'ma Yisra'el* and *Vive la France!*

The Sanhedrin notables were not wrong, but they were not altogether right either. Leveling Judaism to a combination of nationality and religion ignored the only thing Jews had ever said they were: a people. One wonders what the Sanhedrin members thought of their Haggadah when they sat down at their Seder that year. By the standards of the Enlightenment (which the Sanhedrin represented), it is only with great difficulty that the Haggadah can be considered a religious manifesto. Even today, we think of religion in Enlightenment terms, expecting it to address purely private matters of belief, faith, morality, and conscience. That is precisely the approach that had influenced Emerson and Whitman, but they could have gotten it from philosopher Emanuel Kant, a child of German Protestant pietism, who had faulted Judaism explicitly for being a doctrine of law better suited to a nation-state than a religion.

The issue was not just an arcane category of peoplehood, then; it was the fact that peoplehood implies at least customs, if not actual laws, that may run counter to those of the nation-state. Indeed, the Haggadah is filled with such laws *(mitzvot)*. Until modern times no Jew would have taken issue with the statement that properly fulfilling the *mitzvot* is the most important thing about it: wash twice but say the blessing only once; don't eat matzah until nightfall; eat it again as an *afikoman*; lift the cup here but not there; arrange the plate so that the leader need never bypass one symbol to use another; and so on. The popularity of the Seder papers over this legal essence, but for nearly two thousand years, and still today, in traditionalist circles, whatever else the Seder is, it is above all a carefully orchestrated set of legal requirements having virtually nothing to do with the Kantian view of religion that still dominates American consciousness.

Rabbinic Judaism (and the Haggadah it spawned) had been a legal thing from the very start. Look at the Mishnah and Tosefta, our two earliest rabbinic discussions of the Seder (c. 200 and 250, respectively—see Appendix I, *My People's Passover Haggadah*, Volume 2, pp. 225–234). They are law codes. The Mishnah centers on the obligation to tell the tale of Israel's deliverance. For the Tosefta, the matters of moment are the sacrificial rules that had ceased by the Tosefta's time but would, it was hoped, be someday reinstated.

At no point prior to modernity does Judaism cease being a people *governed by legal prescription*. Jewish liberals after Napoleon had a twin object of complaint: not just that Jews were a people, not a religion, but that peoplehood was external and legal, not internal and spiritual.

The Middle Ages only emphasized the legal focus of the Haggadah. In the post-Crusade era for example, Jews codified the specificities of Seder regulations. To this day, we accompany the Haggadah with *Kadesh urchats* (see *My People's Passover Haggadah*, Volume 1, p. 107), an ordering mnemonic that came into being then, so as to guarantee the proper rules of procedure. We also say part of a poem intended originally as a rundown of Passover detail to be mastered on *Shabbat Hagadol*, the Sabbath before the Seder: *Chasal siddur pesach k'hilkhato*, "The Passover celebration has concluded appropriately, *with all its laws and rules*" (see *My People's Passover Haggadah*, Volume 1, p. 187).

Judaism is hardly the only religion to insist on legal detail, especially concerning ritual. Kant had castigated Roman Catholicism for it too. But legal structures are essential to all of Judaism, not just its ritual. Kant was also not wrong to see Judaism as more nationality than religion, insofar as law is at the core of nation-statehood and altogether inimical to religion as defined by Protestant pietism. It would not have mattered had Kant not been representative of the trend in European thought at the very time that Jews were seeking the right to citizenship. France may be highly Catholic, but it was the Protestant Enlightenment, not Catholic traditionalism, that governed Napoleonic thinking. For the next century, Catholic monarchists fought Enlightenment republicans on that score. By 1897 Jews were caught in the middle with the Dreyfus incident, where a Jew, Alfred Dreyfus, was framed with trumped-up charges of treason; his accusers were Catholic traditionalists and recidivist monarchists, and his defenders were liberal champions of Napoleonic republicanism.

Dreyfus was acquitted: the liberals won that round, but the victory was short-lived. The next hundred years replaced the Enlightenment ideal of a universal religion of reason with a set of conflicting and vindictive nationalisms. Still, we Jews in the West never gave up the liberal dream. There were exceptions—there always are, to everything—but overall, wherever Jews established diasporas, we committed ourselves to being a religion. We bracketed peoplehood as a definition to debate among ourselves.

It is not that Jews are not still a people. We are. And it is not that there is anything wrong with Halakhah. There isn't. But living in a modern Western culture where no one else thinks that way makes us a cognitive minority of one. And that is a very lonely position to be in. However much we may go about our business internally as a people, we require some additional self-identity that others understand. As the need for alternative models of "who we are" became stronger, it was inevitable that the nature of the Haggadah, literally, "the telling [of who we are]," would change.

PEOPLEHOOD, RELIGION, AND ETHNICITY

Before looking at those alternative models, we need to understand what we mean by "peoplehood," "religion," and "ethnicity." Peoplehood is not antithetical to religion. It is just something larger, a category that includes religion but a whole lot more as well. With its dissolution as a sufficient rationale for modern Jewish identity, most people confuse it with ethnicity. But as much as Judaism is not just a religion, it is even less an ethnicity. If Jews are a people, then by our own definition we are a *single* people, which has *many* ethnic groups. The confusion arises out of limited historical consciousness.

Ethnicity was once akin to peoplehood in that the term, which goes back to the Greek *ethnos*, denoted the various peoples who constituted the Mediterranean. What made each *ethnos* special was its particular combination of language, history, customs, folklore, and so forth—all the things that do, in fact, constitute peoplehood, as long as we limit peoplehood to a single geographical time and place. As long as "Jews" meant the people who practiced Judaism in Judea (later, Roman Palestine), people who shared a common past going back centuries, Jews were an *ethnos*. But when Josephus tells us that Jews showed up from Babylonia dressed as archers on horseback, with such different customs that he did not know what to make of them, we see how *ethnos* and people eventually must part ways.

In our time, self-conscious ethnicity is a product of the nineteenth and twentieth centuries. Like the period when Greeks had little good to say about the other peoples whom they met in trade or warfare, this too was an era of local particularism. In part, it arose as a reaction to Napoleon, for whom ethnic identity was as irrelevant as peoplehood, although he at least knew what ethnic groups were. The problem was that he tried to squeeze the ethnicity out of them by merging them all into his definition of nation-statehood; they were hardly thrilled. When Napoleon's enemies prevailed, they expressed their antagonism by advancing a countercultural trend called romanticism—no longer a denunciation, but a celebration, of ethnic difference. Whereas the Enlightenment had celebrated the unity of all human beings by virtue of their underlying rationality, romantics highlighted the uniqueness of languages, customs, and history. In the developing Prussian state, Germans explored Teutonic myths; Wagner wrote operas about them. Similar developments occurred elsewhere, as nation-states reveled in ethnic roots that were sometimes as much invented as discovered but, in any case, considered necessary, the very essence of what people are.

Ironically, German romanticism, which mostly hated Jews, understood the Jewish claim to being a people. It was the same thing as the German *Volk*, living on patrimonial lands where Jews, as outsiders, had no right to reside. The only hope for Jews was to hold out the ideal of being a religion, deserving of representation there because of the Jewish contribution to German spirituality.

But as much as nation-statehood encouraged ethnic identity (Germany for Germans, for instance), its imperial outreach squashed it. The two trends are fundamentally at odds with one another. Ethnicities are intensely local. Nation-states were intensely imperial. Imperialism and localism are poor bedfellows. The First World War was fought over empires, and when it was over, the multiple ethnicities that had been suppressed by the imperial ambition of the losers came out again to play. Czechs, Slovaks, and Magyars (Hungarians)—to name just a few—emerged from the Austro-Hungary empire as independent states with their own ethnic particularism. Jews were again caught in the middle, no less than in the days of Alfred Dreyfus. This time they epitomized enemy ethnicity sullying lands that sought ethnic purity. On the positive side of the ledger, the State of Israel was largely shaped by emigration of Jews from such centers, especially Poland, when a Polish state cast off German hegemony in 1918. On the negative side, anti-Semitic rioting occurred throughout most of the new areas of ethnic solidarity—which is why so many Jews left in the first place.

These Jews of eastern Europe did not have to wait for the end of World War I to know they did not belong. They were made perfectly aware of that by the czar, who was molding numerous ethnic states into a Russian empire. Jews were like Georgians and White Russians, but without a state. Zionists went "home" to Jerusalem to found one. Their rivals, Jewish territorialists, also wanted a state but hoped to create it within the Russian empire, using Yiddish as their official language. Yet a third group gave up on statehood altogether and came to America, where, like the Germans before them, they were told that they were a religion.

The German Jews they met had already set the religious agenda: to do what is expected of religions—build synagogues (like churches) with worship at their core. Primarily Reform in orientation, they had dropped whatever they could of Jewish ethnicity in favor of their newly attained religious identity. They remained ethnic in their own way, but German ethnics. Germany had provided high culture, after all. They were Jewish by religion, American by nationality, and German by ethnicity.

Eastern European Jews, however, were either Jewish by peoplehood and law, or anti-czarist socialists and freethinkers, making them, in either case, neither ethnic Germans nor religious Jews. So they maintained their own ethnic roots in Judaism. Eventually the bulk of them had also to bow before America's demand that they declare themselves a religion, but the religion most of them adopted was Conservative Judaism, which remained ethnic through and through. Reform Judaism never went that route because its ethnic preference was German, not Jewish. Entering the war against Germany in 1917 made German ethnicity problematic. So western European Jews became full-fledged religionists, dropping ethnicity altogether. Eastern European Jews, however, remained Jewish ethnics.

Until then the Haggadah had been a matter of *mitzvah*. But the splintering of non-Orthodox Jews into the Reform Movement (rooted in religion) and the Conservative Movement (rooted in ethnicity) gave birth to two alternatives: Haggadah as religion and Haggadah as ethnicity.

HAGGADAH AS RELIGION OR ETHNICITY

The Haggadah as religion came first. The die had been cast in 1885, when founding representatives of the American Reform rabbinate met in Pittsburgh to ratify a statement of religious belief. The very idea of voting in a creed of Jewish faith was novel, even radical. Being a religion, Christianity had done it many times. Not being a religion, however, traditional Judaism never had. Some statements of belief had been associated with Jews as individuals—Maimonides' Thirteen Principles of Faith, for example—but no one had ever voted on them, and more people had rejected them than accepted them. Yet here were Reform rabbis, convinced they were a religion and acting like one by adopting a corporate definition of religious faith.

The Pittsburgh Platform does not even mention peoplehood. It takes the religious basis of Judaism for granted in its very first lines when it announces, "We recognize in every religion an attempt to grasp the Infinite." The Jewish People's trials and tribulations provide passing mention, but their subject is Judaism, not Jews, in that "Judaism presents the highest conception of the God-idea" and "Judaism preserved and defended, midst continual struggles and trials and under enforced isolation, this God-idea as the central religious truth for the human race." We are left to imagine that Judaism, not the Jewish People, suffered from these "struggles and trials and enforced isolation." What matters is the doctrine, not the people holding it.

The point here is that the Protestantized version of religion is about belief, and it exists regardless of whether there are any Protestants around to believe it. By contrast, the traditional Haggadah is less about Judaism than it is about Jews. It was, therefore, no easy feat to make it over into a religious manifesto rather than an exercise in *mitzvah*. But that is what Reform Jews did in 1907.[3]

The traditional Haggadah text had been filled with references to the experience of the Jewish People, and given the old model of Haggadah as *mitzvah*, that meant a heavy accent on doing the Seder properly. The best example, as we saw, is the final prayer affirming, "The Passover celebration has concluded appropriately, with all its laws and rules." That conclusion was omitted by the Reformers. Since the fourteenth century yet another line had been tacked onto the ending: "Next year in Jerusalem." Jerusalem was indeed a religious symbol of peace and hope, but a symbol specific to the Jewish People, hardly the world; so the 1907 Haggadah omits it, praying instead that "all the wrongs that still prevail be righted in the coming year" (p. 46). An added final song says, "Speed the day of freedom's reign o'er all the human race"—"all the human race," note, not just the Jewish people. Another example is that traditionally, the wise son asks, "What are the precepts, statutes, and laws that Adonai our God commanded you?" and is provided with the answer that according to Halakhah "it is forbidden to conclude the *afikoman* after the Passover offering." The 1907 Reform Haggadah does not tell us what the wise child asks, but the answer couldn't be less legal or more religious: "This service is held in order to worship the Lord our God."

I do not want to imply that Reform Jews abandoned the Jewish People. Their Haggadah was still Jewish to its core and retained echoes of that People's ancient story. But the accent had subtly shifted. Religion had been secondary to the Jewish People who keep it; now the men and women who kept it were secondary to the religion that they kept. Jews became to Judaism what Christians are to Christianity. Napoleon would have understood this. So too did Americans among whom German

Jews made their homes, as did the celebrants, Jews and non-Jews alike now, who met for Seders in those homes.

It is always a mistake to generalize too much. Reform Judaism, for example, is said to have opposed Zionism—precisely because if Judaism is a religion, it can hardly be a nationality. Protestants have no national homeland; why should Jews have one? And to some extent, that is an accurate assessment. But in 1937, the movement officially endorsed building up a Jewish homeland, and even before that, Supreme Court Justice Louis D. Brandeis (1856–1941) was a Reform Jew who directed the World Zionist Organization between 1914 and 1918; so too were Rabbis Stephen S. Wise (1874–1949) and Abba Hillel Silver (1903–1963). Silver led the Zionist Organization of America in the critical pre-state years of 1945 to 1947, while simultaneously serving as the president of the Reform rabbinate—it was obviously possible to be the most respected Reform rabbi among peers and also to champion Zionism, even in the movement that was supposedly anti-Zionist. So too, here, with the Reform experience of the Seder. In general it is indeed true that Reform Judaism transformed its Passover Haggadah into an experience of Judaism as a religion. It is also true, however, that many Reform Jews celebrated Seders with or without the official Reform Haggadah, and with or without understanding the subtle change that the Reform Haggadah entailed.

A parallel story can be told of the people who identified as Conservative. By and large, these were the Russian Jews who found religion a difficult concept to buy, since the people selling it were German and Reform. Decades of distrust had separated the two groups. Jews throughout the cultured classes of Germany considered their eastern cousins uncouth, uncultured, and unkempt. Here in America, they feared also that a tidal wave of easterners would set back the progress they had made in convincing Americans that Jews (by religion) could make good citizens. Their 1885 Pittsburgh Platform was a direct response to the first wave of Russians to arrive here. Moreover, by 1907 Germans were becoming a minority, while eastern European immigration had yet to peak. The Haggadah's insistence on Judaism as religion was only heightened by the fear that the rising swell of eastern Jewish ethnics would call the religious enterprise itself into question.

So, faced with the Reform Movement's emphasis on Judaism as religion without ethnicity, eastern European Jews who wanted to become socialized as Americans chose Conservatism. But they did more than choose it; they invented it. The Conservative Movement would eventually trace its origins back to conservative Reformers in Germany, but that is an ex post facto analysis. Conservative Judaism here came into being as the brain child of Classical Reformers, who were put off by eastern European Jewish ethnicity, who therefore bought up a lazy little seminary on New York's Upper West Side, and who constituted themselves as a board and established a training ground for eastern European rabbis there. Its first rabbinic graduates reached adulthood in the Depression and then World War II, hardly the time to assert movement ideology. It was not until 1946 that the Reform board was sent packing so that graduates of the Jewish Theological Seminary itself could establish what the seminary, and they, would stand for. That is when and how today's American Conservative Movement reached adulthood. But no movement Haggadah came out until 1982, following a new Reform Haggadah in 1974.[4] Both of these Haggadot reflected events involving Israel and the Soviet Union.

More than a quarter of a century after the fact, it is hard to convey what the Six-Day War of 1967 meant to Jews in America. Without instant satellite news coverage, we waited all night long to find out if important battles had been won or lost. The war broke out for me during exam week at rabbinic school. Like everyone else, I sat the whole night before watching Israeli ambassador Abba Eban on television as he addressed the United Nations—in my case, instead of studying for a final exam. I failed it; no one cared. Jews from every walk of life were jumping on planes to volunteer for nonmilitary duty while the citizen army went to war. When Jerusalem was liberated, we cried.

But we never quite forgot the possibility that the war might have ended differently. And in 1973, when we awoke on Yom Kippur morning to hear that Egyptians were pushing back Israeli troops in the Sinai, we thought again that it really could. Simultaneously, Americans discovered Jews behind the iron curtain. Annual marches down New York's Fifth Avenue taught a whole generation of Jews to shout, "Let My people go." The threats to Israel and Soviet refuseniks affected all Jews equally. And all of this was happening as a new generation of Reform rabbis (most of them by now from eastern European heritage) was beginning to occupy senior positions in large and influential congregations; the president of the movement, Rabbi Alexander Schindler, was himself from eastern Europe. The very distinction between eastern and western Europeans had dissipated. No one much remembered that they hadn't liked each other once.

Again history altered age-old identity. Being a religion was no longer enough for Reform Jews. So it issued a new Haggadah in which Jewish Peoplehood loomed larger. "Next year in Jerusalem" was back; so was Hebrew; and there were echoes of the Holocaust and Hebrew literature too. Chaim Nachman Bialik, poet laureate of the Jewish People, and an eastern European Jew if ever there was one, spoke from the pages of this new Haggadah. Eighteen illustrations decorated the pages, most with decorative Hebrew, but no English; two of them accompany Bialik's poem, picturing the return to Zion and the city of Jerusalem. In its first six years of print, ninety-five thousand copies were sold! The old Haggadah as religion had become a broken mirror. It was hard to imagine a time when Hebrew was out, English songs were in, and Jerusalem was not in the forefront of Passover consciousness.

At the same time, this Reform Haggadah retained and even reemphasized its movement's religious message. It resurrected an ancient custom of having a fifth cup of wine, as a symbol of religious hope in the coming of a messiah. The ten plagues were accompanied by a mitigating midrash in which God warns Israel not to gloat over the death of the Egyptians. A new introductory prayer tells everyone at the Seder that "we gather for our sacred [!] celebration" and "heed once again our divine [!] call to service, living a story that is told for all [!] peoples." The particularism of peoplehood is merged with the universalism of religion. Most Reform Jews exchanged the old Haggadah for the new one, because it so eloquently presented the kind of post-1967 Jew they thought they were.

The parallel story for Conservative Judaism is quite different. Common wisdom has it that there is little or no difference any more between Reform and

Conservative Jews. But despite significant overlap, people who self-identify as one or the other attend synagogues with radically different cultures. Liturgically, for example, Reform Jews adopt novelties that Conservative Jews may find "faddy." Conservative Jews expect a preponderance of Hebrew prayer (even if they do not understand it). Reform Jews stress the understanding of prayers, so welcome the feel of Hebrew here and there, but only alongside a good deal of English—the Hebrew they read may be in transliteration. Reform Jews go to services that start "on time" and end at a "reasonable" hour thereafter. Conservative Jews arrive late for services but leave only after sitting (and standing) for a long, long time. Emphasizing personal meaningfulness, Reform Jews pare and alter service content and style; Conservative Jews keep the liturgy intact, even, sometimes, at the expense of aesthetic fulfillment.

Even where the two movements use the same language to describe themselves, they may mean it differently. Conservative Jews accent the study of text; Reform Jews study text too but do not see it as the center of their spirituality, the way Conservative Jews do. It is important for both groups to know they are doing things right. But Reform Jews believe "right" is a negotiation between tradition and personal meaningfulness, while Conservative Jews grant more authority to the tradition. Both groups claim to keep standards high but measure standards differently. For Conservative Jews, high standards mean a demonstrated ability to daven well, handle the Hebrew, know the choreography of prayer (when to bow, how to stand), and be comfortable in a traditional milieu anywhere in the world. Reform Jews measure services by the spirituality they offer, part of which demands continuity with tradition; but part also requires personal investment of professionals and worshipers in mastering new congregational melodies, integrating quiet moments of individual meditation, and leaving with a personal sense of healing and hope.

That is not to say that all Jews join the two movements with these factors in mind. Some, for example, affiliate with synagogues because of the preschools they have. Some Jews cannot even say for sure what denomination their synagogue is. But both movements have an elite tier of members who take their choice very seriously and who strive to live up to their respective movement's ideals.

We do not know how public worship preference impacts private family celebrations, especially the Seder, where people worry about the sensitivities of guests and the need to keep children occupied. Conservative Jews who are perfectly able to follow lengthy synagogue services conducted entirely in Hebrew may balk at leading a Seder that way. It is hard to know, therefore, how much denominational difference impacts Haggadah choice; and even if we know what Haggadah is used, there is no way to predict how much of it is recited or what portion of the Seder is recited in Hebrew as opposed to English. That is the situation now, however, not fifty years ago.

Before World War II, the distinction between the two Jewish types was more profound. Seders by Conservative Jews were likely still led by the second-generation adults or their parents, the original immigrants. Reform Judaism appeared cold and churchy to them. Most Conservative homes (using the term "Conservative" loosely) would have continued the normal immigrant custom of using a traditional Haggadah of one sort or another—after 1934, a Maxwell House Coffee version. There was no official Conservative Movement liturgy of any sort, a Haggadah included. Only after the war did Conservative Judaism publish its own prayer literature, and not until 1982 did the Rabbinical Assembly (the Conservative organization of rabbis) publish a Haggadah—its purpose writ large in the preface: it is the first Haggadah "that faithfully reflects Conservative ideology" (p. 6), by which the editor means "it is deeply committed to preserving the classic tradition," albeit counterbalanced by innovation, "responding to new developments and developing new dimensions."[5] Work on this Haggadah had begun five years earlier, in 1977, ten years after the Six-Day War and four years after the Yom Kippur sequel.

Even more than the new Reform Haggadah of 1973, this one fairly breathes the heady peoplehood decade that it marks. Reform Jews had had to make a radical turn from religion back to peoplehood, exchanging all-English prayers for an English/Hebrew mixture and reincorporating such staples as "Next year in Jerusalem." This was old hat to Conservative Jews, who had used the traditional Haggadah all along. Their 1982 Haggadah simply replicated what people were used to, including "Pour out Your wrath," the prayer for vengeance instituted by European Jews in the wake of the first Crusade.

Aside from a few small, albeit important, textual changes—like altering the Haggadah's focal midrash and bringing in Miriam—what is mostly new here is additional readings, marginal commentary, and a creative page design. It all adds up to a heightened identification with Israel under siege and Soviet refuseniks trying to escape, precisely the events that the Reform Haggadah had echoed. But Conservative Jews were already ethnic and identified far more readily with Jews under siege. Messages about Israel and the Soviet Union are more central to the Conservative Haggadah.

"Pour out Your wrath" had been missing from the Reform text. In the Conservative parallel it is given its own double-page spread, with the explanation that Jews must not "opt conveniently for chronic amnesia" when it comes to our oppressors. The page is to remind us also of "The Hadrianic persecutions [following the destruction of the Temple]. The Crusades. The ritual murder accusations. The Inquisition. The pogroms. The Holocaust" (p. 101). Neither Russia nor the Arabs show up in the prayers here, but they are evident everywhere in marginal commentary: the recollection of a secret Seder in a Soviet Labor camp (p. 96), for instance, and a poignant one-liner recalling the miraculous deliverance of hijacked Jews from a commandeered plane sitting on a runway in Uganda, "From Auschwitz to Entebbe in a single generation" (p. 69).

What distinguishes this Haggadah from its Reform parallel is the extent to which it recalls Jewish suffering, particularly the *Sho'ah*, coupled with proud documentation of a Jewish state with the power to defend itself, "a new breed of Maccabees," as the Haggadah (using words by Theodor Herzl) calls them (p. 97).

This is far from the traditional Haggadah as mitzvah. But it is also far from Haggadah as religion, the manifesto for religious identity from which even Reform Jews in the 1970s were retreating. It is entirely a document celebrating peoplehood, even to the point of citing great mystic and spiritual leader Rav Kook, not on Kabbalah, but to the effect that "the Land of Israel is part of the very essence of our nationhood" (p. 97).

Better than any other Haggadah, the Conservative offering expresses the ethos of the 1980s: the identity that American Jews were working through, with the *Sho'ah* reinforced by the USSR and the Six-Day War. Having moved to the suburbs, where Jews were not at first welcome, we also find an emphasis on the universalist application of Judaism to people of all faiths: the Maggid of Kozhenitz prays for the redemption of "the other nations" (p. 113), not just Jews; Israel's experience in Egypt "has meaning for all times and for all living peoples." The greater lesson, however, is the connection between the Holocaust and Israel. Jews are the "ever-dying people" that manages nonetheless to be history's phoenix ever rising from the ashes. "From Auschwitz to Entebbe" means "from Hitler to Israel."

This was the de facto message of Jewish identity for most Jews at the time. It echoed a lesson that could be inferred also from the two semi-religious holidays that had entered the Jewish year: Yom Hasho'ah (Holocaust Day) and Yom Ha'atsma'ut (Israeli Independence Day). People began seeing them as related. One led directly to the other.

This lesson was being preached by an institution that had become far more powerful than the synagogues: Jewish Federations. Community-aid organizations had been around for decades, but the crisis of Soviet Jewry and the Six-Day War boosted them into prominence. They alone could raise the significant amounts of money required for what was becoming the foreign affairs agenda of the Jewish People in America. Federation became something of a Jewish government, to which all Jews were expected to contribute as a form of voluntary taxation. Its annual G[eneral] A[ssembly] attracted more people than any other Jewish conference—that, everyone knew, was where the action was.

But Federations were far from religious. Their leaders and professionals tended to be eastern European Jews who had great love for Judaism and Jews, but from a secular perspective. It has been called the civil religion of American Jews,[6] a rival to the denominational movements. Its High Holy Day was Super Sunday, when thousands of volunteers staffed phone banks to raise donations. *Am yisra'el cha'i*, not *Sh'ma Yisra'el*, became the watchword of the new faith: "The People of Israel lives."

We arrive at the twenty-first century with three Haggadah models: Haggadah as *mitzvah*, religion, or ethnicity. Before seeing how they are faring today, we need to situate within the trio of options the only other major experiment in Jewish identity through the Seder, Mordecai Kaplan's Reconstructionist Haggadah of 1941.

Kaplan has established his place in history as a bold and prophetic American Jewish voice whose thinking still challenges us now—fully 126 years after his birth. Conservative Judaism declared its movement independence in 1946, only after significant public debate with Kaplan, who had been teaching at the Jewish Theological Seminary since 1909. For many, he became hero, mentor, and prophet. Already in 1934 he had published the book that would make him famous, *Judaism as a Civilization*—obviously, yet a fourth option for the message of Haggadah identity.

Kaplan was an intellectual. From Emile Durkheim, a founder of modern sociology and a Jew (albeit estranged), he had learned that human satisfaction requires membership in a group. The Jewish People, therefore, needs no justification. The Napoleonic Sanhedrin was altogether wrong in thinking Jews are a religion. To be a people is the most natural thing in the world. We are, however, a religious people. And we are more than that. We are nothing short of a civilization. It is a people's civilization that defines its adherents' unique character: "elements like language, literature, arts, religion and laws."[7] We are, then, a religious civilization.

Kaplan's analysis of Jewish life was remarkably honest, even prescient, drawing attention to problems that others would write about only decades later. Like other living organisms, a people too has an inbuilt will to flourish, but as things stand, Jewish life is "superficially conceived." The "urge to Jewish survival must [therefore] be given an inspiring and irresistible motive."[8] Kaplan's solution included new liturgy that demonstrated a reconstruction of Judaism, including, among other things, an accent on ethics and the universalism of Judaism's message. In 1939—the very year the war on Hitler began—Kaplan sat down with his trusted inner circle to plan a Haggadah that would reflect these values.[9] The completed work was successful enough to attract blistering reviews by his colleagues at the Jewish Theological Seminary, some of whom refused to sit next to Kaplan at faculty meetings because they were honoring a decree of excommunication passed by the Orthodox at a meeting in which Kaplan's liturgy was actually burned.

Kaplan's Haggadah was addressed to Jews in the 1930s, overwhelmingly second-generation eastern Europeans, living in second-area settlements, and surviving the Great Depression. Palestine was not yet Israel; Hitler was swallowing up Europe; Stalin (though we didn't fully know it yet) was bent on destroying Jews. Years prior, immigration from western Europe had slowed to a virtual stop, and with the Depression stalemating America at large, Reform Judaism had stagnated. But there was no ideological entity called Conservative yet (that would come only after the war—Kaplan still called it Conservative Reformism, or the Right Wing of Reformism). Kaplan hoped to fill the gap.

Kaplan's Haggadah was a remarkable document for those days. In retrospect it does not seem so far removed from the religious message of Reform, for which Kaplan had a high regard. But he faulted Reform of his time for appealing only to the upper classes who could afford magnificent synagogues and for shrinking Judaism from a religious *civilization* into mere religion. To assume that Judaism was not also a nation (Kaplan's word, at times, for "people") was "a new kind of suicide." Referring to the Cheshire Cat from *Alice in Wonderland*, Kaplan explained that, for Jews, religion without a nation is like a smile without a cat.[10]

But Kaplan's immediate readership was not Reform. It was the "Conservative Reformists" whom he charged with urging loyalty to the nationhood of Israel even though what they were being asked to be loyal to was "nothing more than the memory of a people that once had body but is now a mere haunting ghost."[11] By this, Kaplan meant that Jewish Peoplehood had dissipated into nostalgia, without even knowing what it was nostalgic for. It was, in short, pure ethnicity—not ethnicity with culture, religion, and substance, but ethnicity as pure cat without the smile.

We can therefore categorize Kaplan's Haggadah as an early effort to avoid both extremes: Haggadah of ethnicity and Haggadah as religion. He was ahead of his time. Though some Reform leaders (as we saw) did resonate with the need for Jewish Peoplehood and homeland, it would take the Six-Day War of 1967 for the movement as a whole to get that message. And within the Conservative camp, ethnicity would only be exacerbated by world events from 1939 to 1990. In 1983 Kaplan's Reconstructionist Movement would undergo a revolution from within, as it merged with a loose coalition of *chavurot* that had emerged in the 1960s and 1970s. Much of Kaplan's philosophy was later espoused by leaders within Reform and Conservative Judaism as well. But in its day, the underlying message of the Reconstructionist Haggadah—the need for Jewish Peoplehood beyond ethnicity—went largely unheeded.

We should not imagine that people choose one of the three Haggadah models to the absolute exclusion of the others. Every mainstream Haggadah is likely to display at least some loyalty to the traditional text and its halakhic rules; they will all also have some semblance of religious ambience and at least some attention to theology—perhaps even what people today would call spirituality (more on that word in the next section); and every Seder has some ethnic orientation that dwells on the concerns of the Jewish People worldwide. As to the ritualization of the Haggadah script, any of these Seder models is as likely as another to feature study of text, attention to children, and universalistic reference to Judaism's hope for world redemption. I mean the types simply as ideals, to which Haggadot and the Seders they facilitate more or less end up approximating.

What makes the current moment so fascinating is the extent to which identity is up for grabs. Part of that is the simple fact that the baby-boomers are ceding authority to their children. But even if the generational changeover were years away, too much is happening culturally and demographically in America to imagine that the search for Jewish identity will remain unchanged. So we should conclude this survey of Haggadah types by chronicling changes afoot even now, and what they imply for the future.

AMERICAN JEWISH IDENTITY IN PROCESS

The 1960s brought a deep social cleavage between the right and the left in American religion. In the 1950s mainstream churches and synagogues had supported civil rights, and a decade later they took liberal positions on such issues as the Vietnam War, feminism, and the sexual revolution. By the 1970s, in churches at least, a conservative backlash had developed. They found their left and right wings at ideological war, so that liberals in all denominations had more in common with each other than they did with conservative opponents in the same church. As a liberal coalition across religious lines developed, most Jews joined it. The boundaries of what had once been hermetically sealed religious groupings were becoming porous; what mattered most was the position one took on social issues of the time, not the religion from which one took it.

The 1970s also brought a massive shift of the population south and west, eroding ties with families and traditions. Jews in new environments were free not to join synagogues, not to support Jewish charities, and not even to be Jewish anymore. No one they knew back home—parents, grandparents, and old-time friends of the family—was around to see them. The old pattern had been to live in all-Jewish neighborhoods, attend mostly Jewish schools, marry other Jews, and have Jewish children. But the cycle was breaking down. Birth control pills and changing sexual mores delayed early marriage; economic shifts kept Jews in school longer; feminism sent women pursuing careers. In graduate school, the workplace, bars, and parties, Jews met non-Jews as equals. Jewish identity became peripheral, intermarriage rose, and Jewish numbers fell.

A declining sense of Jewish obligation is no longer just a regional phenomenon. Fear of falling numbers and rising intermarriage has even provided it with a patina of social acceptance, since not attending synagogue, say, seems a minor infraction compared to actual assimilation. But the polarization of the 1960s continues, so the "no" to Jewish responsibility has been met with growing numbers of Orthodox Jews who elect to say "yes." Other than the Orthodox, however, most American Jews have shown a distinct disapproval of even the word *mitzvah*.[12] Conservative Judaism, which considers the inculcation of a sense of *mitzvah* in its members to be utterly critical, has dropped from 42 percent of the population in 1970 to only 32 percent today. Leaders of the largest religiously identified denomination, Reform (42 percent), are less and less apt to use the word at all. Instead, like liberal Jews in general, they opt for "Jewish meaning." Even those who choose Orthodoxy may explain that they find their choice "meaningful."

"Meaning" has become a catch phrase for Americans in general, having both a strong and a weak interpretation. Weakly put, "meaningful" can express nothing more than, "It feels good to do it." Its strong meaning, however, implies the existence of a transcendent basis for what is otherwise just the accident of being here. In this latter sense, used generally for religion, something is meaningful to the extent that it deepens human existence, suggesting a larger purpose to which one is drawn. People are looking for hints of this transcendent human purpose, what sociologist Peter Berger once called "a rumor of angels."

Orthodox growth on the right and the search for transcendent meaning on the left can be explained by the death knell of ethnicity in the center, largely among Conservative Jews. To be sure, young Jews of all sorts still enjoy those ethnic experiences that prove meaningful (a klezmer concert, for instance), but overall, the eastern European heritage of Jewish ethnicity has run its course. Ethnic ties once accounted for what just looked like fealty to *mitzvot*, but Jews were not choosing to be religiously responsible so much as they were going through the ethnic motions of being loyal to the tribe. They did all sorts of things toward that end: attended *shul*, ate lox and bagels, told Jewish jokes, and fasted on Yom Kippur. But as the justification of ethnic continuity is no longer compelling, they leave Conservative Judaism for something else or nothing at all.

But the old Reform justification of religion is in trouble too, despite the fact that America remains a deeply religious country where people are expected to believe in God and follow some religiously moral compass. Here, too, American polarization has proved formidable. Religion is alive and well on the Christian right but not on the left, where, by and large, liberal churches stagnate. They are accused of being religious but not spiritual. Without spirituality, religion is suspect of being mere outward form—just as critics like Emerson, Whitman, and even Kant had charged—lacking the very transcendent meaning it claims to provide.

So as much as the demise of ethnicity threatens Conservative Judaism, expectation of spirituality challenges Reform, which always promised religion but now discovers that religion and spirituality are two separate things. Religious practice (attendance at a Seder, for example) may be spiritual, but it also may not, in which case the practice becomes irrelevant because it is "meaningless." The rise in intermarriage only adds to the number of "spirituality seekers." It brings into a Jewish orbit adults with no Jewish ethnic memories, and no reason, therefore, to participate in the nostalgia of those who do; but coming from a Christian background, they see Judaism as a religion, so expect spiritual meaning from it.

Another trend is the impact of the subtle but significant governmental blurring of the boundary between church and state. America never fully divested its public posture from religion. George Washington tried to make the Commonwealth of Virginia officially Episcopalian. We still have a White House Christmas tree. Presidents are expected to attend church. Atheism is widely considered immoral. And a new era began with the inauguration of faith-based community initiatives, born of the notion that social welfare is not, as the New Deal believed, the responsibility solely of the government. More and more, religious groups are now engaged in "social justice initiatives." Among older Jews, this may ring a familiar bell, especially those who still remember Classical Reform sermons on the prophets and Reconstructionist followers of Mordecai Kaplan's universalism. But it evokes ready assent from Jews in their thirties, too, the generation coming of age in American Jewish affairs. And it surely resonates with the Haggadah's metaphor of slavery in Egypt. To the reasons for the Seder's popularity with which we began, we should add the growing power of Passover's message of social justice.

It has been said that Jews are just like everyone else, only more so. What this means, presumably, is that Jews herald social trends early and then epitomize them more completely. That is clearly not always the case—historically speaking, Jews have been opposed to much that the world has done (although it may be that even then, Jews *suffered* "just like everyone else, only more so"). There are, in any event, some long-term American trends that Jews do epitomize. We are the most educated group in America and probably the wealthiest and most secular. We are also the very model of "take charge" urbanity. As a result, we lead the way in the sense of personal competence and the resulting revolution against passivity as religious "consumers." In Jewish ritual generally, we increasingly want a say in what gets done and a share in doing it.

Here, then, are the trends that throw Jewish identity into question and impact the way we observe our Seders:

1. The growth among non-Jews and converts to Judaism
2. Polarization of response to *mitzvah*
3. The demise of ethnicity
4. The search for meaning, particularly in terms of spirituality and social justice
5. The desire to take an active part in all we do.

If the Haggadah we choose reflects identity, if our identity is in flux, and if we really are so educated and "take-charge," it will be no surprise to find us regularly in the market for new Haggadot. As we said at the outset, there are certain givens: reunions of family and friends, telling a story, and having fun. But beyond that, among those, that is, who want more, what Seders can we increasingly expect to have?

To begin with, Orthodoxy is growing; it is no longer marginal and no longer the default position (as it was thirty years ago) for people who told pollsters they were Orthodox, but only out of habit. For today's Orthodox Jews (who really *are* Orthodox), the Haggadah's status is not in question. Haggadah as *mitzvah* remains more viable than ever. At the same time, Orthodoxy has become more sophisticated. Just using the old text, and using it right, is less likely to satisfy. Orthodox Jews also want meaning from their rituals—hence the plethora of Haggadah translations, along with learned commentaries. The *ArtScroll Haggadah* is probably the best example of this phenomenon, but it is now possible to buy a Haggadah with marginal notes by luminaries of the past like Malbim, Sefat Emet, *Ramban*, Rav Nachman of Breslov, and the Chofetz Chaim, to name but a few; and familiarity with the text and its ritual frees competent people to do all sorts of experimental things. A halakhic Haggadah for today—for Orthodox and also for Conservative Jews who increasingly graduate from day schools—may be filled with commentaries, adapted to families with children, covered with illustrations, equipped with details of Jewish law, or all of the above, equipping the traditional text with whatever it takes to make the fulfillment of the Seder meaningful beyond the basic satisfaction of knowing one has done the right thing.

Jews on the liberal side of the spectrum are less likely to have sufficient familiarity with tradition to be especially intrigued by such things as the Malbim, Chofetz Chaim, and Sefat Emet Haggadot mentioned above. They may be happy enough just to have a Seder that excites children and provides good family time, worthy goals in and of themselves. Toward that end, they are likely to make use of the many Seder aids available, many of them emphasizing the family aspect of the Seder, like Noam Zion and David Dishon's *A Different Night* (Shalom Hartman Institute), David Arnow's *Creating Lively Passover Seders: A Sourcebook of Engaging Tales, Texts and Activities* (Jewish Lights), and Ron Wolfson's *Passover: The Family Guide to Spiritual Celebration*, 2nd ed. (Jewish Lights). Traditionally learned Jews may use them also, of course, but see them as ways to enrich the traditional Haggadah text more than liberal Jews who are not wed to that text do.

There are also lots of Jews without traditional Hebrew and learning skills who want to supplement family goals with adult personal meaning. Not tied to the traditional Haggadah text, they will seek a Haggadah promising spirituality. It is not surprising, therefore, to find another Reform Haggadah being published in 2002 and a Reconstructionist one two years earlier. I have omitted full discussion of them, since it is too early to measure their impact. But it does seem that so far, at least, neither Haggadah has become widespread. In its six years in print (as we saw), the 1974 Reform Haggadah sold ninety-five thousand copies. Reform Jews were only 32 percent of the population then. The parallel figure for its 2002 replacement, when Reform Jews have become 42 percent of the population, is twenty-six thousand copies. It is true that the farther one gets toward the liberal end of the Jewish spectrum, the more dependence on and loyalty to denominations grow. But denominationalism is receding. We are beyond the time when a movement can easily dictate a specific Haggadah for its members.

As an educated, competent, and take-charge generation, liberal Jews will accept their denominational Haggadah only if it satisfies their needs—for family Seders and/or for personal spirituality. The problem with spirituality, however, is that it cannot be mandated in a book. It is not *in a reading* so much as it is in *how the reading is read*, the way reading and speaking and music and movement come together to become a satisfying ritual. Jews seeking Haggadah as religion (but religion with spirituality) will have to contend with the fact that, to some extent, it doesn't matter what Haggadah they buy. As ritual text, the Haggadah can only suggest or constrict ritual possibilities— new Haggadot for them will have to be spiritually expansive, not restrictive. What matters is the Seder that the Haggadah becomes, and that depends on the will and skill of Seder leaders and planners.

Finally, we have the Haggadah as ethnicity. The ethnic Seder once needed no overarching justification; it is the nature of ethnics to do what they do—that is what makes them ethnic to start with. But ethnicity dies after three generations: the European immigrants, their children (who reject it), and their grandchildren (who try in vain to recapture it). Jews who value the ethnic aspect of the Seder will also have to deepen it with Jewish sources and add to it the dimension of spirituality.

MOVING FORWARD

Old distinctions are breaking down. Children of the baby-boomers abhor exclusivities. My three Haggadah categories have helped us think the matter through—that is the point of categories: to help us think. But once we think with them, we are free to unify, dismember, or even trash them, a trend well illustrated elsewhere. In a book called *The Collapse of the Fact/Value Dichotomy*, philosopher of science Hilary Putnam, for example, considers the age-old opposition between "what is" and "what ought to be".[13] Astounded at how everybody nowadays crosses over old boundaries to put the world together, anthropologist Clifford Geertz comments, "One waits only for quantum theory in verse or biography in algebra."[14] Philosophic genius Ludwig Wittgenstein concludes the treatise that made him famous by explaining that he has offered steps that the reader "may climb beyond…. He must, so to speak, throw away the ladder after he has climbed up it."[15]

My three kinds of Haggadah are rungs in a ladder that extends to a bird's-eye view of the ongoing American Jewish struggle with identity. Once we get the picture, however, we can throw the ladder away. The three modes of being Jewish are not necessarily at odds with one another. One can at least hope that we will find our way to a Haggadah experience that provides a little bit of them all. The closer one comes to Orthodoxy, the more *mitzvah* will claim priority; the farther away, the more religion will demand its day. But ethnicity has its own contribution to make: Jewish Peoplehood.

Peoplehood is how the story of being a Jew began. It is the underlying story of every Haggadah. Reform Jews said they were a religion, but they never entirely believed that religion alone was sufficient. How could they, with the Haggadah story ringing in their ears from year to year? Not that the world would have let them do so anyway—Hitler saw to that. And despite official scruples over Zionism, when it came to establishing the state, Reform rabbis were among those who led the way. Certainly after the Six-Day War, Reform ideology made up for lost time with a peoplehood-centered Haggadah that virtually all Reform Jews bought and used.

As for Orthodoxy, even to imagine the absence of peoplehood from Halakhah is absurd. Much of Halakhah applies *only* to Jews, to the point where, traditionally speaking, the Seder is held to be a Jewish-only event, hardly the place where one invites non-Jewish guests for the benefit of a universal message of freedom (see Landes, *My People's Passover Haggadah*, Volume 1, p. 142). The peoplehood of Israel has both halakhic and religious components. Jews of all sorts—not just Orthodox—may come together in what they share: the religion and Halakhah of peoplehood.

It is of course impossible to know exactly what tomorrow's Haggadot will look like. Given American marketing, they will probably include no end of options. But the Haggadah narrative that prompts them all is the story of peoplehood—and not just peoplehood: given our search for meaning and spirituality, we want peoplehood with purpose. Here is where it may turn out that Mordecai Kaplan was the most prescient. His particular solution for the 1930s will no longer suffice, but Kaplan was intent on making over Judaism into an American phenomenon, precisely our goal today—albeit in a different America than Kaplan knew.

I suggested at the outset that every Jewish culture has four stages, the third being *creativity*. We want to leave posterity with our American equivalent of the Babylonian Talmud, Sefardi poetry and philosophy, French commentary (the school of *Rashi*), Kabbalah from Ottoman Palestine, Polish Chasidism, Lithuanian talmudic genius, Enlightenment German scholarship, and the evolving American experience. And we want to leave our mark not just on Jews, but on the world, moving it closer to the redemptive vision that the Haggadah presupposes. To know we do both would be the transcendent meaning we seek. It would be peoplehood with purpose. Hence this book: a guide to peoplehood with purpose. It is *My People's (!) Passover Haggadah*.

Where Have All the Women Gone?

Feminist Questions about the Haggadah

Wendy I. Zierler

In the spring of 1976, while the rest of America was gearing up for the bicentennial of American independence, a group of prominent American feminists celebrated their own Jewish women's independence rite, in the form of the first New York feminist Seder. Held in the Upper West Side apartment of pioneering feminist psychologist Phyllis Chesler and co-led by Chesler and author E. M. Broner, the feminist Seder boasted among its attendees such other leading second-wave feminists as Letty Cottin Pogrebin and Gloria Steinem. As Chesler recalls, "We asked women to identify themselves by their first names and by their mother's and grandmother's names. We identified the plagues in feminist and political terms and also our own personal plagues.... Within a few years, *Ms.* magazine published a brief Haggadah from this Seder.[1] Each year our Seder was somewhat different and drew upon many feminist and therapeutic styles."[2] According to Broner, the New York feminist Seder constituted an important step toward "changing the order" of male-centered Jewish liturgy and ritual, filling in what had traditionally been omitted and filtering out that which had denigrated women.[3]

To be sure, this was not the first feminist Seder in history, though it seems to have been the first to include such high-profile American feminists. Already in the early 1970s, the idea of the feminist Seder had begun to germinate. Feminist activist Aviva Cantor Zuckoff published the basis of a feminist Haggadah in 1974, the outgrowth of a Seder she had conducted earlier with a group of like-minded feminists.[4] Around this same time, Jewish feminist groups in other locales such as Berkeley and San Diego had begun writing feminist Haggadot and conducting women's Seders of their own. A compilation of liturgies and commentaries from these emergent women's Seders, edited by Reena Friedman, came out in the Spring/Summer 1977 issue of *Lilith* magazine. A new era of feminist Passover ritual invention was clearly underway.

There are several reasons why Passover and the Haggadah provided such fertile ground for this kind of woman-centered innovation. Chief among them is the thematic centrality of both liberation and childbirth in the Exodus narrative. As Michael Walzer would later write in *Exodus and Revolution*, the Exodus narrative was "a story that made it possible to tell other stories"[5]; indeed, many Jewish feminists read their own struggle for women's economic, legislative, and reproductive rights into the Exodus narrative and yet felt that the Haggadah, as traditionally conceived, failed to honor the heroines of the biblical account. For too long, women had "slaved" to prepare Pesach for their families and yet remained marginal if not completely excluded from the Seder learning community. From now on, then, there would be a Miriam's cup commemorating the role of Miriam in the Exodus; the traditional four cups drunk of the Seder would be dedicated to great Jewish women from the past or to milestones of Jewish feminist activism; and the *Dayyenu* prayer would be supplemented with a *Lo dayyenu* text, providing an agenda of freedoms not yet attained by women or other marginal groups.

The women's Seder movement has resulted in the private production of scores of feminist and LGBT Haggadot, culminating most recently with the publication of *The Journey Continues: The Ma'yan Passover Haggadah*, as well as two women's Seder resource books, edited by Sharon Cohen Annisfeld, Tara Mohr, and Catherine Spector, *The Women's Seder Sourcebook: Rituals and Readings for Use at the Passover Seder* and *The Women's Passover Companion: Women's Reflections on the Festival of Freedom* (both Jewish Lights). The ideas and sensibilities promoted through the women's Seders have taken such deep root within liberal Judaism that many of their rituals and commentaries have been incorporated into "mainstream" Haggadot sponsored by the Reform and Reconstructionist Movements, such as *The Open Door: A Passover Haggadah*, published by the CCAR and edited by Sue Levi Elwell, and *A Night of Questions: A Passover Haggadah*, published by the Reconstructionist Press and edited by Rabbis Joy Levitt and Michael Strassfeld. Effects can be discerned in the modern Orthodox community as well. The Jewish Orthodox Feminist Alliance (JOFA) publishes a yearly Passover newsletter entitled "*Vehigadet levitekh*" ("And you [feminine] shall tell it to your daughters"), the very title of which suggests an aspiration to transform the Seder "telling," formerly construed as an activity for fathers and sons only, into one for mothers and daughters as well. Likewise, Joel B. Wolowelsky's *Women at the Seder: A Passover Haggadah* celebrates the modern-day entry of Jewish women into the community of Jewish scholars by compiling Haggadah commentaries from a variety of learned Orthodox women.

Given these thirty years of creative liturgical and interpretive innovation surrounding the Passover Seder, is there anything left to say? And given the cogent arguments stated and restated by feminists about the pervasive male bias of the traditional Haggadah, why bother with the traditional text at all? Why not follow the lead of those rejectionist feminists who, discerning the male-centered biases of canonical religious texts, conclude these books are "the message and not just the container for it?"[6]

To begin answering these questions, I need to confess my position and lay out my interpretive principles, beginning with my understanding of what constitutes a sacred "text." It is my conviction that rejectionist interpretation paradoxically reinforces the idea that sacred texts inhabit a space above history, interpretation, or context. In contrast, I maintain that these texts "exist" and are constituted only within a community of readers; even those texts with overt masculine bias are open to reformation through the process of engagement, critique, and reconsideration.

If one takes seriously the idea that a text is produced within a cultural context and equally seriously the idea that textual interpretation is radically subjective, then the text that I read and receive today, within my feminist community of readers, is not the same one that might be used to undergird and/or legitimate the oppression of women (or other "Others"). This interpretive orientation is especially applicable to a text such as the Haggadah, which (a) does not pretend, like the Bible, to be the word of God, and (b) is not so much a fixed and rigid liturgy as a work of meta-telling and meta-interpretation. One best reads the Haggadah as a handbook on how to tell the story, providing examples of how one might fruitfully digress about telling, making the experience ever fresh, relevant, and liberating.

If that is the case, though, I must ask again: why be bound at all to the traditional text? Given the Haggadah's obvious lacunae and biases, why not depart from the text entirely or at least largely? And given all of the work on women's Seders, why not cede the whole business of feminist commentary on the Haggadah to the already sizable number of women's Haggadot?

In answering, I confess a traditionalist conviction that if Jews recited the Haggadah for so many generations, then it means something to have a relationship with this ancient book. As for the idea of ceding feminist commentary to the women's Seders, I am reminded of my prior research into the beginnings of Hebrew women's poetry, where I observed a tendency on the part of early Hebrew women poets writing on biblical stories to engage in what I called a "Hermeneutics of Displacement," in which they foregrounded biblical women by completely displacing or ignoring biblical men. While this strategy can be seen as a necessary beginning point to raise feminist consciousness, it perpetuates an age-old system of binary oppositions and exclusions, this time with women excluding men instead of the other way around. Along similar lines, while women's Seders have served the critical function of creating a feminist ritual space, they nevertheless promote a notion of feminist Judaism as a separatist, women's-only affair. As early as 1977, Rabbi Sandy Eisenberg Sasso warned that "out of our frustration with the lack of recognition given women in the past, we mustn't evolve a situation in which we respond in kind by being exclusivistic. The Seder which speaks only for the Jewish woman, centers purely upon her enslavements and liberations, weakens our bond of solidarity with the whole of Jewish civilization and people."[7] Even earlier than that, Aviva Cantor Zuckoff imagined

> … a Seder that focuses on the oppression of Jews and on Jewish liberation
> from a *Jewish feminist viewpoint.* Such a haggada would deal honestly with
> the oppression of women while keeping the main focus on Jewish liberation.
> It would be a Seder for families of all kinds, whether by blood or by choice.
> In such a Seder, women would be as "visible" as men, but neither men nor
> women would be the entire focus of the Seder. This is the kind of Seder I
> would like to take my children to—if and when I ever have children."[8]

In writing this commentary, I have aimed to respond to Cantor Zuckoff's early pluralistic vision. Recognizing that feminism has now become *feminisms*, with its many offshoots and theoretical perspectives, I have attempted to incorporate a range of feminist methodologies and hermeneutics that are both critical and recuperative, deconstructive and reconstructive.

I begin with a *hermeneutics of suspicion*, a term originated by Paul Ricoeur to describe Sigmund Freud's interpretive method. Freud's interpretations of the Bible (as of human behavior) presuppose an elliptical text, with buried or repressed elements that the critic needs to decipher or uncover, sorting out truth from distortion. Though Freud's readings were typically male-centered, focusing on dramas between sons and fathers, his analytic method, especially in *Moses and Monotheism* (1939), has been instructive to many feminist biblical critics who read the Bible in an attempt not merely to expose the masculine bias of the Bible but also its repressed content or counter-traditions.[9] In my reading of the Haggadah, I proceed from a similar assumption that there is a buried under-layer of material, both in the Exodus story and the Haggadah, that we can creatively discern and conjure up in a feminist retelling. While I reckon with the male-centeredness of Haggadah, I make various suggestions in the commentary as to how we can use the framework, rituals, and digressive structure of the traditional text to write women and other marginal groups back into the text. If the Haggadah script conceives of Israel or God in purely masculine terms, I refer to ways in which feminist Haggadot have responded to this material with alternative liturgies. Where the Haggadah presents the table talk of the Seder as an all-male experience, I propose additional material that can bring women and their interests to the table. While many feminist Haggadot simply excise or displace the traditional text, here the feminist commentary and the traditional Haggadah reside side by side, typographically engaging, if you will, in a kind of talmudic argument or dialogue. Significantly, mine is not the only interpretive voice here. In sharing the page with other forms of contemporary interpretation, this feminist commentary becomes one of a plurality of voices, reminding us, as feminist Hebrew Bible scholar Jacqueline L. Lapsley has aptly cautioned, that "[m]any texts are patriarchal in some respects but are *still about something else as well*."[10] Being open to this "something else as well" is itself a feminist idea. As Judith Plaskow insists very eloquently in *Standing Again at Sinai*, feminism entails more than pursuing women's interests alone:

> For me, then, feminism is not about attaining equal rights for women in religious or social structures that remain unchanged, but about the thoroughgoing transformation of religion and society.… Feminism, I believe, aims at the liberation of all women and all people and is thus not a movement for individual equality, but for the creation of a society that no longer construes differences in terms of superiority and subordination."[11]

With this idea in mind, I try, where relevant, to widen my feminist interpretive lens to include such broader feminist interests as the triumphalism and violence of the text, the ideology of "us versus them," the evocation of both human and divine anger, as well as other linguistic and philosophical issues raised in works of feminist theory. Bearing in mind the relationship between feminist and gender studies and the obvious fact that not only women are gendered, I attempt wherever possible to note the effects of masculinist constructions of Israel and/or God not only on women but also on men. Lastly, recognizing that the meanings of the terms "male," "female," "masculine," and "feminine" are far from fixed, I endeavor to call attention to moments of "gender trouble"[12] in the traditional Haggadah, where the very idea of fixed gender categories is called into question.

POSTSCRIPT: WHERE ARE THE WOMEN?

One of the recurrent and most pressing themes in all feminist Haggadot is the need to repopulate the Haggadah text, especially the *Maggid* section, with women.[13] Since it is often noted that the Haggadah barely even mentions Moses, emphasizing instead the role of God as deliverer of the children of Israel, it seems necessary to account for this critical inclination in feminist Haggadot. First, it is important to note that the Haggadah does not omit all reference to humans. In fact, there are many men mentioned in the Haggadah. In terms of biblical men, the Haggadah refers (in order) to Joshua, Terach, Nachor, Abraham, Isaac, Jacob, Esau, Laban, Pharaoh, Moses, and Elijah. It also mentions ten (a traditional prayer *minyan*!) different rabbis: Rabbi Eliezer (twice), Rabbi Joshua, Rabbi Elazar ben Azariah, Rabbi Akiva (twice), Rabbi Tarfon, Ben Zoma, Rabbi Judah, Rabbi Yosei the Galilean, Rabban Gamaliel, and Hillel the Elder. How come so many men, then, and no women at all? Simply put, where are the women?

 The question becomes even more urgent when one considers the significant role played by women in the Exodus narrative. Two midwives, Shifra and Puah, defy Pharaoh's order to kill newborn Israelite males; Yocheved and Miriam, Moses' mother and sister, conspire to save him; and Pharaoh's own daughter sends her slave girl to rescue the infant Moses from the Nile. It might be said that if women were portrayed in the Haggadah as significantly as they are in Exodus itself, the impetus for a feminist critique might not be as urgent, though feminist critics of the Bible disagree as to how to regard the activist role of women in Exodus, some taking issue, for example, with the way women disappear from the text after Moses' safety is ensured.[14] That said, it cannot be denied that in the Exodus story, women occupy prominent positions. In contrast, women are nowhere to be found in the Haggadah's "telling."

 What accounts for this glaring absence? Tal Ilan has shown that aristocratic women were attracted to Pharisaic Judaism and played a role in its development and rising influence. The Rabbis who composed the Mishnah and formed the basis of the Haggadah were heirs to this Pharisaic Judaism that seems to have tolerated and in some cases benefited from the participation of women.[15] Judith Hauptman has similarly demonstrated that the Tosefta often pays charitable attention to women; Tosefta Pesachim 10, for example, which includes a version of a Passover Seder, mentions a husband's obligation to gladden his wife with wine at the Seder, whereas the Mishnah includes no reference to women at all. Hauptman generally argues that Tosefta Pesachim represents a more ancient Seder tradition than that depicted in the Mishnah.[16] All this simply intensifies the question: Where are the women? Why did the editors of the Mishnah edit women out of the Haggadah?

There are a number of possible answers that we can glean from rabbinic sources as well as from recent feminist scholarship. If one considers the Seder first and foremost an occasion for transmitting Torah from one generation to the next, it appears that the Rabbis, like many of their Greco-Roman counterparts, did not envision women as equal participants in this kind of intellectual activity. One need look no further than the famous statement of Rabbi Eliezer ben Hyrcanus, one of the rabbis featured in the Haggadah, that "whoever teaches his daughter Torah teaches her foolishness [sometimes translated as licentiousness]" (M. Sot. 3:4). Ben Azzai disagrees with Rabbi Eliezer in this mishnah, but curiously, he does not appear as one of the sages of the Haggadah. Rachel Adler speaks of the homosocial (men's only) study milieu of the Rabbis and the *bet midrash* (study house) as a state of mind that rejected dependency on women. In her study of rabbinic temptation narratives, she notes an opposition between women and texts:

> Both women and texts may be known, but one represents the knowledge of the body and its passions, while the other represents the knowledge of the spirit, of reason and commandment that rules the passions. [...] A good woman, one who accepts her proper role in the dichotomized worlds of women and of no-women, resigns her claim to visibility in deference to the superior claim of holy text. [...] A bad woman is one who makes herself a rival of the text."[17]

Building on these insights, it seems that if Passover celebrates freedom through an immersion in text, telling, and transmission, and if, for the Rabbis, an ideal (free) man was someone defined in opposition to women, then women could not serve as fitting textual models for the sacred discussion. Their invisibility from the Haggadah in effect buttresses the rabbinic masculine model of freedom.

Additional insight can be derived from Cynthia Baker's work on architecture and gender in Jewish antiquity. In her book *Rebuilding the House of Israel*, Baker addresses the exact question raised here—Where are the women?—and answers that "by all accounts they were *everywhere*."[18] While it is true that married women were often associated in rabbinic literature with the domestic sphere, Baker shows, through an analysis of the ancient architectural environment of Galilean Palestine, that there was a "fluidity, sociality, and multi-utility that characterized domestic space in both its architectural and rabbinic/halakhic expressions."[19] At the same time, she also offers a brilliant critique of the Rabbis' common depiction—she notes the same habit of thought in Greco-Roman culture as well—of wives (both socially and sexually) as houses. For the Rabbis, a wife was a structure built by her husband; sexually speaking, her organs were a domicile that the husband entered and inhabited. Her identity was constituted by her "houseness or inhouseness." And while she was permitted to go out of the house, she was required to do so with her head covered (see Kid. 1:11). As Baker writes, "*[I]t is precisely when she 'goes out'* (presumably from the house) and precisely because she is a wife (that is, a "house") that she requires a hat," an obligation that Baker describes as "the internalization of invisibility."[20] (I have added emphasis to the passage above referring to the rabbinic injunction that even in going out, women have to be "housed" inside a hat, since this seems to bear great relevance to women's participation in the rituals celebrating *y'tsi'at mitsrayim, the going out from Egypt*.) If, in the view of the Rabbis, women were characterized by "inhouseness," how could they serve as proper models and as interpreters of the narrative of going out of Egypt? If when outside, it was necessary for women to be rendered invisible, paradoxically through a visible sign, how could they be expected to occupy a place of visibility within a book that structures the discussion of Israelite deliverance?

The writing of this Haggadah commentary, then, follows in the line of other feminist Haggadot that have attempted to insert women into the text—to bring them "inside" as well as "outside." In demanding that women be visible *inside* the Haggadah, we insist on their ability to circulate in an unrestricted way through the *outside* spaces of freedom and spirituality traditionally occupied by men. In fact, we insist that our celebration of Passover define freedom in the broadest possible way, so that it is not enacted in opposition to or at the expense of any subgroup within our midst.

Moving through the Movements

American Denominations and Their Haggadot

Carole B. Balin

The twin processes of modernity, Emancipation and Enlightenment, penetrated western Jewry at the end of the eighteenth century and later, to some degree or other, eastern European Jews as well. Eventually, here in America especially, evolving views on language, aesthetics, and religion that justified approaches to, or retreats from, practice and observance came to be reflected in the phenomenon of religious denominations (also called movements): Reform, Orthodox, and Positive-Historical (known eventually as Conservative) Judaism in the nineteenth century and Reconstructionism in the twentieth. The same two centuries also ushered in myriad other ways to regard oneself as a Jew, at times altogether separate from religion and God. For instance, a Jew might see him- or herself as part of a nation (Zionism), a political movement (socialism and communism), an ethnic group, or a culture.

These dizzying and countless changes, along with the heightened pace of printing and distribution, resulted in an explosion in Haggadot. Whereas fewer than 250 editions appeared in the eighteenth century, the following century saw nearly 1,300.[1] That number likely doubled in the twentieth century. As printed materials became both more available and affordable, it became common practice for every person at the Seder to hold a copy of the Haggadah, in contrast to days gone by when it was usually only the head of the household and perhaps a couple of others who were privy to its contents, firsthand.[2]

In order for all Jews to comprehend its content, already in the sixteenth and seventeenth centuries, respectively, instructions and vernacular translations of the traditional text made their way into the Haggadah. By the modern era, bilingual, and in some cases trilingual, Haggadot became customary as knowledge of Hebrew diminished among Jews worldwide. Translations of the Haggadah have become as numerous as the Jewish communities that issue them—for example, Hindi (Poona, India, 1874), Afrikaans (Paarl, South Africa, 1943), Braille (America, 1964), Amharic (Israel, 1984), and, ironically, Arabic (Egypt, no date given).[3] By the nineteenth century, incrementally and with a growing self-consciousness, Jews moved beyond mere translation and began to modify the text itself.

The pages of modern Haggadot thus practically beg students of history to unearth layers of the Jewish past: Which elements of the traditional text are emphasized, eliminated, enriched, or otherwise edited? How much Hebrew is preserved in general and which passages in particular? What illustrations appear beside the text? What nonconventional elements (like dedications, musical notations, hymns, national anthems, and the like) are included? How are the Haggadah's age-old themes (e.g., liberation, renewal, redemption) applied by various communities to champion a cause, whether of universal significance or of a particularistically Jewish nature? All of these guided me as I compiled this commentary.

My commentary surveys scores of Haggadot, not just those of the official religious movements and their antecedents, but also those that I found particularly moving, of deep spiritual insight, of unusual thematic interest, or just amusing and even quirky. I covered Haggadot issued by kibbutzniks in pre-state Israel, patriotic Americans, modern-day Karaites, Sefardim, survivors of the Holocaust, communists, vegetarians, and pacifists, as well as advocates for Soviet Jewry and civil rights in 1960s America. I drew, too, from extant parodies of the Haggadah, created by those who wished to subvert the tradition or lampoon themselves (or others) as an assertion of beliefs. All these and more enrich our understanding of the modern Haggadah beyond the boundaries of the four religious movements. But ever since they began, Jews have taken cues regarding identity from the movements. That trend seems to be slowing as the twenty-first century proceeds, but because it was overwhelmingly the norm until now, I have taken special care to examine what denominational Haggadot say about being Jewish. Further detail on them, along with my observations regarding the non-movement Haggadot, can be found in the pages of my commentary. But before dispatching the reader to explore the commentary, an orientation to Haggadot issued by official bodies of the four North American movements is in order.

Predictably, Reformers, with their commitment to adapting Judaism to the times, were the first to publish a thoroughly revised and self-contained Haggadah. It appeared, however, not in Germany, typically regarded as the fount of liturgical innovation, but in England, in 1842. Two years prior, a kind of "Reform Club" formed in London, consisting of twenty-four families, nineteen Sefardi and five Ashkenazi. The group issued a declaration deploring, among other things, "the length and imperfections of the order of services" at the existing synagogues.[4] Consequently, they established their own congregation in the western section of the city, called it the West London Synagogue of British Jews, and hired the Reverend David Woolf Marks (1811–1909), an English-born biblicist who later became professor of Hebrew at University College.

Marks produced *Haggadah Lepesach: Domestic Service for the First Night of Passover.* Critically, the title indicates that the service is intended for only one night of Passover, emulating Marks's own belief that the second day of festivals be shunned altogether.[5] The content of the Haggadah is most unusual in its very lengthy scriptural additions, including Exodus 12:1–20 and Psalm 78, and its elimination of three of the four cups of wine, upon which the Mishnah is so insistent. Those elements and others that hew to biblical tradition led one scholar to consider the Haggadah's strong tendencies toward Karaism, the movement that broke away from rabbinic Judaism on the grounds that true Judaism was purely bibilical.[6]

But Marks's Haggadah proved idiosyncratic and thus fleeting. It was David Einhorn (1809–1879), an ideologue first in Germany and later in America, who came to have a more lasting impact on the American Reform Haggadah, albeit in a very roundabout way. In 1856 Einhorn published a short "Domestic Service on the Eve of Passover" within his well-known prayer book *Olat Tamid*. The all-German Passover service contained only a single phrase in Hebrew (i.e., the oddly constructed *tzevaot Adonai*, "hosts of the Lord"). It followed neither the traditional content nor order of the service and was less a Haggadah with its attendant prayers than a scripted dialogue between the knowledgeable head of household and the inquiring youngest member at the table. Because of the favorable reception accorded *Olat Tamid*, Einhorn issued an English translation of his prayer book in 1872, with the assistance of Reform rabbi Bernard Felsenthal (1822–1908). The "Domestic Service on the Eve of Passover" was included in the translation.

Two decades later, in 1892, the rabbinical arm of the Reform Movement in North America (i.e., Central Conference of American Rabbis [CCAR]) issued a "Domestic Service for the Eve of Passover" (called, parenthetically, *Seder Haggadah*—spelled with two *g*'s) within its proposed official *Union Prayer Book* (*UPB*; in Hebrew: *Seder Tefilot Yisrael*). While the form of the *UPB*'s "Domestic Service" is much like Einhorn's (i.e., a dialogue between parent and child), its content is not at all similar. Rather, the *UPB*'s "Domestic Service" is nearly identical to a Haggadah with, confusingly, an identical name to Einhorn's service (save for the absence of one *g*)— *Seder Hagadah: Domestic Service for the Eve of Passover*. This Haggadah and its subsequent editions (published separately) were the work of Isaac S. Moses (b. 1847), a rabbi involved in the editing of the *UPB* who had received his rabbinical diploma from Bernard Felsenthal, the very rabbi who had assisted Einhorn with the English translation of his "Domestic Service on the Eve of Passover" contained in *Olat Tamid*.

Approximately fifty pages in length, Moses' and the *UPB*'s "Domestic Service for the Eve of Passover" contain Hebrew only for the *Kiddush*, the blessings before eating matzah, and the Grace after the Meal. The English of the service is adapted from the German of *Seder Haavodah* (1882), the Haggadah of Leopold Stein (1810–1882), a moderate Reformer who served as rabbi in Frankfurt-on-the-Main and presided over the second of the three famous rabbinical assemblies held by liberal-leaning rabbis in mid-nineteenth century (pre-state) Germany. The text is a straightforward retelling of the Exodus story, based on biblical narrative, along with descriptions of the Seder symbols and various prayers and songs praising God.

These precursors helped to shape the self-contained *Union Haggadah: Home Service for the Passover Eve* that appeared under the aegis of the CCAR in 1907. According to its introduction, it was meant "to supply the demand of those to whom the old form of the Haggadah no longer appeals." Preceded by a pilot edition in 1905 (which opened from the right and contained traditional elements like Elijah's cup and *Havdalah* for seders falling on *motsa'ei Shabbat* [Saturday night]), the 1907 edition opened like an English book (from the left) and, save for several key passages, was entirely in English. Thumbing through the *Union Haggadah*, one views illustrations such as Moritz Oppenheim's "The Seder Evening," depicting bourgeois domestic life with a family dressed in sumptuous garb gathering in lavish surroundings, and a snapshot of "Religious Liberty" by Moses Ezekiel, set in Fairmount Park, Philadelphia, to commemorate the centennial of American Independence.[7] Aesthetically, this Haggadah was to be a thoroughgoing reflection of modern, especially American, sensibilities.

The *Union Haggadah* was revised in 1923, and then half a century later *The New Union Haggadah* (1974) appeared, with drawings by Leonard Baskin. The latter was not meant as a revision of the old but, as explained in the introduction, a "*renovatio ab origine*: a return to the creative beginning so as to bring forth what is utterly new from what was present in the old." Unlike its forerunners, it would "allow the genius of the original to speak to us again; to permit the discovery of patterns and designs in the texture of the liturgy itself without undue didactic pointing." While updated in the 1980s to make it gender-neutral, *The New Union Haggadah* was succeeded in 2002 by *Kol Dichfin* ["All who are hungry"]: *The Open Door, A Passover Haggadah*, edited by Sue Levi Elwell, with illustrations by Ruth Weisberg and musical revisions by Josée Wolff.

Like the Reformers, the Reconstructionists early on inscribed the Haggadah with their unique ideology. In 1941, nineteen years after the founding of the first Reconstructionist congregation, the triumvirate of Mordecai Kaplan, Eugene Kohn, and Ira Eisenstein published the widely controversial *New Haggadah for the Pesach Seder*, with a decidedly humanistic bent. The text had been updated so that the language and concepts of the ancient rite would "go straight to the minds and hearts of the men and women of [that] day," according to its introduction. Concerned primarily with the progressive improvement of the human personality, it omits "all references to events, real or imagined, in the Exodus story" that conflict with what is taken to be the highest of modern ethical ideals. In 2000, the Reconstructionist Press released *A Night of Questions: A Passover Haggadah*, edited by Joy Levitt and Michael Strassfeld (who two decades earlier had edited an experimental edition of the Conservative Haggadah, as per below). One hundred sixty pages in length, it is accompanied by a CD with thirty Passover songs and provides outlines for Seders geared to different populations: families with older children, families with younger children, families with members who grew up in different religious traditions, and families interested in women's role in the Jewish past, present, and future.

In contrast to Reform and Reconstructionist Jews, those of the Conservative Movement had to wait until the end of the twentieth century for a Haggadah of their own. However, proto-Conservatives Benjamin Szold (1829–1902) and Marcus Jastrow (1829–1903) produced a shortened Haggadah within their domestic devotional *Hegyon Lev* already by 1875.[8] It contained an abbreviated service in Hebrew with

German translation and was likely used by Szold's daughter Henrietta (founder of Hadassah). Within two decades (1891), Jastrow published a "Family Service for the Eve of Passover" in Hebrew and English as part of a larger prayer book known as "Israelite Prayer Book for Domestic Devotion" (*Israelitisches Gebetbuch für die häusliche Andacht*).

Though not published by an official arm of the movement, two Haggadot deserve mention for their connection to Conservative Movement luminaries. The first, *Haggadah of Passover* (Hebrew Publishing Company, 1942), contains an introduction by Louis Finkelstein (1895–1991). At the time of publication, Finkelstein was chancellor of the Jewish Theological Seminary, an expert in Talmud, and professor of theology. He would later become known as "the dominant figure of Conservative Judaism in the twentieth century."[9] He devoted more than half of his lengthy introduction—entitled, "Passover: Instrument of Liberty"—to describing the men involved in developing the Haggadah during the rabbinic period, which he regarded as an age "critical to the history of Judaism, and indeed of all civilization." He brought to life for his readers the "links" in *shalshelet hakabbalah* (the chain of tradition) that stretched from Rabbis Eliezer to Rabban Gamaliel—men of diverse interests and extraordinary erudition, as Finkelstein explained, who "labored in their own way to prevent the political and economic catastrophes [of their day] from involving also the intellectual, moral, and spiritual degradation of their people." The Rabbis' "inspiring example" no doubt guided Finkelstein and his colleagues, who labored to avoid the same fate in their own tragic age. A decade and a half later, Morris Silverman published *Passover Haggadah* (1957, 1972), which, too, might be considered an offspring of Conservative Jewry. Silverman was a Conservative rabbi, and his manuscript of the Siddur had already been published as the movement's *Sabbath and Festival Prayerbook*. By virtue of its near ubiquitous use by Conservative Jewry (until the appearance of *Siddur Sim Shalom for Shabbat and Festivals*, 1998), its author's name had become synonymous with Conservative Judaism's liturgy. Silverman's Haggadah preserves the classic text in its entirety. Meanwhile, the first Haggadah to be published under the official auspices of the Conservative Movement was Hyman Chanover's *A Haggadah for the School* (1964), intended exclusively for instruction at model Seders.

Finally, in 1982, three years after piloting an edition to solicit comments and suggestions, the Rabbinical Assembly of the Conservative Movement issued *Passover Haggadah: The Feast of Freedom* for general use.[10] It claimed to be the first Haggadah "faithfully reflect[ing] Conservative ideology"—a promise it does keep by attending, paradoxically, to both conservation and innovation.[11] On the one hand, it contains much of the classic text of the Haggadah in Hebrew, adhering to the movement's fidelity to tradition (conservation); and on the other, when faced with a problematic text, it may be dropped or reinterpreted (innovation). For example, when the traditional Haggadah cites a midrash that almost seems to take pleasure in multiplying the Egyptians' suffering at the Red Sea, this Haggadah drops the troublesome passage and instead quotes the biblical Song at the Sea (Exod. 15), and concludes with Miriam and the women dancing on the shore of the Sea to celebrate their miraculous salvation. (Ironically, this modification of the classic text adds Miriam but deletes the only mention of Moses' name that occurs in the traditional Haggadah!) Indeed, this duality of conservation and innovation appears as part of the structure itself: the main text of the Haggadah is surrounded by an abundant compilation of explanations, instructions, and commentaries. Taken as a whole, the Haggadah retains a liturgical quality but adds an educational dimension, attempting, perhaps, to raise the level of Jewish observance and consciousness among its constituents.

The same can be said of the latest iterations of the Haggadah compiled and used by many Modern Orthodox Jews. The standard-bearers of the traditional Haggadah for English speakers remain those of Philip Birnbaum and the ArtScroll Mesorah Series.[12] In 1953, Birnbaum edited a Haggadah for the Hebrew Publishing Company that was enlarged in 1976. A year later, ArtScroll Mesorah Series issued its first Haggadah. Capitalizing on the abundant educational opportunities inherent to the Seder, ArtScroll has by now issued over a dozen Haggadot, including first-time translations of classic commentaries from Abarbanel (1437–1508) to the Vilna Gaon (1720–1797), a youth edition, and *The Family Haggadah*. ArtScroll is not alone in its desire to appeal to the widest audience possible. With the growing popularity of do-it-yourself Haggadot, and aided especially by the explosion of available online sources, Jews of all stripes remain committed to building a bridge of spiritual meaning between the Israelites' Exodus of old and the circumstances of average Jews in the twenty-first century. This is a goal to be commended in any work of liturgy, but how much the more so in the Haggadah, an ever-growing chronicle of the Jews' lived experience.

"Good to the Last Drop"

The Proliferation of the Maxwell House Haggadah

Carole B. Balin

In the early 1990s, as the Soviet Union collapsed and fifteen independent republics emerged, one Jew among many emigrated from Moscow to Tel Aviv. Half a dozen Haggadahs—with their signature bright blue covers—were tucked away in his luggage. Although he could read fluently neither the English nor the Hebrew of the bilingual Maxwell House Haggadah, the books had become a treasured possession since being smuggled through customs and delivered to him decades before by American Jews sent on a mission to visit his family, refuseniks of the 1970s. The bizarre odyssey of these Haggadot underscores the widespread proliferation and prevalence of the Maxwell House Haggadah, a symbol of American mass marketing, which, as illustrated by this story, has had even a global impact.

Indeed, like the children of Israel in Egypt, the Maxwell House Haggadah has been "fruitful and increased and multiplied and the land is filled with them" (Exod. 1:7). More than fifty million copies of the Maxwell House Haggadah have been printed to date—reaching one million homes in 2006 alone—making it the most widely used Haggadah in the world. But for a brief one- to two-year interruption during World War II due to paper rationing, it has been reissued continuously since its inception in 1934, making Maxwell House coffee (and its well-known slogan "good to the last drop") a household name among Jews and, according to the latest survey in 1999, the coffee of choice among American Jews (double the figure for non-Jewish homes). Despite popular misconceptions, the Maxwell House Haggadah is, technically, not distributed gratis. As evidenced by "buy one, get one free" stickers affixed to even the latest edition, consumers are invited to pick up a Maxell House Haggadah, but only with the tacit

This essay relies on the archival materials located at Joseph Jacobs Advertising Co. and the generous assistance of its "mighty staff," especially Elie Rosenfeld and David Koch. Thanks as well to Stephen P. Durchslag for use of his first rate Haggadah collection.

understanding that they will also purchase a can of coffee. Originally available only at independent grocers, it has made its way over time into national American supermarket chains like King Kullen and A&P and is nearly ubiquitous in North America today. In addition, between five and ten thousand copies were mailed last year (for the cost of shipping and handling) to households requesting them who did not have access to the Haggadah. Besides homes, they are used in schools, senior citizen centers, jails, and in every U.S. military campaign since the 1930s.

The Maxwell House Haggadah has come to serve more than a utilitarian purpose. It has become a cherished ritual object for American Jews of all stripes, whose memories of Seders past are evoked by its familiar cover. In fact, in 1997, Hallmark issued a Passover greeting card with a Maxwell House Haggadah cover gracing its front and including the message: "Wishing you a Passover filled with all your favorite traditions." As described on the back of the same Hallmark card, Maxwell House Haggadahs are "cultural icons—prized family possessions that have been handed down through the generations and are a warm reminder of the past."

The Maxwell House Haggadah owes its origins to Joseph Jacobs (d. 1967), who served as advertising manager for the Yiddish *Jewish Daily Forward* during its heyday in the first decades of the twentieth century. Jacobs persuaded mainstream advertisers to recognize the Jewish press as a viable and attractive marketing medium for their products. By 1919 he had become successful enough to branch out on his own and establish Joseph Jacobs Advertising with offices on the Lower East Side and, later, on Madison Avenue (and today on the Upper West Side), where it eventually served clients such as Colgate Palmolive, Quaker Oats, and, of course, Maxwell House (which was originally owned by Cheek-Neal Coffee Company before becoming part of General Foods Corporation and later acquired by Kraft Foods).

In a stroke of marketing genius dating back to March 15, 1923, Joseph Jacobs Advertising, which still publishes the Maxwell House Haggadah, forged a propitious relationship between a people and a product. On that day, a full-page advertisement appeared in the *Forward* emblazoned with the heading *mitzvah alenu l'saper*, echoing the traditional phrasing of the Haggadah that admonishes *va'afilu kulanu chakhamim … mitzvah alenu l'saper biy'tsi'at mitsrayim* ("Even if all of us were smart, all of us wise, all of us experienced, all of us learned in Torah, we would still be commanded to tell of the Exodus from Egypt"). But instead of urging the annual retelling of the Passover story, the reader is told the critical fact that Maxwell House coffee is indeed "kosher for Passover."

As the ad explains, "Rabbi Bezalel Rosen of New York has made the necessary arrangements so that every Jew, even the strictest, should be able to drink the coffee without any doubts." Jacobs had enlisted the assistance of Rabbi Rosen to certify to Jewish coffee drinkers that the coffee bean was akin to a berry rather than a bean, or legume. Ashkenazi Jewish law forbids beans and legumes on Passover, owing to their physical resemblance to the five restricted grains of wheat, oats, barley, rye, and spelt; as a berrylike substance, however, drinking the product of coffee "beans" is permissible during the festival.

The fact of the matter is that while coffee is halakhically allowed at Passover, decaffeinated coffee is not necessarily kosher at any time, because its production involves alcohol. Responding to the latter, in 1947, Maxwell House introduced its orange-labeled Sanka, the first kosher decaffeinated coffee. That being said, Jacobs's ad of 1923 convinced many a skeptical Jew to drink a daily cup of coffee during Passover without guilt and was the beginning of a massive advertising campaign that persists to this day. In one clever turn, an ad likened a cup of Maxwell House coffee to "the fifth cup at the seder."

By far the most effective tactic of Jacobs's marketing strategy was the complimentary Haggadah (with the purchase of coffee). While his other attempts to win over the consumer with, for instance, free Chanukah candles or an offer to purchase a "Sabbath set"—consisting of Gorham sterling silver candlesticks and a service booklet—fell by the wayside, the Haggadah became a permanent fixture on the American Jewish landscape.

Although not nearly as successful, other companies attempted to commercialize the Haggadah prior to the advent of the Maxwell House Haggadah and even distributed them for free. For instance, the Haggadah given away by the State Bank of New York was reprinted many times over the course of the first decade of the twentieth century and contained an English translation by Lillie G. Cowen (wife of the publisher Philip Cowen, who printed the Haggadot on Fifth Avenue in New York). Noting the "typographical blunders, bad grammar, and mis-translations which abounded in the [Haggadot] used ... in all the books obtainable in this country," Mrs. Philip Cowen set for herself the goal of "the improvement of the English diction." Accordingly, her lengthy Haggadah had an idiomatic English translation, notes concerning the festival and the service, and, as she put it, "the first attempt, in an English Haggada [sic] to give adequate attention to the choral part of the service," which meant musical arrangements for the standard Seder songs. The text was aimed at the upper crust, it would seem, as an introductory instruction indicates: "It is customary to have the Jewish servants of the household present at least during the first part of the service." While Mrs. Cowen's Haggadah was among the earliest marketing tools used by a company, others followed, including those of the B. Manishewitz Company in 1943 (with a circulation of five hundred thousand by 1954) and Streit's Matzos and Chase & Sanborn Coffees by at least the 1950s.

None, however, prevailed like the Maxwell House Haggadah, whose popularity is due in large measure to the confluence of three factors:

- *Need:* the tremendous and ever-growing interest in the Passover Seder among American Jews, which, of course, requires for even the least observant some sort of "script" in order to enact the domestic meal-oriented ritual.
- *Availability:* the ready availability of the Maxwell House Haggadah, able to be had for nothing but a trip to the local supermarket.
- *Design:* its "script" in user-friendly English and Hebrew—namely, straightforward in form and innocuous in content.

When Jacobs introduced the Maxwell House Haggadah in 1934, the Jewish populace was made up largely of second- and third-generation Americans eager to partake in the traditional Seder of the old world with its attendant symbols and story intact but in a language that could be understood by younger generations. As English came to replace Yiddish as the "Jewish vernacular" and knowledge of Hebrew was on the wane, American Jews turned to the original Maxwell House Haggadah, which promises in its introduction to provide a "new up-to-date edition of the Hagadah [sic], arranged in a most simplified and attractive form." Indeed, the form is what makes this Haggadah up-to-date: it is arranged as two parallel columns, the traditional Hebrew on the right and a complete English translation on the left, with instructions given only in English. In order to help readers maneuver between the columns, the opening word of each Hebrew section precedes the start of each English section, so that, for instance, the Four Questions in English begins with the word *mah* in Hebrew followed by "Wherefore is this night distinguished from all other nights?" In this way, the less educated Jew might feel more at ease negotiating the ancient tongue.

In terms of its content, the Maxwell House Haggadah opens in the conventional right-to-left fashion, hews to the traditional text, and furnishes references to biblical verses on the Hebrew side. The few illustrations are unoriginal, such as the famous drawing of the four sons taken from the *Amsterdam Haggadah* (1695), which was copied more than any Haggadah in history.[1] While the translator is not identified, the English is characteristic of its day, with its formal "thees" and "thous," masculine God language, and gender-specific references to a male reader. Only the sequencing at the conclusion of the service is inconsistent with the traditional Haggadah. For some inexplicable reason, after *Hallel* but even before the fourth cup of wine and the concluding petition for the Seder to be accepted on high *(nirtsah)*, the Maxwell House Haggadah inserts *lashanah haba'ah birushalayim* ("Next year in Jerusalem"). This errant order was retained in later editions of the Maxwell House Haggadah until 1998, when the entire book was revamped in appearance and the phrase in question was transferred to its standard place at the very end of the Seder service.

Twice in its history, Joseph Jacobs Advertising significantly revised its Haggadah. The changes made to the 1960s edition seem largely aesthetic but are, importantly, a subtle indicator of the changing socioeconomic status and identity of its readership. Some three decades after its debut, it is spiffier, polished, more refined. For sure, it reflects the improved financial status of many American Jews, who had moved, seemingly en masse, to the suburbs and joined the middle class. Three decades after its debut, the Maxwell House Haggadah received its striking azure cover (formerly, it had been an unremarkable dull green) with accents of the same color throughout. The new graphic illustrations depict among other things a "normal" American Jewish family in the style of "Ozzie and Harriet." The increased overall dimension to its now-standard 5½ x 8½ inches allowed for larger and clearer fonts with more spacing between words and subheadings in enlarged Hebrew block letters. Significantly, however, the Hebrew on the cover is eclipsed by large English words that read "Passover Haggadah."

Deemed a "DeLuxe Edition," the Maxwell House Haggadah's congratulatory introduction of the 1960s boasted that Maxwell House Coffees had distributed "millions of Passover Haggadahs over a period of many years." Moreover, it promised readers a "complete text"—assumed by acculturating, midcentury American Jews to mean both Hebrew *and* English. Thus, as stated in the introduction, "There are no deletions from the *traditional* version, in either Hebrew or English" (emphasis added). Had the Maxwell House Haggadah now aggregated to itself the mantle of tradition?! Given its proliferation among American Jews, this may not have been far from the truth. Whatever the case, lest more observant readers fret, the introduction explicitly mentioned for the first time that "Orthodox Rabbis and scholars … worked … many hours on this book." They had given the Maxwell House Haggadah their blessing, as had Rabbi Bernard Levy, whose kosher-certifying organization with its familiar insignia of the letter "K" inside a circle (K) ensured that the growing line of Maxwell House coffees remained kosher for Passover. Notably, the English and Hebrew text contained in the 1960s version of the Haggadah is an exact replica of its predecessors; word-for-word, they are identical to earlier editions—though, alas, the page numbering is not the same, wreaking havoc for those families with multiple editions of the Haggadah. (From a marketing perspective, of course, that meant families with old ones had to acquire a new set.)

The 1960s Maxwell House Haggadah does, however, add brief instructions for preparing the Seder table, as well as transliterations of major prayers. The latter was obviously a tool to enable non-Hebrew readers, whose numbers had surely mushroomed, to participate as fully as possible in the Seder service. And the former betrays the growing number of years separating new generations from the old ones, who knew full well how to do what the new Haggadah now feels it is necessary to explain.

Absent altogether is any reference whatsoever to the two main historical events of the century: the *Sho'ah* and the founding of the State of Israel.

Thirty years later, as the twentieth century came to a close and Bill Gates and Steve Jobs had forever changed the way we look at text, Joseph Jacobs Advertising issued its latest edition of the Maxwell House Haggadah. As explained by the chief operating officer, Elie Rosenfeld, there was a desire in the 1990s to re-typeset the Haggadah for the first time since its inception, a likely response to the brave new world of desktop publishing. Moreover, lengthy discussions ensued among the executives of both Joseph Jacobs Advertising and Kraft Foods to alter its "traditional" text, perhaps abbreviating it or making it more contemporary. After consulting a variety of Haggadot, including those of the official versions of the Reform and Conservative Movements, which are in point of fact far lengthier, the decision was made to maintain the "tried and true." In order to attract the largest following possible, the creators of the Maxwell House Haggadah understood that neutrality was their best friend. They steered clear of controversy, so as not to be "offensive across the spectrum," in Rosenfeld's words. That is to say, the more generic the contents, the larger the readership it could attract.

In the end then, except for correcting the errant sequencing of *Nirtsah* (as mentioned above), the wording of the 1990s Maxwell House Haggadah remains virtually unchanged in the English and Hebrew prayers. Thus, the introduction to the 1990s edition can accurately state, like its 1960s antecedent, "This Haggadah is complete. There are no deletions from the traditional version, in either Hebrew or English." In format, too, it borrows from the past, retaining the dual columns, making the subheadings and font clearer still, and inserting a new table of contents to help lost readers find their place.

Yet modernizing influences are felt ever so slightly. With a nod to feminism, the Haggadah's erstwhile masculine-specific instructions of the 1960s ("He then elevates the dish containing the matzahs") morph into inclusive directives, albeit with clunky passive voice ("The matzahs are lifted as we recite the following"). The ambiguously worded instructions for "Grace after Meals" allow for a "company of ten" to count as a *minyan* rather than the traditionally prescribed quorum of ten men. However, the Maxwell House Haggadah perpetuates the myth of a heterosexual, married couple reigning over each and every Jewish household—as evidenced in the same post-meal prayer, which is addressed to "the wife" and "the husband." In a tiny concession to the State of Israel, a photograph of the *Kotel*, the Western Wall, appears at the Haggadah's end to illustrate *lashanah haba'ah birushalayim*, which is translated as "The Following Year Grant us to be in Jerusalem."

At the same time, the cover is something altogether new. The signature blue is shrunk to a 2½ x 3 inch rectangle, resembling a label on a jar of Maxwell House coffee, inscribed with "Passover *Haggadah*" in Hebrew and English along with the Maxwell House logo. The rectangle floats in a virtual photo album of snapshots of three generations of a family in their formal best partaking in a Seder and using, of course, copies of the famous blue-covered Maxwell House Haggadah!

Part II

The Passover Haggadah

A. SETTING THE STAGE
1. PREPARING THE HOME

On the night of the fourteenth of Nisan, the night before the Seder, it is customary to conduct a symbolic search for leaven. Prior to the search, bits of leaven are hidden here and there. It is traditional to use a candle and a feather to sweep up the crumbs. If the Seder falls on Saturday night, the leaven is hunted on Thursday night and burned Friday morning, to avoid doing either on Shabbat.

A. "The Checking of Leaven" *(B'dikat Chamets)*
סֵדֶר בְּדִיקַת חָמֵץ

Before the search begins, recite:

[1] Blessed are You, Adonai our God, ruler of the world, who sanctified us with His commandments and commanded us about burning the leaven.

בָּרוּךְ אַתָּה יְיָ אֱלֹהֵינוּ מֶלֶךְ הָעוֹלָם אֲשֶׁר קִדְּשָׁנוּ בְּמִצְוֹתָיו וְצִוָּנוּ עַל בִּעוּר חָמֵץ:

After the search is concluded, recite:

[2] Let all kinds of leaven in my possession that I have not seen and removed be rendered null and void, like dust of the earth.

כָּל־חֲמִירָא וַחֲמִיעָא דְּאִכָּא בִרְשׁוּתִי דְּלָא חֲמִתֵּהּ וּדְלָא בַעַרְתֵּהּ לִבְטִיל וְלֶהֱוֵי כְּעַפְרָא דְאַרְעָא:

Before burning the leaven the next morning, recite:

[3] Let all kinds of leaven in my possession, whether or not I have seen it, and whether or not I have removed it, be rendered null and void, like dust of the earth.

כָּל־חֲמִירָא וַחֲמִיעָא דְּאִכָּא בִרְשׁוּתִי דַּחֲמִתֵּהּ וּדְלָא חֲמִתֵּהּ דְּבַעֲרְתֵּהּ וּדְלָא בַעֲרְתֵּהּ לִבְטִיל וְלֶהֱוֵי כְּעַפְרָא דְאַרְעָא:

In the Diaspora, Jews traditionally have two Seders, which sometimes fall on Thursday and Friday, making Shabbat the very next day. When that occurs, two kinds of food (a piece of matzah and a cooked dish) are combined and set aside on Wednesday, as if the cooking for Friday night's Shabbat dinner has already begun.

B. Permission to Cook for Shabbat: "The Mixing of Foods" *(Eruv Tavshilin)*
סֵדֶר עֵרוּב תַּבְשִׁילִין

[4] Blessed are You, Adonai our God, ruler of the world, who sanctified us with His commandments and commanded us about the commandment of mixing.

בָּרוּךְ אַתָּה יְיָ אֱלֹהֵינוּ מֶלֶךְ הָעוֹלָם אֲשֶׁר קִדְּשָׁנוּ בְּמִצְוֹתָיו וְצִוָּנוּ עַל מִצְוַת עֵרוּב:

[5]With this *eruv*, may we be permitted to bake, cook, and warm food; kindle [Shabbat] light; and prepare during the festival all our needs for Shabbat—for us and for all others who live in this town.

בַּהֲדֵין עֵרוּבָא יְהֵא שָׁרֵא לָנָא [5] לְמֵפָא וּלְבַשָּׁלָא וּלְאַטְמָנָא וּלְאַדְלָקָא שְׁרָגָא וּלְמֶעְבַּד כָּל־צָרְכָנָא מִיּוֹמָא טָבָא לְשַׁבְּתָא לָנוּ וּלְכָל־הַדָּרִים בָּעִיר הַזֹּאת:

c. **Arranging the Seder Plate**

Prior to the Seder, arrange the contents of the Seder plate and place it on the table.

Preparing the Home
Haggadah Shel Pesach: Otsar Perushim V'tsi'urim, J.D. Eisenstein, Drawings by Lola, New York, 1920

93

BALIN (Modern Haggadot)

[5] *"Permitted to bake, cook"* Sophie Trupin was born in Russia in 1903 and made her own exodus of a sort in 1908 when her family immigrated to the plains of North Dakota. She recalls the arduous preparations for the Seder:

> My mother kept a kosher home, observing every holiday. This was never easy, but here it was even harder than it had been in the Old Country. Several days before Passover, when the melting snow had run into the narrow valley at the south side of the hill we lived on, my mother, sister, and I set about getting our homes ready for the holiday. Mother whitewashed all the walls and scoured the floors. She made the utensils kosher for Passover with *(p. 96)*

BRETTLER (Our Biblical Heritage)

[1] *"Blessed are You, Adonai our God, ruler of the world"* This standard rabbinic blessing formula has biblical roots but is post-biblical in origin. Its initial three Hebrew words are found in late biblical texts (Ps. 119:12; and 1 Chron. 29:10, "David blessed *(p. 96)*

GRAY (Medieval Commentators)

"The Checking of Leaven" Rambam (Moses Maimonides, Spain and Egypt, 1135–1204) points out that it is a positive commandment of the Torah to remove all *chamets* from the home prior to the time it becomes forbidden for eating. *Rambam* understood this to *(p. 97)*

J. HOFFMAN (Translation)

"The Checking of Leaven" Others, "searching," presumably because the traditional way of checking for *chamets* is by searching. But there is a Hebrew word for "searching," and this is not it. "Leaven-check" would be another possible caption. We choose "checking of" rather than "checking for" to make it possible to translate other captions in parallel (e.g., "the mixing of foods"). Our text has, literally, "The *seder* of...." *Seder* means "order" and is also the word we use to name what even in *(p. 100)*

[For prayer instructions, see pages 92–93.]

1. PREPARING THE HOME

A. "The Checking of Leaven" *(B'dikat Chamets)*

[1] Blessed are You, Adonai our God, ruler of the world, who sanctified us with His commandments and commanded us about burning the leaven. [2] Let all kinds of leaven in my possession that I have not seen and removed be rendered null and void, like dust of the earth. [3] Let all kinds of leaven in my possession, whether or not I have seen it, and whether or not I have removed it, be rendered null and void, like dust of the earth.

L. HOFFMAN (History)

[2] *"All kinds of leaven [chamira v'chamiya]"* Two nouns, roughly synonymous, denoting leaven. *Chamira* has the connotation of "strong" and appears, halakhically, as *chumra*, meaning "the strong [as opposed to the lenient] position." In English too, "Do you want something strong?" denotes alcohol ("strong drink"). *Chamiya* is more straightforward. A Hebrew *tsadei* regularly becomes the Aramaic *ayin*, making *chamiya* the Aramaic translation of the Hebrew *chamets*.

KUSHNER AND POLEN (CHASIDIC VOICES)

"The Checking of Leaven" Rabbi Ya'akov Leiner of Izbica (*Sefer Hazmanim, Haggadah shel Pesach* [Lublin, 1903], p. 7) asks why the search for leaven must take place the *night* before the Seder using a candle or lamp and not— at the more obvious time—during the day leading up to Seder eve. To put it another way: what are we *really doing* when we search the house with a lamp during the night?

The explanation is that the first step in preparing for the Seder is finding out

(p. 101)

(p. 101)

סֵדֶר בְּדִיקַת חָמֵץ

בָּרוּךְ אַתָּה יְיָ אֱלֹהֵינוּ מֶלֶךְ הָעוֹלָם אֲשֶׁר קִדְּשָׁנוּ [1]
בְּמִצְוֹתָיו וְצִוָּנוּ עַל בִּעוּר חָמֵץ: כָּל־חֲמִירָא [2]
וַחֲמִיעָא דְּאִכָּא בִרְשׁוּתִי דְּלָא חֲמִתֵּהּ וּדְלָא בַעַרְתֵּהּ
לִבְטִיל וְלֶהֱוֵי כְּעַפְרָא דְאַרְעָא: כָּל־חֲמִירָא וַחֲמִיעָא [3]
דְּאִכָּא בִרְשׁוּתִי דַּחֲמִתֵּהּ וּדְלָא חֲמִתֵּהּ דְּבַעַרְתֵּהּ
וּדְלָא בַעַרְתֵּהּ לִבְטִיל וְלֶהֱוֵי כְּעַפְרָא דְאַרְעָא:

LANDES (HALAKHAH)

"Burning the leaven [chamets]" Regarding the destruction of *chamets*, the Mishnah commands:

1. "On the night of the fourteenth [of Nisan], search for *chamets* by the light of a candle …" (M. Pes. 1:1).
2. "Burn [any remaining *chamets*] at the beginning of the sixth hour [the next day]" (M. Pes. 1:4). (A rabbinic day is figured from sunrise to sunset; that amount is divided by twelve to get an "hour," which can *(p. 101)*

(p. 101)

SIGNPOST: PREPARING THE HOME

PRIOR TO THE SEDER, IT IS CUSTOMARY TO SEARCH OUT AND THEN BURN ANY LEAVEN LEFT IN OUR POSSESSION.

IF SHABBAT FOLLOWS PASSOVER, SHABBAT DINNER WOULD HAVE TO BE PREPARED ON PASSOVER DAY. BUT THE RABBIS FORBADE COOKING ON A HOLIDAY FOR THE NEXT DAY. THAT WOULD OCCASION NO PROBLEM FOR A WEEKDAY, WHICH REQUIRES NO ADVANCE PREPARATION FOR SUPPER. SHABBAT DINNER, HOWEVER, IS DIFFERENT. SO IF THE NEXT DAY IS SHABBAT, THE RABBIS PRESCRIBE AN ERUV TAVSHILIN *(PRONOUNCED AY-ROOV TAHV-SHEE-LEEN), SETTING ASIDE A MIXTURE OF BREAD AND COOKED FOOD UNDER THE LEGAL FICTION THAT*

(p. 104)

(p. 104)

ZIERLER (FEMINIST VOICES)

"The Checking of Leaven" What does it mean for us to eschew *chamets*, even if temporarily? An ecofeminist interpretation might view the practice of searching out and abstaining from fermented foods that expand and puff up over time as a commitment to a more careful and efficient use of our time and resources. It seems especially pertinent in the springtime, just as the earth renews and replenishes itself, to engage in a symbolic repudiation of waste and excess. Modern technology has enslaved us to habits of over-indulgence and misuse. At the time of year when the natural world is most glorious and full of promise, we need to answer the urgent call of conservation and renewal. By pronouncing *(p. 104)*

(p. 104)

B. Permission to Cook for Shabbat: "The Mixing of Foods" (*Eruv Tavshilin*)

סֵדֶר עֵרוּב תַּבְשִׁילִין

[4] Blessed are You, Adonai our God, ruler of the world, who sanctified us with His commandments and commanded us about the commandment of mixing.

בָּרוּךְ אַתָּה יְיָ אֱלֹהֵינוּ מֶלֶךְ הָעוֹלָם אֲשֶׁר קִדְּשָׁנוּ בְּמִצְוֹתָיו וְצִוָּנוּ עַל מִצְוַת עֵרוּב: [4]

[5] With this *eruv*, may we be permitted to bake, cook, and warm food; kindle [Shabbat] light; and prepare during the festival all our needs for Shabbat—for us and for all others who live in this town.

בַּהֲדֵין עֵרוּבָא יְהֵא שָׁרֵא לָנָא לְמֵפָא וּלְבַשָּׁלָא וּלְאַטְמָנָא וּלְאַדְלָקָא שְׁרָגָא וּלְמֶעְבַּד כָּל־צָרְכָנָא מִיּוֹמָא טָבָא לְשַׁבַּתָּא לָנוּ וּלְכָל־הַדָּרִים בָּעִיר הַזֹּאת: [5]

C. Arranging the Seder Plate

Prior to the Seder, arrange the contents of the Seder plate and place it on the table.

BALIN (MODERN HAGGADOT)

scalding hot water. A stone was first heated in the range until it was very hot. It was then put into a very large pot of boiling water, making the water sizzle and hiss. The utensils were boiled for some time in this water. In addition, every piece of furniture was carried down to the slew and scrubbed and allowed to dry on the bank where the young grass was just beginning to appear.[1]

—◆—

BRETTLER (OUR BIBLICAL HERITAGE)

Adonai in front of all the assemblage; David said, 'Blessed are You, Adonai, God of Israel our father, from eternity to eternity'"), while *melekh olam* (rather than *melekh ha'olam*) is found in Jeremiah 10:10 and Psalm 10:16. In the Bible, however, *olam* always means "eternity," while in rabbinic literature it refers to the geographical world as well.

[2] *"Leaven"* The Bible contains several laws concerning leaven (starter dough that contains natural yeast, or dough that has been left out to absorb yeast from the environment—see Exodus 12:34, "So the people took their dough before it was leavened") during Passover. Compare, for example, the following three verses

concerning the exact prohibition and when it begins:

> Exodus 12:15: Seven days you shall eat unleavened bread; on the very first day you
> shall remove leaven from your houses….
> Exodus 13:7: no leavened bread shall be seen with you, and no leaven shall be seen
> in all your territory….
> Deuteronomy 16:3: You shall not eat anything leavened with it; for seven days there-
> after….

The rabbinic law that insists that all leaven must be removed before the festival commences reflects stringencies of each of these biblical passages. The Bible knows of no ritual similar to the one suggested here for searching and burning *chamets*.

[2] *"Let all kinds of leaven"* This formula is in Aramaic, rather than Hebrew. Already during the Babylonian exile (586–538 BCE) many Jews began to use Aramaic, the lingua franca of the ancient Near East at that time, and several late biblical books (e.g., Ezra-Nehemiah, Daniel) are written in a mixture of Aramaic and Hebrew. Exactly when Aramaic fully replaced Hebrew as a spoken language is uncertain, although the destruction of the Second Temple (70 CE) likely accelerated this process. The phrases "in my possession" and "seen" reflect a literal understanding of Exodus 13:7: "no leavened bread shall *be seen with you*, and no leaven shall *be seen*…."

"Eruv tavshilin" This ritual is post-biblical in origin.

———◆———

GRAY (MEDIEVAL COMMENTATORS)

mean "that he [the owner of the *chamets*] should nullify it in his heart, consider it like dust, and resolve in his heart that he has no *chamets* in his domain at all" (Laws of *Chamets* and Matzah 2:2). Although these mental resolutions are biblically sufficient, the talmudic Sages ruled that people must actually search for *chamets* (the search is called *b'dikat chamets*, or "checking of leaven") in the crevices and hidden places in their homes by the light of a candle on the evening of the fourteenth of Nisan. Even though the date and time of day of the search are derived from scriptural verses, *Rambam* also quotes the Sages as saying that nighttime is a good time for the search, since most people are home. Moreover, candlelight is good for conducting the search—particularly in crevices and hidden places (Laws of *Chamets* and Matzah 2:3, based on BT Pes. 4a). When the search is over and the *chamets* has been collected, it is carefully kept in one place in preparation for its destruction the next morning.

David Abudarham (Spain, fourteenth century) asks why the Torah and rabbinic Sages required us to undertake the effort of searching for, mentally nullifying, and then physically destroying the *chamets*. Why are we not required to do the same with other items we are forbidden to eat? His answer is that while most Jews stay away from the well-known forbidden foods all the time and thus are accustomed to avoiding them, *chamets* is different. In the case of *chamets*, we are dealing with a temporarily forbidden food that in essence is permitted. Thus, since we are unaccustomed to the prohibition of *chamets*, we may forget and accidentally eat it if we find it during Passover. To avoid this possibility, we search for it, destroy it, and mentally nullify it in advance.

[1] *"Burning the leaven"* The search for *chamets* is preceded by a blessing ending "... burning the leaven." The Hebrew reads *al bi'ur chamets*. The version of the blessing found in the Haggadah is the one marked by the Talmud as the "law" (Pes. 7b; Laws of *Chamets* and Matzah 3:6). *Hagahot Maimuniyot* (Rabbi Meir Hakohen of Rothenberg, Germany, late thirteenth century) points out that Rabbi Shmuel ben Chofni Gaon (Baghdad, d. 1034) was accustomed also to recite the *Shehecheyanu* blessing in connection with the search for *chamets* but notes that "we [the Jews of Germany and northern France] are not so accustomed" (note 5 to Laws of *Chamets* and Matzah 3:6). Abudarham asks why the blessing formula is *al bi'ur chamets* ("to burn the leaven") and not *al bitul chamets* ("to nullify the leaven") or *al b'dikat chamets* ("to search for the leaven"). He answers that *al bitul chamets* would be an inappropriate formulation of the blessing because nullification of the *chamets* is a matter of the heart, which does not have to be recited aloud. That being so, nullification is not legally considered an "act," and blessings are not recited over *mitzvot* that do not entail acts. Abudarham holds that the blessing formula *al b'dikat chamets* is also inappropriate because searching for *chamets* is a rabbinic, rather than a biblical, requirement. This is odd because we do in fact recite blessings over rabbinic *mitzvot*, such as reading the *Megillah* on Purim. Perhaps what Abudarham means is that although we do recite a blessing over the search for *chamets*, the text of the blessing must reflect the biblical *mitzvah* that is the point of the search—the removal *(bi'ur)* of the *chamets*—rather than the rabbinic act of searching, which is only the means through which we fulfill the biblical requirement to remove leaven from our dwellings.

[2] *"Let all kinds of leaven in my possession"* This recitation to nullify *chamets* appeared in a number of differing, although essentially similar, versions in the Middle Ages. Beginning with the Talmud, Rav Judah in the name of Rav (Pes. 6b) is the source of the notion that one must nullify the *chamets* for which one searched. The Talmud does not, however, preserve a nullification text. The absence of such a text from the Bavli likely led the *Ran* (Rabbenu Nissim Gerondi, Spain, fourteenth century) to write that the nullification formula we have was "received from the hands of the Geonim of blessed memory."[1] Yet *Ramban* (Nachmanides, Spain and Land of Israel, 1194–1270) earlier pointed out that the Talmud Yerushalmi—which is earlier than the Bavli—does contain nullification language. In Hebrew (not Aramaic), it reads, "All *chamets* that I have in my house and of which I do not know—let it be nullified" (PT Pes. 2:2, 28d).[2] Joseph Caro (Spain and Land of Israel, 1488–1575) later opined that despite the existence of this early nullification formula in the Yerushalmi, *Ran* called the nullification formula we use a "geonic tradition" because it is in Aramaic and, more importantly, is more expansive than the earlier formula (*Bet Yosef* to *Tur*, O. Ch. 434).

[2] *"In my possession"* The geonic-era work *Sheiltot* (mid-eighth century) preserves a version of the nullification that reads, "All leaven there is in my possession [*b'reshuti*] in this house [*b'veita ha-dein*] that I have not seen and of which I do not know, let it be nullified [*levteil*] from my possession and be like the dust of the earth" (*Tzav, Sheilta* 74). *Machzor Vitry* (Rabbi Simchah of Vitry, France, twelfth century) presents three versions of the nullification. The first two refer respectively to "this dwelling place" *(hada dirah)* and "this house" *(veita hadein)*. The contemporaneous Ashkenazi scholars *Raban* (Rabbi Eliezer ben Nathan, Germany, 1090–1170) and *Ravyah* (Rabbi Eliezer ben Joel Halevi, Germany, twelfth to thirteenth century) also present versions of the nullification that refer to "this house." *Machzor Vitry* quotes its third version, which uses the more inclusive term "my possession" *(r'shuti)*, from the geonic law code *Halakhot G'dolot* (Shimon Kayyara, Basra, Iraq, ninth century). It labels this third version "the essential one" (Laws of Passover 1). *Kol Bo* (Aaron ben Jacob Hakohen of Narbonne, France, thirteenth to fourteenth century) also points out that the reference to "my possession" is better because it is more inclusive (Laws of *Chamets* and Matzah 48): this term takes in *all* properties owned by the person doing the search, which is not the case with the other terms.

[2] *"Like dust"* Some versions of the Haggadah (not the one in this volume) close this recitation with the Hebrew phrase *"v'lehevai hefker* ("ownerless*") k'afra d'ara,"* literally, "let it be ownerless like the dust of the earth." An item that is declared to be *hefker* by its owner is capable of being possessed by anyone; this willingness to allow someone else to possess the item makes the original owner's renunciation of ownership complete. The presence of the word and concept of *hefker* in some versions of this recitation appears to be traceable to one strand of medieval Ashkenazi tradition. *Ravyah* required a specific reference to *hefker*, although apparently *Ravyah's* own father Rabbi Joel Halevi did not require it. One version of *Raban's* nullification text does not include a reference to *hefker*, while another version does.

[2] *"Like dust of the earth"* This ending, "dust of the earth," is the ending of the nullification as presented in a number of medieval sources, including the *Sheiltot* (*Tzav, Sheilta* 74) and *Rif* (Rabbi Isaac Alfasi, North Africa and Spain, 1013–1103), although many other medieval sources simply end "as dust." *Maharil* (Rabbi Jacob Moellin, Germany, fourteenth to fifteenth century) pointed out that "some end" with "as the dust of the earth" (*Sefer Maharil*, Laws of Checking Leaven 7), and *Rashbetz* (Rabbi Shimon ben Tzemach Duran, North Africa, fourteenth century) also included "as the dust of the earth" in his version of the nullification *(Ma'amar Chamets)*.

[3] *"Let all kinds of leaven in my possession"* Our Haggadah contains two nullifications: one to be recited on the night of the fourteenth of Nisan, after the *b'dikat chamets*, and the other to be recited the following morning, after the burning of the *chamets*. While the nullification at night is ultimately rooted in the Talmud, the morning nullification is not, and some scholars felt that it required justification. *Ritzba* (Rabbi Yitzhak ben Rabbi Abraham, France, d. 1210) ruled that it is a "kosher" custom to do the second

nullification, since people were accustomed either to buy *chamets* to eat that morning (which would not have been included in the nullification the night before) or to reacquire possession of the leaven they had nullified the night before by taking it as food.[3] *Rosh* (Rabbi Asher ben Yechiel, Germany and Spain, 1250–1327) agreed with this rationale, according to the report of his son, Rabbi Jacob ben Asher (Germany and Spain, c. 1270–1340) in the *Arba'ah Turim* (O. Ch. 434).

———◆———

J. HOFFMAN (TRANSLATION)

English is called a "Seder." Here it is used technically for a part of a ritual. Because we have no such word in English, and because we can indicate the role of the words "Checking of Leaven" by typographic means, we leave the word untranslated.

"Leaven" Chamets is a technical term that defies a perfectly accurate translation, but "leaven" seems to be the best we can do.

[1] *"Blessed"* Others, "praised." We are presented with two important issues when translating the Hebrew *barukh*. The first relates to the English distinction between "bless" (generally what God does) and "praise" (generally what people do). The Hebrew word means both. The second issue has to do with the grammatical form of *barukh*. It is a passive particle, but, unlike most passives, it has no active counterpart.

Ideally, we would use "BLESS-ed" (two syllables) for *barukh*, to distinguish it from "blest," because the former, like the Hebrew, is no longer the passive of any active verb. But because the hyphenated "bless-ed" is not available to us, both English verbs (bless-ed and blessed) are spelled the same way. Our choice comes down to "praised" or "blessed." Because there is no clear indication that we are praising God here, we opt for "blessed."

[1] *"Adonai"* We presume that "Adonai" is a name for God, so we transliterate it, rather than translate. Those who do translate it usually opt for "Lord," a tradition that goes back at least twenty-three hundred years to the Greek *kyrios* in the Septuagint. Translators who wish to avoid the masculine connotations of "Lord" sometimes substitute "Eternal." (Interestingly, in the British caste system, "lord" is gender-neutral, and both men and women can be a "lord." The first female mayor of London, Dame Mary Donaldson, insisted upon the traditional title "Right Honourable Lord Mayor." Similarly, women who own manors are the "lords" of the manors.)

[1] *"Ruler"* Or "king." But the Hebrew referred to a familiar, powerful figure, while the modern "king," for most people, refers either to a fictional character in a fable or to a powerless figurehead. Neither image is appropriate here.

[1] *"Burning the leaven"* Better would be just "burning leaven," but that phrase might also refer to leaven that is already ablaze.

"The Mixing of Foods" Again (see "The Checking of Leaven," *My People's Passover Haggadah*, Volume 1, p. 94) we have, literally, "The *seder* of the mixing...."

[4] *"Mixing"* That is, "mixing the food." This sort of elliptical reference is common in the liturgy. While it is less common in modern English, no better alternative presents itself.

———◆———

KUSHNER AND POLEN (CHASIDIC VOICES)

who we *really* are: where is our place in the world, and what we have been placed in the world to repair? Now, in this unredeemed world, he explains, we suffer because we don't know what we need to repair. But, in the future time of redemption, God will show us that even when we were *in the dark,* we were fulfilling a divine plan. In seeking out leaven by candlelight, we are, both literally and metaphorically, giving ourselves a glimmer of light amidst the darkness, in that the light that is used for the search reminds us that we already have the direction we seek.

"The contents of the Seder plate" Placing an egg (roasted or hardboiled) on the Seder plate is required. But many also follow the tradition of serving each guest a hardboiled egg. Rabbi Ya'akov Leiner of Izbica (*Sefer Hazmanim, Haggadah shel Pesach,* [Lublin 1903], p. 55) reports that his father, Rabbi Mordecai Yosef Leiner, was impelled by a constant yearning to accomplish more and grow spiritually. He never did something today that he had done yesterday, merely because he had done it yesterday.

He once interpreted the passage in Deuteronomy 16:22, "You shall not set up a pillar ..." to mean, "You must not set your concepts in stone." And, likewise, he read the injunction, "Let there be no graven images" (Lev. 20:4) to mean, "Do not pour your service of God into *fixed* molds." And this is the reason, he taught, that we eat an egg at the Seder. An egg symbolizes an intermediate stage between the hen and the chick. It is perpetually in a state of *about-to-become*—no longer a hen, not yet a chick. In this way an egg hovers between the generations, just as we constantly hover between who we were and who we will become.

———◆———

LANDES (HALAKHAH)

fluctuate from forty to eighty minutes. The "sixth hour" would be six rabbinic hours after sunrise, roughly at noon.)

The *Shulchan Arukh* (O. Ch. 433:3) rules that any room one might have entered carrying *chamets* is to be searched. Based on the *Ran* (Nissim ben Reuven of Gerona,

c. 1310–c. 1380), the *R'ma* (Moses Isserles, 1530–1575, Poland) concludes (O. Ch. 433:11) that we should even search places where eating is not customary, because bread might have been carried there, or crumbs may have fallen from clothing.

The Mishnah prescribes searching by candlelight, to the exclusion of the light of the sun, the moon, or a torch (for us, a flashlight). The Talmud (Pes. 8a) explains that because candlelight is focused, it forces one to concentrate on the search, and Maimonides (Laws of *Chamets* and Matzah 2:3) adds that a candle is better for checking crevices.

The blessing before the search *(b'dikah)* is "… who … commanded us about burning the leaven." The *Rosh* (Asher ben Yechiel, c. 1250–1328, Germany and Toledo, Spain; on Pes. 71a) discourages speaking about other matters during the search so as to maintain concentration on the task at hand. The *Maharil* (Ya'akov ben Moshe Levi Moellin, 1365–1427, Mayence, Germany) proposes hiding crumbs prior to searching in order to prevent a *b'rakhah l'vatalah* ("a superfluous blessing"). The *Ari* (Rabbi Isaac Luria, 1534–1572, Safed) hid ten pieces of matzah, symbolic of the ten *s'firot* that constitute the divine emanations by which the universe was formed and that parallel the universe we inhabit. The *R'ma* disagreed, on the grounds that one does not need to worry if no *chamets* is found, because the *mitzvah* is the *searching*, not the *finding*. Even though we search at night, we may eat *chamets* until the fifth hour (roughly 11:00 A.M.) the next day. To ensure that no *chamets* is spread after the nighttime search, the *Shulchan Arukh* advises keeping it in a centralized area and covering it, lest a "mouse" drag some away before the time of burning.

When the fourteenth of Nisan falls on Shabbat, the search is moved back to the night of the thirteenth.

The language for the declaration is presented in plain Hebrew in the Yerushalmi (PT Pes. 5:2), but the Siddur of Saadiah Gaon (882–942, Egypt and Sura, Babylon, p. 132) changes the language to Aramaic, and *Otzar Hageonim* (compilation of geonic responsa and interpretations) concurs, claiming that Aramaic will be understood by a common person (Pes. 16).

Bi'ur is understood as meaning "to destroy" or "remove completely." In trying to explain the opinions of the Mishnah (Pes. 2:1), the Gemara (Pes. 21a) discusses the tannaitic dispute over the proper way to dispose of it. Rabbi Judah compares *chamets* to *notar* (what remains of a sacrifice after its prescribed time of consumption), which we are prohibited from eating, owning, benefiting from, or seeing. *Notar* is destroyed only through burning; *chamets* is destroyed similarly. The majority view, however (the *chakhamim* ["sages"]), disagrees, stating that one can "crumble it, throw it to the wind, or toss it into the sea." *Rashi* agrees with Rabbi Judah; Maimonides and the *Shulchan Arukh* (O. Ch. 445:1) follow the *chakhamim*. The *Gra* (the Vilna Gaon, Rabbi Elijah of Vilna, 1720–1797) quotes the Yerushalmi in support of the *chakhamim*, but holds that if the time of burning has elapsed, or if one is unable to burn the *chamets* in the first place (on Shabbat, for instance), the other methods are acceptable. Today, the custom is to burn it *(R'ma)*.

If the fourteenth of Nisan is Shabbat (so burning is not allowed), the *Mishnah B'rurah* (following the *Rif* [Rabbi Isaac Alfasi, 1013–1103, Fez] and Maimonides) prescribes keeping enough *chamets* (from the time of the search, no later than Friday noon) to last for two meals (Friday night and Saturday morning) and then stop eating by the end of the fourth hour (around 10:00 A.M.). During the fifth hour (from 11:00 A.M. to noon), any remaining *chamets* is fed to outdoor animals or flushed away—it must be gone by the beginning of the sixth hour (noon). The *Rosh* (Rabbi Asher ben Yechiel, c. 1250–1328, Germany and Toledo, Spain) views the essential *bitul* (declaration of nullification) to be at night but recommends a second *bitul* after burning the *chamets* during the day. *Magen Avraham* (commentary on the *Shulchan Arukh* by Avraham Halevi Gombiner, 1637–1683, Kalisch) views the essential *bitul* as the one in the morning. But since one is already doing the *b'dikah* (the search) at night, one should declare a *bitul* at the same time, lest they forget to nullify their *chamets* again in the morning and violate the prohibition of owning it when the time arrives.

In sum, the laws of searching for *chamets* are as follows:

1. The prohibition against eating *chamets* extends to owning it, seeing it, and keeping it in our dwellings.
2. We search at night on the fourteenth of Nisan by candlelight.
3. We search wherever food or crumbs could have fallen off clothing.
4. There is a custom to "hide" ten pieces of *chamets* around the house, in order to find them.
5. Once all the pieces are found, one declares the *Kol chamira* formula (the *bitul*), making ownerless any remaining *chamets*.
6. By noon the next day, any remaining *chamets* is destroyed (preferably by burning), after which one repeats the nighttime formula, *Kol chamira*.

[3] *"Like dust"* Because of the prohibition against owning *chamets* during Pesach, we make this declaration so as to render any residual *chamets* as *hefker*, "legally ownerless" (Pes. 6b). Nachmanides (Moshe ben Nachman, 1194–1270, Gerona) thinks that just making it ownerless is insufficient. It must be declared nonexistent, like dust.

"Arrange the contents of the Seder plate [k'arah]" There are various ways of setting the plate (see *The Seder Plate: The World on a Dish*, pp. 37–46). The *R'ma* (Moses Isserles, Poland, 1530–1575) placed the items next to the celebrant in order of their usage: first, *karpas* and salt water; then matzah; then *maror* and *charoset*. Farthest away are the *z'ro'a* (shank bone or chicken wing, commemorating the *pesach* offering) and the *betsah* (roasted egg, commemorating the holiday sacrifice).

The *R'ma* follows a literal reading of a general halakhic principle, *ein ma'avirin al hamitzvot*, "We may not pass over one *mitzvah* in order to do another." Thus, if the matzah were closer to the celebrant than the *karpas*, he would have to reach over the matzah to get to the *karpas*—considered "an embarrassment" (so to speak) to the matzah. Other authorities disagree. They posit that the principle applies only when both *mitzvot* are commanded simultaneously: since matzah is not commanded at the moment that *karpas* is eaten, stretching your hands over the former creates no embarrassment. These authorities allow other ways of ordering the Seder plate, often according to kabbalistic design.

One variation especially should be mentioned. Following the talmudic practice, the *Gra* (the Vilna Gaon, Rabbi Elijah of Vilna, 1720–1797) did not require three matzot. Breaking one of the two replicates the way the poor must eat bread: broken. Halakhah demands a whole piece of matzah, but taking the perspective of the poor as his standard, the *Gra* considers the "broken" matzah "whole."

Additional laws of the Seder plate are as follows:

1. It should be set out before the Seder begins, preferably allowing others to help to engage them in the *mitzvah*.
2. Minimally, there must be one plate for the Seder leader; but if possible, each family present should have its own. Each person should be able to easily see one.
3. The plate is not only for show; it should be eaten from. This includes the roasted egg, but not the *z'ro'a* (shank bone) that symbolizes the paschal lamb, which we are forbidden to eat if not slaughtered in the Temple (see section on paschal lamb)

———◆———

SIGNPOST: PREPARING THE HOME

COOKING FOR SHABBAT HAS ALREADY BEGUN AND MAY THEREFORE BE CONTINUED, EVEN THOUGH COOKING ANEW WOULD NOT BE.

THE SEDER PLATE, A SPECIAL DISH OR TRAY BEARING THE SYMBOLIC FOODS THAT WILL BE EATEN OR DISCUSSED DURING THE EVENING'S PROCEEDINGS, IS ARRANGED AND PLACED ON THE TABLE BEFORE THE SEDER BEGINS (SEE "THE ARRANGEMENT OF THE PLATE," MY PEOPLE'S PASSOVER HAGGADAH, VOLUME 1, P. 43.)

———◆———

ZIERLER (FEMINIST VOICES)

that the leaven formerly in my possession is now "like the dust of the earth," we affirm our awareness that everything we do and amass affects the earth and its future.

"Eruv Tavshilin" If Passover begins on a Thursday or a Friday, the halakhic device of the *eruv tavshilin* allows one to cook food on *yom tov* for Shabbat, even though it is normally permissible to cook food on a festival for use only on that day. Literally, *eruv tavshilin* means "mixing of cooked foods." By taking a matzah and another cooked food, putting them together on a plate, and saying a blessing, one symbolically begins the process of cooking for Shabbat before the festival. The device of *eruv* thus hinges our ability through ritual to blend or blur otherwise fixed categories, a notion that seems

particularly relevant to the Exodus story. Feminist Bible scholar Jacqueline Lapsley notes in her commentary on the early chapters of the Book of Exodus that "crossing social boundaries of class, ethnicity, and gender figures prominently in these early accounts of rescue," as evidenced in the cooperation of a Hebrew sister and mother, an Egyptian princess, an adopted Egyptian prince (Moses), a Midianite priest, and his seven daughters. According to Lapsley, "these features are prominent enough to suggest that the puncturing of human social constructions is a significant part of what deliverance entails."[1] Performing the *eruv* ritual, with its connotations of mixing and blurring boundaries, can thus be seen as symbolic of a desire to bring about human deliverance on a broader, more enduring level.

"The contents of the Seder plate [1]*"* The contents of the Seder plate have been interpreted in many ways. Traditionally, the shank bone and the meat on the Seder plate have been understood as reminiscent of the *pesach* and *chagigah* sacrifices in the Temple. Talmud scholar Yael Katz Levine, who has done a great deal of work in recent years uncovering as well as creating liturgical and ritual materials of relevance to women, adds an additional perspective on these Seder symbols, noting that Rabbi Sherira Gaon of tenth-century Babylon referred to a custom of putting three cooked foods on the plate: a shank bone, an egg, and a fish item. According to one explanation offered by Rabbi Sherira Gaon, the shank bone and the egg are symbolic of the leadership of Moses and Aaron, while the fish item commemorates Miriam, thereby recalling the words of the prophet Micah, "I brought you up from the Land of Egypt, I redeemed you from the house of bondage, and I sent before you Moses, Aaron, and Miriam" (Micah 6:4).[2]

The idea of including fish on the Seder plate finds further support in a midrash that avers that the children of Israel were taken out of Egypt because of the righteousness of the Israelite women, who were associated with fish. According to this midrash, found in Sotah 11b, when the Israelite women drew water from the river, God caused small fish to swim into the water jugs. The women cooked the fish, washed and fed their husbands in the fields, and encouraged them to have children, despite Pharaoh's decree. This midrash seems to fix the idea of feminine righteousness within the maternal and caregiving spheres. It is worth noting, however, that immediately preceding this midrash, Rabbi Samuel bar Nachmani suggests that the Egyptians tormented the Israelites by making the men do women's work and the women do men's work. This gender confusion, though imposed upon the Israelites as a punishment, allowed the Israelite women to become sexual initiators, thereby defying social convention and Pharaoh's expectations.

"The contents of the Seder plate [2]*"* A number of years ago, feminist scholar Susannah Heschel was introduced to a feminist Haggadah that suggested placing a crust of bread on the Seder plate to symbolize the marginalization of gays and lesbians in Judaism. Heschel rejected this idea on the grounds that it associated homosexuality with ritual violation. Instead, she advocated placing an orange on the Seder plate to symbolize the fruitful benefits to Judaism that can come from the full participation of gays and lesbians in Jewish life. Including the orange on the Seder plate has now become a standard addition to many liberal and feminist Haggadot.[3]

קַדֵּשׁ · וּרְחַץ · כַּרְפַּס · יַחַץ ·

מַגִּיד · רָחְצָה · מוֹצִיא מַצָּה ·

מָרוֹר · כּוֹרֵךְ · שֻׁלְחָן עוֹרֵךְ ·

צָפוּן · בָּרֵךְ · הַלֵּל · נִרְצָה:

The Order of the Seder
Haggadah Shel Pesach, Berlin, 1927
Otto Geismar, illustrator

2. THE ORDER OF THE SEDER:
KADESH URCHATS ...

[1]Sanctify	KADESH	קַדֵּשׁ [1]
[2]and Wash	URCHATS	וּרְחַץ [2]
[3]Parsley	KARPAS	כַּרְפַּס [3]
[4]Break	YACHATS	יַחַץ [4]
[5]Narration	MAGGID	מַגִּיד [5]
[6]Washing	ROCHTSAH	רָחְצָה [6]
[7]Blessing over Bread	MOTSI	מוֹצִיא [7]
[8]Matzah	MATZAH	מַצָּה [8]
[9]Bitter Herbs	MAROR	מָרוֹר [9]
[10]Sandwich	KOREKH	כּוֹרֵךְ [10]
[11]The Set Table	SHULCHAN OREKH	שֻׁלְחָן עוֹרֵךְ [11]
[12]Hidden	TSAFUN	צָפוּן [12]
[13]Bless	BAREKH	בָּרֵךְ [13]
[14]Praise	HALLEL	הַלֵּל [14]
[15]Found Acceptance	NIRTSAH	נִרְצָה [15]

BRETTLER (OUR BIBLICAL HERITAGE)

"Kadesh urchats" The recitation of the order of the Seder most likely had a mnemonic function; no similar mnemonics for complex rituals have been preserved in the Bible.

———◆———

L. HOFFMAN (HISTORY)

[2] *"Kadesh urchats"* Only with the invention of printing could average householders dream of owning separate copies of a Haggadah for everyone sitting around the table. In the early years, the leader of the household might own a handwritten version on parchment, but even that was rare, given the cost: a single Haggadah required the hides of two to three sheep or calves—that's twenty to thirty animals for a family Seder of ten—not to mention the labor for curing the hides into something to write on, and copying prayers letter by letter. Only in the thirteenth century did Europe's textile industry produce linen rag paper, and only three hundred years later was scribal art finally rendered obsolete by printing presses. So, for much of the Middle Ages, our Haggadah had to be repeated from memory.

In the eleventh century, people began devising mnemonics of the Seder's order, presumably as an aid to memory. There were many of them, but one, in particular, stuck, and is used nowadays almost universally. Almost every printed Haggadah begins with it, arranging it in word pairs that are often sung as part of the actual Seder ritual. A "table of contents" has become part of the "contents" for which it was once the "table."

Kadesh urchats ("Kiddush and hand-washing")

Karpas yachats ("[eat the] *karpas* [nowadays, parsley, other greens, or even potatoes and] break [the matzah into two, hiding one half as *afikoman*]")

Maggid rochtsah ("tell [the Passover account, and] wash [again]")

Motsi matzah ("[say the] *Motsi* [blessing over bread and eat] matzah")

Maror korekh ("[eat] *maror* [bitter herbs and make a] sandwich [the 'Hillel sandwich,' combining *maror*—and in some homes, *charoset*—with matzah]")

2. THE ORDER OF THE SEDER: *KADESH URCHATS*....

[1]KADESH [2]URCHATS, [3]KARPAS [4]YACHATS, [5]MAGGID [6]ROCHTSAH, [7]MOTSI [8]MATZAH, [9]MAROR [10]KOREKH, [11]SHULCHAN OREKH, [12]TSAFUN [13]BAREKH, [14]HALLEL [15]NIRTSAH.

Shulchan orekh ("set the table [and eat the meal]")

Tsafun barekh ("[eat what is] hidden [the *afikoman*] and say *Birkat Hamazon* ["Grace after Meals"]")

Hallel nirtsah ([say the] *Hallel* [and the prayer called] *Nirtsah* ["It is accepted" by God].

For discussion of why precisely in the eleventh century Jews began to be so concerned with order, see *My People's Passover Haggadah*, Volume 2, Hoffman, "The Passover celebration has concluded appropriately," p. 196.

Additional commentary on the translation of these terms can be found in J. Hoffman's commentary as the terms appear in the Haggadah.

LANDES (HALAKHAH)

"Kadesh, Urchats, Karpas" This "ordering" of the Seder is referred to as *simanei haseder*, "the signs of the Seder." They are the guideposts upon which the Seder is conducted. The order we have here is found in *Machzor Vitry* (Laws of Passover 65) of the *Rashi* school (eleventh century, France) and attributed to Samuel of Falaise, a French tosafist. A similar, but somewhat different order is found in Abudarham (fourteenth century, Spain). Note that we have fifteen signs, symbolic of the fifteen steps in the Temple leading up to

קַדֵּשׁ ¹ וּרְחַץ, ² כַּרְפַּס, ³ יַחַץ, ⁴
מַגִּיד ⁵ רָחְצָה, ⁶ מוֹצִיא ⁷ מַצָּה, ⁸
מָרוֹר ⁹ כּוֹרֵךְ, ¹⁰ שֻׁלְחָן עוֹרֵךְ, ¹¹
צָפוּן ¹² בָּרֵךְ, ¹³ הַלֵּל ¹⁴ נִרְצָה. ¹⁵

the place where the Levites sang the *Hallel* while the *pesach* offerings were being slaughtered.

The *simanei haseder* are recited so that "one should not deviate from the established ordering of the Pesach [Seder]" (*Seder Tikun Hapesach*, Ya'akov Yisrael Kaneivsky, "the Steipler," twentieth-century luminary in Lithuania and B'nai B'rak, Israel). The custom today is to sing the entire order joyously and then, throughout the Seder, to announce with great drama our arrival at each new *siman*—that is, before making *Kiddush*, we announce, *Kadesh!*; before washing, we say, *Urchats!*; and so on. In this way, we awaken curiosity and wonder in the children. I was introduced to a fine *minhag*   (p. 110)

(p. 110)

SIGNPOST: THE ORDER OF THE SEDER

A TRADITIONAL MNEMONIC GOVERNS THE ORDER OF THE SEDER, AND BY NOW, IN MANY HOMES, RECITING OR CHANTING IT HAS BECOME PART OF THE SEDER ITSELF.

ZIERLER (FEMINIST VOICES)

"The Order of the Seder" According to Michael Walzer, the Exodus story is a "political history with a strong linearity, a strong forward movement."[1] The ordered recitation of the elements of the Passover Seder at the beginning of the evening seems to affirm the kind of linear narrative structure that French feminist theorists have identified with a "phallic position."[2] And yet, there are many circular or nonlinear aspects to both the Exodus narrative and the Haggadah. The story of Israelite redemption can be seen as a recapitulation of earlier events from Moses' early life. As a baby, Moses is drawn out of the Nile by Pharaoh's daughter; the text returns in a circular fashion to this initial moment, when God splits the waters of the Reed Sea and draws the people out onto dry land. Moses flees Egypt for the wilderness of Midian, and then returns to Egypt only to escape once again into the wilderness, this time with the entire people of Israel. Zipporah saves Moses and/or their first-born son Gershom from death when she circumcises the baby and touches his feet with the bloody foreskin, an act that is recapitulated when the Israelites place the paschal blood on   (p. 110)

(p. 110)

LANDES (HALAKHAH)

at the home of Rabbi Moshe Hier of Los Angeles, where they sing all the *simanei haseder* before each stage and then repeat it a second time, stopping at the action to be performed.

———◆———

ZIERLER (FEMINIST VOICES)

the lintels of the door, thereby diverting death from their doorsteps. Likewise, there is considerable circularity as well as disorder within the purported "order" of the Seder. The roundness of the wine goblet, the egg, the handmade matzah, and the traditional Seder plate all convey the sense of circularity that is echoed in the pronouncement that in every generation we reexperience the redemption of the Exodus story. And the digressive quality of the *maggid* section indicates that storytelling can assume diverse forms. The hybrid nature of the Haggadah teaches that to tell the story of redemption one needs to meaningfully conjoin a plurality of voices and social tendencies.

————◆ ◆ ◆————

3. BEGINNING THE SEDER

A. Lighting Candles

Light the candles, and recite the blessing:

On Friday night, include the words in parentheses.

[1]Blessed are You, Adonai our God, ruler of the world, who sanctified us with His commandments and commanded us to light (a Shabbat and) a festival candle.

בָּרוּךְ אַתָּה יְיָ אֱלֹהֵינוּ מֶלֶךְ הָעוֹלָם [1] אֲשֶׁר קִדְּשָׁנוּ בְּמִצְוֹתָיו וְצִוָּנוּ לְהַדְלִיק נֵר שֶׁל (שַׁבָּת וְשֶׁל) יוֹם טוֹב:

B. Defining Sacred Time (*Kiddush and the First Cup*)

KADESH: Reciting Kiddush

קַדֵּשׁ. כּוֹס רִאשׁוֹן

Pour the first cup of wine for each participant.

On Friday night, begin Kiddush here:

([2]There was evening and there was morning: The sixth day. [3]Heaven and earth and everything associated with them were completed. [4]On the seventh day, God completed the work He had done. On the seventh day, He rested from all the work He had done. [5]God blessed the seventh day and sanctified it, for on it He rested from all the work God had created to do.)

(וַיְהִי־עֶרֶב וַיְהִי־בֹקֶר: יוֹם הַשִּׁשִּׁי: [2] וַיְכֻלּוּ הַשָּׁמַיִם וְהָאָרֶץ וְכָל־צְבָאָם: [3] וַיְכַל אֱלֹהִים בַּיּוֹם הַשְּׁבִיעִי מְלַאכְתּוֹ [4] אֲשֶׁר עָשָׂה וַיִּשְׁבֹּת בַּיּוֹם הַשְּׁבִיעִי מִכָּל־מְלַאכְתּוֹ אֲשֶׁר עָשָׂה: וַיְבָרֶךְ [5] אֱלֹהִים אֶת־יוֹם הַשְּׁבִיעִי וַיְקַדֵּשׁ אֹתוֹ כִּי בוֹ שָׁבַת מִכָּל־מְלַאכְתּוֹ אֲשֶׁר־בָּרָא אֱלֹהִים לַעֲשׂוֹת:)

Other than Friday night, begin Kiddush here:

[6]With our masters' and teachers' approval:

[7]Blessed are You, Adonai our God, ruler of the world, creator of the fruit of the vine.

[8]Blessed are You, Adonai our God, ruler of the world, who chose us from every other nation and exalted us above every other people and sanctified us with His commandments. [9]Adonai our God, You lovingly gave us (Shabbat for rest and) holidays for happiness,

סָבְרִי מָרָנָן וְרַבּוֹתַי: [6] בָּרוּךְ אַתָּה יְיָ אֱלֹהֵינוּ מֶלֶךְ הָעוֹלָם [7] בּוֹרֵא פְּרִי הַגָּפֶן: בָּרוּךְ אַתָּה יְיָ אֱלֹהֵינוּ מֶלֶךְ הָעוֹלָם [8] אֲשֶׁר בָּחַר בָּנוּ מִכָּל־עָם וְרוֹמְמָנוּ מִכָּל־לָשׁוֹן וְקִדְּשָׁנוּ בְּמִצְוֹתָיו. וַתִּתֶּן־לָנוּ יְיָ אֱלֹהֵינוּ בְּאַהֲבָה [9] (שַׁבָּתוֹת לִמְנוּחָה וּ) מוֹעֲדִים לְשִׂמְחָה

festivals and times of the year for rejoicing; [10]You gave us (this day of Shabbat and) this Festival of Matzot, the time of our freedom (in love), a holy occasion, a memorial of the Exodus from Egypt. [11]For You have chosen us and sanctified us above all nations, (lovingly and adoringly and) joyfully and joyously granting us Your holy (Shabbat and) holidays as our inheritance. [12]Blessed are You, Adonai, who sanctifies (Shabbat and) Israel and the times of year.

אֶת־יוֹם [10] חַגִּים וּזְמַנִּים לְשָׂשׂוֹן. (הַשַּׁבָּת הַזֶּה וְאֶת־יוֹם) חַג הַמַּצּוֹת הַזֶּה זְמַן חֵרוּתֵנוּ (בְּאַהֲבָה) מִקְרָא־קֹדֶשׁ זֵכֶר לִיצִיאַת מִצְרָיִם. [11] כִּי־בָנוּ בָחַרְתָּ וְאוֹתָנוּ קִדַּשְׁתָּ מִכָּל־הָעַמִּים. (וְשַׁבָּת) וּמוֹעֲדֵי קָדְשֶׁךָ (בְּאַהֲבָה וּבְרָצוֹן) בְּשִׂמְחָה וּבְשָׂשׂוֹן הִנְחַלְתָּנוּ. [12] בָּרוּךְ אַתָּה יְיָ מְקַדֵּשׁ (הַשַּׁבָּת וְ) יִשְׂרָאֵל וְהַזְּמַנִּים:

Drink the wine while reclining ceremoniously to the left.

C. Distingushing Times of Holiness (Havdalah)

הַבְדָּלָה

On Saturday night, continue here with Havdalah:

[13]Blessed are You, Adonai our God, ruler of the world, creator of the lights of fire.

[14]Blessed are You, Adonai our God, ruler of the world, who distinguishes between holy and ordinary, between light and dark, between Israel and the nations, between the seventh day and the six days of work. [15]You distinguished between the holiness of Shabbat and the holiness of the holidays. [16]You sanctified the seventh day above the six days of work. [17]You distinguished and sanctified Your people Israel in Your holiness. [18]Blessed are You, Adonai, who distinguishes between holy and holy.

בָּרוּךְ אַתָּה יְיָ אֱלֹהֵינוּ מֶלֶךְ הָעוֹלָם [13] בּוֹרֵא מְאוֹרֵי הָאֵשׁ: בָּרוּךְ אַתָּה יְיָ אֱלֹהֵינוּ מֶלֶךְ הָעוֹלָם [14] הַמַּבְדִּיל בֵּין קֹדֶשׁ לְחֹל בֵּין אוֹר לְחֹשֶׁךְ בֵּין יִשְׂרָאֵל לָעַמִּים בֵּין יוֹם הַשְּׁבִיעִי לְשֵׁשֶׁת יְמֵי הַמַּעֲשֶׂה. [15] בֵּין קְדֻשַּׁת שַׁבָּת לִקְדֻשַּׁת יוֹם טוֹב הִבְדַּלְתָּ. [16] וְאֶת־יוֹם הַשְּׁבִיעִי מִשֵּׁשֶׁת יְמֵי הַמַּעֲשֶׂה קִדַּשְׁתָּ. [17] הִבְדַּלְתָּ וְקִדַּשְׁתָּ אֶת־עַמְּךָ יִשְׂרָאֵל בִּקְדֻשָּׁתֶךָ. [18] בָּרוּךְ אַתָּה יְיָ הַמַּבְדִּיל בֵּין קֹדֶשׁ לְקֹדֶשׁ:

D. **Gratitude for Being Here**
   (Shehecheyanu)

שֶׁהֶחֱיָנוּ

[19]Blessed are You, Adonai our God, ruler of the world, who has kept us alive, sustained us, and brought us to this time of year.

בָּרוּךְ אַתָּה יְיָ אֱלֹהֵינוּ מֶלֶךְ הָעוֹלָם [19]
שֶׁהֶחֱיָנוּ וְקִיְּמָנוּ וְהִגִּיעָנוּ לַזְּמַן הַזֶּה:

E. **The First Washing** *(Urchats)* **and**
   Dipping *Karpas*

   URCHATS: Washing without a Blessing

וּרְחַץ

Participants wash hands without a blessing.

   KARPAS: Dipping and Eating Greens

כַּרְפַּס

Participants dip parsley or another green leafy vegetable—or even potatoes—in salt water, reciting the blessing below and then eating the greens:

[20]Blessed are You, Adonai our God, ruler of the world, creator of the fruit of the earth.

בָּרוּךְ אַתָּה יְיָ אֱלֹהֵינוּ מֶלֶךְ הָעוֹלָם [20]
בּוֹרֵא פְּרִי הָאֲדָמָה:

F. **"Breaking the Matzah"** *(Yachats)*
   and Reserving the *Afikoman*

   YACHATS:

יַחַץ

The Seder leader breaks the middle matzah, reserving the larger piece for the afikoman.

Note: Customs involving the afikoman vary. In some homes, the Seder leader hides the afikoman, which children later find and hold for ransom. In others, the leader leaves the afikoman on the table for children to "steal" and hold for ransom. In either case, adults may pretend to search for the afikoman and, not finding it, only then negotiate the ransom price.

Lift the broken matzah for all to see and recite Ha lachma anya, *"This is the bread of affliction":*

G. **"Bread of Affliction,"** *Ha Lachma*
   Anya: Begin *MAGGID* **("Telling")**

מַגִּיד

[21]This is the bread of affliction our ancestors ate in the Land of Egypt.

[22]Let all who are hungry come and eat.

[23]Let all who are in need come and observe Pesach.

[24]This year here, next year in the Land of Israel.

[25]Now enslaved, next year free.

הָא לַחְמָא עַנְיָא דִּי אֲכָלוּ אַבְהָתָנָא [21]
בְּאַרְעָא דְמִצְרָיִם. [22] כָּל־דִּכְפִין
יֵיתֵי וְיֵכֻל. [23] כָּל־דִּצְרִיךְ יֵיתֵי וְיִפְסַח.
[24] הָשַׁתָּא הָכָא לְשָׁנָה הַבָּאָה בְּאַרְעָא
דְיִשְׂרָאֵל. [25] הָשַׁתָּא עַבְדֵי לְשָׁנָה הַבָּאָה
בְּנֵי חוֹרִין:

Pour the second cup of wine.

ARNOW (THE WORLD OF MIDRASH)

[7] *"Fruit of the vine"* The Sages of the Talmud understood drinking four cups of wine at the Seder to be an expression of freedom, *cherut* (Pes. 117b). Wine also filled in for at least some of the joy of the missing paschal offering in the post-Temple era: "Now that the Temple no longer exists there is no rejoicing except with wine" (Pes. 109a). But the abundance of wine at the Seder also reflects the general esteem in which the Rabbis held the fruit of *(p. 118)*

BALIN (MODERN HAGGADOT)

"Kadesh" The marriage of Jewish and American values finds an ideal home in the pages of the Haggadah. The "Domestic Service for the Eve of Passover" (American Reform, 1892) retained the traditional Hebrew of the *Kiddush* but *(p. 120)*

BRETTLER (OUR BIBLICAL HERITAGE)

[7] *"Fruit of the vine"* The ritual of drinking four cups of wine during the Seder is post-biblical in origin. Although there are many references to getting drunk from wine in the Bible, there are references *(p. 121)*

GILLMAN (THEOLOGICALLY SPEAKING)

"Kadesh" The term *Kiddush* stems from the Hebrew root *k.d.sh*, which means "set apart." The same root yields *kadosh* and *k'dushah*, conventionally translated respectively as "holy" or "sacred," and "holiness." What is "set apart" eventually becomes "sacred," just as the English term "distinguished" *(p. 124)*

GRAY (MEDIEVAL COMMENTATORS)

"The First Cup" Shibbolei Haleket (by Zedekiah ben Abraham Anav, Italy, thirteenth century) quotes *Rashi's* explanation (Rabbi Solomon ben Isaac, France, 1040–1105) that we do not recite the blessing "who did miracles for us" *(she'asah nisim la'avoteinu)* after the festival *Kiddush* because, prior to *Hallel*, we praise God, "who did all these miracles for us and for our ancestors" *(My People's Passover Haggadah*, Volume 2, p. 93).

"Yachats: Breaking the matzah" Abudarham asks why we *(p. 126)*

[For prayer instructions, see pages 111–113.]

3. BEGINNING THE SEDER

A. Lighting Candles

[1]Blessed are You, Adonai our God, ruler of the world, who sanctified us with His commandments and commanded us to light (a Shabbat and) a festival candle.

B. Defining Sacred Time (*Kiddush* and the First Cup)

KADESH: Reciting Kiddush

([2]There was evening and there was morning:

GREEN (PERSONAL SPIRITUALITY)

[10] *"Holy occasion"* The word *mikra* derives from the root *k.r.alef*, "to call." As a *mikra kodesh*, the festival is literally a "holy calling," as though the day itself calls forth to us to respond to it. Each of the festivals has its own "call." On Pesach we are *called to freedom*. The sense of call makes for a different type of freedom than that of simply breaking all restraints. We respond to it by examining our own enslavements and asking how we can become more free and bring others more freedom. As Jews we understand that "more *(p. 128)*

J. Hoffman (Translation)

[1] *"Light"* Others, "kindle," but "kindle" seems too rare an English word for the common Hebrew word.

[1] *"Candle"* The singular here is surprising; most translations emend "candle" to "the candles" in the form of "… (the Shabbat) and the festival candles," but the Hebrew is clearly singular and does not contain the definite article "the." Moreover, the word *ner*, which in modern Hebrew means "candle," predates the invention of wax candles. When the prayer was written, a *ner* was an (oil)   *(p. 129)*

בָּרוּךְ אַתָּה יְיָ אֱלֹהֵינוּ מֶלֶךְ הָעוֹלָם אֲשֶׁר קִדְּשָׁנוּ בְּמִצְוֹתָיו וְצִוָּנוּ לְהַדְלִיק נֵר שֶׁל (שַׁבָּת וְשֶׁל) יוֹם טוֹב:

קַדֵּשׁ. כּוֹס רִאשׁוֹן

(וַיְהִי־עֶרֶב וַיְהִי־בֹקֶר:[2]

L. Hoffman (History)

[10] *"The time [z'man] of our freedom"* See below, "And brought us to this time [z'man]."

[12] *"Who sanctifies Israel and the times of year"* One of the earliest strands of Jewish liturgy is the *Kiddush* ("Sanctification"), more correctly called *K'dushat Hayom* ("Sanctification of the Day"), the liturgical means to welcome or affirm sacred time. Its signature last line (the *chatimah*, "seal") sheds light on the Jewish understanding of the sacred. Times (like Shabbat), places   *(p. 131)*

SIGNPOST: BEGINNING THE SEDER

SOME OPENING PRAYERS ARE RELEVANT TO EVERY HOLIDAY: CANDLES AND KIDDUSH; AND HAVDALAH TO END SHABBAT, IF THE PASSOVER SEDER FALLS ON SATURDAY NIGHT. (FOR ADDITIONAL COMMENTARY ON THE PORTIONS OF KIDDUSH ONLY RECITED WHEN PASSOVER FALLS ON SHABBAT, SEE MY PEOPLE'S PRAYER BOOK, VOLUME 7, SHABBAT AT HOME, PP. 91–115, AND FOR MORE ON HAVDALAH SEE PP. 164–180 OF THAT VOLUME.)   (p. 136)

LANDES (Halakhah)

[7] *"Creator of the fruit of the vine"* This blessing is recited before each of the four cups *(arba kosot)*.

Wine in ancient times was prepared in a concentrated form, almost a syrup. To drink it straight was not pleasant; it needed to be mixed with water. In his *Mishneh Torah* (Laws of *Chamets* and Matzah 7:9), Maimonides (Moshe ben Maimon,   *(p. 136)*

ZIERLER (Feminist Voices)

"Kadesh" According to the Rabbis, are women obligated to drink the four cups of wine at the Seder? In both Mishnah and Tosefta Pesachim (10:1), the Rabbis insist that an *adam* is obliged to drink no less than four cups; this obligation extends to poor and rich men alike. But does the word *adam* include women? The Mishnah is silent on the issue; the Tosefta refers to the *adam*'s obligation to gladden his children and the members of his household on the festival by giving them wine to drink, with Rabbi Judah expressing a   *(p. 142)*

The sixth day. [3]Heaven and earth and everything associated with them were completed. [4]On the seventh day, God completed the work He had done. On the seventh day, He rested from all the work He had done. [5]God blessed the seventh day and sanctified it, for on it He rested from all the work God had created to do.)

[6]With our masters' and teachers' approval:

[7]Blessed are You, Adonai our God, ruler of the world, creator of the fruit of the vine.

[8]Blessed are You, Adonai our God, ruler of the world, who chose us from every other nation and exalted us above every other people and sanctified us with His commandments. [9]Adonai our God, You lovingly gave us (Shabbat for rest and) holidays for happiness, festivals and times of the year for rejoicing; [10]You gave us (this day of Shabbat and) this Festival of Matzot, the time of our freedom (in love), a holy occasion, a memorial of the Exodus from Egypt. [11]For You have chosen us and sanctified us above all nations, (lovingly and adoringly and) joyfully and joyously granting us Your holy (Shabbat and) holidays as our inheritance. [12]Blessed are You, Adonai, who sanctifies (Shabbat and) Israel and the times of year.

[3]יוֹם הַשִּׁשִּׁי: וַיְכֻלּוּ הַשָּׁמַיִם וְהָאָרֶץ וְכָל־צְבָאָם: [4]וַיְכַל אֱלֹהִים בַּיּוֹם הַשְּׁבִיעִי מְלַאכְתּוֹ אֲשֶׁר עָשָׂה וַיִּשְׁבֹּת בַּיּוֹם הַשְּׁבִיעִי מִכָּל־מְלַאכְתּוֹ אֲשֶׁר עָשָׂה: [5]וַיְבָרֶךְ אֱלֹהִים אֶת־יוֹם הַשְּׁבִיעִי וַיְקַדֵּשׁ אֹתוֹ כִּי בוֹ שָׁבַת מִכָּל־מְלַאכְתּוֹ אֲשֶׁר־בָּרָא אֱלֹהִים לַעֲשׂוֹת:

[6]סָבְרִי מָרָנָן וְרַבּוֹתַי:

[7]**בָּ**רוּךְ אַתָּה יְיָ אֱלֹהֵינוּ מֶלֶךְ הָעוֹלָם בּוֹרֵא פְּרִי הַגָּפֶן:

[8]בָּרוּךְ אַתָּה יְיָ אֱלֹהֵינוּ מֶלֶךְ הָעוֹלָם אֲשֶׁר בָּחַר בָּנוּ מִכָּל־עָם וְרוֹמְמָנוּ מִכָּל־לָשׁוֹן וְקִדְּשָׁנוּ בְּמִצְוֹתָיו. [9]וַתִּתֶּן־לָנוּ יְיָ אֱלֹהֵינוּ בְּאַהֲבָה (שַׁבָּתוֹת לִמְנוּחָה וּ) מוֹעֲדִים לְשִׂמְחָה חַגִּים וּזְמַנִּים לְשָׂשׂוֹן. [10]אֶת־יוֹם (הַשַּׁבָּת הַזֶּה וְאֶת־יוֹם) חַג הַמַּצּוֹת הַזֶּה זְמַן חֵרוּתֵנוּ (בְּאַהֲבָה) מִקְרָא־קֹדֶשׁ זֵכֶר לִיצִיאַת מִצְרָיִם. [11]כִּי־בָנוּ בָחַרְתָּ וְאוֹתָנוּ קִדַּשְׁתָּ מִכָּל־הָעַמִּים. (וְשַׁבָּת) וּמוֹעֲדֵי קָדְשֶׁךָ (בְּאַהֲבָה וּבְרָצוֹן) בְּשִׂמְחָה וּבְשָׂשׂוֹן הִנְחַלְתָּנוּ. [12]בָּרוּךְ אַתָּה יְיָ מְקַדֵּשׁ (הַשַּׁבָּת וְ) יִשְׂרָאֵל וְהַזְּמַנִּים:

C. Distinguishing Times of Holiness
   (Havdalah)

הַבְדָּלָה

[13]Blessed are You, Adonai our God, ruler of the world, creator of the lights of fire.

[13]בָּרוּךְ אַתָּה יְיָ אֱלֹהֵינוּ מֶלֶךְ הָעוֹלָם בּוֹרֵא מְאוֹרֵי הָאֵשׁ:

[14]Blessed are You, Adonai our God, ruler of the world, who distinguishes between holy and ordinary, between light and dark, between Israel and the nations, between the seventh day and the six days of work. [15]You distinguished between the holiness of Shabbat and the holiness of the holidays. [16]You sanctified the seventh day above the six days of work. [17]You distinguished and sanctified Your people Israel in Your holiness. [18]Blessed are You, Adonai, who distinguishes between holy and holy.

[14]בָּרוּךְ אַתָּה יְיָ אֱלֹהֵינוּ מֶלֶךְ הָעוֹלָם הַמַּבְדִּיל בֵּין קֹדֶשׁ לְחֹל בֵּין אוֹר לְחֹשֶׁךְ בֵּין יִשְׂרָאֵל לָעַמִּים בֵּין יוֹם הַשְּׁבִיעִי לְשֵׁשֶׁת יְמֵי הַמַּעֲשֶׂה. [15]בֵּין קְדֻשַּׁת שַׁבָּת לִקְדֻשַּׁת יוֹם טוֹב הִבְדַּלְתָּ. [16]וְאֶת־יוֹם הַשְּׁבִיעִי מִשֵּׁשֶׁת יְמֵי הַמַּעֲשֶׂה קִדַּשְׁתָּ. [17]הִבְדַּלְתָּ וְקִדַּשְׁתָּ אֶת־עַמְּךָ יִשְׂרָאֵל בִּקְדֻשָּׁתֶךָ. [18]בָּרוּךְ אַתָּה יְיָ הַמַּבְדִּיל בֵּין קֹדֶשׁ לְקֹדֶשׁ:

D. Gratitude for Being Here
   (Shehecheyanu)

שֶׁהֶחֱיָנוּ

[19]Blessed are You, Adonai our God, ruler of the world, who has kept us alive, sustained us, and brought us to this time of year.

[19]בָּרוּךְ אַתָּה יְיָ אֱלֹהֵינוּ מֶלֶךְ הָעוֹלָם שֶׁהֶחֱיָנוּ וְקִיְּמָנוּ וְהִגִּיעָנוּ לַזְּמַן הַזֶּה:

E. The First Washing *(Urchats)* and
   Dipping *Karpas*

URCHATS: *Washing without a Blessing*

וּרְחַץ

KARPAS: *Dipping and Eating Greens*

כַּרְפַּס

[20]Blessed are You, Adonai our God, ruler of the world, creator of the fruit of the earth.

[20]בָּרוּךְ אַתָּה יְיָ אֱלֹהֵינוּ מֶלֶךְ הָעוֹלָם בּוֹרֵא פְּרִי הָאֲדָמָה:

F. "Breaking the Matzah" (*Yachats*) and Reserving the *Afikoman*
YACHATS:

G. "Bread of Affliction," *Ha Lachma Anya*: Begin MAGGID ("Telling")

[21]This is the bread of affliction our ancestors ate in the Land of Egypt.

[22]Let all who are hungry come and eat.

[23]Let all who are in need come and observe Pesach.

[24]This year here, next year in the Land of Israel.

[25]Now enslaved, next year free.

יַחַץ

מַגִּיד

[21]הָא לַחְמָא עַנְיָא דִּי אֲכָלוּ אֲבָהָתָנָא בְּאַרְעָא דְמִצְרָיִם. [22]כָּל־דִּכְפִין יֵיתֵי וְיֵכֵל. [23]כָּל־דִּצְרִיךְ יֵיתֵי וְיִפְסַח. [24]הָשַׁתָּא הָכָא לְשָׁנָה הַבָּאָה בְּאַרְעָא דְיִשְׂרָאֵל. [25]הָשַׁתָּא עַבְדֵי לְשָׁנָה הַבָּאָה בְּנֵי חוֹרִין:

ARNOW (The World of Midrash)

the vine. "A person in whose house wine does not flow like water has not reached the ultimate stage of blessedness!" (Eruv. 65a). A third-century text compares wine to *aggadah*—the beloved rabbinic art of telling stories and finding ever new meaning in ancient texts—because both exert "a pull on one's heart" (*Sifre Deut.* 317). In rabbinic parlance, *aggadah* and *haggadah* are generally interchangeable. Drinking wine provides the perfect accompaniment to exploring the Haggadah (literally, "telling") as we celebrate *z'man cheruteinu*, "the time of our freedom."

[8]*"Who chose us"* The idea of Jewish chosenness constitutes a central motif in the evening *Kiddush* for festivals and Shabbat. An important question involves whether God's choosing "us from every other nation" was arbitrary or a reflection of merit. In giving no reason for God's choice, a statement from the *Mekhilta D'rabbi Shimon bar Yochai*, an early midrash, may embody the first view: "Because God took [only] them from Egypt and redeemed [only] them from the house of slavery—that is why God said, 'You shall be My treasured possession among all the peoples (*mikol ha'amim*), (Exod. 19:5)."[1] A midrashic parable from Midrash Samuel (8:2; tenth century or earlier) illustrates the latter position: "A Roman matron said to Rabbi Yosei [second century]: 'Your God arbitrarily brings near to Himself whomsoever He pleases!' He brought her a basket of figs, and she examined them well, picking the best and eating. He said to her: 'You, apparently, know how to choose, but the Holy One does not? God chooses and brings near those in whom God sees good deeds.'" Here, God chooses those who act in godly ways.

"Washing without a Blessing" In the days of the Temple, priests washed before offering sacrifices on the altar. That would have been true for the *pesach* offering as well. After the Temple was destroyed, the Sages likened one's table to the altar, making the stipulated symbolic food of the Seder meal the equivalent of the missing *pesach*. Symbolically, beginning the Seder by washing thus makes sense. We wash here also because the Talmud (Pes. 115a) requires washing prior to touching anything dipped in liquid (i.e., parsley dipped in salt water). *Numbers Rabbah* (2:15) provides a parable linking washing to reconciliation with God: "A king sent his son to school, but instead, the boy went to play in the street. His father found out and scolded him. Afterwards, however, his father said, 'Wash your hands and come and dine with me.'" Israel is the wayward son, and God the king; by washing we prepare ourselves to be worthy of our annual dialogue with God on the question of redemption.

"Eating Greens" Although many use parsley here, the ninth-century prayer book of Amram Gaon lists a variety of acceptable spring vegetables: radishes, lettuce, arugula, cilantro, and parsley.[2] Folkloric associations relating to each of these doubtless augmented their significance on the Seder plate. According to the Talmud, radishes are good for fever and help dissolve food (A.Z. 28b). Lettuce seen in a dream portends either rapid growth or bitter decline of business (Ber. 56a). Arugula benefits the eyes (Shab. 109a). Eating cilantro produces stout children, and eating parsley guarantees beautiful ones (Ket. 61a)!

[21] *"Bread of affliction"* The Hebrew equivalent of the Aramaic *lachma anya* is *lechem oni* (Deut. 16:3). Because here *oni*, עֳנִי, lacks the letter *vav*—it is usually spelled עוֹנִי—its meaning is ambiguous, a fact not lost on the Sages. Shmuel (third century CE) said the Torah designates matzah as the bread of *oni* because it is the "bread over which we recite [*onin*] many words," that is, we retell the story of the Exodus. Rabbi Akiva reads *lechem oni* as *lechem ani*—not "bread of *affliction*," but "bread of *poverty*" (Pes. 36a). His reading links matzah directly to the Haggadah's invitation to the hungry.

[22]*"Let all who are hungry come and eat"* This invitation's style is reminiscent of that proffered by Rav Huna, a third-century sage from Babylonia. Impoverished in his early life, Rav Huna never forgot the poor when he became wealthy: "When he had a meal he would open the door wide and declare, 'Let all who are in need come and eat'" (Ta'an. 20b). *Leviticus Rabbah* (34:9) put it this way: "The poor man stands at your door, and the Holy One stands at his right hand." The life of the body and the spirit cannot be separated. Oppressive poverty "deprives an individual of knowing his creator" (Eruv. 41a).

[25]*"Next year free"* Why the expectation that "next year" so much will change? Because, Rabbi Joshua (first and second centuries CE) taught: "In Nisan [the month when Passover falls] they *were* redeemed: and in Nisan they *will be* redeemed" (R. H. 11a). Although Rabbi Eliezer disagreed and held that the future redemption would occur in Tishrei, when the autumn holidays fall, Jewish messianic expectations have historically been overwhelmingly associated with Passover and Nisan.

paraphrased the English to extol Jews' adopted country as the best venue to live out shared American and Jewish ideals of freedom and justice:

> We give thanks to Thee, O God, for the many blessings Thou hast bestowed upon us. We thank Thee for the good land in which we live, for the liberty which we enjoy, and for the grace with which Thou continuest to watch over us.

In a similar vein, I. S. Moses' "Domestic Service for the Eve of Passover" (American Reform, 1898) contains the music and all verses to both "America" and the "Star-Spangled Banner," only nine years after the latter was adopted officially by the Navy and (prophetically?) a full thirty-three years before being made the national anthem by congressional legislation.

"Urchats" In keeping with the antireligious campaign underway in the 1920s, members of the *Yevsektsiia*—the Jewish section of the Commissariat of Nationalities of the Communist Party—were charged with the task of directing the cultural fate of Soviet Jewry. Deeming Jewish nationalism and religion to be outmoded obstacles to proletarian progress, the *Yevsektsiia* (supported by government agencies) initiated and executed the liquidation of Zionism, Hebrew culture, and Judaism. Yiddish was the only tolerated Jewish language, but it was used largely as a means to indoctrinate Communist ideology, as abundantly evident in this excerpt from a parody of the Haggadah, *"Hagodeh far gloiber un apikorsim"* (Haggadah for Believers and Atheists, Moscow, 1927):

> Wash away, workers and peasants, the entire bourgeois filth, wash off the mildew of the ages and say—not a blessing—but a curse. May annihilation overcome all the outdated rabbinic laws and customs, yeshivas and cheders, which blacken and enslave the people.[1]

"Yachats" The text of *A Sephardic Passover Haggadah* (1988), edited by Marc D. Angel, is much in keeping with that of Ashkenazim but includes commentary explicating rituals unique to Sefardim. According to Shem Tov Ganguine, a twentieth-century Sefardi rabbi in England, it is customary in many Sefardi households to wrap the *afikoman* in a sack and for each participant to have the opportunity to sling it over his or her shoulder. This symbolizes the Israelites carrying their burdens as they left Egypt. Some have the custom of actually standing up and walking around the table with the sack on their shoulder. Those present ask: From where are you coming? The answer: From Egypt. Then they ask: Where are you going? The answer: To Jerusalem. Others have the custom of carrying this sack around the room while reciting the statement, "Thus did our ancestors when they left Egypt."

[21] *"This is the bread of affliction"* The Reconstructionists' *New Haggadah for Pesach* (1941) retains the traditional wording of *Ha lachma anya* but adds a passage arguing that human beings can be enslaved to themselves when they permit harmful habits to tyrannize them:

> When laziness or cowardness [*sic*] keeps them from doing what they know to be right, when ignorance blinds them so that … they can turn round and round in meaningless drudgery. When envy, bitterness and jealousy sour their joys and darken their brightness of their contentment—they are slaves to themselves.[2]

Sometimes, people have felt afflicted just by the difficulty of procuring the "bread of affliction," as we see from an interesting morsel of American Jewish history. In 1849, Jews followed the Gold Rush to California, where unleavened bread became a necessary commodity come spring. The following newspaper account shows the fiery controversy unleashed by such sales in San Francisco:

Revolt Against Matzoth Prices

The high prices charged last Passover by the matzoth bakers of this city has [*sic*] induced a number of coreligionists to form an association for the purpose of selling matzoth at a reasonable price. This society is called the "People's Matzoth Association of San Francisco," and at a meeting recently held, the following gentlemen were appointed a committee to make the necessary arrangements to start the society: Aaron Levy, F. Henry, E. Belasco, S. Samuels, J. Hartman, D. Steinbach and H. Solomon. The society has funds to commence operations, the following amounts have been advanced: H. and S. Solomon, $1,500; Mr. Steinberg, $150; C. Hess, $150; A. M. Cohn, $100.[3]

The Jews of the former Soviet Union compose the third largest Jewish community in the world, after the United States and Israel. In the early 1970s, still under Communist rule, they began an active fight for the right to maintain their religious language and culture and, for some, to leave the country. As relations between Washington and Moscow reached a nadir, the National Conference on Soviet Jewry (NCSJ) was created as the central coordinating agency for policy and activities on behalf of the Jews of the USSR. Jews worldwide joined the battle to liberate their coreligionists from the shackles of intolerance, and as part of that effort, thousands of American-Jewish households remembered Soviet Jewry especially and aptly at Passover, with an innovative ritual called "The Matzah of Hope." Based on the thousands of pamphlets distributed by the NCSJ, Jews are enjoined to recognize that "Soviet Jews are not free" and that "they have not been forgotten" by setting aside a piece of matzah as "a symbol of hope."

◆

BRETTLER (Our Biblical Heritage)

to wine as a common drink; this was typical in pre-modern times, when the purity of water could not be assured.

[8] *"Who chose us"* The idea of chosenness is especially prominent in Deuteronomy, e.g., 7:6, where like here it is connected to Israel's sanctification: "For you are a people consecrated [or: sanctified] to Adonai your God: of all the peoples on earth Adonai your God chose you to be His treasured people." In Deuteronomy, however, Israel is intrinsically holy rather than "sanctified … with … commandments"; that concept is found especially in Leviticus 17–26, a legal collection often called the Holiness Collection, which introduces legislation by stating (Lev. 19:2): "You shall be holy, for I, Adonai your God, am holy," offering the idea that following God's legislation, the *mitzvot*, makes Israel holy. "Who chose us from every other nation and exalted us above every other people" is in typical biblical poetic parallelism, where the second phrase

repeats and, in this case, extends the first: not only is Israel chosen, but it is also better than all the other nations, an expansion of Deuteronomy's notion of chosenness. The novelty of the phrase "and exalted us above every other people" is also seen in the use of *lashon*, which in the Bible means "tongue" or "language," to mean a "people" by metonymy.

⁹*"You lovingly"* The mutual love between God and Israel is a significant theme of Deuteronomy (see, e.g., 10:12, 10:15), though there Israel's love of God may not represent an emotional attitude, but obedience (see *My People's Prayer Book*, Volume 1, *The Sh'ma and Its Blessings*, p. 101), and the mitzvot are never explicitly depicted in the Bible as a sign of God's love for Israel, though this notion might be implicit (see Deut. 4:37–40), and elsewhere Deuteronomy connects Israel's love for God and performance of commandments (e.g., Deut. 30:16, 30:20).

⁹*"Holidays for happiness, festivals and times of the year for rejoicing"* Deuteronomy 16:14 notes, "You shall rejoice in your festival [singular!]," referring to Sukkot, which celebrated the very end of the harvest, half a year after Passover, when people no longer had major agricultural responsibilities and could truly rejoice; this commandment to rejoice, expressed in typical biblical parallelism, is applied here to all festivals. Perhaps this development occurred after sacrifices at the Temple ceased; contrast Deuteronomy 16:7, which notes that after coming to the Temple to offer the paschal lamb, "in the morning you may start back on your journey home," presumably to engage in crucial agricultural tasks—this was not as of yet a time for relaxed joy, since the outcome of the harvest was still uncertain.

¹⁰*"Festival of Matzot"* In much of the Bible, the Festival of Matzot refers to the seven-day festival beginning on the fourteenth of Nisan, while *pesach* refers to the paschal lamb, and perhaps to the time when it was sacrificed, on the eve of the fourteenth. (See especially Lev. 23:5–6: "In the first month, on the fourteenth day of the month, at twilight, there shall be a Passover offering to Adonai, and on the fifteenth day of that month Adonai's Feast of Unleavened Bread. You shall eat unleavened bread for seven days.") Deuteronomy 16:1–8 combines these two festivals, and in later Jewish tradition, "Passover" and "the Festival of Matzot" are typically used interchangeably. (See *My People's Passover Haggadah*, Volume 1, pp. 10–14.)

¹⁰*"Freedom"* A post-biblical word used within a prayer that is otherwise typically biblical in style and vocabulary. The use of the phrase here refers to political freedom only. Although the Bible often refers to God taking or redeeming Israel from Egypt, it does not view this as freedom in the broadest sense, but shifting from a situation where Israel was the vassal of Egypt to being God's vassal. This idea is reflected in several rabbinic statements that discuss Israel going from slavery (in the physical sense in Egypt) to slavery (being subservient to God).

¹⁰*"A memorial of the Exodus from Egypt"* Though found elsewhere, the word cluster "memorial" (related to "remember"), "Exodus," and "Egypt" typifies Deuteronomy, as

in 16:3, "You shall not eat anything leavened with it; for seven days thereafter you shall eat unleavened bread, bread of affliction—for you departed from the Land of Egypt hurriedly—so that you may remember the day of your departure from the Land of Egypt as long as you live."

[11] *"For You have chosen us and sanctified us above all nations, (lovingly and adoringly and) joyfully and joyously granting us Your holy (Shabbat and) holidays as our inheritance."* A summary of the previous ideas, repeating much of the earlier vocabulary.

[12] *"Who sanctifies (Shabbat and) Israel and the times of year"* There is some confusion in the Bible about whether Israel is intrinsically holy or must be holy; this prayer follows Exodus 31:13, "… that you may know that I Adonai have consecrated you"; Leviticus 20:8, "I Adonai make you holy"; and related passages (Ezek. 20:12, 37:28). In the Bible, God never sanctifies the festivals; the idea found here is an extension of Genesis 2:3, "And God blessed the seventh day and declared it holy" (see also Exod. 20:11), where the festivals are analogized to the Shabbat.

"Urchats" This is likely a reflection of the biblical idea that one must be ritually pure before performing certain cultic actions; this is why the priests had a laver in the sanctuary (Exod. 30:18–21), and various texts in Leviticus 15 (but see also Deut. 23:12) note that washing removes minor ritual impurity from an Israelite.

[20] *"Fruit of the earth"* In rabbinic literature, the "fruit of the earth" refers to vegetables, as opposed to the "fruit of the trees," which refers to fruit. Jeremiah 7:20, which distinguishes between these two, mentioning both *p'ri ha'adamah* (fruit of the earth) and *p'ri ha'ets* (fruit of the trees), may suggest that this distinction is biblical as well, though in some cases, *p'ri ha'adamah* seems to be used generically in the Bible for all produce.

"Yachats" Although matzah is an important part of Passover already in the biblical period, no comparable rituals of splitting matzah in half are noted in the Bible.

"Maggid" This section, *maggid*, "telling," is the core and longest section of the Haggadah. Its name is based on Exodus 13:8, in the middle of the Passover legislation: "Tell [*v'higadta*, from the root *n.g.d*, the same root as in Haggadah and *maggid*] your child on that very day: 'This is what Adonai did for me when I left Egypt.'" There is no evidence, however, that a complex story was told in the biblical period; this verse says simply, "This is what Adonai did for me when I left Egypt." Deuteronomy 6:21–25 suggests a longer answer beginning, "We were slaves to Pharaoh in Egypt …" as an answer to the child who asks (v. 20), "What are the precepts, statutes, and laws that Adonai our God commanded you?"—a question not clearly associated with the Passover festival and its rituals.

[21] *"Bread of affliction"* A translation of Hebrew *lechem oni*, found only in Deuteronomy 16:3, "for seven days thereafter you shall eat unleavened bread, bread of affliction," where the eating of matzah seems to be connected to the food that slaves or poor people would eat, rather than the tradition that matzah commemorates the lack of

time for the dough to rise (e.g., Exod. 12:39). On the use of Aramaic, see "Let all kinds of leaven," *My People's Passover Haggadah*, Volume 1, p. 97.

[22] *"Let all who are hungry come and eat"* The custom of inviting others to partake may derive from Temple times, when large groups joined together to eat a single lamb that needed to be consumed by the morning (Exod. 12:10).

———◆———

GILLMAN (THEOLOGICALLY SPEAKING)

meaning "separate" eventually comes to mean "special." The *Kiddush* prayer, typically recited at sunset at the beginning of the Sabbath and the Festivals, thus serves to set the new day apart from the "profane" (or "ordinary") days of the week that precede it. Similarly, the prayer recited at the conclusion of the Sabbath and Festivals, *Havdalah* (see p. 110), also means "separating out." It also works to distinguish, this time between the special day that is now ending from the ordinary days of the week that are about to begin. Thus *Kiddush* and *Havdalah* are synonyms. They form the liturgical parentheses around the special days of the liturgical year.

Kiddush marks one example of "set-apartedness"; the festival day is set apart from the ordinary days of the week. But the *Kiddush* liturgy asserts another example, Israel from the nations. We praise God who "chose us from every other nation and exalted us above every other people and sanctified us with His commandments." This doctrine of Israel as the "chosen people" is omnipresent in the Bible and in the later rabbinic tradition and its liturgies. Jewish traditionalists view this as God's expression of exclusive affection for the Jewish people. Israel is God's "treasured possession among all the peoples" (Exod. 19:5). Liberal theologians view it as our ancestors' self-perception, stemming probably from their attempts to account for Israel's unique historical experience of redemption. Deuteronomy 4 is the classical textual reference for this perception. Here, God is portrayed as having allotted the sun, moon, and stars to the other nations to worship, "but you Adonai took and brought out of Egypt ... to be His very own people ..." (Deut. 4:19–20).

Not surprisingly, the doctrine has frequently been viewed as offensive to modern sensibilities because of its overtones of racism. However Amos 9:7—"To me, O Israelites, you are just like the Ethiopians, declares Adonai"—would seem to mitigate that conclusion. Frequently, modern apologists for the doctrine resort to the distinction between status and function. Israel is "chosen" from among the peoples not because it is superior, but rather because it has a unique function or responsibility: to represent the One God among the nations of the world. Add to that the notion that because of Israel's unique destiny, it will be judged more severely than the other peoples of the world, and the doctrine loses some of its offensiveness. Still, all references to the doctrine of Israel as God's chosen people were eliminated from the Reconstructionist prayer books.

The doctrine of Israel as holy/set apart reaches its pinnacle in Leviticus 19:2, "You shall be holy, for I, Adonai your God, am holy." In what sense is God set apart? From the other gods? Possibly. Or, the sense here may also be closer to the two senses of "distinguished." God is special in the sense that God transcends anything in the created world and is thus unique. With that as a model, Israel is also to transcend all other peoples and achieve a unique standing. The *Kiddush* makes the further point that it is through fulfilling God's mitzvot that Israel achieves that unique standing, echoing Deuteronomy 4:8, "What great nation has laws and rules as perfect as all this Teaching that I set before you this day?"

"Havdalah" This is the *Havdalah* prayer that we append to the *Kiddush* when the festival occurs on Saturday night. We include the blessing over light, but not the one over spices that we would recite at the close of Shabbat. The main *Havdalah* prayer emphasizes, as noted above, the set-apartedness of Shabbat from the rest of the week, but it views this as one of a series of "set-apartnesses": the holy and the everyday, Israel and the nations, light and darkness, the holiness of the Sabbath and that of the Festivals. It also makes explicit what had been implicit until now: to "sanctify" and to "distinguish" are synonyms—"You distinguished and sanctified Your people Israel in Your holiness."

The issue is one of structures. To set apart, to distinguish, to sanctify is to divide (the literal meaning of *Havdalah*), and they all mean to structure, to order, to bring cosmos out of chaos, order out of anarchy. As in the creation myth in Genesis 1, God is portrayed here as the source of order. God orders nature, time, society, history, and human life. The grand purpose of religion implied here is to order our experience of the world.[1] Our celebration on the night of Passover reflects this in its very name, *Seder*, which means "order."

"Yachats" The Haggadah quickly introduces the theme of brokenness. Its trajectory will take us from brokenness at the outset to wholeness at the end. In the words of the Mishnah (Pes. 10:4), when we instruct our children, we "begin with the disgrace and end with the praise." That trajectory is expressed verbally throughout the Haggadah, but frequently, in Judaism, theological reflections are also articulated in another language, ritual behavior. Here, we echo the opening words of the Haggadah—"This is the bread of affliction …"—by the ritual of breaking the middle matzah. It will eventually be made whole again through the act of eating: the first half at the beginning of the festive meal, and the other half at its conclusion, for the *afikoman*.

[25] *"Now enslaved"* Slavery is one aspect of the broader category of exile. Exile begins in the Torah as a historical event, the climax of the punishments to be visited on Israel for breaching the covenant (Deut. 28:64ff.). Redemption from exile, following repentance and return to God, is the mark of God's renewed favor. The enslavement in Egypt is not specifically referred to as exile—that term appears in the later tradition to accompany the destruction of Jerusalem and the Temple and the experience in Babylonia, and later after the destruction of the Second Temple at the hands of Rome. But if the natural state is for a people to occupy its own territory, then Egyptian slavery is by extension an experience

of exile. We can, by extension, understand Adam and Eve's banishment from Eden as the original manifestation of "exile." Exile, thus, is the opposite of being "at home." The Haggadah speaks to both dimensions of exile when it says "now enslaved, next year free." To the compilers of the Haggadah, this last phrase referred to exile from Israel.

Much later, in the teachings of the Safed kabbalists in the wake of the expulsion of the Jews from Spain and Portugal at the end of the fifteenth century, exile becomes a metaphysical state; the world, and even God, are in exile. To say that the world is in exile means that the world is flawed, imperfect, that chaos still hovers over the periphery of the world. And to say that God is in exile means that even God is not fully God. Here, the kabbalists expanded on a rabbinic tradition. The talmudic Rabbis used the term *galut Shekhinah* ("the exile of the *Shekhinah*") to indicate that God accompanied Israel into exile—in Egypt, as well as after the destruction of the Temple and Jerusalem. This myth of cosmic exile served to provide the exiled community with a modicum of consolation.

To the kabbalists, then, Israel's historical situation mirrors a broader, more cosmic state of affairs. And as Israel needs to be redeemed, so does the world and God.[2]

[25] *"Next year free"* This is the ultimate eschatological hope. Hope is a theological category. Not the everyday kind of hope, not the hope that I will pass my exam or that the Red Sox will win the pennant, but what we can call "hope against hope"—hope when all the indications counsel despair, when the statistics are against you, when the diagnosis suggests that all is lost. Yes, in the face of all of this, there surges within us hope. The prophet Zachariah (9:12) describes us as "prisoners of hope," suggesting that we hope against our own better instincts.

That kind of hope has theological weight, for we can legitimately ask, where does that hope come from? What within us impels that kind of hope? It stems from a persistent dissatisfaction with the world as we find it, from a sense that even God is dissatisfied with the world as it is. This is the impulse that produces eschatologies, visions of a world and a social setting perfected. Thus we can proclaim, "Next year free."

GRAY (MEDIEVAL COMMENTATORS)

break the middle matzah prior to beginning our recitation of the *Maggid*. He answers that this is so we can recite, "This is the bread of affliction" (p. 113) over a broken matzah. The Talmud says that just as a poor person is accustomed to eat only broken-off pieces of bread, so here, too, as we recall our slavery, we must make do with a broken-off piece of matzah (Pes. 101a).

[21] *"Bread of affliction"* This passage is not found in the Talmud and appears to have been first mentioned in *Seder Rav Amram Gaon* (our first prayer book; c. 860 CE). *Ravyah* points out that the passage is largely in Aramaic rather than Hebrew, because that was the vernacular of the Jews in earlier times. The advantage of using Aramaic was so that children and women could understand what was being said—Hebrew being a

learned language that might not be accessible to them.[1] *Ritba* (Rabbi Yom Tov ben Abraham Ishbili, Spain, c. 1250–1330) quoted the explanation of *M'yuchas l'Rashi*, a commentary attributed to *Rashi*, that we recite this passage in Aramaic to make sure that demons will not understand it (particularly the invitation *kol dikhfin*, "all who are hungry" [v. 22]) and so will not enter the house. Perhaps out of a disinclination to resort to demon-oriented explanations, *Ritba* endorses an interpretation similar to that of *Ravyah*: the passage is in Aramaic because it was not part of the original Mishnaic order but was added in the vernacular during the amoraic period so that everyone could understand it. *Ritba* also suggests (based on Shab. 12b) that this passage is in Aramaic so that angels will not understand it and then seize upon the occasion to argue in heaven that our sins make us unworthy of redemption (Haggadah commentary). *Ravyah* explains that the last words of the passage ("next year free" [v. 25]) are in Hebrew so that the non-Jews among whom the Babylonian Jews lived would not understand that the Jews were looking forward to leaving them and returning to Israel, which could cause tensions between the communities.

[22] *"Let all who are hungry"* The Talmud recounts that *whenever* Rav Huna would eat a meal—not just on Pesach—he would open up his gate and say, "Whoever is in need, let him come and eat" (Ta'an. 20b). Abudarham quotes a scholar named Rabbi Matityah who said—perhaps because of Ta'anit 20b—that the line "Let all who are hungry" stems from an old custom of opening one's doors at mealtimes, raising up one's table, and calling out to the hungry to join in the meal.

[23] *"Come and observe Pesach"* Shibbolei Haleket (by Zedekiah ben Abraham Anav, Italy, thirteenth century) quotes Rabbi Isaiah DiTrani (Italy, c. 1180–1260), who sensibly pointed out that this line probably should be omitted, since literally it refers to an actual Passover sacrifice—which we no longer have—and to which, in any case, people had to have been specially invited beforehand, not at the last minute, as is implied here. Nevertheless, *Shibbolei Haleket* follows the view of Zedekiah's older brother, Rabbi Benjamin Harofei, who said that we must retain this line even though there is no longer an actual *pesach* sacrifice. We may surmise that this is because we are hereby memorializing the ritual as it was.[2]

Abudarham adds a touching interpretation of "Let all who are in need come and observe the Pesach." He points out that this applies to the poor Jews, but also to those who have enough money to acquire nourishing food for themselves on most days (and so are technically not "hungry") but who do not have enough money to acquire the other requirements of the Seder: *charoset, maror,* or wine for the four cups. This invitation is directed at these people so that they have a home in which they can celebrate the Seder properly. Abudarham adds that after the Seder, the head of the household should speak kindly to these guests and tell them that there is no need for them to be embarrassed about having relied on others.

[25] *"Next year free"* Abudarham and *Machzor Vitry* (Laws of Passover 95) point out that "next year" is probably meant literally: the Talmud says that Israel was redeemed

from Egypt in Nisan and will be redeemed in the month of Nisan in the messianic future (R. H. 11a).

———◆———

GREEN (PERSONAL SPIRITUALITY)

free" means "more free to live in God's presence" or less subjugated to those forces—whether they be social, economic, political, or even "religious"—that keep us from God. Pesach calls out to us to renew our commitment to freedom on these most profound levels, both for ourselves and for others.

"First cup" This is the first of the Seder's four cups of wine. Most Haggadah commentators relate the four cups of wine to four terms used for redemption in the Exodus narrative. But that is a wholly internal coordination of symbols and does not really tell us much. The kabbalists refer them to four rungs of "shell" or defilement that the Israelites had to overcome in order to be redeemed. Their years in Egypt had taken them down to the lowest of spiritual rungs. They needed to be purified step by step before they could be taken forth. (As the later Torah narrative proceeds, we might wonder whether this process was really quite successful.)

But my favorite interpretation of the four cups is found on an old glass goblet I treasure. Made in Bohemia in the eighteenth century, it is inscribed *arba kosot neged arba imahot*: "four cups standing for the four mothers." This interpretation is already found, it turns out, in the Haggadah commentary of the Maharal of Prague, who lived two centuries earlier. I wonder what it was about those Bohemian Jewish mothers that inspired such a thought!

Playing it out, we can understand how the first cup represents Sarah. This is the cup of hospitality, welcoming the guests, the way Mother Sarah kept the flaps of her tent ever open to welcome sojourning strangers. The second cup is that of Rebekah, who switched her sons before Isaac's blessing. The cleverness, even trickery, she showed also protected Israel's sons in Egypt and allowed them to leave, deceiving Pharaoh and his armies both in Egypt and at the shore of the sea. Sometimes liberation requires trickery. But how about Leah and Rachel? How do the last two cups apply to them? I leave that for conversation around *your* Seder table.

[25] *"Now enslaved"* This phrase sets up the dramatic tension that embraces the entire Seder. In a moment we will say: "We were slaves to Pharaoh in Egypt…. If the Holy One of Blessing had not brought our ancestors out of Egypt we … would still be enslaved." Liberation happened long ago, and as good faithful Jews we still remember it. But first, in this opening to the Seder, we say the opposite: We are *still* slaves! Next year may we be *really* free! We recognize, in other words, that our liberation from "Egypt" never quite succeeded; we are still on the road to liberation, not quite wholly free.

Both of these versions of liberation are true. When seen from the viewpoint of our onetime total bondage in Egypt and that of Jews and others within our own memory, we indeed have every reason to be grateful. We live in a society that offers us freedom and opportunities that were far beyond the dreams of prior generations. But the human condition is such that we still, and always, struggle to be free. Conversation at the Seder table should attempt to encompass both of these truths and highlight the tension between them.

———◆———

J. HOFFMAN (TRANSLATION)

lamp. But because *ner* was such a familiar concept for the original authors of the prayer, we use a familiar concept in translating it. "Light" is another good option. Finally, our translation leaves open two possibilities: either one candle in total is lit for both Shabbat and the festival, or one is lit for each; the Hebrew is likewise ambiguous.

"Kadesh" This is the first of fifteen traditional sections of the Passover Seder. In English, captions tend to be formed from nouns, but because the Hebrew has both nouns and verbs, we use both in English, too, as on p. 107, "Sanctify."

[2] *"The sixth day"* Or "a sixth day." The Hebrew is actually ungrammatical. In Hebrew, both adjectives and nouns can take the word "the" (marked with an initial *heh*), but when they do, they have to match. So the grammatical way to say "the sixth day" is "the day the sixth" *(hayom hashishi)*. By contrast, "a sixth day" is "day sixth" *(yom shishi)*. This text, from Genesis *(yom hashishi)*, combines both constructions. (*Rashi* notices the extra *heh* and offers midrashic explanations for it, including a suggestion that the *heh*, whose numerical value in Hebrew is "5," is an oblique reference to the five books of Torah.)

[3] *"Associated with them"* Others, the literal "their host," but the connotations of the English "host" (e.g., the convener of a party) are so wrong that we prefer not to use this word. One possibility is that "their host" is the planets and other celestial bodies.

[4] *"Rested"* The Hebrew word for "rested" *(shavat)* is from the same root as "Sabbath" *(shabat)*—the Hebrew *v* and *b* are different forms of the same letter. The result is a word play that we cannot capture in English. The basic idea is similar to "He rested on the day of rest" or "He sabbathed on the sabbath."

[5] *"Had created to do"* That is, God created work to do ("the work God had created to do"), and having done it, on the seventh day God rested from it. This somewhat awkward phrase is probably the result of the author trying to include both the verb *bara* ("create") and the verb *asah* ("do").

[6] *"With our masters' and teachers' approval"* This line is in the (then) commonly spoken vernacular Aramaic, not Hebrew. Probably it was at first an informal invitation, along the lines of "shall we …" or "let's …"

[8] *"Every other"* Or simply "all." The Hebrew is ambiguous. Our translation suggests that God chose "us" above all other nations, in accord with the next phrase.

[8] *"People"* Literally, "tongue," but used metonymically in a way that doesn't quite work in English. (Metonymy is using a word to refer to something related to that word.) In English, we use "tongue" to refer to a language, that is, something spoken by the tongue. In Hebrew, *lashon* ("tongue"), in what is actually a sort of double-metonymy, is used to refer to the group of people who speak what is spoken by the tongue.

[9] *"Holidays"* Hebrew, *mo'adim* (sing., *mo'ed*), which is a little more general than the technical "festival" (one of Passover, Shavuot, Sukkot), but less general than the English "holiday." We have no English words for these technical terms, so we cannot translate exactly or even consistently.

[10] *"You gave us"* The Hebrew doesn't repeat "you gave us," but it does include a word that indicates a direct object, making it clear that what follows is indeed a continuation of the verb "gave" in verse 9. To make the passage readable in English, we repeat the verb.

[10] *"Festival of Matzot"* That is, Passover.

[10] *"Memorial"* Frequently, "remembrance," though the point is marking the Exodus, not simply remembering it.

[11] *"Joyfully"* We would prefer "happily" here, but common usage of "happily" does not mean "in a happy way." Rather, it is roughly the opposite of "grudgingly."

[11] *"Joyously"* We need two words in English, to match the two in Hebrew. Unfortunately, the pair "joyfully and joyously" creates alliteration in English where there is none in Hebrew. But we have no better choice. (Rare words such as "gleefully," "mirthfully," etc., seem out of place.)

[11] *"Holidays"* A poor English translation, but the best one we have. *Yontif*—the Yiddishized version of the Hebrew *yom tov*, literally, "good day"—is what we want, because it lets us differentiate among holidays. Chanukah is a holiday, but it is not *yontif*; only the first and last days of the holiday of Passover are *yontif*; etc. But translating "Hebrew in English" by using Yiddish seems like a misstep.

[12] *"Times of the year"* Or "seasons." (See below, "time of year.")

[14] *"The nations"* Or, "the other nations." Hebrew frequently omits the word "other" where it is required in English. Our reading assumes that "the nations" are "the ordinary nations," while "Israel" is a "special nation," and therefore not part of "the nations."

[19] *"Time of year"* Others, "festive times" (which isn't quite right, because the Hebrew does not specifically refer to anything festive) or "season." "Season" has two meanings in English. According to one meaning, there are four seasons in the year. According to a second meaning (which we see, e.g., in "baseball season"), it's more generally any time of the year. The second meaning captures the meaning of *z'man*, but because the first meaning is so much more common, we opt for "time of year."

"Urchats" On page 107, we translate *Urchats* more or less literally—"and wash"—including the word "and," even though it is not clear why, of the fifteen sections of the Seder, this one alone is preceded by "and." Perhaps the "and" was added so that this, like the other fourteen, would consists of an even number of syllables (to make singing and other mnemonics easier.) Alternatively, the purpose of the "and" may be to distinguish this caption from *Rochtsah* "Washing"; see *My People's Passover Haggadah*, Volume 1, p. 107.

"Karpas" Parsley (p. 107). Others, "greens" or "green vegetables." The word may have been more general or may, as our translation suggests, have denoted a specific green vegetable, and if so, "parsley" is one good guess. The other is "celery"—in fact, the English word "parsley," which comes from Greek, actually means "rock celery." (There are two, presumably unrelated, Hebrew words *karpas*. We see one here. The other, appearing only once in the Bible, in the Book of Esther, denotes a kind of linen. It probably comes from the Greek word *karpasos*, a kind of woven flax.)

[20] *"Fruit of the earth"* By tradition, usually green vegetables or potatoes.

"Yachats" Breaking (Volume 1, p. 107). The Hebrew is of unclear origin. It may be a back-formation from the verb "to halve," *chatsah. Yechtseh* means "he will halve" (or, more generally, "he will divide"). From this word a new root may have been formed, incorporating the prefix *yod* and the remaining two strong consonants *chet* and *tsadi*.

◆

L. HOFFMAN (HISTORY)

(like the Temple of old), and things (like a Torah scroll) may be:

A1 *inherently* sacred, made so by God, so that nothing we do can alter their nature;
A2 sacred *only when we recognize* them as such, so that holiness becomes something we and God arrange together; or
A3 *sacred only when we project* holiness upon them—so we create holiness ourselves.

The issue arises because the *chatimah* varies with the occasion (paralleling A1 and A2 above):

B1 The Shabbat version ends, *Barukh ... m'kadesh hashabbat* ("Blessed [is God] who sanctifies the Shabbat").
B2 On Sukkot, Shavuot, and Passover, we say *Barukh ... m'kadesh yisra'el v'hazmanim* ("Blessed ... who sanctifies Israel and the times of year").[1]

The holiday blessing (B2), "Blessed ... who sanctifies Israel and the times of year," reflects the fact that Jewish months are truly lunar—between twenty-nine and thirty days long. So a new month can fall either thirty or thirty-one days after the beginning of the last one. In antiquity, the court followed lunar sightings to declare which one it was, so in practice, the day became holy only if the court said it was. But the court sometimes deliberately postponed a new month from the thirtieth to the thirty-first day, to make sure, for example, that Yom Kippur did not directly precede Shabbat (making it impossible to prepare Shabbat dinner). So the holiness of holidays seems to be partly determined by God, but somewhat variably set by us: a partnership (as in A2). It is not inherently holy then (A1), although the People Israel is. God sanctifies us, and we sanctify the holidays, by declaring when they fall.

Shabbat, by contrast, falls every seven days, regardless of our opinion, making it inherently holy (A1), a fact expressed by the conclusion (B1), "Blessed ... who sanctifies the Shabbat"—without mentioning Israel.

That, at least, follows from *our* wording, which we inherited from Babylonian Jews. Palestinian Jews prior to the Crusades ended their Shabbat blessing as we do our holiday one: "Blessed ... who sanctifies Israel and the Shabbat"). They also had a *Kiddush* for each new month (Rosh Chodesh): "Blessed ... who sanctifies Israel and the new months [*roshei chodashim*]").

Theologically speaking, the blessings thus address the important issue of human agency. What are humans alone capable of doing? Do we work alone or with God? How much authority do we have to determine the metaphysical status of reality?

"Havdalah" The *Havdalah* separating Shabbat from Passover differs from the usual version separating Shabbat from weekdays. The usual blessing over spices is missing, a deficit traditionally explained by the assumption that their sweetness continues during the Seder and the festival it introduces. More likely, the issue is tied to the fact that spices originated in the custom of burning incense after dinner, to mask the smell of food. Since incense involved fire, it could not be prepared until after sundown on Saturday, when Shabbat was over. In our case, however, Saturday night inaugurates Passover—a holiday, not a week day; and some question existed as to whether incense could be burned if the following day was sacred.

The blessing over wine seems to be missing, but in actuality, it is just merged into the cups of wine already associated with dinner.

The Talmud debates the order of *Havdalah* when it is inserted here. Eventually, Halakhah establishes it with the Hebrew mnemonic *YKNHZ*, pronounced *YaKeNHaZ* (or *YaKNeHaZ*):

Y for *yayin*, the cup of "wine" we use for *Kiddush*

K for *Kiddush* that follows

N for *ner*, the *Havdalah* candle

H for the *Havdalah* blessing that thanks God for separating (*havdalah* means "separation") holy from profane—here, "holy from holy"

Z for *z'man*, "time," referring to the *Shehecheyanu*, technically known as *Birkat Haz'man*, "Blessing of Time" (see below, "And brought us to this time [*z'man*]")

In the Middle Ages, *YaKeNHaZ* reminded people of the German word for the commonplace pastime of hunting rabbits: *jagen-has* (pronounced yagenhas), "hare-hunt." Illustrated Haggadot sometimes supplied pictures of hunters chasing rabbits into a net! We are left wondering whether Jews actually hunted for sport then (even rabbits, which were not kosher, so had to be eaten by others) or whether illustrators were just being humorous.

Top: Jagen-has—The Hunting of Hares
Bottom: Jagen-has—The Hares Elude Their Pursuers
Haggadah Shel Pesach, Augsburg, Germany, 1534
Library, The Jewish Theological Seminary of America

[19] *"And brought us to this time [z'man]"* The blessing commonly named *Shehecheyanu* is more properly called *Birkat Haz'man* ("Blessing of Time"). Of the several Hebrew words for "time," *z'man* is used for "holidays," in particular the three Pilgrimage Festivals (Passover, Sukkot, and Shavuot). On those days, pilgrims once brought their harvest to Jerusalem.

Relatively early on, with the rise of cities, the Rabbis superimposed a historical layer of interpretation onto the agrarian one.

- Passover commemorated the Exodus.
- Shavuot became the day of receiving Torah.
- Sukkot's harvest revelry, in a lavish "water drawing" ceremony said by the Mishnah to exceed all others in joy, was muted, and Jews were reminded instead of trekking through the wilderness on the way to the Promised Land of Israel.

Birkat Haz'man later became generalized to apply to any annual event, not just pilgrimage occasions. Nowadays, liberal Jews are apt to say the blessing over practically everything of a celebrative nature, but halakhically, it is still largely limited to *annual* occasions of joy—including a new harvest, and even wearing new clothes. Some Jews say it on their birthdays as well.

The blessing's name relies on astrological beliefs that Jews once shared with their non-Jewish neighbors. Astrology depends on the steady movement of heavenly bodies and the belief that some alignments are more auspicious than others—depending on the astrological "sign" under which one is born and the project pursued at the time. Such and such a time may be romantically favorable for Leos (born July 23–August 21), say, but not for Virgos (born August 22–September 23). Virgos will prosper commercially, however, while Leos should avoid investing that day.

The word "constellation" notes specific stellar arrangements like the Big Dipper and Orion the Hunter, which seem to change positions vis-à-vis the earth. The Hebrew word for "constellation" is *mazal.* When we wish someone *mazal* ("good luck"), we mean, more literally, "Have a good constellation." *Mazal tov* ("congratulations") acknowledges the "lucky" constellation that has brought about a celebratory moment. A *z'man* is the stellar moment characterized by a specific arrangement of *mazalot* (plural of *mazal;* "constellations"). By definition, every *z'man* recurs only once a year, when the stars reassemble precisely the way they appeared one year prior.

As a set of *mazalot,* a *z'man* was considered astrologically auspicious for some things, but not for others. That is why the holiday *Kiddush* varies with regard to the *z'man* it celebrates.

- For Sukkot, we recall the extraordinary autumn festivity of the water drawing ceremony mentioned above, "the time of our joy" *(z'man simchateinu).*
- Shavuot reminds us of "the time we received Torah" *(z'man matan torateinu).*
- Passover is the time of our freedom *(z'man cheruteinu).*

Rabbinic thought influenced the Christian biblical Book of Acts, which designates Shavuot as the time (the *z'man*) when the early Christians were visited by the Holy Spirit (divine knowledge akin to Torah).

[21] *"This is the bread of affliction"* [*Ha lachma anya*] We are uncertain as to when this formula over matzah entered the Haggadah. Since its first appearance elsewhere does not predate the geonic age (c. 750–1038), the dominant view (1) is that it was not added to the Haggadah until then. Others (2) date it all the way back to the first or second century, explaining it as a polemic against Jesus' words at his last supper, "This is my body." Contrary to Christians, who identified matzah with their *second* covenant (the one instituted by Jesus), Jews made a liturgical point of tying it to the first (and *only*) covenant that began with our forebears who ate "bread of affliction" (Deut. 16:3).

Alternatively (3), *Ha lachma anya* is indeed tannaitic but has nothing to do with Christianity. If anything, the polemic is the other way around—Jesus' words, "*This is* my body," being a deliberate variant on the Passover formula, "*This is* the bread of affliction."

According to this third opinion, *Ha lachma anya* is a remnant of the days when a real Passover sacrifice was possible. For financial reasons, and because an entire lamb is so large, families would band together in a fellowship—or, better, a "tableship"—group called a *chavurah* to consume a single sacrifice. (According to Josephus, an average gathering held ten to twenty people.) But to count as a valid sacrifice, it had to be legally owned by all the participants. The Mishnah provides examples of legal formulae that bring about joint ownership. Eventually (see "This Bread: Christianity and the Seder," p. 21), matzah took the place of the Passover sacrifice (the *pesach*). *Ha lachma anya* is an application of the *pesach* ownership formula to matzah.

Some medieval Haggadot provide the verses in different order, and even add an introductory line, "We left Egypt hastily" *(biv'hilu yatsanu mimitsrayim).*

In the Middle Ages, some communities said *K'ha lachma anya,* "This is *like* the bread of affliction." In all probability, the change reflected a growing fascination by Christians with the host used for mass; more and more it was viewed as the *actual* (not just symbolic) body of Christ. Once a year on the feast of Corpus Christi (established 1246), Christians paraded through the streets displaying "the body of Christ." Believing that Jesus had been stabbed in the side while he lay suspended from the cross (John 31:34), Christians sometimes testified that they saw Jews of their time stabbing the host until blood flowed once again. A common result was anti-Jewish riots.

"This *is* the bread of affliction" seemed to imply that some Jews too believed in "real presence." So it was changed to say, "This is [only] *like* the bread of affliction that our ancestors ate in the Land of Egypt."

[23] *"Observe Pesach"* Literally, "offer the Passover sacrifice," possibly a genuine wish for the restoration of sacrifices. The first four verses are poetically arranged so that lines 1 and 4, and lines 2 and 3, are parallel. Line 1 (enslaved "in the Land of Egypt") matches line 4 (redeemed "in the Land of Israel"). Lines 2 and 3 may mean exactly the same, repeated to ensure the poetic device of internal coupling. "Observe Pesach" would then mean "eat the Passover [sacrifice]." Since the last bit of food had to be part of the sacrifice, it appears in line 3, after the more general "eat" of line 2, which included anything else that was consumed.

Signpost: Beginning the Seder

*The Seder adds a ritualized act of handwashing and eating a green vegetable (*karpas, *generally pronounced kahr-*PAHS, *but, commonly,* KAHR-*pahs). A piece of matzah is then halved and the leader identifies it as the bread of affliction (*lachma anya *[commonly pronounced* LAKH-*mah an-yah]). One piece is set aside as the* afikoman *(the piece to be eaten as "dessert"), which makes up in symbolism what it lacks in sweetness.*

On the first night, we also say Shehecheyanu *(pronounced sheh-heh-khee-yah-noo), the blessing praising* God *for keeping us alive to reach this day.*

———◆———

Landes (Halakhah)

1135–1204, Fustat, Egypt), explains, "Drinking these four cups with unmixed wine fulfills [the obligation of drinking] four cups, but not the obligation of experiencing freedom [*cherut*]. Drinking all four cups with mixed wine but all at the same time fulfills [the obligation of] *cherut*, but not [the obligation of drinking] four cups."

The *Gryz* (Yitzchak Ze'ev Halevi Soloveitchik, Lithuania, Israel, 1886–1959) confirms these two separate obligations. One is to experience *cherut*, "freedom." Wine gives pleasure and induces a feeling of liberation. Symbolically, moreover, when we drink wine at *Havdalah*, we say, *Kos y'shu'ot esa*, "I lift up the cup of salvations" (see My People's Prayer Book, *Shabbat at Home*, Volume 7, p. 164). This is the essential part of the *mitzvah*, as Maimonides states, "On that night, each and everyone … is obliged *to drink* the four cups of wine … [ibid. 7:7]." *To drink* is a means of experiencing *cherut*.

But there is a second aspect to these four cups. Each one is an organizing anchor for a different section of the Seder. The first cup is the *Kiddush*, which declares the sanctity of the day, an obligation on every sacred day. Over the second cup we recite the *maggid*, "the telling" of the Passover story, the central purpose of the Haggadah. A third cup is added to the *Birkat Hamazon* ("Grace after Meals"), not just at the Seder but on all august occasions. The fourth cup is connected to *Hallel* ("praise"), which concludes the Seder. Thus, drinking all four cups at once fulfills *cherut* but detracts from the *mitzvah* of connecting individual cups to parts of the Seder.

Both elements need to be honored. *Cherut* implies a choice wine (or grape juice) that only individuals who are free can enjoy. Everyone should drink, for no one can experience this freedom for another. Second, each individual cup should be drunk. One should not pass on the third or fourth, saying he has finished drinking. Each cup constitutes a separate *mitzvah* with its own blessing.

The *Gryz's* formulation juxtaposes an experiential approach *(cherut)* with a formulistic, legal one (the need for four separate cups [*arba kosot*]). But this is a well-known traditional dialectic: The Decalogue was said to be *engraved* on the stone tablets. The Rabbis read the Hebrew for engraved, *ChaRuT*, as *CheRuT* ("freedom"). Law is formal, but it must lead to freedom. The Seder itself means "that which is *ordered, fixed,*" so potentially formalistic and dull. But done properly, it leads to the greatest of all experiences: leaving Egypt.

In this context, a story regarding Rabbi Chayim Soloveitchik of Brisk has relevance. A man asked him if he could fulfill his obligation of *arba kosot* with milk, for wine was too expensive. Technically this is possible, for the Halakhah allows *chamar m'dinah* (whatever happens to be the popular local drink) in such situations. But Reb Chayim gave him money to buy wine. The rebbetzin later noted that he had given a greater sum than needed to secure even the best wine. Reb Chayim responded, "If he asked about using milk, it shows that he doesn't have enough funds for his family to eat meat." That, too, is part of *cherut.*

In sum, the laws of the *arba kosot* are as follows:

1. All are obliged to drink the four cups.
2. They should be drunk at their designated place, as they are separate *mitzvot,* each one corresponding to a different part of the Seder.
3. As all at the Seder are free people, the custom is to have each participant have another person there (also a free Jew who is obliged to drink) pour for him or her. Thus, no one has to pour for him- or herself.
4. The best practice is to drink red wine or superior white wine, if one prefers that taste. Wine from Eretz Yisrael is preferred.
5. All Seder tables must have sacramental kosher grape juice for children and for those who have difficulties with wine, since the wine is to be "pleasant" for the individual (heard from my teacher, Rabbi Joseph B. Soloveitchik, based on PT Shek. 47:3).
6. Tradition measures the obligation of drinking wine according to a talmudic measure called a *rivit.* According to Rabbi Moshe Feinstein (late twentieth century, Russia, New York), a *rivit* is 4.42 fluid ounces. Rabbi Abraham Chaim Na'eh (early twentieth century, Israel) measures it as 2.91 ounces; and for the Chazon Ish (Abraham Isaiah ben Shmaryahu Joseph Karelitz 1878–1953, Kosov, Lithuania, and B'nai B'rak, Israel), it is 5.07 ounces. Ideally, one drinks the entire cup, or at least the majority of the cup *(rov kos).* The minimum quantity, in any event, is *rov rivit,* the majority of 2.9 or 4.42 fluid ounces.
7. But Rabbi Moshe Feinstein distinguishes Seder on Friday night from Seder on any other night of the week. *Kiddush* on Shabbat is a Torah obligation *(d'ora'ita),* necessitating the full 4.42 ounces. When the Seder falls any other night, *Kiddush* is a rabbinic enactment *(d'rabbanan),* and one can be more lenient with the quantity—2.9 ounces. In either case, the remaining three cups need to be a minimum of 2.9 ounces.
8. One drinks while reclining and within a short period of time, not sipping slowly throughout the meal.

[12] *"Who sanctifies (Shabbat …)" Kiddush* is a liturgical fulfillment of the Torah requirement "to remember Shabbat by sanctifying it." Even when they do not fall on Friday/Saturday, holidays are considered as a "Shabbat"—a day of rest.

Kiddush may be said by the leader on behalf of everyone present, under the principle *shome'a k'oneh*, listening with the intent to fulfill is the same as fulfilling. Alternatively, the leader can make *Kiddush* first, followed by heads of families for their family, or all can make *Kiddush* together.

[19] *"Who has kept us alive"* Everyone should say *Shehecheyanu*, having in mind both the sanctity of the day and performance of the *mitzvot* of the night, especially the recitation of the Haggadah.

Reciting *Shehecheyanu* with the Haggadah in mind connects the normal recitation of *Kiddush* to the *arba kosot* (the four cups). Maimonides states (Laws of *Chamets* and Matzah 7:1), "It is a positive *mitzvah* of the Torah to tell of the miracles and wonders that were done for our parents in Egypt on the night of the fifteenth, as it says, 'Remember this day when you went free from Egypt' (Exod. 13:3), which is likened to the verse, 'Remember the Sabbath day' (Exod. 20:8)." The comparison with the Sabbath, Reb Chayim of Brisk says, implies the need to specify that it is *this* very day in which the miracle took place. *Kiddush* here is both the "normal" sanctification of a holy day and part of the recitation of the Haggadah. Unlike a regular Shabbat and other holidays, where *Kiddush* can usher the holy day in before nightfall, this *Kiddush* must be said after nightfall, for it is time-specific—it must designate *this* day, which begins only with sundown.

"Urchats: Washing without a Blessing" The guests at the Seder table rise to do the ritual washing but do not make the usual blessing *(al n'tilat yada'im)*. They then eat only a vegetable dipped in salt water! All of this is puzzling—"puzzlement" being the whole point of the Seder ritual, which depends on raising questions in the minds of the celebrants.

This is, however, more than a contrivance. The washing over wet vegetables is a sister ritual to washing over bread.

Both practices presuppose the rabbinic understanding of *tum'ah v'tohorah*, "ritual/spiritual impurity and purity." Associated primarily with death, *tum'ah* is a state of ritual and spiritual alienation in which one cannot enter the Temple or come into contact with (or eat) a holy object associated with the Temple. One who is *tamei* (ritually/spiritually impure, or "alienated") can, upon contact, make others *tamei*. But this is not a permanent status. Temple rituals can change the status of *tamei* to *tahor* (ritually/spiritually pure or "integrated"). With the end of the Temple, most of the rituals were no longer operative, but the Rabbis retained a number of elements of *tum'ah v'tohorah*,

Ritual/spiritual impurity *(tum'ah)* can exist as a primary or secondary condition. A person's hands are a case of *sh'niyot l'tum'ah* ("a secondary state of impurity"), because they are "busy" *(askaniyot)*, inadvertently touching things that might themselves be impure (in a state of *t'umah*) or even just dirty *(Rashi)*. Hands unwashed must therefore refrain from touching and eating that which is *kadosh*, the sacrifices. Later the Sages extended the prohibition to *t'rumah*, produce set aside as a gift to the priest. Still later this was extended to all non-consecrated bread.

So before eating bread (defined as that which requires the blessing of *hamotsi*), the hands must be washed. As Maimonides says, "[This is so] even though it is profane bread, and even though a person's hands are not soiled and not knowingly [touched by] *tum'ah*. [No matter what,] he should not eat until he washes his two hands." But Maimonides then adds, "Similarly, for anything that has been dipped in liquid, it is necessary to wash one's hands at the beginning [before eating]" (Laws of Blessings 6:1).

The practice of washing over bread has remained in effect. Theoretically it still exists for food dipped in liquid, as we saw in Maimonides. But Alfasi does not mention any blessing for such food, and both the *Shulchan Arukh* and *Bet Yosef* (both by Joseph Caro) discourage making a blessing (sec. 160). So even though this washing over liquids remains "on the books," it generally goes unobserved. The only real occurrence is on Seder night, where we wash without blessing (even though there are those who, following Maimonides, call for it).

But why do we keep it for the Seder? The Seder is a commemoration of several periods of Jewish history. At its core is the remembrance of the Exodus, but many of the rituals recollect also *aliyah laregel*, "making a holiday pilgrimage," a practice of the Temple period. Here we have a primary example, reenacting through our Seder the sacrificing and consumption of the *korban pesach*, the sacrificial paschal lamb. In that mode, we revert to the customs of the Temple era. One is preserving *tohorah* and avoiding *tum'ah*. By arising to wash, even over vegetables dipped in salt water, we place ourselves in the company of the *olei laregel*, the holiday pilgrims. One night a year, one can maintain this heightened consciousness of one's ritual state. Some contemporary spiritual giants go so far as to make the blessing (heard from Rabbi Moshe Lichtenstein regarding his father, Rabbi Dr. Aharon Lichtenstein, Rosh Yeshivah of Yeshivat Har Etzion).

The rules of washing are as follows:

1. Washing over liquids is virtually the same as washing over bread.
2. One's hands should be clean and dry before washing ritually.
3. Using one's left hand, one pours a cup of clean water over the right. One then places the cup in the right hand and pours over the left. Repeat. (Alternatively, pour twice over the right hand and then over the left.)
4. The water need only be sufficient to cover the full hand.
5. It is customary to fill the cup for the next person.
6. One then raises one's hands, fingers pointing up, allowing the water to drip downwards toward the wrists as one dries one's hands on a clean towel.
7. The general practice is not to say a blessing (the blessing is reserved for washing before eating bread).
8. With one's hands in a state of ritual purity, one should not touch one's hair, shoe soles, or anything dirty or greasy.
9. With one's hands in such a ritually pure state, one eats the *karpas*.

"Karpas" The vegetable is dipped in water. The custom is to have a green vegetable such as parsley or celery (reminiscent in Roman times of the victor's laurels). The

Lithuanian custom is to have a cooked potato. One can set the *karpas* in salt water in individual bowls to give it taste and then lift it out in order to dip it when reciting the blessing. But *karpas* was originally a form of *maror* (bitter herbs), so while saying the blessing, one should also have *maror*, eaten later, in mind.

The general *minhag* is that the *karpas* should be less than *k'zayit* (literally, the size of an olive, taken nowadays to be less than an ounce), because anything more would necessitate a blessing after eating as well.

"Yachats" One breaks the middle matzah and hides the larger piece as the *afikoman*. One might imagine that we should break the matzah only later, when, as part of the meal, we turn to it as our actual food. That was indeed what Maimonides did, but following Hai Gaon (969–1038) the custom is to break it here, before the *maggid* section, which portrays our finding freedom. The point is still to be able to say, in effect, "This is the bread of affliction, just as the poor have only a piece [a 'crust'], so here too we only have a piece [of the whole]. We break the bread to render ourselves [as if we are] poor."

The Tzemach Tzedek (Menachem Mendel Schneersohn, 1789–1866) says that since *yachats* is to ensure that the matzah be indeed *lechem oni* ("the bread of affliction"), as described in the Torah (Deut. 6:3), it must be a Torah requirement *(d'ora'ita)*.

The laws of *yachats* are as follows:

1. The larger broken part is put aside as *afikoman*.
2. While hiding and seeking the *afikoman*, one should be careful not to break it further.
3. It should not be so well hidden that it cannot be found.
4. According to the *Gra*, only two pieces of matzah are used. After *yachats*, one has only one and a half pieces left.

"Maggid ['Telling']" Reb Chayim of Brisk distinguishes between the daily *mitzvah* of *zakhor* ("remembering" the Exodus [Num. 15:41]) and the Passover night *mitzvah* of *sippur* ("recounting" it [Exod. 15:18]), which is referred to rabbinically as *maggid* (the verb "to tell") and *haggadah* (the noun meaning "telling").

1. The daily remembering *(zakhor)* is not listed by Maimonides as a *mitzvah*, while the Passover act of *sippur* is. This is because *zakhor* is already part of the daily *mitzvah* of *k'ri'at sh'ma* ("reciting the *Sh'ma*"), which includes a remembrance section. That is to say, the daily *zakhor* is not so much its own *mitzvah* as it is a means to fulfilling the larger *mitzvah* of reciting the *Sh'ma*. By contrast, *sippur* is an independent *mitzvah*, not a vehicle for another one.
2. *Zakhor* is fulfilled by just remembering the general whole of the Exodus; *sippur* requires a full telling in detail, from beginning to end.
3. *Zakhor* is one's own remembering; *sippur* is in response to a question that provokes a telling.
4. *Zakhor* is done on one's own; *sippur* is a telling to someone else, especially one's own children (or students).

Rabbi Joseph B. Soloveitchik (1903–1993, Belarus and Boston/New York), grandson of Reb Chayim, adds:

5. *Zakhor* is a mental remembering; *sippur* involves "props" used to evoke the story (the Haggadah is said over the *z'ro'a*, matzah, and *maror*).
6. *Zakhor* is simply remembering the facts; *sippur* involves praise *(Hallel)* and acknowledgment of God's act of saving us.
7. *Zakhor* is passive; *sippur* is active—we utilize reclining, the four cups, and the like to *show* ourselves as if we ourselves had left Egypt (Maimonides).

[21] *"This is the bread of affliction"* Three *mitzvot* are incorporated in this recitation:

1. As indicated by the invitation, "Let all who are hungry come and eat" (v. 22), first and foremost is the *mitzvah* of *hachnasat orchim*, "welcoming guests," which includes providing for their needs. This is a subcategory of *g'milut chasadim*, "doing acts of loving-kindness" (Shab. 127b). This, in the end, is derived from "Love your fellow as yourself" (Lev. 19:18), which is understood as "Everything you would wish to be done for you by others, you should do for them" (Maimonides, Laws of Mourning 14:1). The overall commandment is biblical, while the details are elucidated by the Rabbis. The *mitzvah* applies to those who are poor and wanting. One must greet these guests warmly and "with a gracious countenance," *b'sever panim yafot* (*Sefer Hayirah* of Rabbenu Yonah, Jonah ben Abraham of Gerona). This is exemplified by our holding up the matzah and saying, "This is the bread of affliction our ancestors ate in the Land of Egypt." By directly stating that both host and guest share a common history, the guest is put at ease.
2. The second *mitzvah* is *v'samachta b'chagekha*, "You shall rejoice in your festival." Halakhically speaking, real joy entails providing happiness for one's family. Maimonides expands:

Thus children should be given roasted grain, nuts, and other treats; women should have clothes and jewelry bought for them, according to one's means; and men should eat meat and drink wine, for there can be no real rejoicing without meat to eat and wine to drink. And while one eats and drinks himself, it is his duty to feed the stranger, the orphan, the widow, and other poor and unfortunate people, for he who locks the door to his courtyard and eats and drinks with his wife and family, without giving anything to eat and drink to the poor and bitter in soul—his meal is not a rejoicing in a divine commandment, but a rejoicing in his own stomach. (Laws of Repose on the Festivals 6:18)

The Seder is the paramount and paradigmatic meal of all the holidays. For it to be a true Jewish *simchah*, it must include the "poor and bitter in soul," and it must serve to liberate people, even for an evening, from the imprisonment of their circumstances.

Hachnasat orchim is a universal commandment applicable at all times; but it is also the second mitzvah of *simchah* for every *yom tov* festival.

3. The third *mitzvah* is specific to Passover evening, for only then do we recite *kol dits'rich yeitei v'yifsach,* "Let all who are in need come and observe Pesach" (v. 23). The social organization of Seder night in Greco-Roman times was the *chavurah,* a group that gathered to share in the paschal lamb; one member of the group would offer it as the sacrifice, and the entire group would eat it. These groups were often large, but care was taken that each participant would receive the minimal amount. The *chavurah* was exclusivist too—one was not allowed to eat in two of them (Pes. 86a). To be legally considered part of a *chavurah,* one needed to be "appointed" before the lamb was slaughtered (Pes. 61a). When the *Ha lachma anya* announcement invites "all who are in need," it refers to the need to belong to a *chavurah* in order to perform the *mitzvah* of *korban pesach* ("the Passover offering"). This select group is composed of Jews alone, for "this sacrifice is a commemoration of our freedom and our coming into a true covenant [*b'rit*] with God" (*Sefer Hachinukh* 14:17, attributed to Aaron Halevi of Barcelona, 1235–1290).

The Seder is thus a covenantal experience that binds Jews together through commemoration of freedom in service to God. Not only does *Ha lachma anya* allow us to fulfill the great *mitzvot* of welcoming guests (in this case, those especially needy) and sharing with them the joy of the holiday. It also assures that all Jews have an opportunity to share in this crucial ritual, thereby creating identity as it binds us together in a covenantal ceremony.

———◆———

ZIERLER (FEMINIST VOICES)

dissenting opinion that women and children should only be given an amount of wine according to what is appropriate for them, indicating a concern, perhaps, that like children, women might not be able to tolerate four cups. The Talmud (Pes. 108a) speaks much more directly to this, however, insisting upon women's obligation: "Rabbi Yehoshua ben Levi said: Women are obligated [to drink] these four cups, for they too were part of that miracle."

In Megillah 4a, Rabbi Yehoshua ben Levi asserts women's obligation to hear the reading of the *Megillah* on Purim on the same grounds. These statements by Rabbi Yehoshua ben Levi have been very important sources of support for the idea of greater women's participation in public ritual. Because women were "there" for those miracles, they need to be "there" for the commemorations thereof. Viewed differently, however, Rabbi Yehoshua's statements can also be seen as exceptions that prove the rule of women's historical and ritual marginality. The Tosafot on Pesachim 108 states explicitly that if not for the reasoning supplied by Rabbi Yehoshua ben Levi, women would not be obligated in the four cups, since it is a time-bound commandment. The general rule remains that women have generally not "been there" and are generally not obligated to perform time-bound rituals.

The custom that has evolved from the women's Seders to dedicate each of the four cups to a different group of historical or contemporary women thus takes on particular significance. Indeed, this feminist ritual can be seen as a direct rejoinder to this idea, as implied in the Talmud, that women have generally not played significant roles in Jewish history and ritual life. Ritualwell.org, a Web project sponsored by Kolot, the Center of Women and Gender Studies at the Reconstructionist Rabbinical College, prefaces its four cups ceremony with this statement:

> Tonight we will drink four cups of wine, traditionally linked to God's four promises to Israel.
>
> As it is written, "I will bring you out from under the burdens of Egypt. I will deliver you from bondage. I will redeem you with an outstretched arm and great judgments. I will take you to be My people and I will be your God." (Exod. 6:6–7)
>
> In this seder the four cups of wine are also linked to historical and living Jewish women, who in their own eras have acted as God's partners in fulfilling the divine promises of redemption and freedom.
>
> As it is written, "It was for the sake of the righteous women of that generation that we were redeemed from Egypt." (Babylonian Talmud, Sotah 9b)[1]

"Urchats" In performing the ritual of *urchats*, everyone at the Passover Seder acts as though the Temple purity laws are still in effect. Jewish law typically places the burden of family "purity" at the doorstep of women; here the entire family shares equally in the ritual, cleansing his or her hands in preparation for the sacred meal.

"Karpas" There is a strong critical strain within feminist religious thought that blames the monotheism of the Hebrew Bible for eradicating the feminine spirituality of fertility goddess worship. The centrality of childbirth and of spring to the Passover story, however, provides an opportunity to revere the fecundity of earth and woman within the framework of Jewish faith. The Exodus story is replete with reference to the Genesis creation accounts. The daughter of Levi looks at her baby, as God looks upon the created elements of the world, and "sees that he is good" (Exod. 2:2). Eve celebrates the birth of her first-born son, Cain, by proclaiming, *Kaniti ish et Adonai*, "I have created a man with God (Gen. 4:1). Likewise, in the Song of the Sea (Exod. 15), Moses describes the Israelites passing through the split waters as *am zu kanita*, "this nation, whom You have created." The Exodus story is thus not only about the liberation of the Israelites from slavery but also about their birth as a nation, ready to receive the Torah. The *karpas* ritual of eating a leafy vegetable dipped in salt water connects us to notions of universal as well as national rebirth: to the rejuvenation of nature that occurs in spring, as well as to the delivery/birth of the nation of Israel from the slavery of Egypt and the threatening waters of the Reed Sea.

The salt water, in which we dip the vegetable, is typically associated with the tears of the slaving Israelites before their liberation. In dipping the vegetable in salt water, we temper the joy of the spring festival with our awareness of the historical afflictions of the Jews as well as all those who have suffered injustices. In *A Journey Towards Freedom: A Haggadah for Women Who Have Experienced Domestic Violence*, the salt water and the tears it represents are evoked not as a sign of suffering but of blessing:

Blessed are the tears, for they represent my freedom to feel
Blessed are the tears, for they indicate that I am self-aware
Blessed are the tears, for they prove to me that I have found myself
Blessed are the tears for they are proof that I am alive.[2]

"Yachats" In women's and LGBT seders, the ritual of breaking and hiding the middle matzah has become an opportunity to consider the symbolic meaning of breaking and brokenness. Some feminist Haggadot use *yachats* as a call to break the shackles of domestic abuse and of *aginut,* a condition suffered by women who are chained in marriage by recalcitrant husbands who refuse to grant a *get* (Jewish divorce). In a lesbian Haggadah produced by Congregation Beit Simchat Torah in New York, breaking the matzah symbolizes the shattering of rigid social structures that exclude gays, lesbians, and transgendered Jews as well as other marginal groups; by breaking the middle matzah, "we create space, room to welcome" (p. 8).

The act of hiding the middle matzah recalls Yocheved's hiding her newborn baby and then placing him in the *teivah* (reed basket), an act that in turn recalls Noah's building of a *teivah* to save his family and the animals in Genesis 6–7. As a social symbol, hiding the middle matzah can also be seen as representative of the ways in which we hide aspects of ourselves, fearing punishment at the hands of an intolerant society. We look forward, therefore, to finding the *afikoman,* to sharing with our community what we've hidden away, and to restoring wholeness.

"Maggid" In Exodus 10:1–2 God tells Moses that He has hardened Pharaoh's heart "in order that I may display these My signs in the midst of them, and that you may tell in the ears of your son and your son's sons what I have wrought upon Egypt." According to these verses, God intervenes in history specifically to provoke a telling of this intervention. If telling is the stated end of the story, then the question of who tells and how is of critical religious importance. For too many generations, women did all of the preparation for the Seder but took no active or leaderly role in the Seder telling. All this, despite the consensus in the halakhic literature that women are obligated in the *mitzvah* of *sippur y'tsi'at mitsrayim* (e.g., *Shulchan Arukh,* O. Ch. 172:14). Rabbi Moses Isserles (commentary on *Shulchan Arukh,* O. Ch. 173:6) instructs the Seder leader to tell the story in a language that women and children understand, indicating both a determination to include women in the telling and an assumption that women (like children) do not know enough to be full-fledged tellers in their own right. The ordination of women rabbis, however, and the burgeoning movement of women's Torah study have created an entirely new contemporary Jewish reality, with women and daughters becoming active tellers in ways we have never seen before.

[21] *"This is the bread of affliction"* Scholars have differing views as to why this passage was written in Aramaic. According to one theory, the intention was to extend the invitation to the Seder in a language that was broadly spoken. Others maintain that the Geonim simply liked to use Aramaic for liturgical purposes. Suffice it to say, Aramaic is now a relatively unknown language, understood only by those with an elite talmudic

education. *Ha lachma anya* thus impels us to consider the need in every generation to create means of education and communication so that the truly democratic and pluralistic messages of our tradition can reach the largest numbers of people.

Our translation renders the Aramaic phrase *di akhalu avhatana* as "our *ancestors* ate," but many Haggadot translate this as "our *forefathers* ate."[3] The masculinely gendered nature of this common translation is disturbing, especially given Jewish women's historical involvement in preparing for the Seder. In the memoirs of Pauline Wengeroff, a Russian woman who lived in the nineteenth century, much of the section devoted to her memories of Passover concerns the Seder preparations done by the women of her family. Considerably less attention is devoted to describing the Seder itself, except to note the ways in which the women in the family served the men:

> Father settled comfortably into his seat … asking Mother to hand him the individual dishes as needed. The younger men followed his example. When he asked for red wine, she filled his goblet, and my married sisters filled the goblets of their husbands. Our older unmarried sister filled the cups of all the other people at the table including the children and Shimshon the *meshores* [servant].[4]

One thus sees that the gendering of language has real-life implications. A ritual meant to commemorate liberation from slavery ought not use language that presumes that one part of the group prepares and serves the food while the other part eats and declaims over it.

[22] *"Let all who are hungry"* This passage begs us to consider that even in the free world so many people go hungry and that the majority of the hungry are women. As Celine Mizrahi writes, "The feminization of poverty is a tragic reality in the United States today, where poor single mothers make up the largest proportion of people in poverty."[5]

[25] *"Now enslaved"* One of the great paradoxes of the Haggadah is that while it ostensibly commemorates our liberation from bondage in Egypt, it includes passages such as this, in which we openly declare our continued enslavement. This admission creates a context in which we can openly discuss those areas where we feel that our communities have not yet succeeded in living up to our hopes and ideals and consider what fetters us and others in the present day. To what extent has our society still failed to deliver on the promise to women of equal work for equal pay? What can we do to ensure that our Western patterns of consumption do not depend on the enslavement of children or unfair labor practices in other countries? What can we do to advocate for equal rights for gays, lesbians, and other minority groups? What measures can we take to stop the trafficking of woman in countries all over the world, including Israel?

◆ ◆ ◆

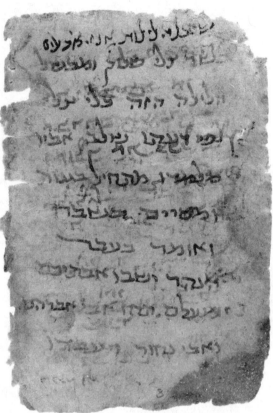
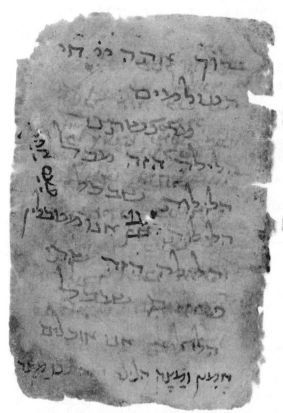

Mah Nishtanah
Israel, Tenth or Eleventh Century (See My People's Passover Haggadah, Volume 2, Appendix II)
The University of Pennsylvania Center for Advanced Jewish Studies
Cairo Genizah Collection, Halper 211 (The Dropsie Haggadah)
Mah Nishtanah begins on the third line of the left-hand page.

4. QUESTIONS OF THE NIGHT: *MAH NISHTANAH*, "WHY IS THIS NIGHT DIFFERENT?"

At this point it is customary to remove the Seder plate from the table—to encourage children to ask why. One of the younger Seder participants recites the Mah Nishtanah.

[1]Why is this night different from all other nights?

[2]—In that on all other nights we eat leaven and matzah, this night, only matzah.

[3]—In that on all other nights we eat various vegetables, this night, bitter herbs.

[4]—In that on all other nights we don't dip things even one time, this night, two times.

[5]—In that on all other nights we eat either regularly or ceremoniously, this night, we all eat ceremoniously.

מַ֫ה־נִּשְׁתַּנָּה הַלַּ֫יְלָה הַזֶּה מִכָּל־הַלֵּילוֹת? [1]

שֶׁבְּכָל־הַלֵּילוֹת אָנוּ אוֹכְלִין חָמֵץ וּמַצָּה. הַלַּ֫יְלָה הַזֶּה כֻּלּוֹ מַצָּה: [2]

שֶׁבְּכָל־הַלֵּילוֹת אָנוּ אוֹכְלִין שְׁאָר יְרָקוֹת. הַלַּ֫יְלָה הַזֶּה מָרוֹר: [3]

שֶׁבְּכָל־הַלֵּילוֹת אֵין אָנוּ מַטְבִּילִין אֲפִלּוּ פַּעַם אֶחָת. הַלַּ֫יְלָה הַזֶּה שְׁתֵּי פְעָמִים: [4]

שֶׁבְּכָל־הַלֵּילוֹת אָנוּ אוֹכְלִין בֵּין יוֹשְׁבִין וּבֵין מְסֻבִּין. הַלַּ֫יְלָה הַזֶּה כֻּלָּנוּ מְסֻבִּין: [5]

Return the Seder plate to the table.

ARNOW (THE WORLD OF MIDRASH)

[1]*"Why is this night different"* Traditionally the Four Questions are known as *arba kushyot*, literally "four difficulties." In rabbinic discourse, a *kushya* is a difficulty arising from one's expectation or a deviation from the norm.[1] Here's an example of a *Mah Nishtanah*-style *kushya* that teaches an important lesson related to the Exodus. The Tosefta (B. K. 7:5) explains the biblical requirement (Exod. 21:6 and Deut. 15:17) to pierce the ear of an individual electing to remain a slave beyond the normally allotted term of servitude. "*Mah Nishtanah*—Why is the ear so different from all other bodily parts that it [rather than they] should be pierced? Because it heard from   *(p. 150)*

BALIN (MODERN HAGGADOT)

[1]*"Why is this night different"* "Out of the mouths of babes" goes the well-known expression. Indeed, the (scripted) questions asked by the youngest child in order to elicit an informative response from elders tell us much about modern Haggadot and the communities that used them.   *(p. 151)*

BRETTLER (OUR BIBLICAL HERITAGE)

[1]*"Why is this night different"* Four and its multiples are important in the Bible, where we have, for example, four rivers in Eden (Gen. 2:10–14) and Moses staying on Mount Sinai for forty days and nights (Exod. 24:18). Of the four differences noted here, only the first,   *(p. 152)*

GILLMAN (THEOLOGICALLY SPEAKING)

[1]*"Why is this night different"* Education begins with questions. Questions emerge when familiar patterns are disturbed. These four questions are stimulated by changes in the familiar patterns of the meal. Theological questions are stimulated by disturbances in the familiar patterns of life. Why do bad things happen to good people? Why do we have to die? How can we believe in a God that we can't see? The simple recitation of the Haggadah will stimulate these and   *(p. 152)*

[For prayer instructions, see page 147.]

4. QUESTIONS OF THE NIGHT: *MAH NISHTANAH*, "WHY IS THIS NIGHT DIFFERENT?"

[1]Why is this night different from all other nights?

[2]—In that on all other nights we eat leaven and matzah, this night, only matzah.

[3]—In that on all other nights we eat various vegetables, this night, bitter herbs.

[4]—In that on all other nights we don't dip things even one time, this night, two times.

GRAY (MEDIEVAL COMMENTATORS)

[1]*"Why is this night different"* The Mishnah's list includes a question about the eating of roasted meat—a reminder of the Passover sacrifice—and omits the question found in our Haggadah about reclining. *Rambam* logically explains that we do not recite the question about the Passover sacrifice because we do not have one at present (Laws of *Chamets* and Matzah 8:3).

Can one fulfill the requirement of asking questions by asking *any* questions, or must the   *(p. 152)*

J. HOFFMAN (TRANSLATION)

[1] *"All other"* Literally, just "all." See "The nations," Volume 1, p. 130.

[2] *"In that"* This phrase (*she-* in Hebrew) introduces the first of four parts of the question. The frequent term "Four Questions" is somewhat of a misnomer, because we really have, at most, one question with four parts. In its original context in the Mishnah, it may not have been a question at all. (See L. Hoffman, below.)

[2] *"All other"* Again, literally just "all," here and below. *(p. 153)*

SIGNPOST: QUESTIONS OF THE NIGHT

THE STAGE HAVING BEEN SET, AS IT WERE, THE DRAMA OF THE SEDER OPENS WITH A PARTICIPANT (USUALLY A CHILD) ASKING THE "FOUR QUESTIONS," A RITUALIZED WAY TO ESTABLISH THE UNIQUENESS OF PASSOVER EVE. THE SPECIFIC CONTENT OF THE QUESTIONS IS RELATIVELY UNIMPORTANT, AND HAS EVEN VARIED THROUGH TIME. WHAT MATTERS IS THAT EVEN THE YOUNGEST PERSON IN THE ROOM CAN AWAKEN THE DINERS TO THE MYSTERY OF THIS NIGHT OF NIGHTS.

[1] מַה־נִּשְׁתַּנָּה הַלַּיְלָה הַזֶּה מִכָּל־הַלֵּילוֹת?

[2] שֶׁבְּכָל־הַלֵּילוֹת אָנוּ אוֹכְלִין חָמֵץ וּמַצָּה. הַלַּיְלָה הַזֶּה כֻּלּוֹ מַצָּה:

[3] שֶׁבְּכָל־הַלֵּילוֹת אָנוּ אוֹכְלִין שְׁאָר יְרָקוֹת. הַלַּיְלָה הַזֶּה מָרוֹר:

[4] שֶׁבְּכָל־הַלֵּילוֹת אֵין אָנוּ מַטְבִּילִין אֲפִלּוּ פַּעַם אֶחָת. הַלַּיְלָה הַזֶּה שְׁתֵּי פְעָמִים:

LANDES (HALAKHAH)

[1] *"Why is this night different"* Formal questions asked by the youngest present provoke the entire sequence of *maggid*—telling the story. But how much must be asked?

Rabbi Simcha Ziskind Broide (late twentieth century, Rosh Yeshiva of Hebron Yeshivah, Jerusalem) pointed *(p. 155)*

L. HOFFMAN (HISTORY)

[1] *"Why is this night different [Mah Nishtanah]"* How many questions were there when the Seder began? If *Mah Nishtanah* means "Why is this night different?" then, added to the four questions that follow, we would have *five*. Regardless of how the Haggadah words it, however, the Mishnah suggests *Mah Nishtanah* was originally no question at all. Its instructions for the Seder stipulate, "The father poses questions to the son, but if the son lacks [the necessary] understanding *(p. 154)*

ZIERLER (FEMINIST VOICES)

[1] *"Why is this night different"* The Four Questions have played an extremely important part in the feminist encounter with Passover. Feminists have resonated greatly with the idea that we only begin to make sense of our past and out present by first asking questions, that is, by engaging in critical inquiry. In women's Haggadot, specifically, the Four Questions have been rewritten to address issues pertaining to women's role at the Seder and in Jewish life writ large. *(p. 158)*

5—In that on all other nights we eat either regularly or ceremoniously, this night, we all eat ceremoniously.

⁵שֶׁבְּכָל־הַלֵּילוֹת אָנוּ אוֹכְלִין בֵּין יוֹשְׁבִין וּבֵין מְסֻבִּין. הַלַּיְלָה הַזֶּה כֻּלָּנוּ מְסֻבִּין:

ARNOW (THE WORLD OF MIDRASH)

Mount Sinai, 'To Me the Israelites are servants [slaves]: they are My servants, whom I freed from the Land of Egypt' (Lev. 25:55). Yet [the ear] broke away from the yoke of heaven and accepted the yoke of human beings. Therefore Scripture says, 'Let the ear come and be pierced, for it disobeyed [the commandment] that it heard.'" To refuse freedom is to mishear the word of God.

2 *"Leaven and matzah"* Chamets means "leavened" or "sour" (as in sourdough). Even in ancient times, the distinction between leavened and unleavened bread had been understood in metaphoric terms. Psalm 73:21 describes the heart as soured, embittered, or in a state of ferment (כִּי-יִתְחַמֵּץ לְבָבִי). Philo, the first-century Jewish philosopher from Alexandria, interprets the general prohibition of leaven from the altar: "Leaven is forbidden on account of the rising that it causes; this prohibition again having a figurative meaning, intimating that no one who comes to the altar ought ... to allow himself to be ... puffed up by insolence ... and [should] discard all treacherous self-conceit" (Special Laws 53:293).2 Likewise, rabbinic tradition forged a link between leaven and the evil inclination, the *yetser hara*. One sage concluded his prayers with an entreaty that God "break the yoke of the evil inclination" so that no "fermenting of the dough" would interfere with serving God "with a whole heart" (PT Ber. 33a, 4:7:d). During Passover we cleanse home *and* heart of the unwholesome effects of that "fermenting dough."

3 *"Bitter herbs"* Although the Sages acknowledged that the commandment to eat bitter herbs, *maror*, could be fulfilled by many vegetables, their favorite was *chazeret*, a variety of lettuce that initially produces tender leaves but eventually develops a tough, woody stalk. The Talmud compares the Egyptians to *chazeret* because they were soft in the beginning and hard in the end (Pes. 39a): initially they paid the Israelites for their labor, but later they forced them to work without pay. The generic word for "lettuce" is *chasah*, so the Talmud also advises lettuce "because the Merciful One took pity [*chas*] upon us [and took us out of Egypt].

5 *"Eat ... ceremoniously"* Said Rabbi Levi (early third century), "Because it is the custom of slaves to eat standing, here [we are required] to eat reclining to proclaim that [we] have left slavery for freedom" (PT Pes. 68b, 10:37:b).

◆

BALIN (MODERN HAGGADOT)

The questions formulated by the beleaguered *m'lamdim* (teachers), whose thankless task it was to teach Jewish children in the *cheders* of eastern Europe, composed a Hebrew parody known as *Haggadah Lem'lamdim* (Haggadah of Teachers, Odessa, 1885). In it, they compared themselves to slaves in Egypt):

How does teaching differ from all other professions in the world?

All the other professions enrich, and their practitioners eat and drink and are happy all the days of the year. But teachers groan and sorrow even on this night.

In all other professions the workers do not dare to be brazen before their employers. But in teaching, the boys and girls [*habanim v'habanot*] constantly disrupt, and yet all find the teacher to be guilty.

In all other professions there is peace … But among the teachers the opposite is true.

All professions earn their livelihood with honor and receive their salary in full. But teachers acquire only a crust of bread and water, along with insults and abuses, and instead of a salary they receive hunger and famine.[1]

Note as well how the parody undoes conventional wisdom by acknowledging that girls studied in *cheders* along with boys. How's that for liberation!

The Freedom Seder—known by aficionados as the "Hippie Haggadah"—appeared in 1969, complete with unorthodox readings by such men as "Allen Ginsberg the *tzaddik*," "Rabbi Henry David Thoreau," and "*Shofet* [judge] Nat Turner." Although it includes some of the traditional text, it is more a montage of peace songs and inspirational readings than it is a conventional Haggadah. It turns the direction of intergenerational dialogue on its head when it instructs children to chide their parents: "Elders! We have heard your lessons so far, and believe them. But as the prophet Dylan sang: The times they are a-changin'. We have lessons of our own to teach you."[2] This Haggadah was actually used in a Seder held on the third night of Passover, April 4, 1969, the first anniversary of the death of Martin Luther King, Jr., in the basement of an African American church in Washington, DC. Approximately eight hundred people participated, half of them Jews. The rest were Christians. In the decades that followed, freedom seders of all types emerged, including Jewish-Chrisitan interfaith seders, gay seders, and feminist third seders, which are the fastest growing permutation in recent years.

In *Haggadah for a Secular Celebration of Pesach* (Philadelphia, 1982), secular humanists interrupt their Seder with the following question: "I believe in liberation— for everyone. But why must I believe in it as a Jew? I want to believe in it as a human being. I don't want a Jewish celebration of liberation. I just want people to be people and to be free. That's a real question. Answer that one!"

In response, they quote the classical Yiddish writer Y. L. Peretz:

Don't assume you are fulfilling your obligation by working only for the greater entity, for so-called humanity-at-large. Humanity-at-large is an abstraction. On the world stage today are individual groups, distinct peoples, differing cultures…. We too hope for a common humanity, but we shall never achieve it by destroying unique languages, or by annihilating separate peoples, or by cutting down cultures…. We have not endured these thousands of years in order now to forget our way of life. We wish to continue it, so that we may later unite with the company of mankind as equal partners.... Working for one's own hearth and one's own kinsmen does not mean relinquishing the banner of common humanity. We hope for a tomorrow in which there will be a common granary for mankind ... but we also want to bring our bit of corn and wheat to this common storehouse. On the day of the great harvest we do not want our people to stand aside and weep over lost years or beg for alien bread.[3]

BRETTLER (OUR BIBLICAL HERITAGE)

concerning the eating of matzah and prohibition of *chamets,* is biblical. In its earlier form, one of the questions also dealt with the paschal offering, and thus three of the questions were based on Exodus 12:8, "They shall eat the flesh that same night; they shall eat it roasted over the fire, with unleavened bread and with bitter herbs."

GILLMAN (THEOLOGICALLY SPEAKING)

many other questions of this kind. They may not be in the text, but they will be in the air. Let them emerge. Use them for educational purposes. And don't worry if they are not answered. Most significant theological questions have no easy answers.

GRAY (MEDIEVAL COMMENTATORS)

Mishnah's formulaic questions be asked? The Talmud recounts that Abaye witnessed the plate being taken from before Rabbah and asked why that was being done. Rabbah responded that Abaye's question had exempted them from reciting *Mah Nishtanah* (Pes. 115b). But was Rabbah referring only to the Mishnah's opening observation about how different Pesach night is or to the entire set of questions? *Rashbam* (Rabbi Shmuel ben Meir, France, twelfth century) understood Rabbah to mean that he did not need to go over the Mishnah's questions but could proceed immediately to "We were slaves" (*My People's Passover Haggadah*, Volume 1, p. 161).[1] In some manuscript versions of *Rambam*'s Laws of *Chamets* and Matzah 7:2, the text reads, *Haben sho'el v'omer hakorei mah nishtanah,* "The son asks and the reciter [of the Haggadah] says, '*Mah nishtanah,*'" clearly implying that the child asks whatever he wishes, while the Seder leader recites the formulaic questions. In other manuscripts, the text reads, *Haben sho'el v'omer lakorei mah nishtanah,* "The son asks and says to the reciter [of the Haggadah], '*Mah nishtanah,*'" thus clearly indicating that the son recites the formulaic Four Questions.

[5] *"Ceremoniously"* Literally, the root *s.b.h* means to "recline." Mishnah Pesachim 10:1 already says that neither a poor person nor anyone else may eat without reclining, which *Rashbam*, among other *Rishonim*, understands to be because reclining during a meal is a sign of freedom.[2]

The Talmud (Pes. 108a) says that a woman should not recline in the presence of her husband, although an "important woman" may do so. The *Sheiltot* (*Tzav, Sheilta* 77) states that women must not recline at the Seder because it is not customary for them to mix cups of wine, and the four cups are one of the Seder rituals for which reclining is required. *Rashbam* explains that women should not recline in their husbands' presence because "the fear of her husband is upon her, for she is subservient to him."[3] The definition of the "important woman" who does recline is likely sociologically determined. Rabbi Joseph Caro (*Kesef Mishneh* to Laws of *Chamets* and Matzah 7:8) quotes Rabbi Manoah of Narbonne (fourteenth century), who offered the following definitions of the "important woman": (1) a woman without a husband, who is the mistress of the house, (2) a woman who has accomplished much in business, (3) a woman who is the daughter of great ones of the generation, (4) a pious, God-fearing woman, or (5) a woman who has many servants and who thus does not ordinarily busy herself with housework.

◆

J. HOFFMAN (TRANSLATION)

[3] *"Bitter herbs"* That is, *maror*.

[4] *"Two times"* Or "twice," but we prefer to follow the Hebrew more literally here. In Hebrew, as in English, "twice" is usually greatly preferred to "two times." We translate somewhat odd Hebrew with somewhat odd English. Probably the number "two" was meant to be emphasized.

[5] *"Regularly"* Literally, "sitting" or "sitting up." We have two possible ways to translate this word (*yoshvin*) and the next (*m'subin*). One would be "sitting/reclining." The other is "regularly/ceremoniously." The point of *m'subin*, next, is probably both "ceremoniously" and "reclining," but we don't have any way to express that in English. Because the ceremonious aspect seems more important to us than the physical posture of the diners, we opt to reflect manner instead of posture in our translation. The word *m'subin*, from the root *s.b.b*, sometimes simply means "dining," while other verbs from the same root seem to mean "reclining." The situation is similar to our English "dining" and "diner." Though they are clearly related etymologically, "dining" involves significantly more ceremony than one expects at a "diner." (The related Modern Hebrew word *m'siba* means "party.")

[5] *"Ceremoniously"* Or, "reclining." See above, "Regularly."

◆

L. HOFFMAN (HISTORY)

[to do so], the father instructs him "How [*mah* can also mean 'how'] different this night is from all other nights!'" The father then "instructs the son in accordance with his level of understanding."

Originally, then, there were no questions at all. The whole sentence says, "The father instructs the son in accordance with his level of understanding,

1. beginning with [Israel's initial] *degradation (mat'chil big'nut)*,
2. then concluding with *praise* [of God] *(m'sayem b'shevach)*,
3. and sealing [the whole thing] with [reference to Israel's] *redemption (v'chotem big'ulah)*."

The story had to go from degradation to praise to redemption.

So originally, any son able to understand his role would pose random questions. Any query would do. If none emerged, the father explained the Haggadah's basic lesson: Israel's degrading servitude, its Exodus that prompted grateful praise of God, and the miracle of its redemption.

Before written texts, the Haggadah, "the telling," was improvised on the spot, but it had to follow this threefold formula: from degradation to praise and redemption.

By the talmudic era (200–c. 550) a set of standard questions had been determined. But nonetheless, asking an unusual question cancelled the need to recite them. People ate on personalized movable tables (like TV trays), and we hear of a Rabbi questioning a servant who removed his table early (Pes. 115b). The Talmud rules that his real-life question takes the place of the standardized ones. Eventually, however, most authorities held that the actual *Mah Nishtanah* text was necessary, even if other questions were asked. Maimonides (among others) makes sure that happens by instructing the leader, not the son, to say it, lest the son ask something novel and forget to say the necessary text.

The Seder is the Jewish version of festival banquets common throughout the Greco-Roman world called *symposia* (singular: *symposium*). These dinners began with a meal and then turned to conversation, often prompted by a rhetorical question posed regarding the food just consumed. Originally, the Seder meal was eaten first, and questions about the food would have arisen naturally.

In the second century, however, as a response to guests who "ate and ran" without staying to hear the Passover story, the meal was postponed until later in the evening (as we have it). Even a clever child might not come up with a real question about the food, which hadn't appeared yet. That is when stock questions were added.

Our four questions were common in Babylonia. Palestinian Jews had only three, one of which ("Why do we eat meat that is roasted, not boiled?") fell out of use. Also, the Palestinians did not ask why people reclined, since reclining took place at all fancy dinners in Roman society. The Babylonians added that one, since reclining was unusual where they lived. Similarly, dipping lettuce as an hors d'oeuvre was usual at Roman banquets, whereas the Seder called for dipping both *karpas* and (later) *maror* (bitter lettuce, in those days). So Palestinians asked why people usually dipped once, not twice.

In Babylonia, where no dipping was the rule, the question became, "Why [normally] do we *never* dip, whereas at the Seder, we dip twice?"

◆ ———

LANDES (HALAKHAH)

to a case in the Talmud (Pes. 115b–116a) where Rabbah removed the small table on which they had eaten, whereupon the child Abaye asked, "We haven't eaten and you nonetheless pull the table away?" Rabbah responded, "You have exempted us from saying *Mah nishtanah!*" Rabbi Broide reads *Rashbam's* explanation of the story to imply that even the manipulated question drawn from the child is sufficient to trigger the response of *Avadim hayyinu* ("We were slaves …"—the section following this one and the beginning of the tale [see *My People's Passover Haggadah*, Volume 1, p. 161]). Tosafot disagrees: the surprise of the child must lead to *Mah nishtanah* itself. *Rashbam* sees the *Mah Nishtanah* as nothing but a particular formalized presentation of questions, inferior to the "real" question of what actually is happening. Tosafot sees the formal questions as crucial. Maimonides has a third opinion: "… We pour the second cup, and here the son asks and the *leader* says, *Mah nishtanah*" (Laws of *Chamets* and Matzah 8:2)—not the child at all! According to Rabbi Broide it is sufficient for the child to ask any question that triggers the response of *Avadim hayyinu*, since that paragraph alone includes the answer that the child needs. But before the answer is given, the leader of the Seder reads the Four Questions, for this is the official Seder language.

I suggest another answer. The child asks her or his own question because its genuineness is prized. The leader then reads the formal questions teaching this child the types of queries she or he may decide to ask one day. This fits with the Mishnah (Pes. 10:4): "And if the child has no knowledge, the parent teaches *Mah Nishtanah*…." My colleague, Rabbi Arie Strikovsky (one of the *chokhmei Y'rushalayim*—current "sages of Jerusalem" renowned for knowledge and wisdom) points out that the questions of *Mah Nishtanah* are those of the wise child, involving a detailed understanding of the Seder. Eliciting from children a genuine question and teaching them how to probe further are two educational tasks of the parent.

[5] "*This night, we all eat ceremoniously*" Part of *cherut* is reclining while drinking the four cups and performing the major *mitzvot* of the evening, such as eating matzah. Its origin is Mishnah Pesachim 10:1: "Even the poor of Israel should not eat without reclining." *Rashi* (Rabbi Solomon ben Isaac, 1040–1105, Troyes, France) comments, "As is the way of free people on a bed and at a table—a commemoration [*zekher*] of freedom."

The Yerushalmi (PT Pes. 10:1) reports, "Rabbi Levi [stated]: It is the way of slaves to eat standing. So here [at the Seder, it is obligatory] to eat while reclining, to show that one has passed from slavery to freedom."

Indeed Maimonides (Laws of *Chamets* and Matzah 6:7) recasts the famous phrase

"In each and every generation people must regard [*lirot*—literally, 'to see'] themselves as though they personally left Egypt" as "In every generation a person is obligated *l'harot* ['to *show*'] him/herself as if he/she has personally now left the enslavement of Egypt. Therefore, when one dines on that night, he/she must eat and drink reclining, that being the manner of freedom." Reclining is not only how we *experience* freedom; it is also a way to *demonstrate* that we are free.

The question arose in the Middle Ages, when it was no longer customary for even "royalty and great people" (Maimonides, *Commentary on the Mishnah*) to recline on beds and the like, as to what the halakhic requirement should be for a seemingly anachronistic practice. Some, such as the *Ravyah* (Eliezer ben Joel Halevi, d. 1225, Cologne) felt that the practice was no longer obligatory at all and "one should sit in one's customary posture." Others such as the *Ravnai* (Abraham ben Nathan Hayarchi, b. mid-twelfth century, Lunel, France) concluded that any manner of reclining suffices. The *Maharil* (Jacob ben Moses Halevi Moellin, 1365–1427, Worms) actually prohibited full reclining, for "what aspect of freedom can be associated with it? The very opposite [is true]! It makes one look sick!" (*Sefer Maharil* 18b). Nonetheless, both the *Tur* and the *Shulchan Arukh* (O. Ch. 472:2) require reclining, evidently considering it not to be dependent upon practice of their time, but a special practice of Passover freedom (see Menachem M. Kasher, early to mid-twentieth century, Lithuania and Israel, *Haggadah Sh'lemah* [1967], pp. 68–76).

The case of women is especially interesting. The Talmud states, "A woman in front of her husband does not need to recline, but if she is an important woman [*ishah chashuvah*] she must do so" (Pes. 108a). Why does a woman in front of her husband not need to recline? Are women without husbands obligated to recline? And what constitutes an *ishah chashuvah*?

To begin with, the Talmud does not *forbid* women from reclining. The question revolves around whether they are *required* to do so. The *Rashbam* (Samuel ben Meir, 1085–1158, Provence) comments that "a woman does not need to recline, because the fear of her husband is upon her and she is subject to him." If a woman is subject to her husband, it would be a burden for her to recline, as she would need to jump up to serve him. Given this reason, the *Or Zarua* (Isaac ben Moses of Vienna, 1200–1270, and a student of the *Ravyah*) concludes that widows, divorcees, and single women are required to recline just as men are.

Rabbenu Manoach (twelfth century, England) responds to all three concerns: "A [married] woman burdened by the preparation of the meal is exempt from [the requirement of] reclining, just as she is exempt from positive time-bound commandments. But an *ishah chashuvah*, who has servants who are burdened by the meal preparation while she sits on a proper seat—she must recline." For Rabbenu Manoach, the question revolves around economic status and convenience. The Rabbis are loath to require those who possess neither to recline.

The Mordecai (Mordecai ben Hillel, c. 1250–1298, Nuremburg, Germany) quotes the Tosafot: "All of our women [i.e., of our locale] are important [*chashuvot*]. They must recline." The Mordecai and the Tosafot go beyond economics to existential status and declare full equality. Nonetheless, the *R'ma* (Moses Isserles, 1530–1572, Cracow, Poland), referring to the Mordecai and the Tosafot, states, "But I have not seen women reclining these days. Perhaps they have accustomed themselves to be lenient by basing themselves on the [aforementioned] *Ravyah*, who wrote that 'in our time [nobody] is required to recline'" (*R'ma* on *Shulchan Arukh*, O. Ch. 572:4).

Today the custom is for everyone to recline. We see halakhic precedent for this move when the Talmud allows a son to recline while in the presence of his father (Pes. 108a); as the *Meiri* (Menachem Meiri, 1249–c. 1310, Provence, France) explains, "for the father wishes him to, and forgoes his own honor.") The Talmud is stricter regarding a student in front of his rabbi, but all agree that if the rabbi gives permission, he should recline (*Bet Yosef* of Joseph Caro, O. Ch. 473). Finally, a waiter must recline when he consumes the matzah. As the *Meiri* explains, "The only burden of fear that the waiter has is regarding his work [to serve properly, for that is his vocation, but he is to have no 'fear' of anyone else]. This night is a call of freedom for all."

The logic of the Seder thus calls for reclining by everyone. The *K'tav Sofer* (Abraham Benjamin Sofer, 1815–1871, Bratislava), an opponent of the Enlightenment, would bring a special bed to the table so that his wife would recline.

Rules of reclining are as follows:

1. One reclines on one's left side. One can recline by leaning against the back of one's chair; the best practice is to recline on a pillow.
2. Everyone should recline.
3. People with back difficulties or injury can recline slightly, and to any direction. If that is troublesome, they are exempt.
4. One is obliged to recline while consuming: (a) the four cups of wine; (b) the minimal amount of matzah *(k'zayit)*; (c) the same amount of *korekh*; (d) the same amount of the *afikoman*.
5. It is customary *not* to recline (a) during the actual recitation of the Haggadah, so as to be sure to say it with attention and seriousness (*Mishnah B'rurah* 473:71, Israel Meir Hakohen Kagan 1838–1933, Radom, Poland, quoting the *Sh'lah*, Isaiah Horowitz, 1565–1630, Safed); (b) while fulfilling the *mitzvah* of *maror*—an experience of slavery; (c) during Grace after Meals, which is to be said with awe and fear (*Shulchan Arukh*, O. Ch.183:9).
6. If one forgot to recline while engaged in an act for which there is a blessing (eating the prescribed foods, for example), one has not fulfilled his obligation and must repeat the *mitzvah*, albeit without the blessing. An exception is *korekh*, for since it includes *maror*, some do not have the custom to recline to begin with.

Zierler (Feminist Voices)

The Four Questions that appear in Elaine Moise and Rebecca Schwartz's *The Dancing with Miriam Haggadah* are noteworthy in that they highlight women's issues while also maintaining a focus on the community as a whole:

> At all other seders, we hear the stories of our forefathers,
> But the voices of our mothers are silent.
> *Tonight they will be heard.*
> At all other seders, the heroic deeds of our sisters
> Miriam, Yocheved, Shifra and Puah are kept hidden.
> *Tonight we will celebrate their courage.*
> At all other seders, we denounce the Pharaoh of the past.
> *Tonight we will also examine the pharaohs of our own day.*
> At all other seders we rejoice only in our liberation as a people.
> *Tonight we also celebrate our empowerment as Jewish women.*[1]

The Four Questions have also played an important role in pioneering works of Jewish feminist literature. In "Leilei Pesach," Hava Shapiro (1878–1943), one of the first Hebrew women prose writers, expresses frustration over the fact that despite her knowledge of Torah and her reading proficiency, she is prevented from reciting the Four Questions for her family:

> I also know the Questions by heart, but no one pays attention to me; the main object of attention is my brother. My heart murmurs within me. I would have asked better than he did. But me, they send to the women's table. Only my mother sees my pain, pacifying me with caresses from her wondrous eyes.[2]

In contrast to the complaint of Hava Shapiro's essay, Jo Sinclair's 1949 Harper Prize–winning novel *Wasteland* imagines a scenario where a younger sister takes over the asking of the Four Questions and the brother protests! When Jake Brown, the protagonist of the novel, boycotts the family Seder, Debby, his lesbian sister, asks the Four Questions in his stead. Debby's asking of the Four Questions—which Jake perceives as an act of ritual theft—precipitates an identity crisis in Jake and compels him on a quest of psychoanalytic self-discovery; here, remarkably, it is a Jewish lesbian who teaches the male protagonist about self-acceptance and the value of a reinvigorated Jewish identity.

[5] *"We all eat ceremoniously"* Is there a way to conceptualize freedom that doesn't presuppose an antithetical realm of subjugation? This question becomes especially pertinent when one considers the practice of *haseivah*. Though translated here as "eating ceremoniously," the usual translation and the practice still today is "reclining," which originated with the ceremonial dining practices of ancient Greece and Rome. The last of the four questions states that on Passover *kulanu m'subin*—we all recline. But who belongs to this universal category of *kulanu*? According to Blake Layerle, in the Greco-Roman world, reclining was a hierarchical practice of the male elite. If women, children, or other socially inferior people were present at a festive meal, they were

expected not to recline, rather to sit at the end of the man's couches or on lower couches or benches.[3] The Mishnah and Tosefta undermine much of this hierarchy, insisting that even the poor people of Israel must recline while eating matzah and drinking wine at the Seder. A woman in the presence of her husband, however, does not need to recline, unless she is an *ishah chashuvah*, an important woman, and then she must recline (Pes. 108a). The *Rashbam* (Rabbi Shmuel ben Meir, 1085–c. 1174) explains that a "regular woman" does not recline in the presence of her husband because the fear of her husband is upon her, and she is subservient to him. The *Meiri* (Menachem ben Solomon, Provence, 1249–1316) concurs, asserting that there is no freedom for a wife in the domain of her husband. Over time, talmudic interpreters and codifiers amend this position: the Mordecai (Mordecai ben Hillel Hakohen, thirteenth century) asserts that "all of our women are important and must recline," and in his gloss on the *Shulchan Arukh*, Rabbi Moses Isserles (the *R'ma*) reiterates this position. The *R'ma* adds, however, that women customarily do not recline. Indeed, a certain male-only attitude persists around the practice of *haseivah* both in Sefardi and Ashkenazi circles.

Leah Shakdiel (the first woman to be elected to a Religious Council in Israel) comments trenchantly about the implications of women's continued exclusion from the practice of *haseivah:*

> The Jewish woman is seen as a dual creature. First, she is a Jew who shares the historical fate of the Jewish man as well as the national and spiritual consciousness that derives from that special history. She is expected to be present at the commemoration of her people's liberation, the Passover seder. But because she is also a woman, she is subject to the secondary and subservient role—at the seder and elsewhere—of women in all patriarchies…. The Rabbis tell us that we, Jewish women, are free as Jews but not free as women.[4]

In order for the practice of *haseivah* to continue to be a meaningful ritual, we need to make sure that indeed *kulanu m'subin*—that we all recline and relax, celebrating the leisure of conversation and festive eating. Unless we want our notion of freedom to derive its meaning from a sense of lording over others, we need to affirm that *kulanu hashuvim*—we are all deemed equally important in the eyes of Jewish law and custom.

◆ ◆ ◆

B. FROM ENSLAVEMENT ...

5. A SHORT ANSWER: ENSLAVEMENT IS PHYSICAL— *AVADIM HAYYINU*, "WE WERE SLAVES"

[1]We were slaves to Pharaoh in Egypt, and Adonai our God brought us out of there with a strong hand and an outstretched arm. [2]If the Holy One of Blessing had not brought our ancestors out of Egypt, we and our children and our children's children would still be enslaved to Pharaoh in Egypt.

עֲבָדִים הָיִינוּ לְפַרְעֹה בְּמִצְרַיִם
וַיּוֹצִיאֵנוּ יְיָ אֱלֹהֵינוּ מִשָּׁם בְּיָד
חֲזָקָה וּבִזְרוֹעַ נְטוּיָה. וְאִלּוּ לֹא הוֹצִיא
הַקָּדוֹשׁ בָּרוּךְ הוּא אֶת־אֲבוֹתֵינוּ
מִמִּצְרַיִם הֲרֵי אָנוּ וּבָנֵינוּ וּבְנֵי בָנֵינוּ
מְשֻׁעְבָּדִים הָיִינוּ לְפַרְעֹה בְּמִצְרָיִם.

We Were Slaves
Kibbutz Ein Gev, Israel, 1951
The Kibbutz Haggada,
published by
Yad Izhak Ben Zvi

ARNOW (THE WORLD OF MIDRASH)

[1] *"We were slaves to Pharaoh"* The plethora of explanations the Sages offered to explain Israel's ordeal in Egypt suggests that they found none of them fully satisfying. Perhaps they were enslaved because Jacob favored Joseph over his brothers (Shab. 10b)—such is the damage done when a parent treats one child with favoritism. Alternatively, slavery was God's punishment for the Israelites' desire to "become like the Egyptians," abandoning the covenantal rite of circumcision (*Exod. Rab.* 1:8). In another source (*Midrash on Psalms* 10:3), "[God] said to Jacob's sons: You sold Joseph into slavery ... so year after year you will be reciting, *We* were slaves to Pharaoh in Egypt." *Pesikta Chadta* (p. 164)

BALIN (MODERN HAGGADOT)

[1] *"We were slaves"* When the first Passover after World War II arrived, large numbers of Jews of the *sh'erit hapletah* ("surviving remnant") gathered to celebrate at Seders of every variety. Among the Haggadot created by survivors themselves for this first Passover was one used by a (p. 164)

BRETTLER (OUR BIBLICAL HERITAGE)

[1] *"We were slaves ... and an outstretched arm"* This is quoting a variant of the Hebrew text of much of Deuteronomy 6:21: "We were slaves to Pharaoh in Egypt and Adonai our God brought us out of there with a strong hand." The Haggadah adds the words "and an (p. 164)

GILLMAN (THEOLOGICALLY SPEAKING)

[1] *"We were slaves to Pharaoh in Egypt"* The Hebrew word *haggadah* means "telling." When we recite the Haggadah, we are telling a story. The story is an extended answer to the Four Questions. It is also a way of doing theology. We are more familiar with the kind of theology that is articulated in abstract statements, such as that of the giant of medieval Jewish philosophy, Moses Maimonides (Spain and Egypt, 1135–1204), the Thirteen Principles of Faith. This was Maimonides' attempt to (p. 165)

5. A SHORT ANSWER: ENSLAVEMENT IS PHYSICAL—*AVADIM HAYYINU*, "WE WERE SLAVES"

[1]We were slaves to Pharaoh in Egypt, and Adonai our God brought us out of there with a strong hand and an outstretched arm. [2]If the Holy One of Blessing had not brought our ancestors out of Egypt, we and our children and our children's children would still be enslaved to Pharaoh in Egypt.

GRAY (MEDIEVAL COMMENTATORS)

[1] *"We were slaves"* After instructing the pouring of the second cup of wine, setting out *mah nishtanah*, and pointing out that a father must instruct his son at a level appropriate for him, the Mishnah (Pes. 10:4) says that the father (the Seder leader) is to "begin with disgrace [*g'nut*] and conclude with praise [*shevach*]." The Talmud naturally asks what it means to "begin with disgrace." Two answers are offered in the names of two Rabbis, but due to wildly differing manuscript readings of (p. 166)

J. HOFFMAN (TRANSLATION)

[2] *"Holy One of Blessing"* We take "Holy One of Blessing," instead of the more common "Holy One, Blessed be He," from Congregation Beth El of Sudbury's 1980 prayer book *V'taher Libeinu*. "The Holy One who is Blessed" might be another good option.

[2] *"Ancestors"* Others, wrongly, "fathers." The Hebrew is clearly inclusive.

[2] *"Children's children"* Or "[descendents and our] descendents' descendents," or maybe even "grandchildren." The line is purposely redundant.

◆

עֲבָדִים הָיִינוּ לְפַרְעֹה בְּמִצְרָיִם וַיּוֹצִיאֵנוּ יְיָ אֱלֹהֵינוּ[1] מִשָּׁם בְּיָד חֲזָקָה וּבִזְרוֹעַ נְטוּיָה. וְאִלּוּ לֹא הוֹצִיא[2] הַקָּדוֹשׁ בָּרוּךְ הוּא אֶת־אֲבוֹתֵינוּ מִמִּצְרָיִם הֲרֵי אָנוּ וּבָנֵינוּ וּבְנֵי בָנֵינוּ מְשֻׁעְבָּדִים הָיִינוּ לְפַרְעֹה בְּמִצְרָיִם:

L. HOFFMAN (HISTORY)

[1] *"We were slaves.... At first, our ancestors engaged in false service [My People's Passover Haggadah, Volume 1, p. 213]"* We saw above, "How different [*Mah nishtanah*]," p. 154, that the original "answer" in the Haggadah had to:

1. begin with [Israel's initial] *degradation (mat'chil big'nut)*,
2. then conclude with *praise* [of God] *(m'sayem b'shevach)*,
3. and seal [the whole thing] with [reference to Israel's] *redemption (v'chotem big'ulah)*.

(p. 167)

SIGNPOST: A SHORT ANSWER— ENSLAVEMENT IS PHYSICAL

THE ANSWER TO THE QUESTIONS BEGINS TO EMERGE—NOT TO EACH QUESTION PER SE, BUT TO THE DEEPER CONCERN THEY SYMBOLIZE, SUMMARIZED BY THE RABBIS IN A THREEFOLD RECIPE FOR TELLING OUR TALE: WE BEGIN WITH (1) AN ACCOUNT OF ENSLAVEMENT AND THEN PROCEED THROUGH (2) PRAISE OF GOD WHO SAVED US AND (3) AN AFFIRMATION OF THE REDEMPTION WE ENJOY. THE EARLY PART OF THE HAGGADAH PROVIDES TWO SHORT ANSWERS ON THE NATURE OF ENSLAVEMENT (1). THE FIRST IS ENCOUNTERED NOW: ENSLAVEMENT IS PHYSICAL—"WE WERE SLAVES TO PHARAOH IN EGYPT."

◆

ZIERLER (FEMINIST VOICES)

[1] *"We were slaves"* The masculinely gendered nature of the language of the traditional Haggadah is a stumbling block for many feminists. Many women's Haggadot address this simply by feminizing all the nouns and verbs, but that makes the text usable only for women. The solution adopted in "והיינו כולנו שם" *We Were All There: A Feminist Passover Haggadah* is to combine both genders in the representation of both God and community: "We were slaves and bondswomen to Pharaoh in Egypt, and God, She took us out from there with a strong hand and an outstretched arm, and if She had not taken us out of Egypt ... even if we were all [fem.]

(p. 168)

THE PASSOVER HAGGADAH

ARNOW (THE WORLD OF MIDRASH)

traces the enslavement back to the fact that the children of Jacob's wives, Rachel and Leah, degraded the children of Jacob's maidservants, Bilhah and Zilpah. "Said the Holy One, 'How can I make them accept the maidservants' children?' I will send them down to Egypt, where they will *all* be slaves. When I redeem them I will give them the commandments of Passover to observe…. When they all say *avadim hayyinu* ('We were slaves to Pharaoh'), they will see they are all equal."[1]

BALIN (MODERN HAGGADOT)

group of 200 DPs ("displaced persons") meeting in the Deutsches Theatre Restaurant in Munich for a Seder conducted by U.S. Army Chaplain Abraham J. Klausner. *A Survivors' Haggadah*, as it became known, is written in Hebrew and Yiddish translation by the Lithuanian writer Yosef Dov Sheinson and accompanied by woodcut illustrations by Hungarian artist Miklós Adler. It interweaves the tale of their modern-day Exodus with that of the Bible, as explained in the preface by Klausner:

> In their hearts they felt very close to all that which was narrated. Pharaoh and Egypt gave way to Hitler and Germany. Pitham and Ramses faded beneath fresh memories of Buchenwald and Dachau. The driving spirit of the victory they felt was the same, but the leadership had changed. Great Allied armies replaced the ancient handful and in the sacred conviction of Moses now stood General Dwight D. Eisenhower. Just beyond the sounds of the Seder, in the wreckage of the city, the former slave sat in company with his tantalizing memories and celebrated his first Passover since the liberation … [reciting the ancient words now invested with his own experience]: "We were slaves to Hitler in Germany."[1]

BRETTLER (OUR BIBLICAL HERITAGE)

outstretched arm," which are found in the Septuagint, the pre-Christian translation of the Bible into Greek, which was rendered from a text slightly different from the Masoretic text, the Hebrew text that we now use. The consonantal frame of the Masoretic text likely crystallized by the early second century CE, suggesting that this passage is earlier. There are several other such cases in the Haggadah, suggesting that parts of it go back to the late Second Temple period or soon thereafter. This verse from Deuteronomy 6:21 is suitable here since it is preceded by (v. 20) "When, in time to come, your children ask you, 'What are the precepts, statutes, and laws that Adonai our God commanded you?'" The Haggadah is understanding "the precepts …" as referring to the Four Questions.

[2] *"Our children and our children's children"* A slightly unusual phrase, probably meant to recall the following two verses:

Exodus 10:2, "and that you may recount in the hearing of your children and of your children's children how I made a mockery of the Egyptians…."

Deuteronomy 4:9, "But take utmost care and watch yourselves scrupulously, so that you do not forget the things that you saw with your own eyes and so that they do not fade from your mind as long as you live. And make them known to your children and to your children's children."

◆

GILLMAN (THEOLOGICALLY SPEAKING)

reduce the basics of Jewish belief to thirteen propositions (about God, about the Torah, about the hereafter …). Here, Maimonides was writing as most classic philosophers had been doing.

Maimonides may well have been the greatest philosophical mind in Jewish history, but his way of doing philosophy was more a product of medieval culture than of Jewish tradition. The Torah itself, for example, is hardly replete with abstract philosophical or theological statements. Nor is rabbinic literature and the Midrash. Both of these bodies of literature deal extensively with the agenda of theology and philosophy but they do so in the form of stories—the story of creation, of the Exodus from Egypt, of the revelation at Sinai and the rest.

At the Passover Seder, we are commanded to do a number of things: eat matzah, eat bitter herbs, drink four cups of wine—and we are commanded to tell the story of the Exodus. We can do this in many different ways—as long as, following the Mishnah, we begin with the disgrace and end with the praise—and in fact, the Haggadah itself includes different versions of the story. But what is significant here is that the story is a way of communicating the beliefs of Judaism, such as that God redeems enslaved peoples. Everyone loves a story, and as we know quite well, they are also remarkably effective educational devices.

[2] *"We … would still be enslaved"* This is our first encounter with a theme that will reoccur a number of times in the Haggadah. The Exodus from Egypt is not a historical event only, it is also contemporaneous; not only were our ancestors redeemed, so were we. If they had not been freed, we would still be slaves. That is why we must continuously tell the story. The story is not only their story, it is ours as well. The Exodus inhabits an eternal present. All Jews came out of Egypt; all Jews stood at the foot of Sinai. It is worth noting that Christians make the same claim about the resurrection of Jesus of Nazareth. On Easter Sunday, Christians do not say that on this day "Christ arose." Rather, they say "Christ is risen."

The Haggadah is explicit: It was God who took our ancestors out of Egypt—not

Moses, not an angel, no one but God. But the skeptical theologian would ask, "How do we know that?" Our ancestors ordained that we should recite prayers thanking God for the miraculous victories of the Maccabees, but how did they know that it was God who enabled them to win those battles? Similarly, how do we know that it was God who supported the Israeli army in the Israeli War of Independence, though some of us credit God for that victory as well? In fact, how do we know that God does anything? How do we know that God acts in history?

The classical tradition assumes that God acts in history and views the entire panorama of world and Jewish history as guided by God's hidden master hand. More modern, liberal and skeptical thinkers understand this view as historiography, not history—as a subjective, human interpretation of the events of history, not an objective, literal recounting. This more skeptical view suggests that God is present in history when humans put God into the picture, and that this procedure applies not only to our own times but to all of Jewish history, stretching back to the Exodus from Egypt and even beyond.

Denying the objectivity of the Haggadah's account of the Exodus should not for a moment rob it of its power. When we come together at the Seder table and tell the story of the Exodus, it remains our story, the story of how we became a people, and we acknowledge that none of this could be possible without God's intervention in history.

—◆—

GRAY (MEDIEVAL COMMENTATORS)

who said what, we will focus on the answers and not on who allegedly presented them. One view ("view 1") is that we should begin with "At first, our ancestors engaged in false service" (*My People's Passover Haggadah*, Volume 1, p. 213), while the other view ("view 2") is that we should begin "We were slaves to Pharaoh in Egypt" (Pes. 116a).

Rabbi David Abudarham reconstructs the rationale underlying view 2 as follows: Since the whole point of Pesach is to recall the Exodus from Egypt, the only "disgrace" we should recall is that of slavery. The rationale underlying view 1 is that since we are obligated to recall the disgrace and praise of the Egypt experience in order to publicize the praise of God, who "lifts up the needy from the dunghill" (1 Sam. 2:8), we must also mention the historically earlier disgrace that our ancestors worshiped idolatry. This latter disgrace is even more serious than the disgrace of having been slaves. Since the disgrace of idolatry is greater, God is even more to be praised for having brought us near to God's service despite that idolatry.

But what is the talmudic dispute really about? Does the Talmud mean for us to choose between these two views of "disgrace," or is the question one of which disgrace should be mentioned first? Rabbenu Hananel (North Africa, eleventh century) and *Rif* each pointed out that "today, we practice like both of them" (both views 1 and 2).[1] This observation implies that although perhaps the Talmud might have intended for us to choose between those views, we do not choose but follow both. *Ritba* (R. Yom Tov Ishbili, Spain, thirteenth to fourteenth century) explains that views 1 and 2 are not really in conflict, but that the disagreement was about whether we should *begin* with "We were slaves to Pharaoh in Egypt" or "At first, our ancestors engaged in false service." View 1 is that we should begin by referring to our ancestors' early history as idol worshipers, which puts our Haggadah's recitation in chronological order. View 2 is that we should begin with the liberation from Egypt, which was the main miraculous event, and then work backwards in time (Haggadah commentary). View 2 reflects what has become our practice.

[2] *"If" Ritba* asks how we can say "if." Didn't God unconditionally promise Abraham that He would rescue his descendants from Egyptian slavery? *Ritba* answers that were it not for that earlier divine promise, Israel likely would not have deserved to be redeemed because they had become corrupted by the ways of Egypt. Moreover, since that generation would not have been redeemed, their descendants would have become progressively assimilated into Egyptian society, with the result that the Jewish People— ultimately including us—would never have left Egypt. Thus we must consider ourselves as if we had been literally redeemed and must recount this miracle every year (Haggadah commentary).

Abudarham sharpens *Ritba*'s point as follows: If the sins of Israel and the "mixed multitude" (called the *erev rav* in the Torah [Exod. 12:38], a diverse group of people who seized on the opportunity of the Israelite exodus to leave Egypt themselves[2]) in Egypt might have prevented their redemption, how much more so would our sins prevent our redemption if we were now to be sent back in time to Egypt!

◆

L. HOFFMAN (HISTORY)

That is: it went from degradation to praise and redemption.

How this boilerplate outline was carried out in practice varied from place to place. In the traditional Haggadah nowadays, its core is the midrash beginning "My father was a wandering Aramean" (*My People's Passover Haggadah*, Volume 2, p. 1). "We were slaves" (what we have here), and "At first, our ancestors engaged in false service"(*My People's Passover Haggadah*, Volume 1, p. 213) now serve as dual "prologues" to that midrash. In the Talmud, they are alternative responses to the question, "What [do we mean by] degradation?" But originally, each section was probably an "answer" unto itself. Each one begins with "degradation" and ends with "praise and redemption." Here, the first line says it all: "We were slaves ... and God brought us out of there with a strong hand and an outstretched arm."

◆

ZIERLER (FEMINIST VOICES)

sages, and full of understanding [fem.] and elders [masc.] and knowers of the Torah [masc.]...."[1]

[1] *"With a strong hand"* The description of God as saving the people with a strong hand and an outstretched arm seems to support an "andro"pomorphic (i.e., manlike) view of God as a phallic "man of war." However, a closer examination of the grammar of this expression complicates this picture. In Hebrew, both *yad* and *z'ro'a* are femininely gendered nouns, a grammatical detail that creates a more textured, even androgynous image of God as savior. We might want to reorient our thinking about God's strong hand as referring, then, to that of a father or mother, who is used to lifting and carrying around his/her children; the outstretched arm might be equally be thought of as that of a parent or loving friend, ever prepared and accustomed to pulling his/her loved ones out of harm's way. We are reminded, in this regard, of Isaiah 49, where God promises to lift a hand before the nations; in the same context, God is compared to an eternally compassionate, nursing mother: "Can a woman forget her sucking child, that she should not have compassion on the son of her womb? Yea, these she may forget, yet will not I forget thee" (Isa. 49:15).

◆ ◆ ◆

6. How We Tell the Tale

A. Everyone Tells the Story: "Even If All of Us Were Smart ..."

[1]Even if all of us were smart, all of us wise, all of us experienced, all of us learned in Torah, we would still be commanded to discuss the Exodus from Egypt. [2]And everyone who really discusses the Exodus from Egypt is praised.

B. Telling at Length: The Five Sages' Seder

[3]The story is told of Rabbi Eliezer, Rabbi Joshua, Rabbi Elazar ben Azariah, Rabbi Akiva, and Rabbi Tarfon, [4]who were dining in B'nai B'rak and spent the whole night discussing the Exodus from Egypt [5]until their students came and said to them, "Rabbis, the time has come to recite the morning *Sh'ma!*"

C. Telling at Night? "*All* the Days of Your Life ..."

[6]Rabbi Elazar ben Azariah said, "I am like a man of seventy, and I never really got to hear a discussion of the Exodus from Egypt at night [7]until Ben Zoma explained it, quoting, 'in order that you remember the day you left the Land of Egypt all the days of your life.' [8]'The days of your life' refers to the days. 'All the days of your life' includes nights." [9]But the Sages say, "'The days of your life' refers to this world. 'All the days of your life' includes the days of the messiah."

וַ֝אֲפִלּוּ כֻּלָּנוּ חֲכָמִים כֻּלָּנוּ נְבוֹנִים כֻּלָּנוּ זְקֵנִים כֻּלָּנוּ יוֹדְעִים אֶת־הַתּוֹרָה מִצְוָה עָלֵינוּ לְסַפֵּר בִּיצִיאַת מִצְרָיִם. וְכָל־הַמַּרְבֶּה לְסַפֵּר בִּיצִיאַת מִצְרַיִם הֲרֵי זֶה מְשֻׁבָּח:

מַעֲשֶׂה בְּרַבִּי אֱלִיעֶזֶר וְרַבִּי יְהוֹשֻׁעַ וְרַבִּי אֶלְעָזָר בֶּן עֲזַרְיָה וְרַבִּי עֲקִיבָא וְרַבִּי טַרְפוֹן שֶׁהָיוּ מְסֻבִּין בִּבְנֵי בְרַק וְהָיוּ מְסַפְּרִים בִּיצִיאַת מִצְרַיִם כָּל־אוֹתוֹ הַלַּיְלָה עַד שֶׁבָּאוּ תַלְמִידֵיהֶם וְאָמְרוּ לָהֶם רַבּוֹתֵינוּ הִגִּיעַ זְמַן קְרִיאַת שְׁמַע שֶׁל שַׁחֲרִית:

אָמַר רַבִּי אֶלְעָזָר בֶּן עֲזַרְיָה. הֲרֵי אֲנִי כְּבֶן שִׁבְעִים שָׁנָה. וְלֹא זָכִיתִי שֶׁתֵּאָמֵר יְצִיאַת מִצְרַיִם בַּלֵּילוֹת עַד שֶׁדְּרָשָׁהּ בֶּן זוֹמָא. שֶׁנֶּאֱמַר: לְמַעַן תִּזְכֹּר אֶת־יוֹם צֵאתְךָ מֵאֶרֶץ מִצְרַיִם כֹּל יְמֵי חַיֶּיךָ. יְמֵי חַיֶּיךָ הַיָּמִים. כֹּל יְמֵי חַיֶּיךָ הַלֵּילוֹת. וַחֲכָמִים אוֹמְרִים. יְמֵי חַיֶּיךָ הָעוֹלָם הַזֶּה. כֹּל יְמֵי חַיֶּיךָ לְהָבִיא לִימוֹת הַמָּשִׁיחַ:

D. Telling the Next Generation: The Four Children

[10]Blessed is God. [11]Blessed is He. [12]Blessed is the One who gave Torah to His people Israel. [13]Blessed is He.

[14]The Torah alludes to four children: one wise, one wicked, one simple, and one who doesn't know how to ask.

[15]What does the wise child ask? [16]"What are the precepts, statutes, and laws that Adonai our God commanded you?" [17]You should respond by answering that according to Halakhah it is forbidden to conclude the *afikoman* after the Passover offering.

[18]What does the wicked child ask? [19]"What is this service to you?"—"you" and not himself. [20]By removing himself from the group, he misses the whole point. You should respond by chastising him and telling him, "This is what Adonai did for me when I left Egypt"—[21]"for me" and not "for him," for had he been there he would not have been redeemed.

[22]What does the simple child ask? [23]"What is this?" [24]Answer him, "With a strong hand Adonai brought us out of the house of slaves."

[25]And the one who doesn't know how to ask? [26]You should start, for it says, "Tell your child on that very day: 'This is what Adonai did for me when I left Egypt.'"

בָּרוּךְ הַמָּקוֹם. [11]בָּרוּךְ הוּא. [12]בָּרוּךְ [10]
שֶׁנָּתַן תּוֹרָה לְעַמּוֹ יִשְׂרָאֵל. [13]בָּרוּךְ
הוּא: [14]כְּנֶגֶד אַרְבָּעָה בָנִים דִּבְּרָה
תוֹרָה. אֶחָד חָכָם. וְאֶחָד רָשָׁע. וְאֶחָד
תָּם. וְאֶחָד שֶׁאֵינוֹ יוֹדֵעַ לִשְׁאוֹל:

[15]חָכָם מַה הוּא אוֹמֵר? [16]מָה הָעֵדֹת
וְהַחֻקִּים וְהַמִּשְׁפָּטִים אֲשֶׁר צִוָּה יְיָ
אֱלֹהֵינוּ אֶתְכֶם: [17]וְאַף אַתָּה אֱמָר־לוֹ
כְּהִלְכוֹת הַפֶּסַח אֵין מַפְטִירִין אַחַר
הַפֶּסַח אֲפִיקוֹמָן:

[18]רָשָׁע מַה הוּא אוֹמֵר? [19]מָה הָעֲבֹדָה
הַזֹּאת לָכֶם: לָכֶם וְלֹא לוֹ. [20]וּלְפִי
שֶׁהוֹצִיא אֶת־עַצְמוֹ מִן הַכְּלָל וְכָפַר
בָּעִקָּר. אַף אַתָּה הַקְהֵה אֶת־שִׁנָּיו
וֶאֱמָר־לוֹ: בַּעֲבוּר זֶה עָשָׂה יְיָ לִי
בְּצֵאתִי מִמִּצְרָיִם. [21]לִי וְלֹא־לוֹ. אִלּוּ
הָיָה שָׁם לֹא הָיָה נִגְאָל:

[22]תָּם מַה הוּא אוֹמֵר? [23]מַה־זֹּאת?
[24]וְאָמַרְתָּ אֵלָיו: בְּחֹזֶק יָד הוֹצִיאָנוּ יְיָ
מִמִּצְרַיִם מִבֵּית עֲבָדִים:

[25]וְשֶׁאֵינוֹ יוֹדֵעַ לִשְׁאוֹל? [26]אַתְּ פְּתַח
לוֹ. שֶׁנֶּאֱמַר: וְהִגַּדְתָּ לְבִנְךָ בַּיּוֹם הַהוּא
לֵאמֹר בַּעֲבוּר זֶה עָשָׂה יְיָ לִי בְּצֵאתִי
מִמִּצְרָיִם:

E. **Telling at the Proper Time: At the Beginning of the Month?**

[27]It might mean on Rosh Chodesh. [28]That's why it says, "on that very day." [29]With just "on that very day," it might mean while it is still day. [30]That's why it says, "this is what…." I say that "this is what …" can only mean the time when matzah and *maror* are put before you.

[27]יָכוֹל מֵרֹאשׁ חֹדֶשׁ. [28]תַּלְמוּד לוֹמַר בַּיּוֹם הַהוּא. [29]אִי בַּיּוֹם הַהוּא יָכוֹל מִבְּעוֹד יוֹם. [30]תַּלְמוּד לוֹמַר בַּעֲבוּר זֶה. בַּעֲבוּר זֶה לֹא אָמַרְתִּי אֶלָּא בְּשָׁעָה שֶׁיֵּשׁ מַצָּה וּמָרוֹר מֻנָּחִים לְפָנֶיךָ:

ARNOW (THE WORLD OF MIDRASH)

[1]*"Commanded to discuss the Exodus"* When the Temple was destroyed, it took time to develop a truly satisfying celebration of Passover without it. People missed the actual *pesach,* the sacrificed lamb. Rabban Gamaliel himself at first recommended roasting a lamb just like the sacrifice (M. Pes. 7:2). When that was declared impermissible, the yearning for a tangible connection to the Passover sacrifice found expression in the ancient version of the last of what had originally been three "questions": "On all other nights we eat meat that is roasted, stewed, or boiled, but on this night only roasted" (M. Pes. 10:4). Eventually this too was given up. Discussing the story of the Exodus was *(p. 176)*

BALIN (MODERN HAGGADOT)

[14]*"Four Children"* Illustrated Haggadot have flourished since the Middle Ages. Images help to draw in participants at the Seder, especially children, as with a picture book. Also, the Passover symbols, the *(p. 179)*

BRETTLER (OUR BIBLICAL HERITAGE)

[1]*"Wise ... learned in Torah"* In biblical texts, wisdom is secular, distinct from righteousness or Torah knowledge. The identification of wisdom with Torah is first attested in the apocryphal book Ben Sirah (second century BCE), which states, for example, in 19:20, *(p. 183)*

GILLMAN (THEOLOGICALLY SPEAKING)

[9]*"The days of the messiah"* The "days of the messiah" is one of the terms used to refer to the era that will follow the familiar world as we know it now. It is synonymous with terms such as "the world [or the age] to come" or "the end of days." The messiah is the being—human or divine—that will introduce that era. The word itself (*mashi'ach* in Hebrew) simply means "anointed." In the Bible, the high priest and the kings of Israel were anointed with oil as part of the ritual of appointment. *(p. 186)*

6. HOW WE TELL THE TALE

A. Everyone Tells the Story: "Even If All of Us Were Smart ..."

[1]Even if all of us were smart, all of us wise, all of us experienced, all of us learned in Torah, we would still be commanded to discuss the Exodus from Egypt. [2]And everyone who really discusses the Exodus from Egypt is praised.

GRAY (MEDIEVAL COMMENTATORS)

[1]*"Even if all of us were smart"* Rashbetz points out that these words are an important corrective. We should not think that the recitation of the Haggadah is only for the children—notwithstanding all the attention paid to them at the Seder. The recounting of the Exodus from Egypt is an adult responsibility as well, even for those adults who are Jewishly learned (Haggadah commentary).

[2]*"And everyone who really discusses"* Abudarham stresses that the *(p. 187)*

GREEN (PERSONAL SPIRITUALITY)

[1] *"Commanded to discuss"* Even if we all know the story, we are commanded to tell it again. The commandment of *haggadah* ("telling") comes from the verse "Tell your child...." But even a person who is childless is bound to tell the story. We tell it to pass it down from generation to generation. But at the Jewish old folk's home, where the youngest participant is seventy-five years old, everyone is still required to tell the tale. Storytelling for its own sake, you might call it, whether there is anyone "new" who needs to hear it or not. *(p. 190)*

THE STORY OF OUR JOURNEY FROM SLAVERY TO FREEDOM HAS BEGUN. BUT IT SHOULD NOT BE TOLD SO SIMPLY AND THEN FORGOTTEN. BEFORE CONTINUING, THEN, WE PAUSE TO CONSIDER HOW WE TELL IT. FIRST, NO ONE IS EXEMPT, EVEN THE MOST LEARNED; AS AN ILLUSTRATION, WE GET A TALE OF FIVE SAGES WHO STAY UP ALL NIGHT CONSIDERING IT, SO ANXIOUS ARE THEY TO TREAT THE TALE WITH RESPECT. WE THEN LEARN WHY WE TELL IT AT NIGHT AND WHY ITS RETELLING MAY BE REQUIRED *(p. 202)*

וַאֲפִלוּ כֻּלָּנוּ חֲכָמִים כֻּלָּנוּ נְבוֹנִים כֻּלָּנוּ זְקֵנִים כֻּלָּנוּ יוֹדְעִים אֶת הַתּוֹרָה מִצְוָה עָלֵינוּ לְסַפֵּר בִּיצִיאַת מִצְרָיִם. ² וְכָל־הַמַּרְבֶּה לְסַפֵּר בִּיצִיאַת מִצְרָיִם הֲרֵי זֶה מְשֻׁבָּח:

J. HOFFMAN (TRANSLATION)

[1] *"All of us were smart, all of us wise"* We find two words in Hebrew, *chakham* and then *navon*. Even though we translate *chakham* as "wise" in "wise child," we translate "smart ... wise" (reversing the order of the adjectives) here to improve the flow of the English text. *(p. 193)*

L. HOFFMAN (HISTORY)

[3] *"The story is told of Rabbi Eliezer"* Why would Rabbis stay awake all night at a Seder? Since the ones mentioned here all lived during the Bar Kohkba revolt against Rome (132–135 CE), popular opinion assumes they were using the occasion as a ruse *(p. 196)*

KUSHNER AND POLEN (CHASIDIC VOICES)

[8] *"All the days of your life"* Rabbi Menachem Nachum of Chernobyl (*Me'or Eina'im, Parashat Shmot,* Vol. 1, p. 140) provides an additional reading to the Haggadah's discussion of *"all* the days of your life."

Ben Zoma contends that the apparently redundant word "all" implies that our leaving Egypt should be mentioned not just during the day but at night too.

Menachem Nachum builds on the idea of "day and night." *(p. 203)*

ZIERLER (FEMINIST VOICES)

[1] *"Even if all of us were smart, all of us wise"* As in the case of the discussion of *kulanu m'subin,* "we all eat ceremoniously" (see *My People's Passover Haggadah,* Volume 1, p. 147), we need to ask what we mean here when we say the words *va'afilu kulanu chakhamim,* "even *(p. 205)*

B. Telling at Length: The Five Sages' Seder

[3]The story is told of Rabbi Eliezer, Rabbi Joshua, Rabbi Elazar ben Azariah, Rabbi Akiva, and Rabbi Tarfon, [4]who were dining in B'nai B'rak and spent the whole night discussing the Exodus from Egypt [5]until their students came and said to them, "Rabbis, the time has come to recite the morning *Sh'ma*!"

C. Telling at Night? "*All* the Days of Your Life …"

[6]Rabbi Elazar ben Azariah said, "I am like a man of seventy, and I never really got to hear a discussion of the Exodus from Egypt at night [7]until Ben Zoma explained it, quoting, 'in order that you remember the day you left the Land of Egypt all the days of your life.' [8]'The days of your life' refers to the days. 'All the days of your life' includes nights." [9]But the Sages say, "'The days of your life' refers to this world. 'All the days of your life' includes the days of the messiah."

D. Telling the Next Generation: The Four Children

[10]Blessed is God. [11]Blessed is He. [12]Blessed is the One who gave Torah to His people Israel. [13]Blessed is He.

[14]The Torah alludes to four children: one wise, one wicked, one simple, and one who doesn't know how to ask.

מַ[3]עֲשֶׂה בְּרַבִּי אֱלִיעֶזֶר וְרַבִּי יְהוֹשֻׁעַ וְרַבִּי אֶלְעָזָר בֶּן עֲזַרְיָה וְרַבִּי עֲקִיבָא וְרַבִּי טַרְפוֹן [4]שֶׁהָיוּ מְסֻבִּין בִּבְנֵי בְרַק וְהָיוּ מְסַפְּרִים בִּיצִיאַת מִצְרַיִם כָּל־אוֹתוֹ הַלַּיְלָה [5]עַד שֶׁבָּאוּ תַלְמִידֵיהֶם וְאָמְרוּ לָהֶם רַבּוֹתֵינוּ הִגִּיעַ זְמַן קְרִיאַת שְׁמַע שֶׁל שַׁחֲרִית:

אָ[6]מַר רַבִּי אֶלְעָזָר בֶּן עֲזַרְיָה. הֲרֵי אֲנִי כְּבֶן שִׁבְעִים שָׁנָה. וְלֹא זָכִיתִי שֶׁתֵּאָמֵר יְצִיאַת מִצְרַיִם בַּלֵּילוֹת [7]עַד שֶׁדְּרָשָׁהּ בֶּן זוֹמָא. שֶׁנֶּאֱמַר: לְמַעַן תִּזְכֹּר אֶת־יוֹם צֵאתְךָ מֵאֶרֶץ מִצְרַיִם כֹּל יְמֵי חַיֶּיךָ. [8]יְמֵי חַיֶּיךָ הַיָּמִים. כֹּל יְמֵי חַיֶּיךָ הַלֵּילוֹת. [9]וַחֲכָמִים אוֹמְרִים. יְמֵי חַיֶּיךָ הָעוֹלָם הַזֶּה. כֹּל יְמֵי חַיֶּיךָ לְהָבִיא לִימוֹת הַמָּשִׁיחַ:

בָּ[10]רוּךְ הַמָּקוֹם. [11]בָּרוּךְ הוּא. [12]בָּרוּךְ שֶׁנָּתַן תּוֹרָה לְעַמּוֹ יִשְׂרָאֵל. [13]בָּרוּךְ הוּא: [14]כְּנֶגֶד אַרְבָּעָה בָנִים דִּבְּרָה תוֹרָה. אֶחָד חָכָם. וְאֶחָד רָשָׁע. וְאֶחָד תָּם. וְאֶחָד שֶׁאֵינוֹ יוֹדֵעַ לִשְׁאוֹל:

[15]What does the wise child ask? [16]"What are the precepts, statutes, and laws that Adonai our God commanded you?" [17]You should respond by answering that according to Halakhah it is forbidden to conclude the *afikoman* after the Passover offering.

[18]What does the wicked child ask? [19]"What is this service to you?"—"you" and not himself. [20]By removing himself from the group, he misses the whole point. You should respond by chastising him and telling him, "This is what Adonai did for me when I left Egypt"—[21]"for me" and not "for him," for had he been there he would not have been redeemed.

[22]What does the simple child ask? [23]"What is this?" [24]Answer him, "With a strong hand Adonai brought us out of the house of slaves."

[25]And the one who doesn't know how to ask? [26]You should start, for it says, "Tell your child on that very day: 'This is what Adonai did for me when I left Egypt.'"

E. Telling at the Proper Time: At the Beginning of the Month?

[27]It might mean on Rosh Chodesh. [28]That's why it says, "on that very day." [29]With just "on that very day," it might mean while it is still day. [30]That's why it says, "this is what...." I say that "this is what ..." can only mean the time when matzah and *maror* are put before you.

חָכָם מַה הוּא אוֹמֵר? [16]מָה הָעֵדֹת וְהַחֻקִּים וְהַמִּשְׁפָּטִים אֲשֶׁר צִוָּה יְיָ אֱלֹהֵינוּ אֶתְכֶם: [17]וְאַף אַתָּה אֱמָר־לוֹ כְּהִלְכוֹת הַפֶּסַח אֵין מַפְטִירִין אַחַר הַפֶּסַח אֲפִיקוֹמָן: [15]

רָשָׁע מַה הוּא אוֹמֵר? [19]מָה הָעֲבֹדָה הַזֹּאת לָכֶם: לָכֶם וְלֹא לוֹ. [20]וּלְפִי שֶׁהוֹצִיא אֶת־עַצְמוֹ מִן הַכְּלָל וְכָפַר בָּעִקָּר. אַף אַתָּה הַקְהֵה אֶת־שִׁנָּיו וֶאֱמָר־לוֹ: בַּעֲבוּר זֶה עָשָׂה יְיָ לִי בְּצֵאתִי מִמִּצְרָיִם. לִי וְלֹא־לוֹ. [21]אִלּוּ הָיָה שָׁם לֹא הָיָה נִגְאָל: [18]

תָּם מַה הוּא אוֹמֵר? [23]מַה־זֹּאת? וְאָמַרְתָּ אֵלָיו: בְּחֹזֶק יָד הוֹצִיאָנוּ יְיָ מִמִּצְרַיִם מִבֵּית עֲבָדִים: [24][22]

וְשֶׁאֵינוֹ יוֹדֵעַ לִשְׁאוֹל? [26]אַתְּ פְּתַח לוֹ. שֶׁנֶּאֱמַר: וְהִגַּדְתָּ לְבִנְךָ בַּיּוֹם הַהוּא לֵאמֹר בַּעֲבוּר זֶה עָשָׂה יְיָ לִי בְּצֵאתִי מִמִּצְרָיִם: [25]

יָכוֹל מֵרֹאשׁ חֹדֶשׁ. [28]תַּלְמוּד לוֹמַר בַּיּוֹם הַהוּא. [29]אִי בַּיּוֹם הַהוּא יָכוֹל מִבְּעוֹד יוֹם. [30]תַּלְמוּד לוֹמַר בַּעֲבוּר זֶה. בַּעֲבוּר זֶה לֹא אָמַרְתִּי אֶלָּא בְּשָׁעָה שֶׁיֵּשׁ מַצָּה וּמָרוֹר מֻנָּחִים לְפָנֶיךָ: [27]

175

one of the ingredients that would take the place of the paschal offering. Words that came out of the mouth would replace the sacrificial meat that had gone into it.

[2] *"And everyone who really discusses the Exodus from Egypt is praised"* Earlier versions of this passage omitted any reference to "really [intently] discuss[ing]." They read, simply, "… we would still be commanded to discuss the Exodus from Egypt and everyone who discusses the Exodus from Egypt is praised." But if discussing the Exodus is a *commandment*, doing so should not be described as praiseworthy; it is just fulfilling our duty. David ben Joseph Abudarham (Spain, fourteenth century) solved this problem by praising those who exceed the commandment's minimum requirement: "Everyone who *elaborates* [*hamarbeh*, in our translation rendered "really"] on discussing the story is praised." Earlier Haggadot of the Geonim from Babylonia, and that of Maimonides as well, had resolved the same issue with a different emendation: "everyone who *lengthens*" (*kol hama'arich*). Abudarham likely preferred his own approach for two reasons. First, the word *marbeh* shares the root *(resh-bet-heh)* of a number of key words in the Haggadah's midrash on "My father was a wandering Aramean " (*My People's Passover Haggadah*, Volume 2, p. 1): *va'yirbu*, "became populous" (v. 8); *vatirbi*, "you were populous" (v. 9); and *yirbeh*, "multiply" (v. 12). These terms are all positive descriptions of the extraordinary fecundity of the Israelites in Egypt, even amidst oppression.[1] Second, the formulation "everyone who elaborates … is praised" seems to appear only twice in rabbinic literature, and the contexts are revealing: "Everyone [all judges] who elaborates [on the prescribed] questions when examining [witnesses in capital cases] deserves praise" (M. Sanh. 5:2) and "Everyone who elaborates on the mourning rituals for his parents deserves praise" (PT M. K. 18b, 3:83:d). In both contexts, the central figures (the accused and the deceased) cannot act on their own behalf and must trust others to preserve their life or the memory of it. Analogously, the story of the Exodus, so full of hope and promise, cannot preserve itself. In every generation that task falls to the Jewish people—to us. Whether the story will be remembered or forgotten, whether it lives or dies, depends on the passion with which we tell it.

[3–5] *"The story … morning Sh'ma"* This gathering in B'nai B'rak may represent the rejection of a central component of Rabban Gamaliel II's Passover celebration. He roasted a lamb (M. Pes. 7:2) in the manner as it had been prepared when the Temple stood and even referred to it as "the *pesach*," the term reserved for the paschal offering. He then followed this repast with study of the laws of the (absent) sacrifice (Tosefta, *Pischa* 10:12). The Sages, however, forbade Gamaliel's culinary approach to the Seder (M. Betsah 2:7). The B'nai B'rak "Seder" argues implicitly that focusing on the Passover narrative represents a healthier adjustment to the post-Temple reality than Gamaliel's "barbecue." Regardless of its dubious historicity, the assembly in B'nai B'rak also brings together the figures who played key roles in briefly deposing Gamaliel, a leader depicted as excessively domineering (see Ber. 27b–28a). Elazar ben Azariah, the youngest of the group, replaced Gamaliel as *nasi*, head of the Jewish community in the Land of Israel. A hint of this may be alluded to in the order in which the five sages are introduced and presumably seated. Elazar ben Azariah sits in the middle. Rabbinic etiquette (Ber. 46b) accords the central seat to the highest-ranking sage present.

[26] *"I am like a man of seventy"* Elazar ben Azariah's reference to being *k'ven shivim shanah* can mean either "nearly" or "like" seventy years old. The second reading alludes to his ascent to power following the deposition of Rabban Gamaliel II as patriarch (head of the Academy). When his colleagues offered him the patriarchate, he consulted his wife, who said, "They might depose *you* later on." He replied with a proverb: "Let a man use a cup of honor for one day even if it be broken the next." She further objected, "You have no white hair." "He was eighteen years old that day, and a miracle occurred—eighteen rows of hair [on his beard] turned white." That is why he said, "I am *like* a man of seventy," not simply "I am seventy years old."[3]

[7] *"Ben Zoma explained"* The Mishnah (M. Sot. 9:15) recognized Ben Zoma's special capacity to expound upon the deeper meanings of Scripture: "When Ben Zoma died, there were no more *darshanim* ['expounders']." Ben Zoma's insistence that we mention the Exodus at night may allude to the need to maintain hope for redemption amidst dark times. *Mekhilta D'rabbi Yishmael* praises "the faith our ancestors maintained in this world which is altogether night."[4] Likewise, *Tanna D'vei Eliyahu* notes, "As Israel's well-being is associated with the day, so Israel's adversity is associated with the night."[5] *Song of Songs Rabbah* (3:1) refers to Israel's exiles as "the night of Egypt," "the night of Edom" and so forth.

[9] *"The days of the messiah"* The Talmud (Ber. 12b) cites a verse from Jeremiah that seems to imply that perhaps the Exodus *will* be forgotten: "Will the Exodus from Egypt be mentioned in the days of the messiah? Was it not long ago said: 'Assuredly, a time is coming—declares Adonai—when it shall no more be said, "As Adonai lives, who brought the Israelites out of the Land of Egypt," but rather, "As Adonai lives, who brought the offspring of the House of Israel out from … all the lands to which I have banished them"''" (Jer. 23:7–8). The discussion resolves with the promise that in messianic times mention of the Exodus will indeed continue, but it will become secondary to recollections of more recent instances of redemption. We don't forget our history in Egypt, but neither does deliverance in the past satisfy our yearning for redemption today. As Shakespeare wrote in *The Tempest*, "What is past is prologue."

[10] *"Blessed is God"* Hamakom, literally "the Place," an early rabbinic name for God associated with the immanence of the divine presence. "Rav Huna said in Rav Ammi's name: 'Why do we … call God "the place"? Because God is the place of the world'" (*Gen. Rab.* 68:9).

[11] *"Blessed is He"* Although the Sages certainly viewed God as the ultimate source of blessing, they assigned human beings an important responsibility in extending blessings to others. In Genesis 12:2, God promises Abraham "I will bless you … and you shall be a blessing." *Genesis Rabbah* (39:11) offers a striking explanation of why God first promises to bless Abraham and then to make *him* a blessing: "God said to Abraham, 'Until now, *I* had to bless My world; henceforth the blessings are entrusted to *you*. Whoever you find deserving of blessing, you shall bless.'"[6]

[14] *"The Torah alludes to four children"* The Torah indeed notes four occasions in which a child poses questions, but unlike the Haggadah (and the *Mekhilta* and the Yerushalmi, which also contain versions of this parable), it passes no judgments on them. No question is more worthy than another; all are words of Torah. Despite the Haggadah's very different approach, however, it still gives each child a seat at the table. In doing so, the Haggadah embodies a profound insight articulated by *Numbers Rabbah* (8:4): "If you estrange those who are distant, you will ultimately estrange those who are near!"

[15] *"The wise child"* Some commentators point out the perfect fit between the wise child's question and the Haggadah's answer. The child inquires about the laws and is given an answer that indeed refers to the Mishnah's laws of Passover, from A to Z. It is worth noting that in the Jerusalem Talmud's version of the four children, the answers given to the wise and the "stupid" child (who there poses the question asked by the Haggadah's "simple child") are reversed![7] Perhaps the Jerusalem Talmud wants to teach us that sometimes one who poses a highly complex question needs a reminder of the fundamental issue on the table, while one who asks a minimalist question needs to learn that things are not quite so simple.

[18] *"The wicked child"* The biblical context of this child's question pertains to the paschal lamb, the first communal sacrifice (Exod. 12:26–27).[8] The Haggadah suggests that denying the meaning of the paschal sacrifice—and its successor, the Seder—is tantamount to excluding oneself from the community, an act the Sages condemned in the strongest terms. By contrast, a medieval midrash cites the young Moses as the exemplar of communal engagement. "'… [W]hen Moses had grown up, he went out to his people and witnessed their labors' (Exod. 2:11).… Even though raised in Pharaoh's palace, Moses went out to see the suffering of Israel. This is what Hillel taught when he said, 'Do not separate yourself from the community' (M. Avot 2:4). If you see the community in distress do not say, 'I will go home, eat and drink, and feel at peace.' Instead, shoulder the burden with your comrade" (*Midrash Lekach Tov* on Exod. 2:11).

[27] *"It might mean"* This passage resolves any possible ambiguity about when to hold the Seder: not on Rosh Chodesh, the beginning of the month, but in the middle of the month; not during the day, but at night—which means the Seder unfolds under the full moon. The Sages identified the waning and waxing of the moon with the vicissitudes of Jewish history. *Kiddush L'vanah*, the blessing of the new moon, which dates back to talmudic times, speaks of God ordering the "moon to renew itself as a glorious crown over those God sustained from birth [i.e., the people of Israel], who likewise will be regenerated in the future …" (Sanh. 42a). Emphasis on conducting the Seder at the proper time evokes midrashic traditions that view the Exodus as the moment when God turned over responsibility for managing the calendar to Israel. "Consider … the analogy," said the Rabbis, "of a physician who had a medicine cabinet and turned the cabinet over to his son when the son grew up" (*Pesikta D'rav Kahana* 5:13). We hold the sanctification of time in our hands—and with it the healing power of the cycle of the Jewish year.

BALIN (MODERN HAGGADOT)

Seder, the biblical events, and the midrashic motifs of the Haggadah all lend themselves to artistic expression. Depictions of the archetypal sons, in particular, provide visual evidence of the human condition and temperament as interpreted by artists over a period of half a millennium. These depictions of "the wise, the wicked, the simple, and the one who doesn't know how to ask" reveal as much about Jews' perceptions of themselves as of those around them.

The "four sons" made their debut in print in a sixteenth-century Haggadah from Prague (1526).[1] Though they appear only in the margin of the Haggadah, these images would prove central to Jews' understandings of what the historian Jacob Katz called "exclusiveness and tolerance," or relations between Jews and others.

Haggadah Shel Pesach, Prague, 1526 Klau Library, Cincinnati Hebrew Union College–Jewish Institute of Religion

Take for instance, the wicked son, or *rasha*. He is clad in military attire, with a sword and a halberd. Here, wickedness and war are paired as in countless Haggadot well into the twentieth century, with the soldier changing his uniform as circumstances dictated.[2] In the medieval world, where Jews were unlikely to serve in armies, the soldier here must be understood as a "Jew in gentile clothing." He dwells beyond the Jewish pale, so to speak, where wickedness lurks.

Over the course of the modern era, illustrators began to depict the wicked son as a contaminant infecting Jews with vices gotten beyond the insular Jewish community. Lest their negative influence spread, they were to be avoided or even removed, as according to such authorities as Rabbi Moses Schreiber of Pressburg (1762–1839), who admonished readers of his Haggadah commentary to distance themselves from these wicked sons in their midst.[3] More commonly known as the Hatam Sofer (after the title of his famous halakhic work), he was a principal leader of the traditionalists who united against Reformers in early nineteenth-century Europe. As such, he argued—though only theoretically—"If we would have the power, it would be my view to expel [the Reformers] from our borders...."[4]

Later visual representations of the four sons found in modern Haggadot depict the *rasha* as having infiltrated the Jewish community. Indeed, he even sits at the head of the Seder table, perhaps connoting his pervasive influence.

Services for the First Two Nights of the Feast of Passover with New Illustrations,
edited by Hayyim Liberman, Chicago, 1883
Collection of Stephen P. Durchslag

In this illustration from nineteenth-century America (*Services for the Two First Nights of the Feast of Passover with New Illustrations*, Chicago, 1883[5]), the wicked son is caught in the notorious act of excluding himself, which earns him his appellation. Right finger pointing, he reproachfully asks, "What is the meaning of this ceremony to *you*?" But not only that. He is beardless, bareheaded, and dressed in black, unlike his "pure-white" mother, father, and wise brother (who is absorbed in a book). He cavalierly puffs on a cigarette and has usurped the head of the table, where he sits at least a foot away, distancing himself as much from his family as from the ancestral observance. He is leaning back, hardly the kind of leaning favored by tradition! Indeed, in our own day, the celebrated playwright David Mamet has written of the *rasha*'s rejection of his own culture in his highly controversial book, *The Wicked Son: Anti-Semitism, Self-Hatred, and the Jews*.[6]

The wicked son, who dominates the field in the detailed and charming black-and-white sketch by the celebrated artist Nota Koslowsky (b. 1906, Poland) demonstrates through body language his hostile attitude toward the wise son's toil. His bottle of booze, open shirt, cigarette, and scowl indicate his lot in life: he is a hoodlum who threatens his brother with some sort of makeshift weapon, while the wise son attempts to block out the disturbance and focus on his traditional studies (even while wearing the apparel of a Westerner).

However, not everyone regarded the wicked son with disdain. At least one ideologue actually extolled the *rasha*, as properly rebellious, ready and eager to fight for his cause and express ideas imported from beyond the Jewish purview. Ber Borochov (1881–1917), a father of socialist Zionism and founder of P'oalei Zion—a forerunner to today's Meretz, Yachad, and Labor parties in Israel—wrote a scathing critique of the Haggadah in which he attacked the wise son (the *chakham*).[8] To Borochov, the *chakham*

*The Haggadah of Passover,
New York, 1944; a gift of the
Labor Zionist Committee for
Relief and Rehabilitation, Inc.[7]
Nota Koslowsky, illustrator
Collection of Stephen P. Durchslag*

represented complacency and acceptance of the status quo. His passivity enabled Jews to remain exiled in foreign countries far from their proper homeland. He admired the wicked son who found inspiration in the secular movements then sweeping Europe.

This new interpretation of the four sons was part of a larger effort, especially among kibbutzim across Eretz Yisrael (and Zionist groups worldwide), to re-conceptualize and rewrite the Haggadah altogether by focusing primarily on its theme of renewal.[9] As an ancient people looked to reinvent itself as a nation, its holy tongue as a vernacular, and its land of origin as a nation-state, the Passover liturgy became a medium for reinvesting symbols and rituals with new ideologically driven meanings that could then be ingested annually around the Seder table. By the end of the 1930s, as these pioneers grew accustomed to handling the daunting, daily hardships of living in this unfamiliar, "old-new land," they turned their attention to the Haggadah's revision.

No part of the finished products was accidental. Each was a carefully crafted part of the whole, aimed at reinforcing their beliefs and championing their cause: the rebirth of their land. Fixing initially on the past as a source for material, the young farmers supplemented the traditional Haggadah by reviving ancient ceremonies, such as the waving of the omer (sheaf of corn). This agricultural focus became a mainstay of the kibbutz Haggadah, with illustrations of men and women reaping the harvest, ringed by artistically rendered verses from the biblical Song of Songs, the well-known love poetry evoking fecundity and springtime renewal typically associated with Passover.

Even after the State of Israel was founded, illustrators of the Haggadah captured this fresh mood on the canvas, as seen in the rendering of the four sons by Zvi Livni (b. Lodz, *aliyah* in 1927, member of the famed artist group at Kibbutz Artzi and later founder of the prominent Art Colony in Safed).

Expressing the youthful exuberance of the early years of statehood, the sons all appear to be just past adolescence. They are accompanied by slightly altered (but insignificantly so) versions of the traditional text in the first-person singular. The wise

Haggadah Shel Pesach, Yavne Publishing
Israel, 1955
Zvi Livni, illustrator

son is figured as a *chaluts*, a pioneer, with a Haggadah in hand, walking purposefully in the direction of the Seder plate in his eagerness to learn the teachings of his heritage. The plate is buttressed by additional symbols for him to study, all related to the new Jewish state: the seven-branched menorah, tablets inscribed with the Ten Commandments (that Israel might be a moral light to the nations), and the *lulav* of agricultural significance. The wicked son is pictured here as a quintessential member of the bourgeoisie, sporting a necktie and a hankie. He is the enemy of socialist Zionism, and his backward-leaning pose (like the smoking son of 1883) demonstrates that he shirks his responsibilities to the new nation, which include defense and farming. The simple son seems overwhelmed by the sheer number of immigrants entering the Land and too paralyzed to engage in the work at hand.[10] Finally, the one who doesn't know how to ask appears as the *(talmid) chakham* of old, with *pe'os* (sidelocks) and the hunched form of the relentless scholar. Overturning traditional interpretations of the sons, *he* is pictured as the ignorant one, unable even to formulate the questions to comprehend the changing circumstances around him.

In our own day, a majority of Jews acknowledge that the four sons must necessarily be recast as "four children." Asking questions, even in traditional Jewish settings, is no longer regarded as the prerogative of boys alone. Accordingly, Ruth Weisberg's lovely artistic midrash of the "four voices" (i.e., the *chakham*, the *rasha*, the *tam*, and the *she'eino yode'a lishol*) allows for a range of different children who might be prompted at

The Open Door: A Passover Haggadah
New York, 2002
The Central Conference of American Rabbis (Reform)
Ruth Weisberg, illustrator[11]

various points in their development to ask particular types of questions.[12] The muted hues of the background soften the subjects' facial features, as well as their bare forearms and hands, allowing them to look like growing children—with their velvety complexions and chubby fingers.

Indeed, hands play a large role in distinguishing these children, one from another. The wise child (far right) demonstrates, through hand gestures and open mouth, participation in lively conversation at the Seder table. The wise child's gender is ambiguous.[13] He or she wears a yarmulke on top of shoulder-length hair, suggesting that both long-haired boys (who are conventionally understood as rebels; read: *rashas*) and girls in yarmulkes (a rebel of an altogether different sort) share in the wisdom of our ancestors. The child who doesn't know how to ask (far left) is a wide-eyed and cherubic toddler, with plump fingers laid ever so gently on the table's surface. The clothes suggest that she is a girl, but that is not definitive. The simple child looks puzzled by it all, but his/her hands are as steady as his/her eyes, betraying an active interest in all that is happening at the Seder. The wicked child, also in a yarmulke, seems more intent on the playfulness of his own hands than with the matter at hand. Distracted by his own antics, as children often are, he is no more wicked than the next child. Tomorrow, or perhaps the day after, he may yet join his siblings in the act of engaging in the traditions of the past.[14]

BRETTLER (OUR BIBLICAL HERITAGE)

"The whole of wisdom is fear of the Lord, and in all wisdom is the fulfillment of the Law." The identification between wisdom, righteousness, and Torah knowledge continued in rabbinic literature.

[2] *"And everyone who really discusses the Exodus from Egypt is praised"* Though the injunction "to really" or "to extensively" *(marbeh)* tell of the Exodus is post-biblical,

probably meant to replace the joyous and extensive eating of the pascal lamb in Temple times, it creates a measure-for-measure observance of Passover: we multiply telling of the Exodus because God "multipl[ied] ... signs and marvels in the Land of Egypt" (Exod. 7:3).

³ *"B'nai B'rak"* Although we think of this only as an ultra-religious suburb of Tel Aviv, it is mentioned in Joshua 19:45 and in an Akkadian text mentioning the conquest by Sennacherib of the Judean countryside in 701 BCE.

⁵ *"The morning Sh'ma"* Following the rabbinic interpretation that the *Sh'ma* needs to be recited upon waking up, interpreting Deuteronomy 6:7, "Recite them when . . . when you lie down and when you get up." Though this phrase might seem idiomatic to us, meaning "during the day and during the evening" or even "all the time," no such idiomatic uses are found in the Bible.

⁶ *"Seventy"* According to Psalm 90:10, "the span of our life is seventy years"; this thus represents old age.

⁸ *"All the days of your life"* Quoting Deuteronomy 16:3, which contains the phrase *kol y'mei chayekha*, "all the days of your life," rather than the shorter phrase "all your days" *(kol yamekha)*. The two seem to be used indistinguishably in the Bible, but most of classical rabbinic interpretation assumes that the Bible contains no extra words, and thus the longer phrase used here must suggest some time even beyond normal daytime. One option, if "day" means daytime, is that the addition means "night" as well; the other, if "day" means "a twenty-four-hour day," is that time beyond this world, namely the world-to-come, is signified by the added word.

¹⁰ *"Blessed is God [hamakom]"* This is a common rabbinic name for God; it may be used in Esther 4:14, where Mordecai says to Esther: "On the contrary, if you keep silent in this crisis, will relief and deliverance come to the Jews from another quarter *[mimakom acher]*, while you and your father's house will perish? And who knows, perhaps you have attained to royal position for just such a crisis." If translated this way, *makom*, or "place," may refer to God.

¹² *"Who gave Torah to His people Israel"* This divine epithet is never found in the Bible, which emphasizes God's role as redeemer from Egypt much more extensively than His role as Torah giver, which became more central in rabbinic theology. The reason for this change of emphasis is unknown. Some biblical scholars believe that the tradition of law giving at Sinai is a secondary biblical tradition and is thus not mentioned often. Others suggest that the Torah emphasizes God's kind acts of redemption, and thus the giving of the Torah, which places Israel under the divine yoke of obligations (rabbinic *ol malkhut shamayim*), is underemphasized.

¹⁴ *"The Torah alludes to four children"* This grouping of four types of sons is never found in the Bible. It is a result of finding four similar biblical texts dealing with questions, children, and the Exodus, and a desire to distinguish between the questions asked and answers proffered by assuming, in typical rabbinic fashion, that each is

distinct, so that each question and answer reflects a different type of questioner. That children are asking these questions is clear from Exodus 13:14 and Deuteronomy 6:20, "If your child asks you tomorrow...."

[16] *"What are the precepts ... God commanded you?"* Quoting Deuteronomy 6:20, "When, in time to come, your children ask you, 'What are the precepts, statutes, and laws that Adonai our God commanded you?'" However, the Hebrew text here is similar to that of *lakhem*, "you," put into the mouth of the wicked child. Just like the wicked child, the wise child uses a second person pronoun, excluding himself; he should thus be rebuked as well. It is very likely that the text read originally "that Adonai our God has enjoined upon us," and the contrast between the wise and wicked son is reflected in the contrast between the first person ("us") and second person ("you") pronouns. In fact, many significant Septuagint manuscripts have a first person pronoun in Deuteronomy 6:20, and it is likely that the exposition of the wise son was based on such a Hebrew text that served as the source for the Septuagint. Eventually, after the Hebrew text stabilized to read "you," the word "us" was changed to "you," even though the exposition no longer made much sense.

[17] *"It is forbidden to conclude the afikoman"* The law told to this son is post-biblical in origin, as reflected in the Greek word *afikoman*. This is deliberate—although the Rabbis often distinguished between laws that they viewed as biblical (*d'ora'ita*) and rabbinic (*d'rabbanan*) in origin, they believed that laws of both types are authoritative.

[19] *"What is this service to you"* Quoting Exodus 12:26, "And when your children ask you, 'What is this service to you?'"; the text assumes that that this son is wicked or contrary, since he uses the second person rather than the first person suffix, thereby excluding himself.

[20] *"You should respond by chastising"* The idiom is taken from Jeremiah 31:29 and Ezekiel 18:2, where both prophets discuss the relevance of the popular saying "Parents have eaten sour grapes and children's teeth are blunted." Corporal punishment was an important part of premodern child-rearing; see, for example, Proverbs 13:24, "He who spares the rod hates his son, but he who loves him disciplines him early."

[20] *"This is what Adonai did for me when I left Egypt"* From Exodus 13:8, "Tell your child on that very day: 'This is what Adonai did for me when I left Egypt.'" This verse is not continuous with the question in 12:26; in fact Exodus 12:27 offers a very different answer to that question: "You shall say, 'The Passover sacrifice is for Adonai, who passed over the houses of the children of Israel in Egypt when He struck the Egyptians but saved our houses." The author of this section chose the discontinuous Exodus 13:8 rather than 12:26 since the latter uses the first person pronoun "me," which contrasts effectively with "you."

[21] *"He would not have been redeemed"* Although it is not explicit, the biblical text strongly suggests that all Israel was redeemed and contains no clear stories of wicked Israelites left behind.

[23–24] *"'What is this?' Answer him"* Quoting Exodus 13:14, "And when, in time to come, your son asks you, saying, 'What is this?' answer him, 'With a strong hand Adonai our God brought us out of the house of slaves.'" The simple two-word nature of this question (in Hebrew, *Mah zot?*) makes it natural to assign this to the simple child. Unlike the question and answer to the wicked son, which come from different contexts, both the question and answer here are from the same verse.

[26] *"'Tell your child ... when I left Egypt'"* From Exodus 13:8, "'Tell your child on that very day: 'This is what Adonai did for me when I left Egypt.'" Unlike the previous three contexts, here the father explains rather than answers, and no question is offered—thus, this verse must be relevant, from the Rabbis' perspective, to the child who does not know how to ask. The explanation given is the same offered to the wicked son, but the pronoun "me" does not have the same power of exclusion, since this son did not ask a question about "you."

[27] *"Rosh Chodesh"* It is likely that this rabbinic exposition concerning the date of the Seder, and thus the date of Passover, is a polemic against reading the word *chodesh* in verses such as Deuteronomy 16:1, "Observe the *chodesh* of Abib and offer a Passover sacrifice to Adonai your God, for it was in the *chodesh* of Abib, at night, that Adonai your God freed you from Egypt" as "new month" rather than "new moon." (See also Exod. 13:4, 23:15, and 34:18.) In fact, the meaning "new moon" is more likely in all of these contexts, and thus at some point Passover switched from a new moon festival to a mid-month festival; this exposition might even be recalling that.

◆

GILLMAN (THEOLOGICALLY SPEAKING)

Originally, according to Isaiah 11, the messianic figure was a king from the dynasty of David. This chapter describes a human figure who is extraordinarily endowed but remains a human being. Eventually, the notion of a human messianic figure evolved into "the messiah," a divine being sent by God to announce the coming end of days. Christianity is founded on the notion that this messiah has arrived in the person of Jesus of Nazareth, and Christians used Isaiah 11 and other scriptural proof texts to support that account. Because none of the prophecies associated with the end of days were fulfilled in Jesus' time, our ancestors rejected that identification and continue to await the messiah's coming.

Passover is the festival of redemption, and the Haggadah is replete with references to the messianic age and the age/world-to-come. We will explore these themes at greater length as we proceed, but for the present, the expectation of the messiah's ultimate arrival was a source of great anxiety among Jews throughout the ages. The Jewish rejection of Jesus of Nazareth was the cause of ongoing suffering for the Jewish community. Numerous "false messiahs" dot the pages of Jewish history through the early and late Middle Ages, most prominent among them the sad story of Shabbetai Zevi (1626–1676), who was acclaimed by masses of Jews and whose later conversion to Islam led to one of the darkest moments in Jewish history.

The central psychological tension is that while Jews prayed daily for the coming of the messiah, they were also taught to be suspicious of anyone who claimed to be the long-awaited savior. To use Maimonides' formulation, in the twelfth of his Thirteen Principles, "We are to believe as fact that the messiah will come and not consider him late. 'If he delays, wait for him' (Habakkuk 2:3); set no time limit for his coming."[1] So we wait, we pray, we work to repair the world, but most Jews remain skeptical of messianic claims.[2]

[18] *"The wicked child"* What makes the wicked child wicked? The fact that he excludes himself from the community. There are three basic forms of Jewish identity, Mordecai Kaplan (United States, 1883–1986) claims: we can identify as a Jew either by believing, behaving, or belonging. For Kaplan himself, the primary form of identity was belonging. Judaism is the religion of the Jewish people; it emerged out of the life experience of a people, and therefore it is the Jewish people who are responsible to shape Jewish religion in every generation. To exclude oneself from the community is to abandon the relationship that above all makes one a Jew and to forsake the responsibility for the fate of Jews. Note also our response to the contrary child: We do all of this because "this is what Adonai did for me when I left Egypt": "'For me' and not 'for him,'" the text comments. The Exodus was not history alone; it is a contemporary event. I too was taken out of Egypt.

❖

GRAY (MEDIEVAL COMMENTATORS)

text of the Haggadah should read "and everyone who really discusses [*v'khol hamarbeh l'saper*] the Exodus from Egypt is praised," not "everyone who discusses ... [*v'khol ha-m'saper*]. Abudarham is urging a textual emendation because we deserve no special praise for doing what we are obligated to do, namely, to discuss the Exodus story. But if we expand on it, take time with it, make it last—*that* is truly praiseworthy. Later, Don Isaac Abarbanel (Spain and Italy, 1437–1508) comments similarly that the *nuscha amitit* (the "true version") of the Haggadah text here is "and everyone who really discusses" *(Zevach Pesach)*. Abarbanel suggests that one proof that "everyone who really discusses the Exodus from Egypt is praised" (as opposed to the one who simply "discusses") is that the Haggadah follows its comment about praiseworthiness with a story about how five great sages stayed up all night to tell the story of the Exodus. We should strive to emulate their efforts to "really discuss" the Exodus!

[4] *"The whole night"* But, Abarbanel asks, why did these rabbis find it necessary to stay up all night? He answers that they wanted to imitate the precise experience of Israel

leaving Egypt. Just as the Israelites had spent the first part of the night preparing to leave and then had remained awake and alert all night, so did the rabbis spend the first part of the night engaged in matzah, *maror*, and the remembrance of the Passover offering, followed by a sleepless night of discussing the Exodus. In this way, they truly fulfilled the Haggadah's injunction to act as though they themselves had left Egypt (*Zevach Pesach*; see *My People's Passover Haggadah*, Volume 2, p. 73, "In each and every generation people must regard themselves as though they personally left Egypt").

[8] *"All the days of your life"* The Haggadah's discussion of Rabbi Elazar the son of Azariah and Ben Zoma is quoted from Mishnah Berakhot 1:5. In the Mishnah, Ben Zoma is interpreting Deuteronomy 16:3, "in order that you remember the day you left the Land of Egypt all the days of your life." Abarbanel explains that Ben Zoma's goal was to establish why the Exodus from Egypt must be mentioned every night of the year. The Talmud (Ber. 12b) already notes that one reason we recite Numbers 15:37–41 as the third paragraph of the *Sh'ma* is the reference in verse 41 to the Exodus from Egypt. But, continues Abarbanel, Numbers 15:37–41 discusses the *mitzvah* of *tsitsit*, which is only obligatory during the day! How then can we recite that paragraph again at night? Ben Zoma's point is that the third paragraph of the *Sh'ma* should be recited at night precisely because it mentions the Exodus, which occurred at night. The proof lies in Deuteronomy 16:3. Although this verse appears in the Torah in a Pesach context, Ben Zoma realized that it could not apply to Pesach, which takes place one week per year, not "all the days of your life." Moreover, the sort of remembrance of the Exodus the verse commands cannot be like the one we engage in on Pesach. The talmudic Rabbis instructed that we study Pesach deeply each year prior to and on Pesach itself, but not all year long. Hence, the remembrance commanded by Deuteronomy 16:3 must be briefer in nature, but how should it be done? The answer, of course, is that we must recite the third paragraph of the *Sh'ma* at night as well as during the day, notwithstanding its focus on the daytime-only *mitzvah* of *tsitsit*.

[10] *"Blessed is God. Blessed is He"* God is referred to here as *makom*, literally the "place," which is a common sobriquet for God in rabbinic literature (Abudarham). Abudarham also points out that if one multiplies each letter of God's Name (Y-H-V-H) by itself, one arrives at the numerical value of the word *makom*, which is 186. That is, the initial *yod* is multiplied by 10 (yielding 100), the *heh* is multiplied by 5 (25), the *vav* by 6 (36), and the final *heh* by 5 (25), yielding a grand total of 186 (*makom*).

[12] *"Who gave the Torah to His people Israel"* Rashbetz (Haggadah commentary) and Abudarham point out that these verses form a sort of Torah study blessing preceding the Torah verses that are coming right up in the paragraphs about the "four children." R. Zedekiah, the author of *Shibbolei Haleket,* quotes his brother's observation that there are four expressions of blessing in this paragraph: (1) Blessed is God, (2) blessed be He, (3) who gave the Torah to His people Israel, and (4) blessed be He. R. Benjamin Harofei explains that these four expressions of blessing correspond to the four scriptural passages (Exod. 12:26–27, Exod. 13:8, Exod. 13:14, and Deut. 6:20–25) that express the

commandment of *haggadah*, the command to recount the Exodus. R. Benjamin went on to query why the recitation of the Haggadah, which is a positive commandment (a "thou shalt"), does not have a unique blessing ("who has sanctified us with His commandments …") like other positive commandments (e.g., *sukkah*, *lulav*). He explains that the Haggadah does in fact have such a blessing, which is found later in the text (see "Blessed are You. . . Who redeemed us. . . ." *My People's Passover Haggadah*, Volume 2, p. 112). But why would the blessing over the *Haggadah's* recitation come so late? R. Benjamin explains that if we recited the redemption blessing first, we would then hesitate to take a step backwards and go over the history of our enslavement. Therefore, we first recount our enslavement and then proceed to the redemption blessing over the Haggadah (*Shibbolei Haleket, Seder Pe*sach, *siman* 218).

[14] *"The Torah alludes to four children"* Abudarham asks why the Haggadah presents the four children in a different order than their respective passages appear in the Torah (Torah: wicked [Exod. 12:26–27], one who doesn't know how to ask [Exod. 13:8], simple [Exod. 13:14], wise [Deut. 6:20–25]; Haggadah: wise, wicked, simple, one who doesn't know how to ask). He answers that the Haggadah presents the children in descending order of wisdom.

[15] *"What does the wise child ask"* The wise child's question is drawn from Deuteronomy 6:20. His wisdom is apparent in his awareness that the Torah's laws are divided into three categories: "precepts" *(eidot)*, "statutes" *(chukim)*, and "laws" *(mishpatim)*. Abudarham explains these three categories as follows: the *eidot* ("precepts" or testimonies) are those Pesach rituals that "testify" to the redemption, such as matzah and *maror*; the *chukim* ("statutes") are those laws that have no discernible rationale, such as not breaking a bone of the Passover offering; and the *mishpatim* ("laws") are those additional Pesach laws the Sages have promulgated, such as those related to *chamets* and the preparation of matzah. The wise child's desire is to understand the fundamental meaning of all the Pesach rituals.

Rashbetz and Abudarham are also puzzled by the similarity between the wise child, who asks, "What are the precepts, statutes, and laws that Adonai our God commanded you?" and the wicked child, who asks, "What is this service to you?" How are these children different? Both scholars answer that by referring to "Adonai *our* God," the wise child has not removed himself from the community. Also, unlike the wicked child, the wise child uses the more inclusive word *etkhem* for "you," rather than the wicked child's exclusive *lakhem*. The wise child, aware that he was not physically present at the redemption, asks what the meaning of the laws was for *etkhem*, "you," meaning those who had been there. His intention in asking the question is not at all to separate himself from the community.

[18] *"What does the wicked child ask"* The Yerushalmi (PT Pes. 10:4, 37d) puts a more pointed question into the wicked child's mouth: "What is this burden with which you burden us every year?" *Ritba* and Abudarham appear to have had additional language in their versions of the Yerushalmi that we do not have: "What is this burden with

which you burden us every year, to delay our festive meal, and to confuse the happiness of the holiday?"

20 *"You should respond by chastising him"* Ritba, whose version of the Yerushalmi included the notion that the wicked child is disturbed by the lateness of his meal, suggests "setting on edge" those very teeth that are so anxious to eat. Abudarham says that by denying the fundamentals of the faith, the wicked child has made herself a "foreigner" and thus placed herself within the prohibition "no foreigner shall eat of it [the Passover offering]" (Exod. 12:43). Having thus made herself a "foreigner," she must now simply have to endure having her teeth set on edge as she watches others eat of what she cannot.

25 *"And the one who doesn't know how to ask"* Rambam, of course, codifies that it is a *mitzvah* to inform *(l'hodi'a)* the children about the Exodus, even if they do not know how to ask (Laws of *Chamets* and Matzah 7:2; citing Exod. 13:8). If the child is small or not intelligent, the father should do what he can to make the story clear. If the child is "wise," then we must "inform him" about all that happened in the Exodus. What is significant is *Rambam's* persistent use of the Hebrew root *y.d.'* (meaning "knowledge") in discussing informing children about the Exodus. This is in contrast to his use of the root *s.p.r* ("to tell," "recount") in connection with our ancestors' idol worship (Laws of *Chamets* and Matzah 7:4). The verb *y.d.'* connotes deep, intimate knowledge (cf. Gen. 4:1, where Adam is said to have "known" Eve). *Rambam* uses *y.d.'* at the very beginning of his *Mishneh Torah* to refer to deep, intimate, *spiritual* knowledge: "[It is a] pillar of the sciences to know [*l'yeda*, of the root *y.d.'*] that there is a First Cause [God]" (Y'sodei Hatorah 1:1). *Rambam's* use of *y.d.'* in Laws of *Chamets* and Matzah 7:2 drives home the point that we are not simply to recite the Exodus story to children by rote, but to teach it to them in a way calculated to instill in them deep, intimate, religious awareness.

26 *"This is what God did for me when I left Egypt"* Abudarham points out that the word *zeh* in the phrase *ba'avur zeh* ("This is done because of") has a numerical value of 12 (*zayin* = 7 and *heh* = 5). This refers to the twelve *mitzvot* that we do on the Seder night: four cups of wine, *charoset*, *karpas*, two ritual washings of the hands, *Hamotsi*, matzah, *maror*, and the "Hillel sandwich."

———◆———

GREEN (PERSONAL SPIRITUALITY)

You might call this the miracle of Pesach. Think about Chanukah for a moment. Its momentous challenge to the Seleucid rulers and the establishment of a small but free Jewish kingdom under the Hasmonean family were grand events that happened on the stage of world history! But we ignore them, preferring to celebrate a growing light that lasted for eight days. That is where we see the miraculous presence of God. We could have chosen to focus on the victory, but we chose the light instead. On Pesach too, the great events are those of our historical saga: liberation, defeat of Pharaoh's army, and so on. But we see the miracle in something else: the telling of the tale. That is why Jews have survived so long and bear such a rich culture: because we love telling stories. So the *mitzvah* here, parallel to the kindling of the Chanukah lights, lies in the telling of the tale.

How will you tell the tale this year? How will you make it come alive, both for yourself and for those who need to hear it? The Haggadah will soon tell us that *"in every generation* they rise up against us to destroy us." Just as the "Egypt" of each generation is unique, so too must the telling of the tale each Pesach be different and renewed.

³ *"Spent the whole night discussing"* Two interpretations are offered to this event. Some see it as the ultimate activists' Seder: Rabbi Akiva was a supporter of Bar Kokhba's rebellion against the Romans, one that ended in a tragedy that included his own martyrdom. The event depicted here is the heady beginning of that revolution. The Rabbis on the rebels' side told the tale of liberation all night long, so ready were they to apply it to the great struggle for freedom that lay directly before them. But my favorite Chasidic Haggadah reads it differently. Here the Rabbis are depicted as entering into the story of inner liberation with such excitement and wholeness that they are caught up in ecstatic fervor. Their "faces shone like the sun" and "their words came forth and flew across the sky" until they lost all sense of time and did not realize that the physical dawn had come.

Both of these strands together make up the best of our tradition—the activist and the ecstatic. How to balance them, or even better, to weave them together—that is the challenge for today's Jewish seeker. But telling the tale all night is probably a good beginning.

"Telling at night" This section teaches that the Exodus from Egypt has to be mentioned (that is, the final paragraph of the *Sh'ma* needs to be recited) at night as well as during the day.

The Chasidic commentators tell us that it is "at night," here in the dark night of exile, when we most need to remember that we have already come out of Egypt. For Jews living in the ghetto or shtetl and under the constant threat of oppression, that was indeed a saving message. The fact that God had already redeemed us from an even worse burden of enslavement held out the hope that another redemption might come as well. For Jews in places of great darkness—the Holocaust among them—no memory was more precious.

But what of us Jews who are not oppressed, or at least not in the obvious ways that our ancestors suffered? We too are commanded to remember the Exodus every day. What is that memory supposed to mean for the likes of us? I look to two ways in which the *commandment* to remember (and it is considered one of the Torah's 248 positive commandments!) applies to us. We need to ask ourselves every day, "To what am I enslaved?" We have neither Pharaoh nor czar restricting our lives, but let's try on a few other categories to see where the shoe might fit. My need for a big monthly paycheck? Is that an "enslavement"? My vision of success, the constant push to higher and higher achievement? Am I enslaved to that? Or worse—am I enslaving my children to it? A life of affluence? Do I suffer from the "affluenza" disease that marks too many Americans? (Are we Jews especially susceptible to that one?) How about addictions? entertainment? the computer screen? Are these not "enslavements" in my life? "In order that you remember" means that we need to ask ourselves these questions every day. Remember each morning and night what it is like to wake up to newly won freedom, and ask yourself how you can get there again, back to that moment of singing at the shore of the sea.

But we who are not obviously oppressed also have to remember that moment each day for the sake of those who still do suffer the old-fashioned kind of Egyptian bondage. There are real slaveries in the world, terrible sites and times of human oppression. I write these words as the situation in Darfur drags on and on, with the world willing to do little about it. In our post-Holocaust memory we have seen one episode after another of terrible human suffering, whether caused by natural disaster or at the hands of brutal humanity. Biafra. Liberia. Bosnia. Kosovo. Cambodia. Afghanistan. Iraq. War, famine, earthquake, tsunami, and war again. Each of these creates misery and oppression, as we live on in comfort, busily securing our own successes.

Remember every day. Be there to extend a hand, even both hands. If we live and thrive in a society where the economic gaps widen every day, we need to tithe—or better—for the poor.

[10] *"Blessed is God [hamakom]"* In Hebrew *makom*, "place," is a name for God. We are not sure exactly how this came about, but it seems related to the rabbinic adage that "God is the *makom* of the world, but the world is not God's *makom*." This means that the universe is located "inside" God, both surrounded and filled by divine presence. All we need to do is to open our eyes to that reality. At the same time, the perceptible universe is not co-extensive with God; the mystery of existence reaches infinitely beyond our grasp.

But why should this particular name of God, almost never used in liturgy, appear in the Haggadah? Perhaps it is to teach us that *every* place is a place of God. There is much in our memory that could make Egypt a detested place, associated only with suffering and enslavement, but the story of Pesach happens precisely there (!), not in the holy Land of Israel, where we might have expected God to be found. To say tonight that God is *hamakom* reminds us that God may be revealed everywhere, even in what may seem the most unlikely places. The Rabbis asked why God was revealed to Moses in a humble thornbush, rather than a more stately tree. Their answer: "To teach you that no place is devoid of God, not even a thornbush." Not even Egypt, not even the house of bondage.

[21] *"He would not have been redeemed"* Why would this person not have been redeemed? Could you imagine either God or Moses being so judgmental as to leave someone behind? What sin is so awful that it would cause one to deserve being left in Egypt?

No, the point is not that they would have abandoned the "wicked child." Rather, this person who denies the community would have refused redemption even when it came! "What do you mean? Should *I* leave Egypt? How could they possible mean *me* when they say 'Jew?' Or "Jude." Or "Zhyd." This refers to the Jews who denied their communal identity or tried to hide themselves from reality. The World War I veteran who stayed in Germany until it was too late, sure that they would never harm a German hero ... The Soviet Jew who could not let herself believe that Communism had betrayed her ... The Syrian or Iranian Jew who could not give up his business interests ... "He would not have been redeemed" because he chose not to leave, even when he knew the time had come.

This lesson too applies to all of our enslavements. The call to liberation comes, but we have to respond to it. That is not always as easy as it sounds. Sometimes liberation is offered us as a gift, and *still* we refuse to leave Egypt.

Still, the judgment of calling such a person "wicked" seems harsh. If he is doing any "wickedness," it is mostly to himself.

◆

J. HOFFMAN (TRANSLATION)

[1] *"Experienced"* Literally, "old," reflecting a culture in which age was an indication of sagacity. Here we use "experienced" as a compromise, hopefully indicating the sort of wisdom that can only come with age.

[1] *"Learned in Torah"* Literally, "knowers of Torah."

[1] *"Discuss"* Or "tell of." It's hard to know for sure, but it seems that the point is to have a discussion, not merely to relate the story.

[2] "Really" A poor translation of the technical term *marbeh*, but we have nothing better. Another reasonable interpretation of this last line, which amounts to almost the same thing, is that the "more one tells of the Exodus from Egypt, the more one is (to be) praised." See Arnow, *My People's Passover Haggadah*, Volume 1, p. 176.

[2] *"Is praised"* Or "is praiseworthy." We do not translate the word *harei* (in other contexts translated awkwardly as "behold"), but it may change the focus of the sentence. Perhaps the point is contrastive, in that there are lots of ways to earn praise, but discussing the Exodus from Egypt is paramount.

[4] *"Dining"* This is the same word that gave us "ceremoniously" above (*My People's Passover Haggadah*, Volume 1, p. 150). Here we feel that "dining" is enough, because the point here is not how they were dining but rather what they did during their meal.

[6] *"Never really got to hear a discussion"* Clearly hyperbole; of course Rabbi Elazar ben Azariah heard many discussions of the Exodus at night. A similar example in English would be "I never really tasted steak [until I went to a really good steak house]." Our translation reflects what the passage means here in the Haggadah. For a discussion of its original context, see L. Hoffman, *My People's Passover Haggadah*, Volume 1, p. 198. Unfortunately, we have to use the word "really," which we used above for *marbeh*.

[7] *"Quoting"* Ben Zoma quotes Deuteronomy 16:3.

[8] *"Refers to"* Literally, just "is."

[8] *"Includes"* Literally, just "is."

[9] *"But the Sages"* Literally, just "Sages." We capitalize the word because it referred to a specific group of people. We use "but" instead of "and" because Ben Zoma is also one of the "Sages." The point appears to be that his is a minority opinion.

[9] *"Refers to"* Literally, "is."

[9] *"Includes"* Literally, "brings in," raising the interesting possibility that remembering the Exodus "all the days of your life" may actually help bring about the messiah.

[10] *"God"* Hamakom—literally, "the place." See *My People's Passover Haggadah*, Volume 1, p. 218.

[11] *"Blessed is He"* We opt for the Hebrew word order here, even though it is slightly awkward in English, to maintain the parallel between "blessed is God" and "blessed is He." Another option would be "God is Blessed"/"He is blessed," but then we would run into difficulty below.

[14] *"Alludes"* Literally, "speaks *k'neged*." *K'neged* is composed of two parts. The first, *k-*, means "like" or "as though." The second part, *neged*, is more difficult to translate, variously meaning "opposite," "equal to," "like," "in exchange for," etc. The general concept expressed by *(k)neged* seems to be the relationship of equality or comparability. In our case, the "speech" of the Torah is like the four children. We translate the concept of "speech being like" with the words "alluding to."

[14] *"Children"* Others, "sons." But the Hebrew word *banim* does not exclude girls, while "sons" in most dialects of English does. We find the word *banim*, in a different grammatical form, in the phrase *b'nei yisra'el*, that is, *banim of yisra'el*. (*B'nei* means "*banim* of.") The usual translation of that phrase is "children [not sons] of Israel."

[15] *"Ask"* Others, "say." But Hebrew uses *omeir* ("say" or "ask") for a variety of speech acts, while in English our verbs are more specialized.

[16] *"Precepts, statutes, and laws"* We need three English words, to match the three Hebrew ones, but our choice is largely arbitrary. While the Hebrew words all have specific connotations, we lack exact English parallels.

[17] *"Answering"* As above ("ask") we have the Hebrew verb *omeir*. In translating into correct English, we necessarily miss the parallelism in the Hebrew: "the son says [*omeir*]"/"you say [*omeir*]."

[17] *"Halakhah"* Or "rules." The Hebrew noun happens to be plural, but, more importantly, it is a technical term for religious rules; we don't have a similar technical term in English.

[17] *"It is forbidden"* Better would be the more colloquial "we don't …," but a recurring theme of the Haggadah (e.g., "In each and every generation") is the concept of "we/us" and who that includes. Therefore, to use "we" here would be misleading. We could resort to "one doesn't …," but in most modern dialects of English, that sounds too stilted.

[17] *"Conclude the afikoman after the Passover"* This is one of the most difficult lines in the Haggadah to understand. We have translated it more or less literally. At first glance, it doesn't make a lot of sense in English, but the English thereby captures the equally opaque Hebrew. It seems that the line was already part of the Seder by Mishnaic times, but even the Rabbis of the Talmud didn't know what it meant. We have three issues.

The first is what *maftirin* ("conclude") means here. *Maftirin* should mean "one concludes," but here (and only here) it is followed by *achar* ("after") and not *b'* ("with"). In general, verbs change meanings when different prepositions are attached to them. (Compare, for example, the English "pick on" [annoy], "pick up" [increase, as a tempo], and "pick up on" [discern].)

If, however, *achar* is not part of the verb, but rather attached to the noun *pesach* ("Passover," almost certainly the Passover offering), we have "after the Passover one doesn't conclude (the) *afikoman*," rather than the expected, "One doesn't conclude the Passover with (the) *afikoman*."

The hardest issue is that we don't know what *afikoman* means. One dubious account relates it to the Greek root *komo* (from which we get our word "comedy," for example) with the Greek prefix *epi*: *epikomon* or *eipkomion*. Accordingly, *afikoman* would mean "playing around" or "carousing," and the line would mean "after the Passover, it is forbidden to conclude by carousing"—a sentiment captured more succinctly today by "don't eat and run." Although the reasoning (etymological and sociological) is dubious, the Talmud seems to conclude that indeed *afikoman* means "carousing" and that it is forbidden after the Passover meal.

To compound the difficulty, however, *afikoman* later came to mean the middle piece of matzah used to conclude the Seder. So not only wasn't "the *afikoman*" forbidden, it was required! One possible reason for the switch is that, whatever *afikoman* originally meant, the word came to refer to a common way of ending a non-Passover meal. But because *afikoman* was forbidden on Passover, the final bit of matzah was seen as a substitute for *afikoman* and then later took on the name *afikoman*. (A similar process might be: There is no *challah* on Passover. Instead we have matzah. One might imagine saying that "tonight, this matzah is our *challah*." Similarly, "tonight, this matzah is our *afikoman*.") In light of the requirement to teach the line only to the wise child, perhaps the whole point is that it's hard to understand. Then again, another account of the four children assigns this line to the simple child. (See L. Hoffman, *My People's Passover Haggadah*, Volume 1, p. 201.)

[19] *"You"* The Hebrew is plural, as in the colloquial "y'all."

[20] *"He misses the whole point"* Hebrew, *kafar b'ikar*. *Ikar* means "the main issue." We do not know exactly what *kafar b'-* means, though it seems to be an idiom. For example, the Talmud teaches (Arakh. 15:2) that people who gossip are as though they *kafar*

b'ikar. Eventually the phrase would come to mean "deny God," though in earlier usage (from which this passage is taken) it appears to be more general. A frequent translation runs along the lines of "denies a basic tenet of Judaism." However, it seems that, unlike "denying God," *kafar b'ikar* is a passive error—a mistake of omission, not commission—so we translate "misses the whole point," which is likewise passive.

[20] *"Chastising"* Others, "set his teeth on edge" and similar variations with the word "teeth." While the Hebrew expression does involve the teeth, it is usually a mistake to translate expressions literally. For example, the English "driving me up a wall" has nothing to do with walls (or driving, for that matter).

[24] *"House of slaves"* Frequently, "house of slavery" or "house of bondage." Though all three translations have merit, the Hebrew is very clearly "house of slaves," raising the interesting possibility that originally the phrase referred to a physical house, perhaps a dormitory in which slaves lived.

[24] *"Start"* The English, like the Hebrew, does not specify what should be started, though from context it is clear that it is a conversation about the Exodus.

[27] *"It might mean"* This abrupt transition begins a short midrashic interpretation of the previous line. The point of the midrash is that the words "on that very day" teach that Passover is not to be held on Rosh Chodesh—that is, the first of the month—but rather on (another) day, that is, the fifteenth.

The words that follow, "that's why" (more literally, "because of this"), teach that even though the previous lesson alludes to "day," the Passover meal can take place at night, when matzah and *maror* have been placed on the table. Unfortunately, the fairly simple message of the midrash is somewhat obscured by the words used to write it. We choose to translate the words as they are, preserving the oblique nature of the text.

[27] *"On"* Literally, "from."

[27] *"Rosh Chodesh"* That is, the first of the month (literally, the "head of the month"), almost certainly the month of Nisan.

———◆———

L. HOFFMAN (HISTORY)

to assemble under the normally watchful eyes of Roman authorities and plan the uprising. But there is no evidence for the claim.

Tosefta 10:12 (c. third century) contains a similar account, featuring Rabbis from a generation earlier, long before the revolt. They are said to have stayed up to fulfill the obligation "to study the law of the Passover offering all night long." Both accounts may be accurate: the earlier one (from while the Temple was still standing) describes the practice of staying up all night to discuss laws pertinent to sacrificing the *pesach* (the paschal lamb). The Haggadah version from the post-Temple period is a similar all-night Seder, but with the sacrificial cult destroyed, the preferred topic became the tale of the Exodus. If this theory is correct, the very idea of relating the Passover *story*, not its sacrificial laws, was revolutionary, a response to the demise of the Temple.

My own view is that we just happen to have two tales that illustrate the common practice of staying up a long time talking about Passover—"all night" may be an accepted exaggeration, as when we say about insomnia, "I was up all night." There were probably other instances that were lost, whereas these two managed by chance to survive in written form. They look and sound the same because they were forced into a common rhetorical structure, if only to facilitate memorization. One was recorded in the Tosefta; the other was circulated orally and was used in rituals for centuries—like the rest of the Haggadah, until the invention of written records. When the Haggadah found its way into print, so too did the story.

Scholars who emphasize literary records alone (without regard for ritual theory) would disagree, reasoning that the story was fabricated in the geonic era, based on the earlier Tosefta account.

In any event, the story is here to illustrate the last line of the paragraph before, "And everyone who really discusses the Exodus from Egypt is praised." The Rabbis were so engrossed in the discussion that they don't even notice the sun rise!

Why have we perpetuated a myth of the Seder being used militarily? Picturing our Rabbis as a revolutionary fifth column may have satisfied post-*Sho'ah* generations who wanted models of Jewish resistance, and who took pride in the successful war of Israeli independence.

The incident also appealed to a generation trained by Marxist thought to see politics everywhere. Scholars had been trained by the person and writing of Louis Finkelstein (then chancellor of Jewish Theological Seminary) who interpreted all of rabbinic history that way. As he saw it (for example), the earliest Rabbis, called Pharisees, were a Jewish proletariat, owing their existence to the urbanization of the Judean economy. Their opponents, large rural landholders called Sadducees, were the old-guard Jewish bourgeoisie, who, appropriately, lost the struggle over the future of Judaism.

The two accounts of the all-night Seders have been forced into a procrustean bed of rigid rhetorical style. They both have five participants, for instance, a symbolic, rather than an actual number. We too use numbers that way. "I could give you a hundred reasons why that is so," I might say, without meaning, literally, 100. Similarly, in antiquity, the number forty represented a transitional period or age (the Israelites wandered forty years in the desert; Jacob married at age forty; the Flood lasted forty days and forty nights; early Christians kept Lent for varying periods of time, but called them all "forty days").

Our number five symbolized scholarship. We hear, for instance, of someone testifying "in the name of five elders" (M. Eruv. 3:5); Rabban Yochanan ben Zakkai had five students (M. Avot 2:8); and Mishnah Avot, the account of the rabbinic chain of tradition, has five chapters—like the Torah, where there are five books of Moses, and like the Gospel of Matthew, which organizes Jesus' life into five parts.

⁸ *"'All the days of your life' includes nights"* The lesson here, discussing the Exodus at night, seems perfectly designed for the Seder. But it is not. From a parallel text (M. Ber. 1:4) we can see that its topic—mentioning the Exodus at night—is associated with the evening recitation of the *Sh'ma*, not the Seder.

Though commonly associated with just its most famous line, "Hear O Israel: Adonai is our God; Adonai is One," the *Sh'ma* is a compendium of three biblical passages, the last of which describes the *tsitsit* (the tassels on a *tallit*), asking us to look at them as a reminder of the Exodus. The *Sh'ma* is mandated morning and evening ("when you lie down and when you rise up"), but because, prior to electricity, *tsitsit* would not normally be seen at night, some of the Rabbis argued that this last biblical section should be omitted from the evening recitation. Most commentators think the point made here is that those Rabbis are mistaken: the paragraph regarding *tsitsit* and the Exodus *should* be included then.

But that had become a dead issue by the time of Rabbi Elazar ben Azariah; neither he nor any of the other Palestinian Rabbis of the time said the third paragraph at night. Only later, in Babylonia, was it included then. Also, they never referred to that paragraph as "the Exodus from Egypt." Had they wanted to allude to it here, they would have said something like, "The passage on *tsitsit* [not 'the Exodus from Egypt'] should not be mentioned at night." An alternative view, then, is that the reference is not to the third biblical passage of the *Sh'ma*, but to the blessing that follows, called *G'ullah* ("Redemption"; see *My People's Prayer Book*, Volume 1, *The Sh'ma and Its Blessings*, pp. 117–119), which includes an affirmation of deliverance from Egypt. Elazar ben Azariah's point is that at night, when we omit the paragraph of the *Sh'ma* that mentions the Exodus, perhaps we should also omit reference to the Exodus in the blessing that follows.

⁹ *"Includes the days of the messiah"* If I insist you say a prayer "throughout your life," I need not say, "throughout *all* your life." Here too, the Hebrew word *kol* ("all") seems unnecessary. "All" is therefore taken as making its own point. For Ben Zoma, "all" implies "nights," not just "days." The sages (a reference to "the majority opinion") think "all" denotes the messianic age.

At stake is a theological debate over the state of affairs that will exist in messianic times. Deliverance at the end of time is assumed to be God's second act of redemption, foreshadowed, however, by the first one, the Exodus from Egypt. For Ben Zoma, once the second redemptive act occurs, we may as well forget the first. For the sages, gratitude for the first will always be in order. That is to say, even ultimate redemption will not in any way negate the need to be grateful for the original miracle by which the Israelites were saved from servitude.

¹⁰ *"Blessed is God [Hamakom]"* This introduction to the midrash of the four sons has nothing directly to do with the passage it introduces. It may just be a generic way of alerting the reader to the fact that a midrashic account is about to begin. However, the word "praised" *(barukh)* occurs four times, perhaps a conscious attempt to allude to the fact that four sons are about to be discussed.

No one knows for sure how God came to be called *hamakom* ("the place"). The name reveals, however, a theological struggle. On one hand, from Deuteronomy, the Rabbis inherited the certainty that God actually dwells in a certain place, the locus of the sacrificial system, Jerusalem. By Second Temple times, the actual dwelling was said to be an innermost sanctum within the Temple precinct, the Holy of Holies, which only the high priest entered, and only on the most holy day of the year: Yom Kippur. "The Place" as a name for God may be a shortening of "the place" where God dwells. On the other hand, the Bible also insists that God dwells everywhere, a belief that the Rabbis enshrined in the format of blessings that call God "ruler of the universe" *(melekh ha'olam)*. The two concepts merge in the notion that God's dwelling presence, the *Shekhinah*, is most at home in Jerusalem, but accompanies Israel into shared exile, wherever Israel goes.

[14] *"Four children"* Four separate times (Deut. 6:20–21; Exod. 12:26–27; Exod. 13:14; Exod. 13:8) the Torah commands us to relate the story of Passover to our children. Assigning each instance to a different kind of child, the Rabbis create this midrash. Though composed in tannaitic times (before 200 CE), it did not make it into the Haggadah until much later, possibly as late as the geonic era (c. 750–1038)—for reasons unknown. Its tannaitic precursor is carried in two places: the Midrash *(Mekhilta D'rabbi Yishmael)*, and the Palestinian Talmud (the Yerushalmi).

The two sources differ significantly (see, especially, below, "It is forbidden to conclude the *afikoman* after the Passover offering" [*Ein maftirin achar hapesach afikoman*]). Among other things, the name of the simple son is given in one place as *tam* and the other as *tipesh*. It has been suggested that classical Greco-Roman literature prefers the typology of three, not four, so we may have a conflation of two lists of three, one using each of the two terms. That would prove interesting, because reliable manuscripts of the Mishnah (reflecting Palestinian, not Babylonian, practice) list only three, not "four questions"; also, people in geonic times washed their hands three times, using three different blessings. There may even have been a time when the elemental Seder had just three cups. Much has been made of the preference for "fours" in the Seder, but it may be that "three," not "four" was once the default figure.

[17] *"It is forbidden to conclude the afikoman after the Passover offering"* As it stands, the sentence makes little sense because the word *afikoman* is a mystery to us. It seems to be Greek, but opinions vary on what the Greek denotes. Our best bet, based on the Talmud and some knowledge about the Greco-Roman feasts called *symposia* after which the Seder was patterned, is that the word has something to do with "carousing," as this summary from a leading scholarly investigation explains:

> The sentence *Ein maftirin achar hapesach afikoman* was intended in opposition to the Greek custom of dining and rejoicing: at the moment when the festivity reached is height people would disperse to other houses and pressure the people living there to join them in singing and gluttony. They called this *epikomion*. The Mishnah warns against concluding the Passover meal and taking leave by *epikomion*.[1]

Where did this idea come from? The usual argument goes like this: Nowhere in classical rabbinic literature is the word *afikoman* identified as matzah. The Rabbis in the Talmud themselves wonder, "What is *afikoman*?" and give three answers: (1) music; (2) fancy desserts; and (3) "not to leave one *chavurah* [the group in which the Seder was being held] and join another one." All three answers coalesce in the understanding that *afikoman* meant "carousing." In *symposia* banquets, people began with dinner and were then expected to settle down for some light but significant after-dinner philosophizing. But with all that eating and drinking, it was not unusual for people to end in the mood for further partying. Sometimes drunkenness became precisely the point. Early on, Plato (438–347 BCE) alludes to the problem, in his account of a *symposium* attended by Socrates:

> When Socrates had settled himself and had his dinner like the rest, we … betook ourselves to drinking. At this point, Pausanius began as follows, "Come now sirs, what will be the least rigorous rule to make about drinking! I don't mind telling you that yesterday's bout has left me in a very poor way…." After this, everyone agreed that the present party should not be pushed to the point of drunkenness, but that we should drink merely as we felt inclined.
>
> "Since, then, we have come to this decision," said Eryximachus, "that each man shall drink merely as much as he chooses, and that there shall no compulsion, I propose in addition that we should send away the flute girl who has just come in—let her play to herself, or, if she likes, to the women of the household—and entertain ourselves today with conversation. (Plato, *Symposium*, 175c, 176e).[2]

Things remained that way for centuries. In the first century CE, for instance, the apostle Paul berates the Christian community in Corinth for the way they celebrate the Lord's Supper (the forerunner of today's Mass, or Eucharist), which, like the Seder, had been influenced by the *symposium*. "When you come together," he charges, "it is not really to eat the Lord's Supper, for when the time comes to eat … one goes hungry and another becomes drunk" (1 Corinthians, 11:20–21).

In Paul's day, the Seder looked very much like a *symposium*: people ate first and only afterward discussed Passover. The Rabbis passed laws to discourage too much drinking—if it didn't entice diners to rowdiness, it put them to sleep. But these measures failed. People still sang bawdy songs or spent the night with entertainers, like Socrates' flute girl—hence the rabbinic interpretation of *afikoman* as "music." Or they ate themselves sick with "fancy desserts." Or they ate and ran, "leaving one *chavurah* and joining another." The whole thing added up to all-night carousing. So the Rabbis prohibited it directly, ruling, in effect, not to conclude the Passover meal by carousing. Finally, when that failed, they postponed the actual meal until after the Haggadah had been recited—which is the way we have inherited it.

Properly celebrated, except for the mandatory final two cups of wine, drinking ceased after dinner, and the normal dessert course was omitted. One was to eat the *pesach* until feeling completely full—the way wealthy people fill up on dinner. It was to be the last thing eaten, since eating anything afterward might indicate that it hadn't satisfied people's appetite.

By the end of the second century, however, if not earlier, the last taste at dinner had become a piece of matzah (as it is for us). The Temple was gone and sacrificing a *pesach* was impossible in any event. Matzah took the place of the *pesach*, even inheriting its laws, so that rules once governing the consumption of the *pesach* were taken to refer to matzah. That is how matzah came to be eaten last. But that last bite was not yet called *afikoman*. That word came to be applied only in medieval Europe when commentators borrowed it from the Mishnah as a convenient designation.

It is, of course, possible that *afikoman* did mean matzah—along with the other desserts, songs and revelry that people engaged in. Matzah was tasty back then, a piece of fresh bread, albeit unleavened—some warm pita bread for instance. In banning revelry, the Mishnah forbids all manner of after-*pesach* food, not just desserts (as we have seen) but extra matzah too. "Do not conclude [the consumption of] the *pesach* [the Passover offering]," the Mishnah might be saying, "even with matzah."

In any event, regardless of whether *afikoman* means carousing directly or something else indicative of carousing—music, desserts, more matzah, or party hopping—it is at least reasonable to conclude that the word was associated with the kind of after-dinner behavior that Plato and Paul denounced. We can properly agree that the problem attacked by the elusive warning *ein maftirin achar hapesach afikoman* was indeed carousing.

With that understanding, we can better understand the advice given to the four children. Outside of the Haggadah, rabbinic tradition records two versions of the "Four Children" narrative, one in the Palestinian Talmud (the Yerushalmi), and one in a midrash known as the *Mekhilta D'rabbi Yishmael*. But they switch answers with regard to the wise and the simple children.

The *Mekhilta* agrees with our Haggadah in picturing the wise child as an "A" student in graduate school. He jumps to the head of the class by asking for all the "precepts, statutes, and laws" of Passover." The answer he receives addresses his insatiable thirst for knowledge—all the pertinent Halakhah, including the elusive instruction from the Mishnah, "It is forbidden to conclude the *afikoman* after [the consumption of] the *pesach* [the Passover offering]."

Both the *Mekhilta* and Haggadah agree also on the simple child, in obvious contrast to the wise child, this is a child who is challenged cognitively. He asks only, "What is this?"—and is given a response that provides just the uncomplicated essence of the Seder, "With a strong hand, Adonai brought us out of the house of slaves."

The Yerushalmi, however, reverses the answers. There, it is the wise child who is told, "With a strong hand Adonai brought us out of the house of slaves," and the simple child who is warned not to follow the *pesach* with *afikoman*—albeit with an important explanatory addendum, "so that he will not leave this *chavurah* and join another one."

The discrepancy in traditions reflects alternative views of human nature.

For the Haggadah/*Mekhilta* version, life is a classroom where learners master objective data, like students pursuing doctorates. The wise son is the graduate student writing a term paper on Passover Halakhah; he gets it all, even the very last law of the Seder—not to party too much. The simple son, unable to handle too much information, but knowing enough to ask what is going on, gets a one-line synopsis—the single thing that everyone has to know: "With a strong hand Adonai brought us out of the house of slaves."

But life is not just a graduate class. It is equally the ability to engage experientially. In this experiential model, wisdom is the ability to behave appropriately, with the full depth of social and emotional (rather than pure cognitive) intelligence. Here, it is precisely the simple child who has to be told not to conclude the evening with improper carousing. The experientially wise child already knows that—so can be expected to go further and identify with history: the Seder experience replicates the experience of our ancestors whom God released from slavery.

[18] *"'You' and not himself"* The wicked child is berated for removing himself from the community as if the Seder matters to others, perhaps, but not to him. He should have asked why the evening's proceedings had anything to do with "himself," as well as the others whom he addresses as "you."

But wait! Didn't the wise child make the same mistake? He asks, "What are the precepts, statutes, and laws that Adonai our God commanded *you*," not "*us*." His answer is taken right out of Torah (Deut. 6:20), so it can hardly be evil. Why, then, berate the wicked child for saying, in effect, the same thing: "you"?

Some early Haggadot foresaw this problem. They have the wise child ask, "What are the precepts … that God commanded us?" And they get their answer from Torah also: the Greek version of the Torah (called the Septuagint) written in the third century BCE reads "us." Apparently some Rabbis knew this alternative reading and borrowed it: the wise child turns out to have been smart enough to choose an alternative Torah reading that included him in the night's proceedings.

—◆—

SIGNPOST: HOW WE TELL THE TALE

EVEN IN MESSIANIC DAYS AHEAD. WE CONCENTRATE NEXT ON AN IMPORTANT GROUP TO WHOM THE TALE IS TOLD: THE NEXT GENERATION, DIVIDED INTO FOUR TYPES OF CHILD, TO REMIND US TO ADDRESS THE STORY NOT BY ROTE, BUT IN A MANNER UNDERSTANDABLE TO EACH LISTENER. WE RETURN, FINALLY, TO THE TIMING OF WHEN WE TELL THE TALE—NOT AT THE BEGINNING OF THE MONTH OF OUR FREEDOM, BUT IN THE MIDDLE, THE VERY NIGHT WHEN THAT LIBERATION OCCURRED.

—◆—

KUSHNER AND POLEN (CHASIDIC VOICES)

He suggests that the word "day" connotes thinking when the mind functions with clarity. During the day, you understand everything. Night, on the other hand, implies when understanding evades us. We are bidden to recall the Exodus at night, that is, during times of darkness and confusion, to call us to mindfulness *(da'at)*: if we can stay mindful of the reality of God and the constant birth of new possibilities, then we can remain hopeful, thereby transforming darkness to light in our own awareness.

[14] *"Four"* Rabbi Eliyahu ben Shlomo Zalman, the Gaon of Vilna (the *Gra*), asks: "Why are there so many sequences of four in the Haggadah—four questions, four children, four cups of wine?"

The answer, he suggests, is hinted at in Berakhot 54b, where we read that there are four people who are obligated to give thanks: one who has returned from a sea voyage; one who has returned from a caravan crossing the desert; one who has recovered from a serious illness; and one who has been freed from prison. Indeed, notes the Gaon, these four correspond to the experiences of the Jewish people in the Passover narrative. The Jewish people *also* left prison; passed through the sea; traveled through the desert; and, when they received the healing of Torah at Sinai, were returned to health as if from a serious spiritual illness.

[14] *"Four children"* It once happened that a disciple of Rabbi Dov Baer, the Great Maggid of Mezerich, had to make a long journey. His master instructed him to take a box of matzah along with him even though it was many months before Pesach. As fate would have it, the disciple became lost and was taken in by a modest but illiterate Jewish family, with whom he celebrated the Seder. When the master of the house came to the passage in the Haggadah about the four children, the disciple was startled to hear him shout out the reference to each one of them—"*One* is wise!" "*One* is wicked!" and so forth. After the Seder he asked his host about this strange custom. The man replied, "I am not learned. But I do remember that my father taught me that when I recite the *Sh'ma*, I need to enunciate, even going so far as to shout out the word "*one*."

Upon his return home, the disciple related this strange custom and its explanation to his master, Dov Baer. The Great Maggid replied, "So you are the *one*! That is why I sent the matzah with you."

"I don't understand," replied the student.

"I saw in a vision," said his teacher, "that someone far away was having an unusually holy Seder and that this person was able to unify *all the children of Israel*. Through his holy intention he was able, at last, to make all Israel *one*. And now I know that you have found him."

[15] *"The wise child"* Rabbi Levi Yitzchak of Berditchev (*K'dushat Levi*, vocalized ed., vol. I [Jerusalem], p. 239–40) explains the "wise child's" question and the Haggadah's scripted answer (from the Mishnah) that "it is forbidden to conclude the *afikoman* after the Passover offering." The Berditchever teaches that in order to understand the question and its answer, we must consider the symbolism of matzah. Matzah at the

Seder invariably evokes the quality of something "newly made." The making of matzah (mixing the flour with water, perforating the dough, and getting it into the oven) must be completed very quickly—in no more than eighteen minutes. *Chamets,* on the other hand, results from a lengthy, delayed process. (Indeed because of the natural fermenting agents in the air, *anything* left lying around will eventually become *chamets.*) Since the production *of matzah* requires immediacy, no delays, it is associated with the ever fresh, brand-new. Kabbalistic imagery characterizes this as *yesh* ("something") from *ayin* ("nothing"). Matzah symbolizes a continuous renewal of the creative process and of the very work of creation itself. And, therefore, to the extent that we internalize this approach of perpetual renewal, we effectively devote ourselves to seeking what is newly born in each moment.

We don't eat anything else after the *afikoman* because we don't want to dilute or dull the memory of the taste of matzah. We want the novelty of each moment, the literally awesome thrill of "something from nothing," to linger in our mouths throughout the entire year.

Of course, after Pesach ends, we revert to eating *chamets.* And that is why, the Berditchever concludes, we need the 248 performative commandments: to remind us of the reality of God during the rest of the year. A truly radical thought: if the taste of matzah—of the ongoing immediacy of God's creative power—could truly stay with us throughout the year, then that would be the only *mitzvah* we would need to remain in the presence of God!

[25] *"The one who doesn't know how to ask* [1]*"* When Rabbi Levi Yitzchak of Berditchev came to the passage in the Haggadah about the fourth child "who doesn't know how to ask," he would say, "'The one who doesn't know how to ask' is me, Levi Yitzchak of Berditchev. I do not know how to ask You, Lord of the universe, and even if I did know, I would not dare to. How could I venture to ask You why everything happens as it does, why we are driven from one exile to another, why our foes are allowed to torment us? But in the Haggadah, the father of the one 'who doesn't know how to ask' is told: 'You should disclose to him' [literally, 'open to him']. And the Haggadah refers to the verse, 'And you shall tell your son.' And, Lord of the universe, am I not your son? I do not beg You to reveal to me the secret of your ways—I couldn't comprehend it! But please show me one thing. Show me the meaning of what is happening to me at this moment. Show me what it demands of me. Show me what You, Lord of the universe, are telling me through it. It is not why I suffer that I want to know, but only whether I suffer for Your sake."[1]

[25] *"The one who doesn't know how to ask* [2]*"* Why do questions play such an important role in the seder? Surely, when watching the observance of any specific commandment, there are many things a reasonable child might ask (cf. M. Avot 5:7). Indeed, one of the main characteristics of a wise person is that he asks questions that are *on topic.*

You might have thought that a truly wise student wouldn't need to ask anything at all. We learn from this therefore that the process of questioning is an intrinsic dimension of the learning process and wisdom itself.

According to Mishnah Avot 6:6, there are forty-eight ways by which Torah can be acquired, and one of them is "making your teacher wise." But, while this is obviously good for the teacher, how could it be good *for the student?* Furthermore, how could a student possibly make the teacher wise?!

We find our answer by imagining a pedagogic situation in which a student puts a question to the teacher that the teacher cannot answer at once. The teacher is thus prompted to increase his or her own learning in order to respond respectfully and appropriately to the student.

Consider, also, this teacher-student transaction kabbalistically. When we study Torah, our comprehension is not merely intellectual. Our grasp of Torah also depends on the ability of our soul to experience Torah's light. And this light is then revealed in the highest levels of our own knowledge (the *s'firah Chokhmah*), where it then grows into deep intuition (the next *s'firah, Binah*). And thus, when we study Torah, we receive intuitive flashes even before we attain intellectual understanding.

In this way we sometimes get an intuitive flash even before we gain full cognitive comprehension. We literally have knowledge even beyond our intellect. The Great Maggid, Dov Baer of Mezerich, calls this kind of knowing *kadmut hasakhel* ("primal knowing").

The student-teacher relationship is about the intersection of student, teacher, and Torah. The student can actually intuit levels of knowing that surpass the teacher's. Questions are intrinsic to learning because they compel the teacher to make manifest what is already latent. This teaching is based on Rabbi Kalonymos Kalmish Shapiro of Piaseczna, known as "the Rebbe of the Warsaw Ghetto." It was delivered in April of 1941.[2]

◆

ZIERLER (FEMINIST VOICES)

if all of us were smart." This passage imagines an ideal condition of universal learnedness and wisdom. What, though, is the assumed universal of the Rabbis? What is our assumed universal today? Clearly, for the Rabbis, wisdom was a trait reserved for men. Scholar Tal Ilan observes that in Second Temple and tannaitic literature only 25 women are mentioned by name, as opposed to 605 men, and the Haggadah does not mention any of them; only one of these women, Bruria, is connected to religious academies or study houses. According to Ilan, "There was no official education system for girls. They learnt to read and write at home if there was someone to teach them."[1] To be sure, the Rabbis' generally skeptical attitude about women's intellectual capacities was a product of their times. As classicist Sarah Pomeroy notes, "the weakness and light-mindedness of the female sex *(infirmitas sexus* and *levitus animi)* were the underlying principles of Roman legal theory that mandated all women to be under the custody of males."[2]

Our times are different, of course, and in marked contrast with the world of the Rabbis, today we can indeed envision a gender-inclusive definition of the words *va'afilu kulanu chakhamim*; with the ordination of women in three of the denominations and with the proliferation of yeshivot for women as well as higher academic Jewish studies, we now live in a Jewish world that is filled with scores of *talmidei chakhamim* and *chakhamot* (learned men and women). That Jewish women's literacy has risen against a backdrop of increasing assimilation, however, is lamentable. The Haggadah's assertion that even those who are learned need to return to the familiar story of the Exodus to uncover new forms of significance should serve as a reminder that we also need to reach out to those who have yet to attain even the basics of Jewish literacy.

[2] *"And everyone who really discusses the Exodus from Egypt is praised"* The Haggadah does not mention a single woman, with the exception of Hadassah (Esther), who appears in a rarely sung song. The Haggadah's exhortation to enlarge upon the telling of the Exodus story, however, furnishes us with an excellent opportunity to fill in its own blanks and add in discussion of the contributions of women to the Exodus story.

One little-noticed example of women's involvement appears in Exodus 3:21–22, where God promises to "give this people [Israel] favor in the sight of the Egyptians" and announces that "each woman shall ask her neighbor and any woman sojourner living in the neighbor's house for jewelry of silver and of gold, and clothing, and you shall put them on your sons and daughters." While it is true that divine intervention precipitates this act of generosity on the part of Egyptian women, this passage nevertheless suggests that divine salvation depends, at least in part, on female activism and cooperation that traverses ethnic and class boundaries. Exodus 3:22 ends with the words *v'nitsaltem et mitsrayim*, which can be translated as "you shall exploit [or spoil] Egypt." This ending is discomfiting, as it suggests that having been exploited by Egypt, the Israelites will now exploit others. It is important to recall, however, the famous incident in Exodus 2 where three unnamed Egyptian and Israelite daughters band together in a common cause against Pharaoh's tyranny: *bat levi* ("the daughter of Levi," later called Yocheved), her daughter (later called Miriam), and *bat par'oh* (Pharaoh's daughter) collaborate in rescuing the Hebrew Levite baby later called Moses. These women, whose namelessness reflects the anonymity of an underclass and thus binds them to a common cause, represent an alternative to the murderous, hypermasculine, narrow-minded ethos of *mitsrayim*, as represented by Pharaoh's decrees. For Pharaoh, only sons matter, with the riches, labor force, and military might they represent. These Egyptian and Hebrew women join forces in ways that defy and, in effect, strip Pharaoh/*mitsrayim* of his purported masculine, material power. The counterintuitive generosity of these Egyptian women adds nuance to a story that is so often simplistically perceived in us-versus-them terms. Together the Israelite and Egyptian women make possible a vision of the world where the weak can seek succor from the strong and where change can occur through cooperation rather than violence.

[3] *"The story is told of Rabbi"* In Tosefta Pesachim 10:12, one sees a similar story about a group of elders who assemble to talk about the laws of Passover and lose track of time. The difference between the Tosefta story and that which appears in the Haggadah is

that in the Tosefta version, the only named character (who does not appear at all in the Haggadah version) is Rabban Gamaliel, leader of the Jewish community. The other characters are referred to simply as "the elders." By limiting the discussants to the Prince and his elder elite, this version imagines a monolithically elite Seder community.

In marked contrast, the version of the story that appears in the Haggadah includes five named sages from the first and second centuries with mixed pedigrees and divergent viewpoints. Eliezer ben Hyrcanus, Elazar ben Azariah, and Tarfon were all priests and men of considerable fortunes. In contrast, Akiva and Joshua came from poor backgrounds. Add to this the fact that Eliezer ben Hyrcanus and Joshua ben Hananiah were the disputants in the Talmud's famous oven of Akhnai story. In Bava Metsia 59b, Eliezer presents his view on the ritual purity of an oven made by Akhnai, but it is rejected by his colleagues. Eliezer appeals to supernatural forces to prove the correctness of his argument, finally saying, "If the halakhah agrees with me, let it be proved from heaven," whereupon a heavenly voice calls out, "Why do you dispute with Eliezer, seeing that in all matters the halakhah agrees with him?" Rabbi Joshua rises up and announces, "'It [halakhic decision] is not in heaven' [Deut. 30:12], we pay no attention to a heavenly voice, for it is written in the Torah at Mount Sinai: 'One must follow the majority' [Exod. 23:2]." The story culminates in the excommunication of Rabbi Eliezer. The Haggadah's placement of Eliezer in B'nai B'rak together with Joshua, Akiva, and his other colleagues thus conjures up a time of rabbinic solidarity before major rifts and breakdowns in communication or seeks to repair them.

The ostensible purpose of this story is to provide an example of how five rabbis carried out the directive to enlarge upon the telling of the Exodus story. It is noteworthy that in this process of enlargement, the Rabbis lose track of time, in effect becoming "like women," incapable—in the Rabbis' own estimation—of carrying out time-bound commandments because of their domestic responsibilities. The story thus shows that the ability to fulfill time-bound commandments is not gender determined and that men and women equally experience the pressures of conflicting obligations and inclinations.

Speaking generally about the male-centeredness of the Haggadah, Judith Plaskow laments the invisibility of "Mrs. Rabbi Eliezer, Joshua, or Akiva. These women hover outside the boundaries of the text, just as they were probably excluded from their husbands' paradigmatic seder."[3] One way to bring these women into the heart of Seder discussion, of course, is to relate what we know about them from other rabbinic sources.

The story of Rabbi Akiva's wife seems especially relevant to a discussion of the circle of sages assembled in B'nai B'rak. What and who enabled these men to spend such a night of study together? Talmudic legend tells us that Akiva's wife Rachel made extraordinary sacrifices so that Akiva, formerly an illiterate shepherd, could achieve greatness in Torah scholarship. According to Nedarim 50a, when her father, Kalba Savua, learns of her betrothal of Akiva, he disowns her. Despite this, she marries him in the winter, suffers great privations, and counsels him herself to leave her to go study Torah. After studying for twelve years under Rabbi Eliezer and Rabbi Joshua, Akiva is on his way home when he overhears someone taunting his wife about Akiva's inferior social status and his shameless abandonment of her; Rachel parries the insults by saying that she would be happy if Akiva stayed away for yet another twelve years, a comment that Akiva takes as permission to return to his teachers. When Akiva finally returns after the second twelve years, Rachel is reduced to such an impoverished state that when she goes out to greet Akiva, his students fail to recognize her and attempt to shoo her away, until Akiva announces that he and they owe all of their learning to her. The story of Akiva and Rachel thus charts Akiva's triumphant journey from humble economic and intellectual beginnings to a position of social superiority and sagacity. Rachel Adler reads the legend of Rabbi Akiva and Rachel as emblematic of the types of rabbinic story that "describe how men extricate themselves from this abject or physically dangerous state and are restored to normality and righteousness—i.e., patriarchal dominance."[4] But why must Akiva's ascent be predicated on Rachel's descent? Why must he leave her to become a great Torah scholar? Is there no way to imagine a circle of learning that is enriched rather than diminished by the presence of women?

The salutary benefit of female learnedness is demonstrated in a talmudic legend told about Imma Shalom (literally, "Mother of Peace"), the wife of Eliezer ben Hyrcanus and sister of Rabban Gamaliel II, the Nasi (Prince). In Bava Metsia, shortly after the story of the oven of Akhnai and the subsequent excommunication of Eliezer (by Rabban Gamaliel II), Imma Shalom is described as attempting to deter her husband from prostrating himself on the ground in prayers, for fear that Eliezer's prostrate prayers would result in the death of her brother (presumably, a divine retribution for Gamaliel's humiliation of Eliezer). On one occasion, Imma Shalom relaxes her watch; immediately she discovers her husband prostrating himself on the ground and calls out, "You have slain my brother!" When asked by her husband how she knew that Gamaliel would die as a result of his prayers, Imma Shalom answers that she has a tradition from her father's house that "all gates are locked except for the gates of wounded feelings." Imma Shalom's correct application of a teaching she learned from her father/husband thus subverts her husband's famously offensive assertion in Mishnah Sotah 3:4 (also Sot. 20a) that "whoever teaches his daughter Torah teaches her foolishness."

Imma Shalom emerges from this story as a learned intermediary, a woman caught between two powerful men, one who wields the force of the community and another who wields the miraculous force of God. Unable to effect reconciliation between the men, she nevertheless attempts to avert further harm and maintain a cold "peace." According to one version of the story, she relaxes her guard because of a mistake in determining the new moon, an ironic mistake given that the New Moon is customarily considered a woman's holiday. According to the other version of the story, what stands in her way is her (feminine) compassion for the poor; while Eliezer is praying, a poor man comes to their door and Imma Shalom leaves her watch to attend to this poor man's needs. In either version, her failure to prevent her brother's death can be traced to her status as a female outsider in a world of powerful, feuding men.

[6] *"Rabbi Elazar ben Azariah said, 'I am like a man of seventy'"* Elazar ben Azariah's statement that he is "like a man of seventy," alludes to another dramatic talmudic story, again featuring a wife in a marginal, yet significant role. This story from Berakhot 28

concerns the ousting of Rabban Gamaliel II (for his mistreatment of Rabbi Joshua ben Hananiah) and the election of a young Rabbi Elazar in Gamaliel's stead. Elazar consults with his unnamed wife as to whether to assume the position; she cautions that he'll be deposed, but he responds that it would be worth having the honor even if for one day. She counters once again, saying, "You have no gray hair," that is, no sign of age, so no one will respect you. In answer to the wife's concern about his youthful appearance, a miracle occurs: Elazar prematurely sprouts gray hairs, hence, the expression, "I am like a man of seventy." Elazar's ascent is celebrated; in opposition to Gamaliel, who restricted admission to the study house to those who met his stringent criteria of *tocho k'voro*—having identical outer and inner aspects, a social status that matched one's scholarship or a physical appearance that accorded with one's intelligence—Elazar, who himself was only "as if" an elder, opens up the study house to a broad array of students. But his miraculous gray hairs fail to keep him in office. In the end, Gamaliel is reinstated, as per Elazar's wife's prediction. Elazar and his wife emerge from this story as opposing personalities: Elazar is idealistic, scholarly, and public in orientation, while his wife, identified as, *d'veito*, literally, "his house," is homey, pragmatic, and skeptical. And yet, both are, in a sense, proven "right": Elazar is correct in esteeming the chance to govern even if briefly, and his wife is correct in her assessment of political realities on the ground.

Both this story and the Haggadah passage citing Rabbi Elazar ben Azariah demonstrate the value of interpretative pluralism. In the story from Berakhot, Gamaliel is ousted from his position because of his authoritarian, univocal approach to leadership. Elazar, in contrast, is shown to be more open to the ideas of others, including those of his wife. Similarly, in the Haggadah passage, Elazar announces that he could not understand (literally, he never "merited" this understanding of) why the Exodus from Egypt should be recounted in the evening service until Ben Zoma explained the basis of this obligation in the verse *kol y'mei chayekha*, "all the days of your life," the seemingly superfluous word *kol* coming to teach the need to recount the story not only in the daytime but also at night. Note that the text does not stop the interpretive process with Ben Zoma's *d'rashah*; the Haggadah also quotes the reading of the Sages, who suggest that the word *kol* teaches that even in the days of the messiah, we will still need to recount the Exodus story. That is, even in that hoped-for era of redemption, we will still need to remind ourselves of our ur-redemption, so that we continue to recognize God's workings to empathize with the strangers in our midst.

[10] *"Blessed is God"* Four is a key number in the Haggadah: there are four cups, four questions, four matriarchs (in the song *Echad Mi Yode'a?*), and here, four repetitions of the word *barukh*, "blessed." The reiteration of the word *barukh* in this passage praising God as *hamakom* (the place) helps emphasize the need for a many-faceted theology. According to *Genesis Rabbah* 68, God is "the place of the universe" but is not delimited by that place or space, nor by the idea of space. Hence, in this passage, God is presented in spatial, personal (*hu*, "He") terms and in historical terms, as the giver of the Torah to the nation of Israel.

Several feminist Haggadot adapt the language of this passage to incorporate a more androgynous theological concept. In *The Open Door: A Passover Haggadah*, the version of this passage included reads as follows:

> Blessed is the One who dwells in every place.
> Blessed is the *Shechinah*, the One who is blessed.
> Blessed is our people's Source of Torah.
> Blessed is God.
>
> *Barukh HaMakom, baruch hu* [he].
> *Shehi HaShechinah, b'ruchah hi* [she].
> *Baruch shenatan Torah l'amo Yisrael.*
> *B'ruchah hi* [she].[5]

[14] *"The Torah alludes to four children"* The use here of the word *k'neged* is noteworthy in that it connotes opposition as well as correspondence. The word *maggid* (the telling) comes from the same word root, *n.g.d*, indicating that a proper telling of the Exodus story requires a group of people who share certain values but also occasionally disagree. The four types of children specified in the Haggadah themselves demonstrate patterns of correspondence and opposition. The simple and unquestioning children both evince a limited desire to question. And the wise and wicked children both separate themselves from the group by referring to the customs "you" practice. Note as well that a correspondence is drawn between the wicked and the unquestioning children in that the Haggadah answers both of them with the same biblical verse.

That said, the Haggadah also draws stark differences between these children. The wise child shows a willingness to use Jewish legal terminology, while the "wicked" child rejects the very terms of this conversation. And the prescribed methods of speaking to the evil and unquestioning children differ widely. The answer to the rejectionist *rasha* is exaggeratedly patriarchal and authoritarian, while the answer to the unquestioning *she'eino yode'a lishol* combines both a maternal and a paternal voice: *at p'tach lo*, literally, "you [fem.] open [masc.] him up" (v. 26).

In *Unheroic Conduct*, a study of rabbinic notions of masculinity, Daniel Boyarin compares medieval and modern illustrations of the four sons, showing how the visual depictions began to change in the mid-nineteenth century. Boyarin observes that as late as the early nineteenth century, Haggadah illustrations depicted the righteous son as a robed, Middle Eastern scholar, carrying a scroll; in contrast, the "wicked son" is repeatedly pictured as a soldier, with a sword or other weaponry. According to Boyarin, these illustrations suggest that a "bad Jew" is one who takes on the martial ideals of the *goyim*, while the "good Jew" is a man more mental than physical, thin and almost feminine looking. With the advent of Zionism, which placed new value on physical labor and military self-defense, this picture began to change significantly. Now the wise son began to look like a physically vigorous kibbutz member, while the wicked son was a "city slicker," a petit bourgeois who has not been won over to the new Torah of Zionist agriculturalism. The representation of the four sons thus offers insight into changing patterns of Jewish masculinity.[6]

Endeavoring to correct the imbalance of common translation of the traditional Haggadah, which speaks only of sons and not of daughters, women's Haggadot include a four daughters section, often focusing on the issues of women in Judaism. The anger and critical disposition demonstrated by the *rasha* is something that feminist Haggadot typically sympathize with rather than condemn. In lesbian Haggadot, for example, the negativity of the *rasha* is explained as stemming from frustration over the exclusion of gays and lesbians from mainstream Jewish life. The Haggadah's answer to the *rasha*—"If you were there, you would not have been redeemed"— can thus be reconceptualized not as a punishment, but as an honest assessment of what happens when one disengages from Jewish group life. Do you leave the community when it challenges your feminist/LGBT identity, or do you try to make change from within, thereby participating in the ongoing redemption of the Jewish people?

◆ ◆ ◆

THE : UNION : HAGGADAH :

"Monumental Egypt and Modern Israel"
The Union Haggadah, Home Service for the Passover Eve
New York, 1907
The Central Conference of American Rabbis (Reform)

7. A SHORT ANSWER:
ENSLAVEMENT IS SPIRITUAL—
WE WORSHIPED IDOLS

[1]At first, our ancestors engaged in false service, and now God has brought us to His service, as it says, [2]"Joshua told the entire nation, 'This is what Adonai, the God of Israel, says: In the past, your ancestors—Terach, Abraham's father and Nachor's father—lived across the river and served other gods. [3]And I took your father, Abraham, from across the river and I led him throughout the entire Land of Canaan and I multiplied his descendants by giving him Isaac, [4]and by giving Isaac Jacob and Esau, and by giving Esau the hill country of Seir as his inheritance while Jacob and his children went down to Egypt.'"

מִתְּחִלָּה עוֹבְדֵי עֲבוֹדָה זָרָה הָיוּ אֲבוֹתֵינוּ וְעַכְשָׁו קֵרְבָנוּ הַמָּקוֹם לַעֲבוֹדָתוֹ. שֶׁנֶּאֱמַר: [2]וַיֹּאמֶר יְהוֹשֻׁעַ אֶל כָּל־הָעָם כֹּה אָמַר יְיָ אֱלֹהֵי יִשְׂרָאֵל בְּעֵבֶר הַנָּהָר יָשְׁבוּ אֲבוֹתֵיכֶם מֵעוֹלָם תֶּרַח אֲבִי אַבְרָהָם וַאֲבִי נָחוֹר וַיַּעַבְדוּ אֱלֹהִים אֲחֵרִים: [3]וָאֶקַּח אֶת־אֲבִיכֶם אֶת־אַבְרָהָם מֵעֵבֶר הַנָּהָר וָאוֹלֵךְ אוֹתוֹ בְּכָל־אֶרֶץ כְּנָעַן וָאַרְבֶּה אֶת־זַרְעוֹ וָאֶתֶּן־לוֹ אֶת־יִצְחָק: [4]וָאֶתֵּן לְיִצְחָק אֶת־יַעֲקֹב וְאֶת־עֵשָׂו. וָאֶתֵּן לְעֵשָׂו אֶת־הַר שֵׂעִיר לָרֶשֶׁת אוֹתוֹ וְיַעֲקֹב וּבָנָיו יָרְדוּ מִצְרָיִם:

213

ARNOW (THE WORLD OF MIDRASH)

[1] *"False service"* When we tell the Passover story, the Mishnah (M. Pes. 10:4) instructs us to "begin with disgrace and end with praise." The Babylonian Talmud's discussion of this includes a difference between two sages about the meaning of "disgrace" (Pes. 116a).[1] The response of each sage reflects a different meaning of the word *avodah*, which can signify worship or religious service on one hand, and physical work on the other. The first sage explained "disgrace" in spiritual terms, with a phrase not overtly connected with the enslavement in Egypt: "At first, our ancestors engaged in false service, *(p. 216)*

BRETTLER (OUR BIBLICAL HERITAGE)

[1] *"Our ancestors engaged in false service"* Although there are many post-biblical stories about the childhood of Abra(ha)m, the Bible is silent on how he "discovered" Adonai and what motivated him to heed the voice of Genesis 12:1, "Go forth from your native land...." The verse that is about to be cited categorizes various people as worshipers of other gods—the text mentions Terach, Abram's father, and Nachor, his brother; it is ambiguous however, as to whether or not Abram is included among these worshipers of other gods.

[2] *"Joshua told"* Quoting Joshua 24:2–4, the introduction to a reprise of the history of Israel that concludes in 24:13, with the entry into *(p. 217)*

GILLMAN (THEOLOGICALLY SPEAKING)

[1] *"At first"* Here begins an alternate version of the story. The first version began, "We were slaves ..." (see Volume 1, p. 161). This version begins, "... our ancestors engaged in false service." Both versions begin with disgrace. But what precisely was the disgrace? Slavery or idol worshiping? Political enslavement or spiritual enslavement? Over the centuries, that debate became the topic of countless Passover sermons. We can presume that before the Haggadah was canonized in its present form, these two versions circulated independently. *(p. 217)*

7. A SHORT ANSWER: ENSLAVEMENT IS SPIRITUAL—WE WORSHIPED IDOLS

[1]At first, our ancestors engaged in false service, and now God has brought us to His service, as it says, [2]"Joshua told the entire nation, 'This is what Adonai, the God of Israel, says: In the past, your ancestors—Terach, Abraham's father and Nachor's father—lived across the river and served other gods. [3]And I took your father, Abraham, from across the river and I led him throughout the entire Land of Canaan and I multiplied his descendants by giving him Isaac,

GRAY (MEDIEVAL COMMENTATORS)

[1] *"At first"* *Rashbetz* points out that this paragraph illustrates the principle in Pesachim 116a that we must "begin with disgrace and end with praise." This is the disgrace—pointing out how our ancestors had originally been idolaters. *Rashbetz* goes on to suggest that this recitation logically follows shortly after our interaction with the wicked child. Since the wicked child wants to separate himself from the community, we now explain exactly what the nature of the *(p. 217)*

J. HOFFMAN (TRANSLATION)

[1] *"Engaged in false service"* That is, they served false gods. Our version of the text specifically refers to the service, not the gods, but other texts use the expression "star servers," focusing on the false gods, not the false service. We want to preserve the distinction, so we translate "false service" here, rather than the more colloquial "served false gods." Below (v. 2, "other gods"), the text refers directly to the gods. If proper service involves both the correct manner of service and service of the correct god, here we first find a reference to doing the service *(p. 218)*

SIGNPOST: A SHORT ANSWER— ENSLAVEMENT IS SPIRITUAL: WORSHIPING IDOLS

ABOVE (MY PEOPLE'S PASSOVER HAGGADAH, VOLUME 1, P. 161) WE SAW ONE INTERPRETATION OF ENSLAVEMENT: ACTUAL PHYSICAL SLAVERY. WE NOW ENCOUNTER A SECOND ONE: THE SPIRITUAL DEGRADATION THAT WE CHOOSE OURSELVES WHEN WE ELECT TO WORSHIP FALSE GODS.

◆———

ZIERLER (FEMINIST VOICES)

[2] *"Terach, Abraham's father and Nachor's father"* Here is another instance of the way the Haggadah narrates history in terms of "men's time." In the beginning, we are told, our ancestors were idol worshipers, but the ancestor story recited consists of an all-male genealogy. To be sure, it was not only our forefathers who made the theological journey from polytheism to monotheism. Our fore-mothers were deeply connected to this religious world, as famously evidenced by Rachel's theft of her father's teraphim in Genesis 31. And yet, this same Rachel, who clings most tenaciously to the religious ways of her father's home, is represented in Jeremiah 31:15 as weeping for the exiled people of Israel, provoking stirring consolation from God: "Thus said Adonai, 'Refrain your eyes from weeping and your eyes from *(p. 219)*

מִתְּחִלָּה עוֹבְדֵי עֲבוֹדָה זָרָה הָיוּ אֲבוֹתֵינוּ וְעַכְשָׁו [1]
קֵרְבָנוּ הַמָּקוֹם לַעֲבוֹדָתוֹ. שֶׁנֶּאֱמַר: וַיֹּאמֶר יְהוֹשֻׁעַ [2]
אֶל כָּל־הָעָם כֹּה אָמַר יְיָ אֱלֹהֵי יִשְׂרָאֵל בְּעֵבֶר הַנָּהָר
יָשְׁבוּ אֲבוֹתֵיכֶם מֵעוֹלָם תֶּרַח אֲבִי אַבְרָהָם וַאֲבִי
נָחוֹר וַיַּעַבְדוּ אֱלֹהִים אֲחֵרִים: וָאֶקַּח אֶת־אֲבִיכֶם [3]
אֶת־אַבְרָהָם מֵעֵבֶר הַנָּהָר וָאוֹלֵךְ אוֹתוֹ בְּכָל־אֶרֶץ
כְּנָעַן וָאַרְבֶּה אֶת־זַרְעוֹ וָאֶתֶּן־לוֹ אֶת־יִצְחָק:

L. HOFFMAN (HISTORY)

[1] *"At first, our ancestors engaged in false service"* The Yerushalmi advises, "Begin with, 'In days of old, our ancestors lived beyond the river,'" a reference to the account of Israelite history given by Joshua (chapter 24). Like "We were slaves" (see *My People's Passover Haggadah*, Volume 1, p. 161), this passage became one of the two prologues to the central midrash (with an added introductory sentence descriptive of ancestral idolatry, "At first, our ancestors engaged in false *(p. 219)*

4and by giving Isaac Jacob and Esau, and by giving Esau the hill country of Seir as his inheritance while Jacob and his children went down to Egypt.'"

וָאֶתֵּן לְיִצְחָק אֶת־יַעֲקֹב וְאֶת־עֵשָׂו.⁴ וָאֶתֵּן לְעֵשָׂו אֶת־הַר שֵׂעִיר לָרֶשֶׁת אוֹתוֹ וְיַעֲקֹב וּבָנָיו יָרְדוּ מִצְרָיִם:

ARNOW (THE WORLD OF MIDRASH)

avodah zarah." The second sage defined disgrace in a physical sense with the words *avadim hayyinu,* "we were slaves" (Deut. 6:21). The Haggadah's embrace of both sages' positions brings to mind a dictum that highlights the interdependence of physical and spiritual well-being: "Where there is no flour, there is no Torah; when there is no Torah, there is no flour" (M. Avot 3:21).

3*"Abraham"* In rabbinic thought Abraham's life prefigured the experiences of his descendants in Egypt. *Genesis Rabbah* (40:6) imagines God telling Abraham to "go forth and blaze a path for your children." The midrash then lists a dozen parallels between the life of the patriarch and his descendants. For instance: "And Abram went down into Egypt" (Gen. 12:10); "Our ancestors went down into Egypt" (Num. 20:15). "Pharaoh commanded his men … and they sent [Abraham] away …" (Gen. 12:20); "The Egyptians pressed the people that they might send them out …" (Exod. 12:33).[2] The midrash reminds us that the travails we face as individuals mirror those we face as a people. At some point along the road, each of us finds ourselves in Egypt, and each of us must struggle to find our way out.

4*"Jacob and Esau"* The Sages held that many events in the lives of the patriarchs occurred on Passover, but one is particularly disquieting. *Pirkei D'rabbi Eliezer* placed Jacob's theft of Esau's blessing on the night of Passover.[3] As Passover arrived, Jacob "brought two kinds of goats … one for a paschal offering" and the other to prepare as a tasty dish for his father. Upon discovering the deceit, Esau poured out so bitter a cry that Mordecai had to pay for it by his own wailing throughout the streets of Shushan (*Gen. Rab.* 67:4 on Esther 4:1). The *Zohar* adds that when Pharaoh's daughter rescued the infant Moses from the Nile, she found him crying also (Exod. 2:6). "Only when the effect of the tears of Esau have been exhausted will redemption begin for Israel" (*Zohar,* Exodus, 2: 12b). More than requiring triumph over oppressors, redemption demands healing the deepest rifts between brothers.

BRETTLER (OUR BIBLICAL HERITAGE)

the Land; given the focus of the Haggadah, only the beginning is repeated. Another short historical reprise will be quoted and interpreted later in the Haggadah; we do not know the function that the half-dozen or so such passages had in ancient Israel.

——◆——

GILLMAN (THEOLOGICALLY SPEAKING)

Eventually, both versions achieved equal standing, and both were incorporated into our text. The issue continues to be debated over our Seder tables.

The choice of the disgrace with which we begin our story is puzzling. The idol-worshiping ancestors referred to in this passage predate Abraham, who is usually credited with being the father of the Jewish people. Why then should their religious practices be part of our story? Why should it be our form of disgrace? On the other hand, the alternative choice of the disgrace, slavery, which was indeed the fate of our own ancestors, is puzzling for another reason. Our ancestors did not choose to be slaves. They were enslaved by others. Why then should it be a form of disgrace?

Or maybe, "disgrace" is not the best translation of the Hebrew term in the Mishnah. The term is *g'nut* (pronounced g'-noot). An inelegant translation of the term would be "the bad things," which does not convey the implications of "disgrace." "Bad things" can happen to us totally independently of someone else actively inflicting it upon us. So the Haggadah's trajectory can be simply from "bad things" to "good things," where the "bad things" can be either slavery or idol worshiping.

——◆——

GRAY (MEDIEVAL COMMENTATORS)

community is from which he wants to be separated. Following Abraham's rejection of idolatry, Abraham formed a covenant with God, who then took him "from beyond the river" and undertook his covenantal obligation to nurture and protect Israel. Abraham's covenant with God was taken up after him by Isaac (and not Ishmael) and then by Jacob (and not Esau). *Rashbetz* points out that God excluded Ishmael from the Abrahamic covenant when God said, "for it is through Isaac that offspring shall be continued for you" (Gen. 21:12 and Ned. 31a). While conceding that Ishmael's exclusion was involuntary, *Rashbetz* creatively reads the Bible so as to impute to Esau a desire to be separated from the Abrahamic covenant and Israelite destiny. Joshua (Josh. 24:4) quotes God as saying that He gave Jacob and Esau to Isaac and that He gave the hill country of Seir to Esau, while Jacob and his family went down to Egypt. Esau was earlier said to have gone "to another land because of his brother Jacob" (Gen. 36:6). This contrasts with Jacob, who "settled in the land where his father had sojourned"

(Gen. 37:1), after which he descended to Egypt. *Rashbetz* seems to interpret these verses as meaning that God later ratified Esau's own decision to separate from Jacob and his family. In *Rashbetz's* words, "[Esau] did not want to accept slavery and affliction like Jacob did…." This slavery and affliction were crucial aspects of the forging of Israel's religious and national identity, which Esau in some sense "voluntarily" rejected (Haggadah commentary). Interestingly, the Talmud supports *Rashbetz's* view of Esau; it refers to Esau as a "Jewish apostate" (Kid 18a), the same term applied to any Jew who forsakes Judaism.

Ritba elaborates further on God's covenant with Abraham and the latter's separation from idolatry. Abraham rejected his father Terach's idolatrous culture, but his brother Nachor did not. Just as Abraham separated himself from his family and all he knew in order to proclaim the one true God, so did God separate him from that idolatrous culture and choose him and his descendants for covenant (Haggadah commentary). Following *Ritba*, we may say that it is precisely from this new, God-centered community that the wicked child wishes to distance herself.

[3] *"And I multiplied His descendents"* In the Yerushalmi (PT Pes. 10:5, 37d), R. Acha points out that the word "And I increased" *(arbeh)* is written without the letter *heh* on the end, as *arb*. R. Acha then interprets this Hebrew root, *a.r.b*, as connected to the root *r.b*, meaning "arguments" or "trials." Basing himself on this notion of "trials," R. Acha then presents a somewhat fanciful interpretation of the verse (reflected elsewhere in rabbinic midrash), according to which God is saying here, "What trials I imposed on Abraham before giving him his seed"—which was Isaac.

———◆———

J. HOFFMAN (TRANSLATION)

wrong (though not necessarily serving the wrong god), and below we find service to the wrong god. Additionally, we are careful to distinguish between "service" in general—which can include worship or sacrifice—and "worship," which is but one kind of service.

[1] *"God"* Hamakom—literally, "the place." See "God," *My People's Passover Haggadah*, Volume 2, p. 33.

[1] *"Brought us"* Literally, "brought us near." But certainly the point is not that we are almost serving God, but that we are actually serving God. Below, in *Dayyenu*, we see this verb again and translate it "brought us together."

[2] *"Served"* Surprisingly, some translations have "worship" here, though worship as we know it is clearly an anachronism in this context.

[3] *"By giving him"* Literally, "and I gave him." But the Hebrew "and" *(v)* frequently has more force than its literal English equivalent.

———◆———

L. HOFFMAN (HISTORY)

service."). In all probability, this was first intended as an alternative "answer" all by itself, not simply an introduction to the midrash. It fulfills the requirement of beginning with degradation ("Our ancestors engaged in false service," and ending with praise ("Blessed is the One") for redeeming us ("who keeps His promise to Israel.") See *My People's Passover Haggadah*, Volume 1, p. 221.

The inclusion of both "prologues" is one of the many Babylonian usages that inform our own practice. Medieval Palestinian Jews said only "At first," not "We were slaves." But ironically, it was Babylonian, not Palestinian, custom that most impacted Jews worldwide. Much of what we consider "Jewish tradition" was canonized by rabbinic leaders in Babylonia (now Iraq) called Geonim (c. 750–1038), who were catapulted into worldwide decision-making power by the fact that the entire Muslim empire radiated out from caliphs in Baghdad. The Geonim invented responsa literature, including *Seder Rav Amram*, our first comprehensive prayer book (c. 860), sent to an outlying Jewish community in Spain, around 860 CE in response to its members' query as to what the proper Jewish liturgy should be. It contained the Babylonian Haggadah, which Jews all over Europe, Africa, and Asia emulated.

The two opinions (slavery or idolatry) are not idle alternatives. Slavery is physical; idolatry is spiritual. The former can be forced upon us; the latter is our own choosing. When I was a rabbinic student, a hospital chaplain once explained that being relegated to bed, wearing only a hospital gown, and scarred from surgery is likely to be experienced by patients as degrading. Identifying degradation as idolatry teaches us that true degradation arises only from within, so that no matter what disease does to our outer appearance, we should not abandon our sense of inner dignity. But under the truly adverse conditions of illness, we are often unable to see that. Hospital visitors need to appreciate how patients are likely to feel, as their independence, even their ability to dress and groom themselves, is taken from them.

———◆———

ZIERLER (FEMINIST VOICES)

tears, for your work shall be rewarded,' said Adonai, 'and they shall come back from the land of the enemy'" (Jer. 31:16).

[4] *"Jacob and his children went down to Egypt"* This section of the Haggadah, which quotes Joshua 24, concludes with the words *v'Ya'akov uvanav yardu mitsrayim*, ("Jacob and his children went down to Egypt.") Among these children is Serach, the daughter of Asher, a woman whose name appears in Genesis 46:17 and who figures prominently in rabbinic literature about the Israelite sojourn in Egypt. According to a fourteenth-century midrash, Serach was the grandchild designated to tell Jacob that Joseph was still alive (see *Midrash Hagadol* 45:26). In *Pirkei D'rabbi Eliezer* 47, Serach emerges as a remarkable female sage, one endowed with a particular understanding of sacred

language and its relationship to Israelite salvation. This midrash identifies the words *pakod pakadeti*, "I will surely remember you" (Exod. 3:16), as a code for redemption from the bondage of Egypt. The code is passed down by Abraham, from son to son, and eventually—remarkably!—to Serach bat Asher. One day, the elders of Israel report to Serach that Moses and Aaron have shown them signs and wonders, but they do not believe there is any substance behind these signs. In the course of conversation, they mention that Moses spoke of God's redemption of Israel, using the words *pakod yifkod etkhem* "God will surely remember you" (Gen. 50:24). Hearing this, Serach proclaims before the elders that "he [Moses] is the one who is destined to redeem Israel from Egypt." Serach is thereby credited with convincing the elders to believe in Moses and his mission and is added to the ranks of Shifra, Puah, Miriam, and Yocheved—women who help secure the deliverance of the people. Among these women, she is singled out by the Rabbis as a *darshanit*, a hallowed female participant in a tradition of sacred interpretation or midrash.

◆ ◆ ◆

8. Promises—Past and Present

A. The Promise to Abraham: "Blessed Is the One Who Keeps His Promise …"

[1]Blessed is the One who keeps His promise to Israel. [2]Blessed is He. [3]After all, the Holy One of Blessing foresaw the end, when He would do what He said to Abraham our father during the splitting covenant, as it says, [4]"He told Abram, 'Know that your descendants will be strangers in a land that is not theirs; they shall be enslaved and oppressed for four hundred years. [5]But I will judge the nation they serve, and then they will leave with great wealth.'"

בָּרוּךְ שׁוֹמֵר הַבְטָחָתוֹ לְיִשְׂרָאֵל [1]
בָּרוּךְ הוּא. שֶׁהַקָדוֹשׁ בָּרוּךְ הוּא [3] [2]
חִשַּׁב אֶת־הַקֵּץ לַעֲשׂוֹת כְּמָה שֶׁאָמַר
לְאַבְרָהָם אָבִינוּ בִּבְרִית בֵּין הַבְּתָרִים
שֶׁנֶּאֱמַר: [4] וַיֹּאמֶר לְאַבְרָם יָדֹעַ תֵּדַע כִּי
גֵר יִהְיֶה זַרְעֲךָ בְּאֶרֶץ לֹא לָהֶם וַעֲבָדוּם
וְעִנּוּ אֹתָם אַרְבַּע מֵאוֹת שָׁנָה: [5] וְגַם
אֶת־הַגּוֹי אֲשֶׁר יַעֲבֹדוּ דָּן אָנֹכִי וְאַחֲרֵי
כֵן יֵצְאוּ בִּרְכֻשׁ גָּדוֹל:

B. The Promise to Us: "This Kept Our Ancestors and Us Going …"

Lift the cups of wine and say:

[6]This kept our ancestors and us going. Not just one group has risen up against us to destroy us, but rather in every generation they rise up against us to destroy us. [7]And the Holy One of Blessing saves us from their hand.

וְהִיא שֶׁעָמְדָה לַאֲבוֹתֵינוּ וְלָנוּ. שֶׁלֹּא [6]
אֶחָד בִּלְבַד עָמַד עָלֵינוּ לְכַלּוֹתֵנוּ
אֶלָּא שֶׁבְּכָל־דּוֹר וָדוֹר עוֹמְדִים עָלֵינוּ
לְכַלּוֹתֵנוּ. [7] וְהַקָדוֹשׁ בָּרוּךְ הוּא מַצִּילֵנוּ
מִיָּדָם:

Replace the cups of wine.

ARNOW (THE WORLD OF MIDRASH)

[3] *"Foresaw the end"* Midrashic literature knows of an earlier, abortive Exodus undertaken by the tribe of Ephraim some years before God's "ordained" time. [The Ephraimites] assembled and went forth to battle, and many of them were slain. Why is this? Because, neither believing in Adonai nor trusting in His salvation, they tried to hasten the end [*hakets*, i.e., the redemption]" (*Song of Songs Rabbah* 2:20).[1] The midrash may also reflect the mark of two disastrous rebellions against Rome. The first in 70 CE led to the destruction of the Temple; the second in 132 CE brought about exile from Jerusalem, which was made into a pagan shrine *(Aelia Capitolina).* (p. 224)

BRETTLER (OUR BIBLICAL HERITAGE)

[3] *"The end"* The same Hebrew word *kets* is used in Daniel to refer to the end of days, after which the decrees of the wicked Antiochus IV would be reversed; it refers to the end of an old era and the beginning of a new (better) one. Only in later Hebrew does it have an unambiguous eschatological meaning. (p. 226)

GILLMAN (THEOLOGICALLY SPEAKING)

[4] *"Know that your descendants"* The major question about our ancestors' enslavement in Egypt, the question that lurks implicitly throughout the Haggadah but is never explicitly addressed, is alluded to in this passage. Abram is told that his descendants will be oppressed before departing with great wealth (Gen. 15:13–14). (p. 226)

GRAY (MEDIEVAL COMMENTATORS)

[1-3] *"Blessed is the One … foresaw the end"* Rashbetz explains this to mean that we are obligated to bless God, who makes and keeps promises. God took Abraham out of his father's house and brought him to the Land of Israel, making him the promise that "I will make of you a great nation" (Gen. 12:2). Afterwards God told Abraham that his descendants would suffer slavery and a great trial, but He promised that this would (p. 228)

[For prayer instructions, see page 221.]

8. PROMISES—PAST AND PRESENT

A. The Promise to Abraham: "Blessed Is the One Who Keeps His Promise …"

[1] Blessed is the One who keeps His promise to Israel. [2] Blessed is He. [3] After all, the Holy One of Blessing foresaw the end, when He would do what He said to Abraham our father during the splitting covenant, as it says, [4] "He told Abram, 'Know that your descendants will be strangers in a land that is not theirs; they shall be enslaved and oppressed for four hundred years. [5] But I will judge the nation they serve, and then they will leave with great wealth.'"

GREEN (PERSONAL SPIRITUALITY)

[6] *"This kept our ancestors and us going"* Literally, this means, "She who stood up for our ancestors and for us...." Kabbalistic tradition insists that the redemption from Egypt has its root in *Binah*, mother of the seven lower divine rungs, the inner womb of God. Exodus/liberation is a rebirth, a new beginning of life in awareness of God's creation, so it has to go back to the place within the godhead that speaks to such a moment.

Let me try to put this (p. 229)

J. Hoffman (Translation)

[3] *"Foresaw"* Or "planned."

[3] *"Splitting covenant"* This refers to God's covenant with Abraham (Gen. 15), cited next, in which Abraham splits several animals. This reference is frequently translated literally along the lines of "covenant between the pieces." The Genizah (see *My People's Passover Haggadah*, Volume 2, p. 240) does not include the word "covenant," giving us instead the more intriguing "what He said to Abraham … between the pieces."

[5] *"They serve"* Or "to which they are enslaved."

(p. 230)

(p. 230)

Signpost: Promises—Past and Present

We have encountered two short answers regarding enslavement: enslavement is physical (see My People's Passover Haggadah, Volume 1, p. 161); enslavement is spiritual (Volume 1, p. 213). A third and longer answer will be forthcoming next (see My People's Passover Haggadah, Volume 2, p. 1). But first, we recall God's promises, to Abraham and to us—God assures us that no enemy will ever utterly destroy us.

בָּרוּךְ שׁוֹמֵר הַבְטָחָתוֹ לְיִשְׂרָאֵל ²בָּרוּךְ הוּא. ³שֶׁהַקָּדוֹשׁ בָּרוּךְ הוּא חִשַּׁב אֶת־הַקֵּץ לַעֲשׂוֹת כְּמָה שֶׁאָמַר לְאַבְרָהָם אָבִינוּ בִּבְרִית בֵּין הַבְּתָרִים שֶׁנֶּאֱמַר: ⁴וַיֹּאמֶר לְאַבְרָם יָדֹעַ תֵּדַע כִּי גֵר יִהְיֶה זַרְעֲךָ בְּאֶרֶץ לֹא לָהֶם וַעֲבָדוּם וְעִנּוּ אֹתָם אַרְבַּע מֵאוֹת שָׁנָה: ⁵וְגַם אֶת־הַגּוֹי אֲשֶׁר יַעֲבֹדוּ דָּן אָנֹכִי וְאַחֲרֵי כֵן יֵצְאוּ בִּרְכֻשׁ גָּדוֹל:

L. Hoffman (History)

[1] *"Blessed is the One who keeps His promise"* The Seder must move from degradation to praise and redemption (see *My People's Passover Haggadah*, Volume 1, L. Hoffman, p. 154). This paragraph is here because originally it was the "praise" and "redemption" unit that completes the "degradation" piece immediately prior ("At first, our ancestors engaged in false service") ended.

[3] *"Foresaw [literally, 'calculated'] the end"* Is ultimate deliverance tied to our

(p. 230)

(p. 230)

Zierler (Feminist Voices)

[6] *"This kept our ancestors and us going"* Because this passage begins with the feminine pronoun *v'hi* (relating back to the feminine noun, *havtachah*, "promise" (v. 1) many women's Haggadot use it as an opportunity to tell of "she who stood fast"—that is, to recount stories of the bravery and stalwartness of Jewish woman throughout Jewish history. Examples might include the prophet Deborah (Judges 4–5), who rose to lead the Israelites to victory over the Canaanites; Ruth, who faithfully stood by her mother-in-law, Naomi; or Emma Lazarus, the formerly assimilated New York poet, who spoke for the cause of Russian Jewish immigrants and for the early dream of Zionism, when few of her assimilated Sefardi fellow New York Jews were willing to take such stands. Others have suggested that the "she" might refer to the *Shekhinah* (the feminine

(p. 231)

(p. 231)

B. The Promise to Us: "This Kept Our
   Ancestors and Us Going ..."

[6]This kept our ancestors and us going.
Not just one group has risen up
against us to destroy us, but rather in
every generation they rise up against
us to destroy us. [7]And the Holy One of
Blessing saves us from their hand.

וְ֜הִיא שֶׁעָמְדָה לַאֲבוֹתֵינוּ וְלָנוּ. שֶׁלֹּא
אֶחָד בִּלְבַד עָמַד עָלֵינוּ לְכַלּוֹתֵנוּ
אֶלָּא שֶׁבְּכָל־דּוֹר וָדוֹר עוֹמְדִים עָלֵינוּ
לְכַלּוֹתֵנוּ. [7]וְהַקָּדוֹשׁ בָּרוּךְ הוּא מַצִּילֵנוּ
מִיָּדָם:

ARNOW (THE WORLD OF MIDRASH)

Together they left a lingering mistrust of human efforts to hasten God's timetable for
redemption.

[3]*"Abraham our father during the splitting covenant"* The Haggadah's reference to the
"splitting covenant" (often referred to as the Covenant between the Pieces) places the
Exodus squarely within the theological framework of covenantal promise and
fulfillment. Indeed, midrashic tradition sets this first covenant on the eve of Passover.[2]
Just prior to it, Abraham utters his first words to God, questioning God's promise that
he will produce offspring and inherit the Land of Israel. The Talmud (Ned. 32a)
explains Israel's enslavement as a punishment for Abraham's lack of faith in God's
pledge. A tenth-century midrash rejects this view. Here, Moses angrily takes God to task
for allowing Israel's servitude: "What has this people done to deserve more enslavement
than all the preceding generations? Is it because our father Abraham said: 'How shall I
know that I am to possess [the land]?' (Gen. 15:8). And You said to him: 'Know well
that your offspring shall be strangers' (Gen. 15:13). Well, if this be so, then Esau [whom
midrashic literature often associates with Rome and Christendom] and Ishmael [in
midrash, the Arab world], also being [Abraham's] descendants, should likewise have
been subjected [to slavery]; moreover, the generation of Isaac or Jacob should have been
subjected rather than my own generation!" (*Exod. Rab.* 5:22).

[4]*"Your descendants will be strangers"* One lesson to learn from our experience as
strangers or sojourners (*ger*; plural, *gerim*) is clear: "And you shall love the *ger*, for *gerim*
you were in the Land of Egypt" (Deut. 10:19).[3] The Rabbis use the word *ger* not just for
"strangers" but for "proselytes," buttressing their generally favorable attitude toward
them by pointing out that key figures in Jewish history applied this very term to
themselves. The eighth-century *Mishnah of Rabbi Eliezer* offers a good example:

"Beloved are *gerim*: All the prophets called themselves *gerim*. [When he bought the burial cave for his wife] Abraham said: 'I am a *ger* among you ...' (Gen. 23:4). [When he named his son Gershom] Moses said: 'I have been a *ger* in a foreign land' (Exod. 2:22). David said: 'Hear my prayer, O Adonai, and give ear to my cry ... for I am a *ger*, as all my fathers were' (Ps. 39:13)."[4] Burton L. Visotzky, professor of midrash at the Jewish Theological Seminary explains: "We all are 'converts' that is, 'strangers' and so, we must respect the 'other' and the 'stranger,' particularly the one who joins our community—for no one is so pure of lineage that they can claim to not be a bit the stranger—not even David or Moses."[5]

[4] *"Four hundred years"* A careful reading of the Bible's chronology reveals that the Israelites remained in Egypt for about two centuries, not four hundred years. *Pesikta D'rav Kahana* (5:7), a midrash from the fifth or sixth century, explains the discrepancy. When Moses told Israel they would be redeemed "this month," they questioned him. "Didn't the Holy One clearly say to our father Abraham, '... Your descendants ... shall be enslaved and oppressed for four hundred years ...' (Gen. 15:13)? According to our reckoning, we have served only two hundred and ten years.[6] Moses replied, 'Since He desires your redemption, He does not heed your reckonings. Instead *He leaps upon the mountains, He skips upon the hills* (Song of Songs 2:8)—that is He contracts the limits of the period before redemption [and ignored your calculations ...] saying, It is my will that you shall be redeemed this month.'"

[6] *"In every generation"* Why has Israel faced so many travails and how has it managed to endure? A midrash imagines the ministering angels warning God that the people of Israel will prove faithless in exile. God compares Israel to the Egyptians, who became extinct after only ten plagues. But "as for Israel, even though I chastise them with troubles in this world, in every generation—even in every hour—they do not recoil from Me. Because they remain steadfast, they will exist for ever" (*Pesikta Rabbati* 35:1). Here, affliction and existence are two sides of the same coin, both a function of Israel's relationship with God. Come what may, Israel refuses to give up on God.

[7] *"And the Holy One of Blessing saves us"* In contrast to the Haggadah's picture of unstinting divine intervention, the Sages often bitterly chided God for failing to act on Israel's behalf. In the Song of the Sea, the Israelites praise God's power in drowning the Egyptians: "Who is like You, Adonai, among the mighty [*ba-eilim*]?" (Exod. 15:11). Using a play on words, the midrash retorts, "Who is like You among the silent ones [*b'ilmim*], who is like You, who sees insult heaped upon Your children but keep silent?"[7] In like manner, *Exodus Rabbah* 5:22 comments on Exodus 5:23: "Still You have not delivered Your people." Legend has it that those Israelites who fell short of their daily quota of bricks were buried in the walls of Pharaoh's construction projects. According to this midrash, Moses argues [with God], "I know that in the future You will deliver them, but what about those who have been buried in the buildings?"

◆

Brettler (Our Biblical Heritage)

[3] *"Splitting covenant"* Genesis 15:10 narrates how various animals were cut in half; this ritual of covenant making is reflected in Jeremiah 34:18, which refers to "the calf which they cut in two so as to pass between the halves." This most likely symbolized that if one of the parties does not fulfill his obligations, he should likewise be cut in half.

[4] *"Four hundred years"* Quoting Genesis 15:13–14. The Rabbis would later be troubled by how this tradition of a four-hundred-year enslavement might be reconciled with 15:16, which states, "And they shall return here in the fourth generation." Most likely Genesis 15 incorporates disparate traditions.

[6–7] *"In every generation they rise up against us ... saves us"* This paranoid conception is alien to the Bible. In fact, after the sin of the golden calf it is God who wants to totally destroy Israel, and a person, Moses, who saves them (Exod. 32:10–14)!

◆

Gillman (Theologically Speaking)

Nowhere does the Torah address the burning question, why did God allow our ancestors to be enslaved? The area of theology that tries to vindicate God's justice in the face of human suffering is "theodicy" (from the Greek: *theos* = "God," *dike* = "justify"). To do theodicy is to justify God's judgment.

In its crudest form, the issue is this: how can an omnipotent, just, and loving God allow innocent and righteous human beings to undergo implacable suffering? That there are innocent people who do suffer terribly is obvious to all of us. This awareness poses the greatest challenge to people of faith in all religious traditions, and much of theology is expended trying to deal with it. In the Torah itself, suffering is understood as punishment for sin. The middle paragraph of the *Sh'ma* (Deut. 11:13–21) spells out that equation: obedience to God is rewarded, disobedience is punished.

But the Book of Job subverts that equation. Job is the story of an innocent and righteous man who suffers terribly simply because God wills it and in order that God may win a bet with "the Adversary" (in Hebrew, *ha-Satan*)! Yet this book is canonized and is part of our sacred tradition. At the end of the book, God tells Job that he must not try to understand God's ways of dealing with creation, and Job seems to accept that answer (Job 42). That the suffering of the righteous is a mystery is frequently invoked as an attempt at theodicy, though it hardly explains anything.

Another version of this response suggests that suffering occurs because God has "hidden God's face." This metaphor for divine abandonment appears numerous times in Scripture usually as punishment, but at times (e.g., Ps. 44:18–27) simply as one phase in God's mysterious relationship with humanity.

These traditional responses have all emphasized that we must preserve God's omnipotence even at the price of suppressing God's righteousness. More recent attempts to deal with the issue suggest the reverse. Unmerited suffering occurs because God simply does not have the power to prevent it. This theology of a limited God was popularized by Rabbi Harold Kushner in his widely read *When Bad Things Happen to Good People.* The extent to which this solution deals with the theological issue is debatable. The broader question is that with this solution in place, how do we feel about worshiping a God who is powerless to deal with the leftover chaos in the universe?

In our own time, the reality of the suffering undergone during the Holocaust experience has simply raised this entire issue to a much more critical level. We will return to this below ("They rise ... to destroy us ... Holy One ... saves us").

Back to the Haggadah. In the case of our ancestors' enslavement in Egypt, what was the sin? In the face of the Torah's silence, the rabbinic commentaries multiply speculative answers—none of them really satisfactory. Was it because the brothers sold Joseph into slavery? But does this punishment really fit the crime? Hardly.

That the Haggadah provides no answers to this question is only one problem; no theologian has ever come up with a satisfactory answer to why bad things happen to innocent people. The more serious problem is why the question is never raised in the Haggadah itself. It should be raised around the Seder table. Now, it is up to us to raise it.

6–7 *"They rise ... to destroy us ... Holy One ... saves us"* Indeed, they do. In every generation, as we know all too well, enemies of the Jewish people rise up to destroy us. That has been confirmed in our own day. But what about the end of that sentence? What about "And the Holy One of Blessing saves us from their hand." That was hardly confirmed in our own day.

Theological responses to the Holocaust fall into two broad categories. One group views these events as one more instance of Jewish suffering, not intrinsically different from similar instances throughout Jewish history, which can be dealt with as our ancestors dealt with these instances in previous generations. A conventional response absolves God from responsibility. The Holocaust is viewed as the work of evil human beings, exercising the free will that was granted to all humans by God at creation. It is as if God is viewed as refusing to interfere in the way human beings deal with each other. After all, God did not stop Cain from killing his brother Abel. One of the many problems with this response is that it ignores God's supposedly unique relationship with Israel. The Holocaust is not simply one more example of humanly perpetrated evil.

The second group of responses views these events as unprecedented instances of a new kind of radical evil that demand equally radical responses from our generation's thinkers. The most radical of these is the "death of God" response, propounded by Richard Rubenstein. Rubenstein is a theologian and scholar of religion, now retired from Florida State University, where he taught for many years. The "death of God" theology was popularized by a group of liberal Protestant theologians in the 1960s as a response to the upheavals in America precipitated by the Vietnam war. The Christian god did die, of course, though he was resurrected on the third day. These Christian theologians posited that the death of their god was a metaphor for God's abandonment of the world and that this sense of abandonment is not temporary but rather permanent. God has abandoned the world and left humanity totally exposed and vulnerable.

Rubenstein adopted this metaphor as the only possible adequate theological response to the Holocaust. He understood that God's death was not a literal, objective claim—who of us could possible know that—but rather a statement about human culture, about our human perceptions of God. What has died is the complex of myths and metaphors with which Jews have understood God's relation to Israel, the heart of which is the notion that God loves, care for, and will preserve Israel. "The thread uniting God and man, heaven and earth has been broken," Rubenstein writes. "We stand in a cold, silent, unfeeling cosmos, unaided by any purposeful power beyond our own resources."[1]

Paradoxically, in an age of the death of God, Rubenstein notes, we need religion all the more. By "religion" he means the rituals, liturgies, rites of passage, and communal gatherings that support us in our age of despair. This Passover seder, then, should be viewed as less a theological exercise and more an expression of family and communal solidarity in this post-Holocaust era.

Not surprisingly, Rubenstein's theology has found little support among Jewish thinkers. More intriguing is Rabbi Irving Greenberg's notion of "moment faith." Greenberg disagrees with Rubenstein's proposal as well as with all conventional post-Holocaust theodicies because of their shared sense of finality. Either nothing has changed or everything has changed, they propose, and Greenberg disagrees with both of these polarities.

In their place, Greenberg suggests that we should embrace a much more subtle view of faith, a view that accentuates its ambiguity. "Faith … ebbs and flows. The difference between the skeptic and the believer is frequency of faith, and not certitude of position. The rejection of the unbeliever by the believer is literally the denial or the attempted suppression of what is within oneself."[2] In other words, there is a believer at the heart of every atheist, and an atheist at the heart of every believer.

Greenberg is fond of quoting a striking comment by Elie Wiesel to the effect that nothing should be said about the Holocaust that could not be uttered in the presence of the burning children. This would seem to preclude the possibility of any adequate Holocaust theology. If so, our only resort is to ritual, liturgy, and community—Judaism's classical resources for coping with suffering. The sharing of the Passover Seder would be a good place to begin.

—◆—

GRAY (MEDIEVAL COMMENTATORS)

come to an end, and set a date—which He kept—for liberating Israel from slavery.

The verse predicting Israel's slavery was "know that your descendants will be strangers in a land that is not theirs … and they shall be enslaved … 400 years" (Gen. 15:13). But Abudarham points out that the Jews were not actually slaves in Egypt for

400 years, but that the 400-year period of exile and persecution was counted from the birth of Isaac. But if that is the case, why would the verse say that the oppression and slavery would last 400 years? *Shibbolei Haleket* offers this reading of the verse that makes sense of all this: "Know that 'stranger-ness' will be decreed on your seed from the time that Isaac is born and that there will also be slavery ad oppression. The end of the 'stranger-ness,' the slavery, and the oppression will come after 400 years" (*Seder Pesach*, *siman* 218). *Shibbolei Haleket* supports his reading by pointing out that the patriarchs did indeed spend most of their days in wandering and unrest. In Genesis 26:16, Abimelech tells Isaac to leave his people, and, in Genesis 47:9, Jacob makes reference to his frequent wanderings. *Ramban* (R. Moses ben Nachman, Spain and Land of Israel, 1194–1270) struggles to make sense of Genesis 15:13 (which refers to 400 years) as well as Exodus 12:40, which states that the Israelites were in Egypt for 430 years. He explains that God's prediction in Genesis 15:13 was that Abraham's descendants' existence as strangers in a place that didn't belong to them (meaning the Land of Israel prior to the descent to Egypt and then in Egypt) would terminate 400 years from the utterance of the prediction. At that point, the Israelites would be fully free. Yet even then they would not immediately return to the Land of Israel, since they had to wait for "sins of the Amorites" to be fulfilled. On account of that waiting period, a "fourth generation" would return to the Land (Gen. 15:15), thus accounting for the additional thirty years mentioned in Exodus 12:40. While this accounts for the scriptural references, *Ramban* also points out that the 40 years the Israelites spent wandering in the desert—which was on account of *their* sins, not those of the Amorites—are not part of the 430 years.[1]

6 *"This kept our ancestors and us going"* Abudarham says that God's promise at the Covenant between the Pieces (Gen. 15:13) about Israel's slavery and redemption sustained both our ancestors, and us. The promise sustained our ancestors who actually saw the promise fulfilled when they left Egypt, and it sustains us, since we view ourselves as if we also had been liberated from slavery. We are also sustained by the promise because we have not had just one oppressor, but many—*Rashbetz* points to, for example, the Babylonians, Persians, Greeks, Romans, and "others." God saves us from all these oppressors because of that very promise that sustained our ancestors and ourselves (Haggadah commentary).

——◆——

GREEN (PERSONAL SPIRITUALITY)

insight into the language of contemporary religious psychology. I have long believed that the journey up the ladder of the ten *s'firot* is really to be seen as a journey inward, through ten successively deeper modes of spiritual consciousness. There is a time, the Haggadah teaches us, when all our outer senses, all the aspects of our own personalities, dwell in darkness. "Jacob and his sons went down to Egypt" means that our entire "household," all the various emotions that we might think compose us as selves, sometimes are "in exile," unable to function. We are shut down; our inner lights are dimmed. The Kabbalist's response to such a moment is to dig a deeper wellspring within the self. There is an inner place that is deeper than any of our wounds, an endless resource from which redemption will yet spring forth. This is *Binah*, the mothering aspect of God active within the self. *Binah* is the place of *t'shuvah*, the rebirthing energy within God, and hence within every human soul. *She* is the One who stands up for us, always.

———◆———

J. HOFFMAN (TRANSLATION)

[5] *"Wealth"* Or "property."

[6] *"Kept our ancestors and us going"* Literally, "stood for …" perhaps akin to the notion of "withstanding the test of time" or maybe "standing in good stead." The word forms a word play with "risen up," immediately below, which is also, literally, "stood."

[6] *"Risen up"* Literally, "stood up," completing the word play begun immediately above with "kept …," literally "stood."

———◆———

L. HOFFMAN (HISTORY)

willingness to practice repentance (do *t'shuvah*), or is it scheduled to occur in God's good time, according to a divine calculus independent of our own actions? Jewish tradition waffles on this, sometimes wanting to link deliverance to human behavior, and sometimes despairing of the possibility that we will ever act with sufficient goodness to merit being saved. The Jewish calendar retains both views. On Rosh Hashanah and Yom Kippur, our titular new year, we link individual deliverance to personal merit. There, all depends on our own personal determination to repent and not repeat our sins. Six months later, in the month that the Bible considers the new year, we celebrate Passover, redemption for the *group*, not the *individual*. There, where we can control only our own actions, not those of others, we affirm God's determination to save us in the end, even if others (presumably not ourselves) do not deserve it.

———◆———

ZIERLER (FEMINIST VOICES)

manifestation of God), who in rabbinic and kabbalistic thought is said to accompany the Jews into exile.

The New York feminist Seder revised this passage to speak for *hi shelo amdah*, for promises made and broken to women: "the promise of eternal beauty; the promise of eternal love, the promise of eternal health; the promise of stability, the promise of the dream, All these and more were broken."[1]

◆ ◆ ◆

Notes

What Is the Haggadah Anyway?

1. George Lakoff and Mark Johnson, *Metaphors We Live By* (Chicago: University of Chicago Press, 1980).

Passover in the Bible and Before

1. Ivan Engnell, "*Paesah-Massot* and the Problem of 'Patternism'" *Orientalia Suecana* 1 (1952): 39.

2. Jan A. Wagenaar, "Post-Exilic Calendar Innovations: The First Month of the Year and the Date of Passover and the Festival of Unleavened Bread," *Zeitschrift für die Alttestamentliche Wissenschaft* 115 (2003): 11.

3. Julius Wellhausen, *Prolegomena to the History of Ancient Israel* (Cleveland: World Publishing Company, 1965), p. 91.

4. William H. C. Propp, *The Anchor Bible: Exodus 1–18* (New York: Anchor Bible/Doubleday, 1999), pp. 398–401. The sense of the word appears in Isaiah 31:5: "Like the birds that fly, even so will Adonai of hosts shield Jerusalem, shielding and saving, protecting [*pasoach*] and rescuing."

5. H. Louis Ginsberg, *The Israelian Heritage of Judaism* (New York: Jewish Theological Seminary of America, 1982), p. 44.

6. Wellhausen, *Prolegomena*, p. 92.

7. How the word *pasach* came to be translated as "pass over" remains a debated question. For a good discussion, see Samuel Loewenstamm, *The Evolution of the Exodus Tradition* (Jerusalem: Magnes Press/Hebrew University, 1992), pp. 197–206, 219–221.

8. For a critical review of theories on the origins of Passover, see J. B. Segal, *The Hebrew Passover: From the Earliest Times to A.D. 70* (London: Oxford University Press, 1963), chap. 3; Tamar Prosic, *The Development and Symbolism of Passover Until 70 CE* (London: T&T Clark International, 2004). Prosic argues for a unitary development of the festival and offers rebuttals for each claim used to justify the "fusion" hypothesis. Prosic goes on to claim that the festival originated in post-exilic times. For a fascinating theory that dates these developments several centuries earlier than Josiah, see Bernard R. Goldstein and Alan Cooper, "The Festivals of Israel and Judah and the Literary History of the Pentateuch," *Journal of the American Oriental Society* 110, no. 1 (1990); Alan Cooper and Bernard R. Goldstein, "Exodus and *Massot* in History and Tradition," *Maarav* 8 (1992). The Cooper/Goldstein thesis has been challenged by Bernard M. Levinson's *Deuteronomy and the Hermeneutics of Legal Innovation* (New York: Oxford University Press, 1997), p. 71.

9. Archeologists doubt that the Assyrian exile of residents from the Northern Kingdom was complete. The Bible supports the archeological evidence. In 2 Chronicles 30:1, Hezekiah,

king of Judah, "sent word to all Israel and Judah" to celebrate Passover in Jerusalem. Writing nearly a century and a half after the destruction of the Northern Kingdom, Jeremiah (41:5) notes that men came from a number of its cities to mourn the decimated Temple.

10. Levinson, *Deuteronomy and the Hermeneutics of Legal Innovation*, p. 74. Levinson also illustrates Deuteronomy's transformation of the celebration of *matzot*: no longer a pilgrimage festival in its own right as in former times, pilgrims who had come to Jerusalem for the Passover sacrifice returned home for a "solemn gathering" on the seventh day of the holiday (Deut. 16:8).

11. For a discussion about who in practice participated in these pilgrimages, see Menahem Haran, *Temples and Temple Service in Ancient Israel* (Oxford: Clarendon Press, 1978), pp. 293, 300–301.

12. Segal, *Hebrew Passover*.

13. Prosic, *Development and Symbolism of Passover*, p. 54.

14. Even with respect to those biblical sources that fix the date near the middle of the month, the precise relationship in ancient times between Passover and the full moon remains a question. See J. W. McKay, "The Date of Passover and Its Significance," *Zeitschrift für die Alttestamentliche Wissenschaft*, 84 (1972); and Jan A. Wagenaar, "Passover and the First Day of the Festival of Unleavened Bread in the Priestly Calendar," *Vetus Testamentum* 64, no. 2 (2004).

15. Engnell, "*Paesah-Massot* and the Problem of 'Patternism.'"

16. Segal, *Hebrew Passover*.

17. J. G. Frazer, *The Golden Bough: Adonis, Attis, Osiris* (London: Macmillan, 1951), vol. 4, pt. 1, pp. 272–75.

PASSOVER FOR THE EARLY RABBIS: FIXED AND FREE

1. "Songs of praise" refers to the *Hallel*.

2. Baruch M. Bokser, *The Origins of the Seder* (New York: Jewish Theological Seminary of America, 2002). Originally published in 1984.

3. Judith Hauptman, "How Old Is the Haggadah?" *Judaism* 51, no. 1 (Winter 2002): 6. Hauptman argues that rather than being a commentary on the Mishnah—as is usually thought—the core of the Tosefta is an earlier code that the compiler of the Mishnah reworked. See also Hauptman's "Does the Tosefta Precede the Mishnah?: Halakhah, Aggada and Narrative Coherence," *Judaism* 50, no. 2 (Spring 2001): 224–39. For Hauptman's complete treatment of this question, see her *Rereading the Mishnah* (Tubingen: Mohr Siebeck, 2005).

4. The elements of the Mishnah's Seder also follow a slightly different order, and it lacks both the Tosefta's specificity concerning the *Hallel* and the worry about sleepy children.

5. For example, Deuteronomy 6:20 states, "When, in time to come, your children ask...." But here the context has nothing to do with the celebration of Passover. It pertains to the meaning of a host of injunctions including the *Sh'ma*. Exodus 12:26 mandates an explanation of the paschal sacrifice, but only if children ask what it means. Likewise, Exodus 13:14 requires an explanation for the ritual of redeeming the first-born males—connected to God's having slain the Egyptian first-born—but again, only if the child asks. Exodus 13:8 is the only of the four familiar verses that specifies an *unsolicited* explanation of the festival. Here the response seems almost formulaic: "It is because of what Adonai did for me when I went out of Egypt." After saying this, the Torah immediately goes on to explain the rationale for phylacteries.

6. Siegfried Stein, "The Influence of Symposia Literature on the Literary Form of the Pesah Haggadah," *Journal of Jewish Studies* 8 (1957): 1–2.

7. Plutarch, *Symposiacs*, book I, question I.

8. See for example, Jay Rovner, "Two Early Witnesses to the Formation of the Miqra Bikurim Midrash and Their Implications for the Evolution of the Haggadah Text," *Hebrew Union College Annual* 75 (2004).

9. See, for example, Lawrence A. Hoffman, *Beyond the Text: A Holistic Approach to Liturgy* (Indiana University Press: Bloomington, 1987), chap. 4.

10. *Sifre Zuta on Deuteronomy: Citations from a New Tannaitic Midrash* (Jerusalem: Hebrew University Magnes Press, 2005), p. 418. See Joshua Kulp, *The Historical Haggadah*, rev. ed. (Jerusalem: Schecter Institute of Jewish Studies, forthcoming).

THIS BREAD: CHRISTIANITY AND THE SEDER

1. This talmudic discussion and the midrash above are discussed by Eugene Mihaly, "The Passover Haggadah as PaRaDiSe," *CCAR Journal* 13 (April 1960): p. 26.

2. Cf. *Didache*, chap. 8; Jerome, *Commentary on Matthew*, 6:11; Ambrose, *Sacraments* 4:5.

3. Eric Werner, "Melito of Sardis, the First Poet of Deicide," *Hebrew Union College Annual* 37 (1966): 192, 193.

THE SEDER PLATE: THE WORLD ON A DISH

1. Bava Batra 16a, said in relation to Job.

2. See Menachem Kasher's *Haggadah Shlemah* (Torah Shlemah Institute: Jerusalem, 1967), pp. 61–67, for a classic compilation on the Seder plate. See also Heinrich Guggenheimer, *The Scholar's Haggadah* (Northvale, NJ: Jason Aronson, 1995), pp. 200–204; and Joshua Kulp, *The Historical Haggadah*, rev. ed. (Jerusalem: Schechter Institute of Jewish Studies, forthcoming).

3. Blake Layerle, "Meal Customs in the Greco-Roman World," p. 47, n. 7, in *Passover and Easter: Origin and History to Modern Times*, ed. Paul F. Bradshaw and Lawrence A. Hoffman (Notre Dame: University of Notre Dame Press, 1999). For a description of Jewish meal customs, see Ber. 46b.

4. Joseph Tabory ("The Household Table in Rabbinic Palestine," *AJS Review* 4 [1979]) notes that specific references to tables or trays in this context appear in Babylonian rather than Palestinian sources, and he cautions against inferring their use at meals in the Land of Israel. It might just as well be the case that these items were so common as not to require mention.

5. The same lack of awareness of the meal customs in the Mishnaic era gave rise to the explanation in the talmudic period that the Seder's two rounds of dippings (first the *karpas* and later the bitter herbs in *charoset*) were designed to prompt the curiosity of children (Pes. 116a).

6. The reference to "two cooked dishes" may be a later addition, since although it appears in the standard or Vilna edition of the Mishnah, the Kaufmann manuscript of the Mishnah does not mention it (see *My People's Passover Haggadah*, Volume 2, Appendix I, p. 226 [10:3]).

7. See *Rashbam*, Pesachim 114b, on "and one as a remembrance."

8. *Seder Olam Rabbah*, chap. 5, a third- or fourth-century midrash.

9. Maimonides, *Hilkhot Chamets U'Matzah* 8:6; Vilna Gaon's commentary on the *Shulchan Arukh, Biur HaGra, Orach Chayim* 473:4.

10. *Orach Chayim* 473:4.

11. These are the definitions according to Marcus Jastrow, *Dictionary of the Targumim, Talmud Babli, Yerushalmi and Midrashic Literature* (New York: Judaica Press, 1996). Herbert Danby identifies these last four as chicory, pepperwort, snakeroot, and dandelion. See Danby's *The Mishnah* (London: Oxford University Press, 1933), p. 138.

12. *Mekhilta D'rabbi Shimon bar Yochai* (Philadelphia: Jewish Publication Society, 2006, translated by W. David Nelson), Pischa 8:3:7, p. 22.

13. See David Feinstein, *Kol Dodi: Laws of the Seder* (Brooklyn: Mesorah Publications, 2000), p. 65.

14. *Lamentations Rabbah* (Prologue: 18) comments on a verse from Lamentations, "He has filled me with *merurim* [bitterness]; sated me with wormwood [a bitter tasting plant]" (3:15): "Rabbi Avin [fourth century] opened his discourse with the text, 'He has filled me with *merurim* [bitterness]' (Lam. 3:15): On the first nights of the Passover festival [because of the requirement to eat bitter herbs]. '[He] has sated me with wormwood' (Lam. 3:15): On the ninth of Av. What He filled me with on the first nights of Passover, therewith He sated me on the nights of the ninth of Av [i.e., wormwood]."

15. *R'ma* to *Orach Chayim* 473:5.

16. Baruch M. Bokser, "Ritualizing the Seder," *Journal of the American Academy of Religion* 56, no. 3 (1988): 446.

17. Jastrow defines *karpas* as an umbelliferous plant, i.e., without a woody stem and with seed pods resembling an umbrella. The word *karpas* appears in Esther (1:6), but there it means a "white cotton" fabric.

18. *Siddur R. Saadja Gaon*, ed. I. Davidson et al. (Jerusalem: Rubin Mass., 2000), p. 136. For Rav Amram's list, see *My People's Passover Haggadah*, Volume 1, Arnow, "Eating Greens," p. 119.

19. Yosef Tabory, *The Passover Ritual Throughout the Generations* (Israel: Hakibbutz Hameuchad Publishing House, 1996), p. 263. See, for example, the *Machzor Vitry*, late eleventh century, pp. 280–81), which includes an early instance of these fifteen terms used to identify parts of the Seder, although they are not yet gathered as a discrete list.

20. Pes. 108b.

21. *Seder Pesach*, section 318.

22. For example, the American Anti-Slavery Group.

23. *The Women's Seder Sourcebook*, ed. Sharon Cohen Anisfeld, Tara Mohr, and Catherine Spector (Woodstock, VT: Jewish Lights Publishing, 2003), pp. 208–12. The practice had originally been to put a crust of bread on the Seder plate! See Rebecca Alpert, *Like Bread on the Seder Plate* (New York: Columbia University Press, 1997), pp.1–3.

24. It is now common to find Seder plates decorated with the Star of David. While this practice has long been said to derive from the *Ari*, as Gershom Scholem demonstrates, this attribution is utterly groundless. The presence of the Star of David on the Seder plate dates to the nineteenth century, when it became popularized as a Jewish symbol and began regularly appearing on ceremonial objects. See Gershom Scholem, "The Star of David: History of a Symbol," in *The Messianic Idea in Judaism* (New York: Schocken Books, 1995).

25. *R'ma*—Rabbi Moses Isserles (which begins with an *alef* in Hebrew); *Ari*—Elohi ("godly," which begins with an *alef*), Rabbi Isaac; *Gra*—Gaon, Rabbi Elijah (which begins with an *alef*).

26. The most commonly cited source for this is Yoma 33b, which deals with the order in which one puts on and removes phylacteries, *t'fillin*. Pes. 64b may be more relevant in that it applies the same concept to explaining certain technical practices associated with the paschal sacrifice. Hoffman demonstrates that many of the Talmud's legal requirements involving this sacrifice were later applied to matzah, allowing unleavened bread to become a symbolic substitute for the missing sacrifice. Applying a rule connected with the sacrifice to the arrangement of the Seder plate, although a much later development, was an entirely natural development. See Lawrence A. Hoffman, "A Symbol of Salvation in the Passover Seder," in *Passover and Easter: The Symbolic Structuring of Sacred Seasons*, ed. Paul F. Bradshaw and Lawrence A. Hoffman (Notre Dame: University of Notre Dame Press, 1999), p. 114.

27. *Mishnah Berurah* 473:26.

28. For an interesting anthropological discussion of the *Ari*'s arrangement see Ruth Gruber Fredman, *The Passover Seder* (New York: New American Library, 1983), pp. 129–148.

29. The force of this concern seems to have diminished. The *Mishnah Berurah* (473:26) comments that "it may be that with respect to the *maror* and the *charoset* ... the prohibition that one must not pass over *mitzvot* is not relevant."

30. Hayim Vital, *Sidrat Kitve Rabenu ha-Ari* (Jerusalem: Yeshivat Kol Yehuda, 1987), vol. 17, "Pri Etz Hayim," part 2, p. 504. *Ba'er Hetev, Orach Chayim* 473:8.

31. *Zohar* I, 85b–86a.

32. *Numbers Rabbah* 13:14.

PEOPLEHOOD WITH PURPOSE

1. For a summary of standard reasons given, see Arnold M. Eisen, *Rethinking Modern Judaism* (Chicago: University of Chicago Press, 1998), p. 247.

2. The four-stage approach to Jewish history came originally from the great pioneer Jewish historian Simon Dubnow. The specific English words used came from my teacher, in rabbinic school, Martin A. Cohen.

3. *The Union Haggadah: Home Service for Passover Eve* (Cincinnati: Bloch Publishing, 1908). It was revised in 1923 but retained its "religious" perspective.

4. *A Passover Haggadah* (New York: Central Conference of American Rabbis, 1974).

5. *Passover Haggadah: The Feast of Freedom* (New York: The Rabbinical Assembly, 1982).

6. Jonathan S. Woocher, *Sacred Survival: The Civil Religion of American Jews* (Bloomington: Indiana University Press, 1986).

7. Mordecai Kaplan, *Judaism as a Civilization* (New York: Macmillan, 1934), p. 180.

8. Ibid, p. 84.

9. The story is told in Eric Caplan, *From Ideology to Liturgy* (Cincinnati: Hebrew Union College Press, 2002), pp. 48–50.

10. Kaplan, *Judaism as a Civilization*, pp. 120, 125.

11. Ibid, p. 132.

12. See Steven M. Cohen and Arnold Eisen, *The Jew Within: Self, Family, and Community in America* (Bloomington: Indiana University Press, 2000), pp. 24, 97.

13. Hilary Putnam, *The Collapse of the Fact/Value Dichotomy and Other Essays* (Cambridge: Harvard University Press, 2002).

14. Clifford Geertz, *Local Knowledge* (New York: Basic Books, 1983), p. 20.

15. Ludwig Wittgenstein, *Tractatus Logico-Philosophicus*, trans. D. F. Pears and B. F. McGuinness (London: Routledge Classics, 2001 [original German, 1921]), 6:54, p. 89.

WHERE HAVE ALL THE WOMEN GONE? FEMINIST QUESTIONS ABOUT THE HAGGADAH

1. See E. M. Broner and Naomi Nimrod, "A Women's Passover Haggadah and Other Revisionist Rituals," *Ms.* vol. 5, no. 10 (April 1977): 53–56.

2. From email correspondence with Phyllis Chesler, June 26–27, 2007.

3. E. M. Broner and Naomi Nimrod, *The Women's Haggadah* (San Francisco: HarperSanFrancisco, 1994), pp. 1, 7.

4. Aviva Cantor Zuckoff, "Jewish Women's Haggadah," in *Sister Celebrations: Nine Worship Experiences*, ed. Arlene Swidler (Philadelphia: Fortress Press, 1974). See also Aviva Cantor, "An Egalitarian Haggadah," *Lilith* 9 (Spring/Summer 1982/5742): 9–24.

5. Michael Walzer, *Exodus and Revolution* (New York: Basic Books, 1986), p. 12.

6. Elizabeth Schussler Fiorenza, *In Memory of Her: Feminist Theological Reconstruction of Christian Origins* (New York: Crossroad Publishing Company, 1983), p. 28.

7. Sandy Eisenberg Sasso, "How Was This Different from All Other Passovers?" ed. Reena Friedman, *Lilith* 1, no. 3 (Spring/Summer 1977), p. 35.

8. Aviva Cantor Zuckoff, "Jewish Women's Haggadah," in *Sister Celebrations: Nine Worship Experiences*, ed. Arlene Swidler (Philadelphia: Fortress Press, 1974), p. 81.

9. See, for example, Fiorenza, *In Memory of Her*; Ilana Pardes, *Countertraditions in the Bible* (Cambridge, MA: Harvard University Press, 1992); Alicia Ostriker, *Feminist Revision and the Bible* (Oxford: Blackwell, 1993).

10. Jacqueline E. Lapsley, *Whispering the Word: Hearing Women's Stories in the Old Testament* (Louisville, KY: Westminster John Knox Press, 2005), p. 7.

11. Judith Plaskow, *Standing Again at Sinai* (New York: HarperSanFrancisco, 1991), p. xv.

12. This expression comes from the title of an influential work of feminist theory. See Judith Butler, *Gender Trouble: Feminism and the Subversion of Identity* (New York: Routledge, 1990).

13. For an early example of this trend in women's Haggadot, see Broner and Nimrod, "A Women's Passover Haggadah and Other Revisionist Rituals," p. 55.

14. See, for example, Ostriker, *Feminist Revision and the Bible*, p. 49; see also J. Cheryl Exum, *Fragmented Women* (Sheffield: Continuum, 1993), p. 97.

15. Tal Ilan, *Integrating Women into Second Temple History* (Tübingen: Mohr Sieback, 1999), pp. 11–42.

16. Judith Hauptman, *Rereading the Mishnah* (Tübingen: Mohr Sieback, 2005), pp. 50–63, 125–142.

17. Rachel Adler, *Engendering Judaism* (Philadelphia: Jewish Publication Society, 1998), p. 11.

18. Cynthia Baker, *Rebuilding the House of Israel: Architectures of Gender in Jewish Antiquity* (Palo Alto: Stanford University Press, 2002), p. 147.

19. Ibid, p. 41.

20. Ibid, pp. 59, 63.

MOVING THROUGH THE MOVEMENTS: AMERICAN DENOMINATIONS AND THEIR HAGGADOT

1. In his monumental bibliography of the Haggadah, *Bibliografiah shel Haggadot Pesah mi-reshit ha-Defus ve-ad ha-Yom* [Bibliography of the Passover Haggadah: From the Earliest Printed Edition to 1960 (Jerusalem: Bamberger & Wahrman), 1960], Abraham Yaari delineates 25 Haggadot printed in the sixteenth century, 37 in the seventeenth century, 234 in the eighteenth century, 1,269 in the nineteenth century, and over 1,100 in the first 60 years of the twentieth century.

2. Yosef Hayim Yerushalmi, *Haggadah and History: A Panorama in Facsimile of Five Centuries of the Printed Haggadah from the Collections of Harvard University and the Jewish Theological Seminary of America* (Philadelphia: Jewish Publication Society, 1975), p. 24.

3. Thanks to Stephen P. Durchslag for use of his magisterial private collection of Haggadot. I am grateful as well to Daniel J. Rettberg of the Klau Library of Hebrew Union College–Jewish Institute of Religion (HUC-JIR) in Cincinnati and the librarians at the library at the Jewish Theological Seminary and at HUC-JIR in New York, especially Tina Weiss.

4. As quoted in Michael A. Meyer, *Response to Modernity* (New York: Oxford University Press, 1988), p. 174.

5. Note the use of the standard Sefardi title of the Haggadah *(Haggadah Lepesach)* rather than the Ashkenazi version *(Haggadah shel Pesach)*.

6. Jakob J. Petuchowski, "Karaite Tendencies in an Early Reform Haggadah," *HUC Annual* 31 (1960): 223–249.

7. For more on illustrations, see my commentary on the four sons devoted exclusively to this topic.

8. Thanks to Professor Eric Friedland for offering this information along with other crucial suggestions. I am grateful as well to Professor David Ellenson for his guidance, along with David Arnow and Larry Hoffman.

9. Ari Goldman, obituary, *New York Times*, November 30, 1991.

10. Edited by Rachel Anne Rabinowicz, with illustrations by Dan Reisinger.

11. The Strassfeld Haggadah appears in *Conservative Judaism* (Spring 1979).

12. Beginning in the late twentieth century, any number of Modern Orthodox Jews have taken up the pen to compile Haggadot of all sorts, including Rabbi Shlomo Riskin, who was instrumental in bringing about a revival in Modern Orthodoxy in the United States and more recently in Israel (*The Passover Haggadah*, 1983), and a group of Yeshivah University students (*The Yeshivah University Haggadah*, 1985).

"GOOD TO THE LAST DROP": THE PROLIFERATION OF THE MAXWELL HOUSE HAGGADAH

1. Yosef Hayim Yerushalmi, *Haggadah and History* (Philadelphia: Jewish Publication Society, 1975), plate 59.

1. PREPARING THE HOME

Carole B. Balin

1. Courtesy of the Jewish Historical Society of the Upper Midwest, on www.ajlegacy.org.

Alyssa Gray

1. *Ran* on Alfasi to Pes. 3a in *Rif*'s pages, s.v. *"amar."*
2. *Chiddushei Ha-Ramban* to Pes. 4b.
3. *Hagahot Maimuniyot* to Laws of *Chamets* and Matzah 3:7, n. 7.

Wendy I. Zierler

1. Jacqueline E. Lapsley, *Whispering the Word* (Louisville, KY: Westminster John Knox Press, 2005), p. 83.
2. See Yael Katz Levine, "Where Is Miriam on the Seder Plate?" *Edah Journal*, http://www.edah.org/levine.cfm. See also Yael Levine Katz, "Placing a Cooked Food on the Seder Table in Commemoration of Miriam," in *All the Women Followed Her: A Collection of Writings on Miriam the Prophet and the Women on Exodus*, ed. Rebecca Schwartz (Mountain View, CA: Rikudei Miriam Press, 2001).
3. Susannah Heschel, "A Woman's Idea," in *The Women's Seder Sourcebook*, ed. Sharon Cohen Anisfeld, Tara Mohr, and Catherine Spector (Woodstock, VT: Jewish Lights Publishing, 2003), pp. 209–210.

2. THE ORDER OF THE SEDER: KADESH URCHATS ...

Wendy I. Zierler

1. Michael Walzer, *Exodus and Revolution* (New York: Basic Books, 1986), p. 12.
2. Julia Kristeva, "Oscillation between Power and Denial," in *New French Feminisms,* ed. Elaine Marks and Isabelle de Courtivron (New York: Schocken, 1980), p. 165.

3. BEGINNING THE SEDER

David Arnow

1. *Mekhilta de-Rabbi Shimon bar Yohai*, trans. by W. David Nelson (Philadelphia: Jewish Publication Society, 2006), p. 218 (on Exod. 19:5).
2. Daniel Goldschmidt, *Seder Amram Gaon* (Jerusalem: Mossad ha-Kook, 1971), p. 81; ninth century, but possibly "updated" by later copyists.

Carole B. Balin

1. Translation by Yosef Hayim Yerushalmi, *Haggadah and History* (Philadelphia: Jewish Publication Society, 1975), plate 144.
2. Moderchai M. Kaplan, Eugene Korn, and Ira Eisenstein, eds. *New Haggadah for the Pesach Seder* (for the Jewish Reconstructionist Foundation); Leonard Weisgard, illus. (New York: Behrman House, 1941).
3. *The Jewish Messenger*, New York, June 6, 1884, p. 3.

Neil Gillman

1. For an extended defense of this thesis, see the seminal monograph "Religion as a Cultural System" by Clifford Geertz in his anthology, *The Interpretation of Cultures* (New York: Basic Books, 1973).
2. On the Safed kabbalists and their beliefs, see Gershom Scholem, *Major Trends in Jewish Mysticism* (New York: Schocken Books, 1954), chap.7.

Alyssa Gray

1. *Sefer Ravyah*, pt. 2, Pes. 525.
2. *Shibbolei Haleket*, Seder Pesach 218.

Lawrence Hoffman

1. The Rosh Hashanah parallel is *Barukh … m'kadesh yisra'el v'yom hazikaron* ("Blessed … who sanctifies Israel and the day of remembrance").

Wendy I. Zierler

1. See http://www.ritualwell.org/holidays/passover/partsoftheseder/kadeshfourcups/primaryobject.2005-06-15.3466931087/view?searchterm=four%20cups.
2. *A Journey Towards Freedom: A Haggadah for Women Who Have Experienced Domestic Violence* (Seattle: Faith Trust Institute, 2003), p. 7.
3. See for example, *The School Haggadah*, trans. Saadyah Maximon (New York: Shulsinger Brothers, 1958), p. 7. See the Passover Haggadah included on chabad.org, http://www.chabad.org/holidays/passover/pesach.asp?AID=1737, which reads: "This is the bread of affliction that our fathers ate in the Land of Egypt."
4. Pauline Wengeroff, *Rememberings*, trans. Henny Wenkart (College Park: University Press of Maryland, 2000), p. 42.
5. Celine Mizrahi, "On Women and Poverty," in *The Women's Seder Sourcebook*, ed. Sharon Cohen Anisfeld, Tara Mohr, and Catherine Spector (Woodstock, VT: Jewish Lights Publishing, 2003), p. 192.

4. Questions of the Night: *Mah Nishtanah*, "Why Is This Night Different?"

David Arnow

1. Nechama Leibowitz, *Studies on the Haggadah: From the Teachings of Nechama Leibowitz*, ed. Yitshak Reiner and Shmuel Peerless (Brooklyn: Lambda Publishers, 2002), p. 29.
2. Paul echoed this approach. "Your boasting is not good. Do you not know that a little leaven leavens the whole lump *of dough?* Clean out the old leaven so that you may be a new lump … let us celebrate the feast, not with old leaven, nor with the leaven of malice and wickedness, but with the unleavened bread of sincerity and truth" (1 Corinthians 5:6–8).

Carole B. Balin

1. Translation by Yerushalmi, *Haggadah and History*, plate 116. The parody was reissued in 1886 with opening accolades by important *maskilim*, including Y. L. Gordon and Moses Leib Lilienblum.
2. Arthur I. Waskow, *The Freedom Seder: A New Haggadah for Passover*. Lloyd McNeil, illus. (Washington, Micah Press, 1969).
3. Elsie Levitan, Max Rosenfeld, Bess Katz, eds. *Haggadah for a Secular Celebration of Pesach*. Ruthie Rosenfeld, illus. (Philadelphia: Sholom Aleichem Club of Philadelphia, 1982).

Alyssa Gray

1. *Rashbam* to Pes. 115b, s.v. *"patratan m'lomar mah nishtanah."*
2. *Rashbam* to Pes. 99b, s.v. *"afilu ani sh'b'Yisrael lo yokhal."*
3. *Rashbam* to Pes. 108a, s.v. *"ishah einah tzerikhah heseibah."*

Wendy I. Zierler

1. Elaine Moise and Rebecca Schwartz, *The Dancing with Miriam Haggadah,* 3rd ed. (Palo Alto, CA: Rikudei Miriam Press, 1999), p. 10.
2. Hava Shapiro, "Leilei Pesach," *Ha'olam* 13:14–15 (April 3, 1925): 283.

3. Blake Leyerle, "Meal Customs in the Greco-Roman World," in *Passover and Easter: The Origin and History to Modern Times*, ed. Paul F. Bradshaw and Lawrence H. Hoffman (Notre Dame, IN: University of Notre Dame Press, 1999), p. 31.

4. Leah Shakdiel, "We Can't Be Free Until All Women Are Important," in *The Women's Passover Companion*, ed. Sharon Cohen Anisfeld, Tara Mohr, and Catherine Spector (Woodstock, VT: Jewish Lights Publishing, 2003), p. 55.

5. A SHORT ANSWER: ENSLAVEMENT IS PHYSICAL

David Arnow

1. A. Jellinek, *Bet HaMidrasch* (Jerusalem: Sifre Wahrmann, 1967), vol. 6, p. 38.

Carole B. Balin

1. Saul Touster, ed., *A Survivors' Haggadah* (Philadelphia: Jewish Publication Society, 2000), pp. 8, 10, 12; originally published in Munich, 1946, and printed by the U.S. Army of Occupation.

Alyssa Gray

1. Rabbenu Hananel to Pes. 116a and *Rif* to Pes., p. 25b in *Rif*'s pages.

2. The mixed multitude had no covenantal investment in their exodus, and the talmudic Rabbis tended to see them as instigators of various post-Exodus Israelite sins.

Wendy I. Zierler

1. William Cutter and Yaffa Weisman, "והיינו כולנו שם," *We Were All There: A Feminist Passover Haggadah* (Los Angeles: American Jewish Congress Feminist Center, 1996.

6. HOW WE TELL THE TALE

David Arnow

1. See Exod. 1:7, Ezek. 16:7, and Exod. 1:10.

2. There is little to support the popular notion that the Sages had gathered in a dark cave—hence their unawareness of sunrise—to plan the Bar Kokhba rebellion. Rabbis Eliezer, Joshua, and Elazar ben Azariah are thought to have died before the rebellion, and modern scholarship now questions the support Bar Kokhba received from the Rabbis. See, for example, Peter Schäfer "Bar Kokhba and the Rabbis," in *The Bar Kokhba War Reconsidered: New Perspectives on the Second Jewish Revolt Against Rome* (Tübingen: Mohr Siebeck, 2003).

3. Ber. 27b–28a.

4. Jacob Z. Lauterbach, *Mekilta de-Rabbi Ishmael* (Philadelphia: Jewish Publication Society, 1933), Beshalach 7:150, vol. 1, p. 254 (hereafter "*Mekhilta*" in the text and *MRI* in notes).

5. Tanna D'vei Eliyahu (*Eliyahu Rabbah*, 155).

6. In *Num. Rabbah* 11:2 a similar midrash explains the basis of the Priestly Blessing.

7. PT *Pesachim* 70a, 10:37:d.

8. Gordon Tucker, "Sacrifices," in *Etz Hayim* (Philadelphia: Rabbinical Assembly and United Synagogue of Conservative Judaism, 2001), p. 1447.

Carole B. Balin

1. A copy of the Prague Haggadah is at Klau Library, Hebrew Union College–Jewish Institute of Religion (HUC-JIR), Cincinnati, and the Library of the Jewish Theological Seminary of America. Its illustrations are ubiquitous on the Web. The first four illustrations are downloadable at Jewish Heritage Online Magazine, www.jhom.com, © 2005. See also www.haggadahsrus.com, a Web site containing excerpts from *A Different Night: The Family Participation Haggadah* by Noam Zion and David Dishon (Jerusalem: Shalom Hartman Institute, 1997), which contains an essay dedicated to illustrations of the four children.

2. Yosef Hayim Yerushalmi, *Haggadah and History* (Philadelphia: Jewish Publication Society, 1975), plate 11.

3. *Seder Hagadah shel Pesach im shnei perushim hadashim: Hatam Sofer v'Hatan Sofer* [Order of the Passover Seder with two new commentaries: Hatam Sofer and Hatan Sofer] (Vienna: Joseph Schlesinger, 1884), p. 22ff. I'm grateful to Professor Wendy Zierler for pointing out the use of the *rasha* as a modern-day villain among commentators. See Zierler's "Four Sons of the Holocaust: Leah Goldberg's 'Keneged arba'ah banim,'" *Shofar* 23, no. 2 (Winter 2005): 34–46.

4. Responsa H. Sofer 6:#89 as cited by Jacob Katz in "The Controversy over the Temple in Hamburg," in *Divine Law in Human Hands: Case Studies in Halakhic Flexibility* (Jerusalem: Magnes Press, 1998), p. 225, as explained in David Ellenson, *After Emacipation: Jewish Religious Responses to Modernity* (Cincinnati: HUC Press, 2004), pp. 67–68.

5. Rev. H[ayim] Lieberman, *Services for the Two First Nights of the Feast of Passover with New Illustrations* (Chicago: No publisher given, 1883); note that the Hebrew title for this Haggadah is *Seder Haggadah Lepesach. Im tziurim hadashim maskimim leda'at hachmenu z'l* [Order of Haggadah for Passover. With new illustrations in agreement with the opinion of our sages of blessed memory]. The latter strikes a defensive tone, suggesting, perhaps, that the editor realized the innovative and likely shocking nature of the illustrations herein and felt it necessary to buttress his choices with approbation from the rabbis of old. This Haggadah is found at the library of HUC-JIR, New York, and in the Durchslag collection.

6. David Mamet, *The Wicked Son: Anti-Semitism, Self-Hatred, and the Jews* (New York: Schocken, 2006).

7. This Haggadah, translated by the renowned Hebrew poet Abraham Regelson (1896–1981) and illustrated by the celebrated artist Nota Koslowsky (b. 1906, Poland) is in the Durchslag Collection.

8. Ber Borochov, *Ketavim*, vol. 3, eds., L. Levite and Sh. Rekhav (Tel Aviv: Hakibbutz Hameuchad, 1966), pp. 333–34.

9. See the comprehensive work by Avshalom Reich, "Changes and Developments in the Passover Haggadot of the Kibbutz Movement: 1935–1971" (Ph.D. dissertation, University of Texas at Austin, 1972).

10. This interpretation of the simple son is included in Zion and Dishon's *A Different Night*.

11. From *The Open Door: A Passover Haggadah,* ed. Sue Levi Elwell (New York: Central Conference of American Rabbis, 2002), pp. 38–39. Many thanks to illustrator Ruth Weisberg for allowing this image to be reproduced here and for sharing generously her insights on the process of creating visual midrashim.

12. Ruth Weisberg primarily works in painting, drawing, and printmaking. She is dean of the Roski School of Fine Arts at USC and the illustrator of *The Open Door: A Passover Haggadah*, ed. Sue Levi Elwell (New York: Central Conference of American Rabbis, 2002).

13. In speaking with the artist, I learned that she did not intend for the genders of these children to be in question. Rather, she felt strongly that they were to be represented as children (not sons alone) and of varying ages. In fact, the artist collaborated with the four children who acted as models for this illustration. The older three children were asked to act out the four attributes of the text, and then the artist picked the model based on which attribute she/he portrayed best (in that moment). Weisberg felt strongly that no child was to be "cast" as wicked. "We all have these characteristics," she explained, "children and adults alike." In fact, Weisberg's wise child is based on a girl, as is the One Who Does Not Know How to Ask; the others are based on boys.

14. In contrast to my interpretation, Weisberg explained that the "wicked child" is pushing away the traditions.

Lawrence Hoffman

1. Shmuel Safrai and Ze'ev Safrai, *Haggadah Shel Pesach: Haggadat Chazal* (Jerusalem: Karta, 1998), p. 44.

2. Walter Hamilton, trans., *Plato: The Symposium* (New York: Penguin, 1951), pp. 38–40.

Lawrence Kushner and Nehemia Polen

1. Based on Martin Buber, *Or Haganuz* (Jerusalem and Tel Aviv: Schocken, 1979), pp. 203–4 (Hebrew).

2. Kalonymos Kalmish Shapiro, *Esh Kodesh* (Jerusalem: Va'ad haside Pi'asetsnah, 1960), pp. 94–95.

Wendy I. Zierler

1. Tal Ilan, *Jewish Women in Greco-Roman Palestine* (Tübingen: J.C.B. Mohr, 1995), pp. 32, 33, 204.

2. Sarah Pomeroy, *Goddesses, Whores, Wives, and Slaves: Women in Classical Antiquity* (New York: Schocken Books, 1975), p. 150.

3. Judith Plaskow, "The Continuing Value of Separatism," in *The Women's Passover Companion* (Woodstock, VT: Jewish Lights, 2003), pp. 10–11.

4. Rachel Adler, *Engendering Judaism* (Philadelphia: Jewish Publication Society, 1998), p. 7.

5. Sue Levi Elwell, ed., *The Open Door: A Passover Haggadah* (New York: Central Conference of American Rabbis, 2002), p. 37.

6. Daniel Boyarin, *Unheroic Conduct* (Berkeley: University of California Press, 1997), pp. 51–52.

7. A Short Answer: Enslavement Is Spiritual

David Arnow

1. Although today's printed versions of Talmud regularly feature Shmuel and Rav in this debate, earlier manuscripts include a variety of different sages and very few include Shmuel.

2. The translation of the last two biblical verses follows *The Jerusalem Bible* (Jerusalem: Koren, 1986).

3. Gerald Friedlander, *Pirke De Rabbi Eliezer* (New York: Sepher-Hermon Press, 1981), pp. 236–37. The midrash builds on the fact that we recite the prayer for dew on the first day of Passover and on the centrality of dew in the blessings Isaac gave his sons. Of course, the story of Jacob and Esau precedes the Passover story by centuries, but the midrash remains unconstrained by the limits of linear time.

Neil Gillman

1. Maimonides, "*Helek*: Sanhedrin, Chapter Ten," in *A Maimonides Reader*, ed. Isadore Twersky (New York: Berhman House, 1972), p. 422.

2. The ensuing tension is explored in a masterful essay, "The Messianic Idea in Judaism," by the eminent scholar Gershom Scholem, included in a volume of the same name (New York: Schocken, 1971).

8. Promises—Past and Present

David Arnow

1. This midrash amplifies on Ps. 78:9–10: "Like the Ephraimite bowmen who played false in the day of battle, they did not heed God's covenant, they refused to follow his instruction...."

2. *MRI*, Pischa 14:78–84, vol. 1, pp. 112–13.

3. Robert Alter translation (*The Five Books of Moses* [New York: W.W. Norton, 2004]).

4. H. G. Enelow, *Mishnah of Rabbi Eliezer* (New York: Bloch Publishing, 1933), chap. 16, p. 301.

5. Personal communication.

6. *Seder Olam Rabbah* chapter 3 arrives at the figure of 210 years for the sojourn in Egypt. It assumes that the 400 years mentioned in Genesis began from the birth of Isaac. Isaac was 60 years old when Jacob was born (Gen. 25:26) and Jacob says (Gen. 47:9) that he was 130 when he arrived in Egypt: 400 − (60 + 130) = 210.

7. *MRI*, Shirata 8:19–25, vol. 2, pp. 60–61.

Neil Gillman

1. Richard Rubenstein, in *The Condition of Jewish Belief*, compiled by the editors of *Commentary Magazine* (Northvale, NJ: Jason Aronson, 1989), p. 199.

2. Irving Greenberg, "Cloud of Smoke, Pillar of Fire: Judaism, Christianity and Modernity after the Holocaust," in *Auschwitz: Beginning of a New Era?* Ed. Eva Fleishner (New York: Ktav, 1977), pp. 26–27.

Alyssa Gray

1. *Ramban* on Exod. 12:40, 12:42.

Wendy I. Zierler

1. E. M. Broner, *The Telling* (New York: HarperCollins, 1993), p. 21.

List of Abbreviations

A. Z.	Avodah Zarah	Isa.	Isaiah
Arakh.	Arakhin	Jer.	Jeremiah
B. B.	Bava Batra	Josh.	Joshua
B. K.	Bava Kama	Ket.	Ketubot
B. M.	Bava Metsia	Kid.	Kiddushin
Ber.	Berakhot	Lev.	Leviticus
BT	Babylonian Talmud, Bavli	M.	Mishnah
Chron.	Chronicles	M. K.	Moed Katan
Chul.	Chullin	Mal.	Malachi
Dan.	Daniel	Meg.	Megillah
Deut.	Deuteronomy	Men.	Menachot
Eccl.	Ecclesiastes	Mid.	Middot
Eduy.	Eduyot	MRI	Mekhilta de-Rabbi Ishmael
Eruv.	Eruvin	MRSBY	Mekhilta de-Rabbi Shimon bar Yohai
Exod.	Exodus		
Ezek.	Ezekiel	Ned.	Nedarim
Gen.	Genesis	Neh.	Nehemiah
Hab.	Habbakuk	Num.	Numbers
		O. Ch.	Orach Chayim

LIST OF ABBREVIATIONS

Pes.	Pesachim		Shab.	Shabbat
Prov.	Proverbs		Shek.	Shekalim
Ps.	Psalms		Sot.	Sotah
PT	Palestinian Talmud, Yerushalmi		Suk.	Sukkah
			Ta'an.	Ta'anit
R. H.	Rosh Hashanah		Ter.	Terumot
Rab.	Rabbah (Midrash Rabbah)		Zech.	Zechariah
Sam.	Samuel		Zeph.	Zephaniah
Sanh.	Sanhedrin			

Glossary

The following glossary presents names and Hebrew words used regularly throughout this volume and provides the way they are pronounced. Sometimes two pronunciations are common, in which case the first is the way the word is sounded in Hebrew, and the second is the way it is sometimes heard in common speech, under the influence of Yiddish, the folk language of Jews in northern and eastern Europe (a combination, mostly, of Hebrew and German). Our goal is to provide the way that many Jews actually use these words, not just the technically correct version.

- The pronunciations are divided into syllables by dashes.

- The accented syllable is written in capital letters.

- "Kh" represents a guttural sound, similar to the German (as in "sprach").

- The most common vowel is "a" as in "father," which appears here as "ah."

- The short "e" (as in "get") is written as either "e" (when it is in the middle of a syllable) or "eh" (when it ends a syllable).

- Similarly, the short "i" (as in "tin") is written as either "i" (when it is in the middle of a syllable) or "ih" (when it ends a syllable).

- A long "o" (as in Moses") is written as "oe" (as in the word "toe") or "oh" (as in the word "Oh!").

Abudarham: David ben Joseph Abudarham, fourteenth-century Spanish commentator on the liturgy. His *Sefer Abudarham* (completed in 1340) is our primary account of Spanish (Sefardi) practice of the time.

Acharonim (pronounced ah-khah-roh-NEEM or, commonly, akh-ROH-nim): The name given to Jewish legal authorities from the middle of the sixteenth century on. The word means, literally, "later ones," as opposed to the "earlier ones," authorities prior to that time who are held in higher regard and are called *Rishonim* (pronounced ree-shoh-NEEM or, commonly, ree-SHOH-nim). Singular: *Acharon* (pronounced ah-khah-ROHN) and *Rishon* (pronounced ree-SHOHN).

Aggadah (pronounced ah-gah-DAH): Literally, "narrative," or "telling," from the same root as *haggadah* ("telling"), but unrelated to the Passover Haggadah; refers to literary "tellings," or tales, like parables, biographical narratives, and short vignettes that are embedded in rabbinic literature less as legal argumentation than as grounds for lessons in extralegal matters such as ethics, history, and theology.

Amidah (pronounced either ah-mee-DAH or, commonly, ah-MEE-dah): One of three commonly used titles for the second of two central units in the worship service, the first being the *Sh'ma* and Its Blessings. It is composed of a series of blessings, many of which are petitionary, except on Sabbaths and holidays, when the petitions are removed out of deference to the holiness of the day. Also called *T'fillah* and *Sh'moneh Esreh*. *Amidah* means "standing" and refers to the fact that the prayer is said standing up.

Amora(im): See *Tannaitic*.

Arba'ah Turim: See *Tur*.

Ari, Ha'ari (pronounced ah-REE, hah-ah-REE): Acronym for Isaac ben Solomon Luria (1534–1572); the initials refer to *Ha'Elohi Rabbi Yitzchak*, "the divine Rabbi Isaac" or *Ha'Ashkenazi Rabbi Isaac*. Renowned kabbalist who lived mostly in Jerusalem, Egypt, and Safed.

Ashkenazi (pronounced ahsh-k'-nah-ZEE, or, commonly, ahsh-k'-NAH-zee): From the Hebrew word *Ashkenaz*, meaning the geographic area of northern and eastern Europe; "Ashkenazi" is the adjective, describing the liturgical rituals and customs practiced there. "Ashkenazim " (plural) refers to Jews from this geographic region. These terms contrast with "Sefardi," meaning the liturgical rituals and customs that are derived from Sefarad, current day Spain and Portugal (see *Sefardi*), and "Sefardim," who trace their roots there—or, now, also to North Africa or the Middle East, where many exiles went in 1492 (from Spain) and 1497 (from Portugal).

Ashkenazim: See *Ashkenazi*.

Avot D'rabbi Natan (pronounced ah-VOHT d'-rah-BEE nah-TAHN): A collection of wisdom akin to Mishnah Avot, providing lessons attributed to the chain of Rabbis who predated the Mishnah (the Tannaim, pre-200). Variously dated from the third to the seventh/eighth centuries.

Bavli: See *Talmud*.

B'dikat chamets (pronounced b'-dee-KAHT khah-MAYTS): The process of searching for leaven on the night before Passover.

Bertinoro, Ovadiah: Italian rabbi (1450?–1516?) whose commentary on the Mishnah has become the standard commentary on that work.

Bet Yosef (pronounced BAIT yoh-SAYF): Commentary to the *Tur* by Joseph Caro, sixteenth century, Land of Israel; and a precursor to his more popular code, the *Shulchan Arukh*. See *Tur* and **Shulchan Arukh**.

Birkat Hamazon (pronounced beer-KAHT hah-mah-ZOHN): Grace after Meals, consisting of four blessings, which thank God for (1) feeding all creatures; (2) giving the Jewish people the Land of Israel; (3) rebuilding Jerusalem; and (4) showing goodness. Embedded within these four blessings are petitions to the "Merciful One" (*harachaman* [pronounced hah-rah-khah-MAHN]). Bracketing the whole is an introduction called *zimmun* (pronounced zee-MOON) and a conclusion on the theme of peace.

Bitul chamets (pronounced bee-TOOL khah-MAYTS): Literally, "nullification of leaven," a phrase related to the ritual of seeking out and burning the leaven in one's possession, so that any leaven still in one's possession is considered "null and void."

Bi'ur chamets (pronounced bee-OOR khah-MAYTS): Literally, "burning the leaven." The act of symbolically burning leavened food *(chamets)* on the night before Passover.

Caro, Joseph: See **Shulchan Arukh**.

Chamets (pronounced khah-MAYTS): Products forbidden on Passover because they are made with wheat, barley, spelt, oats, or rye that may have fermented or leavened through having come in contact with water for more than eighteen minutes.

Charedi (pronounced khah-ray-DEE or, commonly, khah-RAY-dee): Literally "reverently fearful," a diverse group of ultra-Orthodox Jews who reject accommodation with modernity.

Chazon Ish (pronounced khah-ZOHN EESH): A commentary on part of the *Shulchan Arukh* by Avraham Yeshayahu Karelitz (1878–1953, Lithuania and Israel). Karelitz was a student of astronomy, mathematics, anatomy, and botany as well as one of the leading talmudic scholars of his era. Known for his practical approach to matters of Jewish law.

Deuteronomy Rabbah: A midrashic collection containing some twenty-seven homilies corresponding roughly to the triennial cycle of Torah reading that marked Palestinian Jewry prior to the Crusades. With early origins, the text was compiled between 450 and 800.

Dov Baer, The Great Maggid [Preacher] of Mezerich (1710–1772): Leader of Chasidism following the death of the movement's spiritual father, the Baal Shem Tov (1700–1760). Introduced the systematic study of Kabbalah in Chasidism.

Eruv tavshilin (pronounced ay-ROOV tahv-shee-LEEN or, commonly, AY-roov, tahv-SHEE-leen): Literally, "the joining of cooked foods." Ordinarily, food prepared on a festival must be consumed only on the festival itself. Thus when a festival falls directly before the Sabbath, it would be impossible to cook the Sabbath meal. The *eruv tavshilin* solves this problem through a legal fiction: two dishes, one cooked and the other bread (here, matzah), are set aside before Passover, as if Sabbath-meal cooking actually preceded the festival.

Esther Rabbah: A midrashic collection centered on the Book of Esther, containing material dating from the sixth through eleventh centuries.

Exodus Rabbah: A midrashic collection in two parts. Exodus 1–10 (tenth century) is exegetical—it follows the order of the biblical verses on which it comments; Exodus 12–40 (eleventh or twelfth century) is homiletical—it is arranged like a set of sermons.

Gaon (pronounced gah-OHN; plural: *Geonim*, pronounced g'-oh-NEEM): Title for the leading rabbis in Babylon (present-day Iraq) from about 750 to 1038. From a biblical word meaning "glory," equivalent, in a title, to saying "Your Excellence."

Gemara (pronounced g'-mah-RAH, but, popularly, g'-MAH-rah): The commentary on the Mishnah that appears together with the Mishnah on which it comments as the Talmud (Talmud = Mishnah + Gemara). Sometimes, however, used loosely to mean the entire Talmud, the Mishnah included.

Genesis Rabbah: Extraordinarily detailed midrashic collection (fifth or sixth century), sometimes expounding on Genesis word by word.

Genizah (pronounced g'-nee-ZAH or, commonly g'-NEE-zah): Literally, "storing." A place where worn-out ritual objects and books containing the name of God were stored, usually a room connected to a synagogue. The Cairo Genizah, the most famous such storeroom (discovered at the end of the nineteenth century), contained a Haggadah dating back to the tenth or eleventh century CE (see *My People's Passover Haggadah*, Volume 2, Appendix II).

Geonim: See ***Gaon***.

Gra (pronounced GRAH): Acronym for *Gaon Rabbi Elijah* of Vilna (1720–1797), known also as the Vilna Gaon, outstanding halakhic authority of Lithuania and virulent opponent of Chasidism.

Gryz (pronounced griz): Acronym for *Gaon Rabbi Yitzchak Ze'ev* Soloveitchik (1886–1959), also known as Velvel Soloveitchik or the Brisker Rov. Renowned talmudist from the Brisk dynasty, born in Brisk, Lithuania, he emigrated to Palestine during the war and established the Brisk Yeshiva in Jerusalem.

Hagahot Maimuniyot (pronounced hah-gah-HOHT ma'i-moo-nee-YOHT): Literally, "glosses to Maimonides," a set of glosses and brief commentary on Maimonides' compendium of Jewish law, the *Mishneh Torah*, by Rabbi Meir Hakohen of Rothenburg (late thirteenth century).

Halakhot G'dolot (hah-lah-KHOHT g'doh-LOHT): Ninth-century summary of Jewish law, widely but not universally ascribed to Shimon Kayyara, Babylonia (present-day Iraq).

Hallel (pronounced hah-LAYL, or, commonly, HAH-layl): A Hebrew word meaning "praise" and, by extension, the name given to sets of psalms that are recited liturgically in praise of God: Psalms 145–150, the Daily *Hallel*, is recited each morning; Psalm 136, the Great *Hallel,* is recited on Shabbat and holidays and is part of the Passover Seder. Psalms 113–118, the best-known *Hallel*, known more fully as the Egyptian *Hallel*, is recited on holidays and gets its name from Psalm 114:1, which celebrates the moment "when Israel left Egypt."

Hallel Hagadol (pronounced hah-LAYL [or, commonly, HAH-layl] hah-gah-DOHL): Literally, "the Great *Hallel*," which refers to Psalm 136. See ***Hallel***.

Ibn Ezra, Abraham (Rabbi Abraham ibn Ezra, Spain, then various countries, 1089–1164): Grammarian, poet, Bible commentator, astronomer, physician, and philosopher (1089–1164) born in Spain but itinerant from 1140, during which time he wrote most of his works.

Jerusalem Talmud: Another term for the Palestinian Talmud, in Hebrew, the *Yerushalmi*. See ***Talmud***.

Kabbalah (pronounced kah-bah-LAH or, commonly, kah-BAH-lah): A general term for Jewish mysticism, but used properly for a specific mystical doctrine that began in western Europe in the eleventh or twelfth century; recorded in the *Zohar* (see ***Zohar***) in the thirteenth century, and then further elaborated, especially in the Land of Israel (in Safed), in the sixteenth century. From a Hebrew word meaning "to receive" or "to welcome," and secondarily, "tradition," implying the receiving of tradition from one's past.

Kaplan, Mordecai M. (1881–1983): Born in Lithuania, emigrated to the United States in 1890. Kaplan was a rabbi, teacher, theologian, and spiritual father of the Reconstructionist Movement. He rejected most supernatural ideas in Judaism and defined God as the power that made possible the pursuit of fundamental values such as freedom or improving the world.

Kiddush (pronounced kee-DOOSH or, commonly, KIH-d'sh): Literally, "sanctification," hence, a form of *K'dushat Hayom*; in this case, the prayer for the eve of Shabbat and holidays, intended to announce the arrival of sacred time, and accompanied by *Birkat Yayin,* the blessing over wine.

Lamentations Rabbah: Midrashic collection, late fifth century largely about the destruction of the Temple and the question of divine justice in light of innocent suffering.

Lekach Tov: See ***Midrash Lekach Tov***.

Levi Yitzchak of Berditchev (1740–1810): Disciple of Dov Baer, the *Maggid* of Mezerich. Levi Yitzchak expanded Chasidism in central Poland, the Ukraine, and Lithuania, center of opposition to the movement.

Leviticus Rabbah: Midrashic collection (fifth or sixth century) on the Book of Leviticus.

Machzor Vitry (pronounced mahkh-ZOHR veet-REE or, commonly, MAHKH-zohr VEET-ree): Literally, the *machzor* (prayer book containing the annual cycle of liturgy) from Vitry (in France). The most significant early French commentary to the liturgy, composed in the tenth and/or eleventh century, primarily by Simchah of Vitry, a student of *Rashi*.

Maharal of Prague: Acronym *(MaHaRaL)* for Judah Loew ben Bezalel (1525–1609), *Moreinu HaRav* Loew, "Our Teacher, the Rabbi Loew." Known for his piety and asceticism, a great scholar of Talmud, philosopher, prolific writer, and a mathematician who enjoyed a social relationship with the famed astronomer Tycho Brahe.

Maharil (pronounced mah-hah-RIL; Rabbi Jacob Moellin, Germany, fourteenth to fifteenth century): Acronym *(MaHaRiL)* for *Morenu* ("our teacher") *HaRav Ya'akov* ha*Levi*, (1360?–1427, Germany), leading talmudist and outstanding authority who helped shape Ashkenazi custom and tradition.

Maimonides, Moses (known also as *Rambam*, pronounced RAHM-bahm): Most important Jewish philosopher of all time; also a physician and very significant legal authority. Born in Spain, he moved to Egypt, where he lived most of his life (1135–1204).

Masoretic text: Literally, the "transmitted" text of the Hebrew Bible. Toward the end of the first millennium CE, a group of Jews in Tiberias standardized the Bible as we know it. Working from the consonantal text and from the traditions they had received, they added vowels, cantillation marks, and copious notes about the text. It is the Masoretic text that appears in most Hebrew Bibles.

Meiri, Menachem ben Solomon (1249–1316, Provence): Renowned commentator on the Talmud and author of an important treatise on ethics and repentance.

Mekhilta (pronounced m'-KHIL-tah): Shortened reference to either of two parallel midrashic works. See ***Mekhilta D'rabbi Yishmael*** and ***Mekhilta D'rabbi Shimon bar Yochai***.

Mekhilta D'rabbi Shimon bar Yochai (pronounced m'khil-TAH d'rah-bee shee-MOHN bahr yoh-KHA'i or, commonly, m'-KHIL-tah d'-rah-bee SHEE-mohn bahr yoh-KHA'i): Tannaitic midrash (pre-200) similar in style and content to the *Mekhilta D'rabbi Yishmael*.

Mekhilta D'rabbi Yishmael (pronounced m'-khil-TAH d'-rah-BEE yish-mah-AYL or, commonly, m'-KHIL-tah d'-RAH-bee YISH-mah-ayl): One of the tannaitic midrashim, this one on the Book of Exodus (chapter 12 on).

Merkavah (pronounced mehr-kah-VAH or, commonly, mehr KAH-vah): Literally, "chariot"; hence, the name of a school of Jewish mysticism that pictured God seated in a throne-like chariot, surrounded by angels reciting, "Holy, holy, holy."

Midrash (pronounced meed-RAHSH or, commonly, MID-rahsh): From a Hebrew word meaning "to ferret out the meaning of a text," and therefore a rabbinic interpretation of a biblical word or verse. By extension, a body of rabbinic literature that offers classical interpretations of the Bible.

Midrash Hagadol (pronounced meed-RASH hah-gah-DOHL or, commonly, MIHD-rahsh hah-gah-DOHL) Yemenite midrash on the Pentateuch generally thought to have been composed by David ben Amram of Aden between 1300 and 1400, but incorporating many sources.

Midrash Hallel (pronounced meed-RAHSH hah-LAYL or, commonly, MIHD-rahsh HAH-layl): Midrash on Psalms 113–118 composed in the tenth century or later.

Midrash Lekach Tov (pronounced meed-RAHSH LEH-kach TOHV, or, commonly, MIHD-rahsh leh-kach TOV): Late eleventh-century midrashic commentary on the Pentateuch by Tobiah ben Eliezer. Literally, "good instruction" (Prov. 4:2), the midrash alludes to contemporary events such as the Crusades.

Midrash on Proverbs: Mid-ninth-century midrash reflecting customs in Babylonia and Palestine. Polemicizes against the Karaites, a group of Jews who denied the legitimacy of rabbinic law.

Midrash on Psalms: See *Midrash T'hillim*.

Midrash Samuel: Midrashic collection compiled around the tenth or eleventh century but contains much old material, some of it only found in this collection.

Midrash Sekhel Tov (pronounced meed-RAHSH SAY-khel TOHV or, commonly, MIHD-rahsh say-khel TOV): Midrashic anthology following the weekly Torah reading. Literally, "good understanding" (Ps. 111:10). Composed by Menachem ben Solomon in the first half of the twelfth century. Also considered by some to be the first treatise on the Hebrew language.

Midrash T'hillim (pronounced meed-RAHSH t'-hee-LEEM or, commonly, mid-rahsh TILL-im): Literally, "Midrash to Psalms," a midrashic collection variously dated, with material as early as the third century, but reaching final redaction only centuries later. Also called *Midrash Shocher Tov* (pronounced meed-RAHSH sho-KHAYR TOHV or, commonly, mid-rahsh SHO-kheir TOHV), from the opening words of Proverbs 11:27, the first verse it quotes, "Whoever earnestly seeks what is right [*shocher tov*] pursues what is pleasing."

Midrash Vayosha (pronounced meed-RAHSH vah-yoh-SHAH or, commonly, MIHD-rahsh vah-YOH-sha)): Eleventh-century midrash on the Song of the Sea (Exod. 15), named for the expression in Exodus 14:30, "Thus Adonai saved" *(vayosha)*.

Minhag (pronounced meen-HAHG or, commonly, MIN-hahg): The Hebrew word for custom and, therefore, used liturgically to describe the customary way that different groups of Jews pray. By extension, *minhag* means a "rite," as in *Minhag Ashkenaz,* meaning "the rite of prayer, or the customary way of prayer for Jews in *Ashkenaz*"—that is, northern and eastern Europe.

Mishnah (pronounced meesh-NAH or, commonly, MISH-nah): The first written summary of Jewish law, compiled in the Land of Israel about the year 200 CE and, therefore, our first overall written evidence for the state of Jewish practice in the early centuries.

Mishnah B'rurah (pronounced meesh-NAH b'-roo-RAH or, commonly, MISH-nah B'ROO-rah): Halakhic commentary and compendium on laws in that portion of the *Shulchan Arukh* called *Orach Chayim* ("The Way of Life"), containing most of the laws on liturgy; by Rabbi Israel Meir Hakohen Kagan *(Chafetz Chayim)*, Radin, Poland, 1838–1933.

Mishnah of Rabbi Eliezer: Also known as *Midrash Agur* ("The words of Agur ..." [Prov. 30:1]), date unknown.

Mitzvah (pronounced meetz-VAH or, commonly, MITZ-vah; plural: *mitzvot,* pronounced meetz-VOTE): A Hebrew word used commonly to mean "good deed," but in the more technical sense, denoting any commandment from God and, therefore, by extension, what God wants us to do. Reciting the *Sh'ma* morning and evening, for instance, is a *mitzvah.*

Mitnagdim (pronounced mit-nagh-DEEM or, commonly, the Yiddishized mis-NAHG-dim): Literally, "opponents" of Chasidism in the eighteenth and nineteenth centuries. Now sometimes used to designate ultra-Orthodox Jews who are not Chasidic.

Mitzvot: See **Mitzvah**.

Mordecai Yosef Leiner of Izbica (1804–1854): Founder of the Izhbitzer Chasidic dynasty and known for his belief in radical determinism—that God determines everything, including the actions of all human beings.

M'zuzah (pronounced m'-zoo-ZAH or, commonly, m'-ZOO-zah): Literally, "doorpost," and hence, a small tubelike object, generally decorated, containing a tiny parchment scroll, that is affixed to the doorpost of the entrances to Jewish homes and to certain rooms within. On the parchment are written two passages from the Book of Deuteronomy 6:4–9 and 11:13–21). These include the requirement to inscribe the teachings of Torah "on the doorposts of your house and on your gates."

Nachmanides (pronounced nahkh-MAH-nih-deez): Also known as Ramban (pronounced rahm-BAHN), an acronym (RaMBaN) for *Rabbi Moses ben Nachman* (1194–1270, Spain and Israel). Bible commentator, halakhist, and kabbalist of extraordinary influence.

Numbers Rabbah: A midrashic collection with two parts: sections 1–14, from the mid-twelfth century, and sections 15–23, of unknown origin. Both parts were likely combined in the early thirteenth century.

Olah (pronounced oh-LAH): From the Hebrew word meaning "to go up" and, hence, the Temple offering consisting of an animal wholly offered up to God, because it was entirely consumed by sacrificial fire.

Olam haba (pronounced oh-LAHM hah-BAH or, commonly, OH-lahm hah-BAH): Literally, "the world-to-come," a term for one of the three most common eschatological promises of rabbinic Judaism. The others are *y'mot hamashi'ach* (pronounced y'MOHT hah-mah-SHEE-ahkh), "messianic days" (that is, the era after the coming of the messiah); and *t'chi'at hametim* (pronounced t'chee-YAHT hah-may-TEEM), "the resurrection of the dead."

Omer: See *S'firat ha'omer*.

Orach Chayim (pronounced oh-RAKH kah-YEEM or, commonly, OH-rakh KHA-yim): Abbreviated as O. Ch. Literally, "The Way of Life," one of four sections in the *Tur* and the *Shulchan Arukh,* two of Judaism's major law codes.

Orchot Chayim (pronounced ohr-KHOT khah-YEEM): Chief work of Rabbi Aharon ben Rabbi Jacob Hakohen of Lunel (Southern France and Spain, thirteenth to fourteenth century). Literally, "Ways of Life."

Pesikta D'rav Kahana (pronounced p'SIK-tah d'RAV kah-HAH-nah): Literally, "the section [or portion] of Rabbi Kahana"; a midrashic collection from the fifth or sixth century organized around the cycle of Torah and *Haftarah* readings for the festivals and special Sabbaths.

Pesikta Rabbati (pronounced p'-SIK-tah rah-BAH-tee): A midrashic collection organized similarly to *Pesikta D'rav Kahana*, but of unknown origin and date, and containing material on apocalyptic themes.

Pirkei D'rabbi Eliezer (pronounced peer-KAY d'rah-BEE eh-lee-EH-zer or, commonly, PEER-kay d'-RAH-bee eh-lee-EH-z'r): Literally, "Chapters of Rabbi Eliezer," so named because it begins with stories about Eliezer ben Hyrcanus (the same Rabbi Eliezer mentioned in the Haggadah). Composed in the first third of the ninth century, and sometimes called a "rewritten Bible" because it includes an extended narrative rather than exposition on words or phrases of Scripture.

Rabad (pronounced rah-BAHD): Acronym (RABaD) for *Rabbi Abraham ben David*, (c. 1125–1198) of Posquieres, Provence. Talmudist, halakhist, and among the first to write systematic commentaries on midrash.

Raban (pronounced rah-BAHN): Acronym (RaBaN) for *Rabbi Eliezer ben Nathan* of Mainz, Germany (1090–1170). Rabbinic scholar who also lived in Slavic countries and perhaps Russia whose major work *Sefer Haraban* (the Book by Raban) synopsizes and discusses Jewish law and is the oldest complete book to have survived from German Jewry.

Rabban (pronounced rah-BAHN): Rabbinic title of respect (literally, "our master") reserved for "chief" rabbi, head of the central academy, in first- to second-century Palestine.

Rabbenu Hananel (pronounced rah-BAY-noo CHAH-nah-nayl): Hananel ben Hushiel Kairouan, Tunisia (d. 1055/56). Influential commentator on the Talmud, among the first to highlight comparisons between the Jerusalem and Babylonian Talmuds.

Radak (pronounced rah-DAHK): Acronym (RaDaK) for *Rabbi David Kimchi* (1160?–1235?) of Narbonne, Provence. Bible scholar, grammarian, philosopher, and strong proponent of Maimonides' philosophy.

Rambam: See ***Maimonides***.

Ramban: See ***Nachmanides***.

Ran (pronounced RAHN): Acronym (RaN) for *Rabbi Nissim* [ben Reuven], Spain, d. 1380, and for his commentary on Isaac Alfasi (the *Rif*).

Rashbam (pronounced rahsh-BAHM): Acronym *(RaSHBaM)* for *Rabbi Sh*muel *b*en *M*eir (1080/85–c. 1174) of northern France. Grandson and student of *Rashi*, and commentator on the Bible and Talmud.

Rashbetz (pronounced rahsh-BETZ or, commonly, RASH-betz): Acronym (RaSHBeTZ) for *R*abbi *Sh*imon *b*en *Tz*emach Duran (1361–1444) of Majorca. Physician, astronomer, mathematician, philosopher, and prolific rabbinic authority whose works include a commentary on the Haggadah.

Rashi (pronounced RAH-shee): Acronym (RaSHI) for *R*abbi *Sh*lomo [Solomon] ben *I*saac, French halakhist and commentator on the Bible and Talmud, 1040–1105; founder of school of Jewish thought and custom, whence various liturgical works came into being, among them *Machzor Vitry* and *Siddur Rashi*.

Ravyah (pronounced rahv-YAH or, commonly RAHV-yah): Acronym (RaVYaH) for *R*abbi *E*liezer *v*en *Y*oel *H*alevi (1140–1225) of Bonn, Germany. Itinerant rabbinic scholar and pietist, whose major work (named for him, *Ravyah*) provides a major synopsis and discussion of Jewish law.

Rif (pronounced RIHF): Acronym (RiF) for *R*abbi *I*saac of *F*ez [Alfasi] (North Africa, 1013–1103) and his code of Jewish law by the same name.

Rishonim (pronounced ree-shoh-NEEM or, commonly, ree-SHOH-nim): The name given to Jewish legal authorities from the completion of the Talmud to the middle of the sixteenth century. The word means, literally, "earlier ones," as opposed to the "later ones," authorities after that time who are held in lower regard and are called *Acharonim* (pronounced ah-khah-roh-NEEM or, commonly, akh-ROH-nim). Singular: *Rishon* (pronounced ree-SHOHN) and *Acharon* (pronounced ah-khah-ROHN).

Ritba (pronounced riht-BAH or, commonly, RIHT-bah): Acronym (RITBA) for *R*abbi *Y*om *T*ov *b*en *A*braham Ishbili (c. 1250–1330), Seville. Talmudist and philosopher regarded in his later life as the spiritual leader of Spanish Jewry. His many works include a commentary on the Haggadah.

Ritzba (pronounced ritz-BAH or, commonly, RITZ-bah): Acronym (RITZBA) for *R*abbi *Y*itzhak *b*en *A*braham (twelfth century), France. Commentator on the Talmud and author of numerous responsa, that is, legal opinions.

R'ma (pronounced r'-MAH): An acronym for Rabbi Moses Isserles, sixteenth-century Poland, chief Ashkenazi commentator on the *Shulchan Arukh*, the sixteenth-century Sefardi code by Joseph Caro.

Rosh (pronounced ROHSH): The *Rosh* (1250–1328), otherwise known as Rabbeinu Asher, or Asher ben Yechiel, was a significant halakhic authority, first in Germany and later in Spain. His son, Jacob ben Asher, codified many of his father's views alongside his own in his influential law code, the *Tur*.

S'firat ha'omer (pronounced s'-fee-RAHT hah-OH-mehr): Literally, "counting the Omer." *Omer* (literally, "sheaf") refers to the sheaves of barley, the harvest of which coincides roughly with Passover. The Omer period extends from the eve of the second day of Passover to the night before Shavuot. Each day is counted liturgically as part of the evening *(Ma'ariv)* service.

S'firot (pronounced s'-fee-ROTE; singular: *s'firah*, pronounced s'-fee-RAH): According to the Kabbalah (Jewish mysticism, see **Kabbalah**), the universe came into being by a process of divine emanation, whereby the divine light, as it were, expanded into empty space, eventually becoming physical matter. At various intervals, this light was frozen in time, as if captured by containers, each of which is called a *s'firah*. Literally, *s'firah* means "number," because early theory conceptualized the stages of creation as primordial numbers.

Saadiah Gaon (882-942, Egypt and Sura, Babylonia): A prolific gaon, who wrote grammar, liturgy (the second great prayer book), philosophy, poetry, and responsa. Also noted polemicist against Palestinian authorities and Karaites.

Seder Rav Amram (pronounced SAY-dehr rahv AHM-rahm): First known comprehensive Jewish prayer book, emanating from Rav Amram Gaon (c. 860 CE), a leading Jewish scholar and head of Sura, a famed academy in Babylonia (modern-day Iraq).

Sefardi (pronounced s'-fahr-DEE or, commonly, s'-FAHR-dee): From the Hebrew word *Sefarad* (pronounced s'-fah-RAHD), meaning the geographic area of modern-day Spain and Portugal; "Sefardi" is the adjective, describing the liturgical rituals and customs that are derived from Sefarad, prior to the expulsion of Jews from there at the end of the fifteenth century. These terms contrast with Ashkenazi (see **Ashkenazi**), meaning the liturgical rituals and customs common to northern and eastern Europe. Nowadays, "Sefardi" refers also to the customs of Jews from North Africa and the Arab lands, whose ancestors came from Spain and Portugal. "Sefardim" (plural) refers to Jews who trace their roots to these areas.

Sefardim: See **Sefardi**.

Sefer Ha'agur (pronounced SAY-fehr hah-ah-GOOR): Chief work of Rabbi Jacob Landau (fifteenth century, Germany), a compilation of German Jewish scholarship on daily religious practice; among the first to use kabbalistic ideas as an aid for resolving questions of Jewish law.

Sefer Or Zarua (pronounced SAY-fehr OHR zah-ROO-ah): Legal compendium by Rabbi Isaac ben Moses of Vienna (c. 1180–c. 1250), often referred to as Isaac Or Zarua.

Sefer Rokeach (pronounced SAY-fehr roh-KAY-ahkh): Principal halakhic work of Rabbi Eleazer ben Judah of Worms (c. 1165–1230, Germany), harmonizing the doctrines of German pietists with halakhah, and a valuable source for Jewish custom of the time.

Sekhel Tov: See ***Midrash Sekhel Tov***.

Septuagint (pronounced sehp-TOO-a-jint): Latin for "seventy," reflecting the myth that King Ptolemy of Egypt asked seventy-two Jews to translate the Torah into Greek; refers, therefore, to the first Greek translation of the Bible, begun (probably) in the third century BCE. The original Septuagint included only the Torah, but now we use the term to include also translations of other biblical books that were added to it.

Shehecheyanu (pronounced sheh-heh-khee-YAH-noo): Literally, "who kept us alive" and, hence, the popular name for a blessing praising God for "having kept us alive, sustained us, and brought us to this time of year." Also called *Birkat Hazman* (pronounced beer-KAHT hah-z'-MAHN), "the Blessing of the Time." It is recited at the onset of festivals and a variety of "first-time" events, such as eating the fruit of a new season. Used more generally by liberal Jews to express thanks at happy occasions.

Sheiltot (pronounced sh'-ayl-TOHT): Chief work of Achai Gaon (680–752), literally "*Questions*," a halakhic-midrashic work arranged according to the weekly Torah portion.

Shekhinah (pronounced sh'-khee-NAH or, commonly, sh-KHEE-nah): From the Hebrew root *sh.kh.n*, meaning "to dwell," and, therefore, in talmudic literature, the "indwelling" aspect of God most immediately empathetic to human experience. As the feminine aspect of God, it appears in Kabbalah as the tenth and final *s'firah*, or emanation.

Shibbolei Haleket (pronounced shih-boh-LAY hah-LEH-keht): Literally, "The Gleaned Ears," chief work of Zedekiah ben Abraham Anav (thirteenth century). The first attempt in Italy to codify Jewish law, it includes a complete commentary on the Haggadah.

Sh'ma (pronounced sh'-MAH): The central prayer in the first of the two main units in the worship service, the second being the *Amidah* (see ***Amidah***). The *Sh'ma* comprises three citations from the Bible, and the larger unit in which it is embedded (called the *Sh'ma* and Its Blessings) is composed of a formal Call to Prayer (the *Bar'khu*) and a series of blessings on the theological themes that, together with the *Sh'ma*, constitute a liturgical creed of faith. *Sh'ma*, meaning "hear," is the first word of the first line of the first biblical citation, "Hear O Israel: Adonai is our God; Adonai is One" (Deut. 6:4), which is the paradigmatic statement of Jewish faith, the Jews' absolute commitment to the presence of a single and unique God in time and space.

Shulchan Arukh (pronounced shool-KHAN ah-ROOKH or, commonly, SHOOL-khan AH-rookh): The name given to the best-known code of Jewish law, compiled by Joseph Caro in the Land of Israel and published in 1565. *Shulchan Arukh* means "The Set Table" and refers to the ease with which the various laws are set forth—like a table prepared with food ready for consumption.

Sifra (pronounced seef-RAH): One the tannaitic midrashim, this one on portions of the Book of Leviticus. It begins with Rabbi Ishmael's thirteen rules of interpretation.

Sifre (pronounced seef-RAY): One of the tannaitic midrashim. We have one on Deuteronomy and one on Numbers. The *Sifre on Deuteronomy* includes what may be the oldest written version—a much shorter one—of the Haggadah's midrash on the "wandering Aramean" *(arami oved avi)*.

Soloveitchik, Joseph B. (1903–992, Russia and United States): Also known as "the *Rov*" (the rabbi [par excellence]). Revered centrist Orthodox teacher, philosopher, and talmudist, who ordained more than two thousand rabbis in his nearly fifty years at Yeshiva University. Author of such classics as *Halakhic Man* and *The Lonely Man of Faith*.

Song of Songs Rabbah: Fifth- or sixth-century midrash that interprets the Song of Songs as an allegory of the relationship between God and the people of Israel.

Talmud (pronounced tahl-MOOD or, more commonly, TAHL-m'd): Each of two great compendia of Jewish law and lore compiled over several centuries and, ever since, the literary core of the rabbinic heritage: the Yerushalmi (pronounced y'-roo-SHAHL-mee), the "Palestinian" or "Jerusalem Talmud," compiled in the Land of Israel, c. 400 CE; and the Bavli (pronounced BAHV-lee), or "Babylonian Talmud," from Babylonia (present-day Iraq), c. 550–650 CE. "The" Talmud, cited without specifying one or the other, denotes the Bavli.

Tamid (pronounced tah-MEED): From the Hebrew *tamid*, meaning "always, regular"; hence, the "regular sacrifice" offered daily in the Temple, both morning and afternoon.

Tanchuma (pronounced tahn-KHOO-mah): A midrashic collection of literary sermons covering the weekly Torah readings; probably compiled in Eretz Yisrael in the eighth to ninth century, but attributed to Rabbi Tanchuma bar Abba, an earlier rabbinic figure.

Tanna D'vei Eliyahu (pronounced TAH-nah d'-VAY ay-lee-YAH hoo): Also known as *Seder Eliyahu Rabbah* (SAY-dehr ay-lee-ah-HOO rah-BAH or, commonly, SAY-dehr ay-lee-YAH-hoo RAH-bah), and *Seder Eliyahu Zuta* (SAY-dehr ay-lee-YAH-hoo ZOO-tah), "the greater and lesser teachings of Elijah," a unique midrashic work narrated in the first person. Contains parables, prayers, and admonitions written in colorful style. Dated third or mid-ninth century.

Tanna(im): See **Tannaitic**.

Tannaitic: Referring to the rabbinic period or literature composed between about 20 CE (the death of Hillel) or 70 CE (the destruction of the Second Temple) and 200 CE (the redaction of the Mishnah). A rabbi who lived is this era is called a Tanna (one who hands down orally, learns, or teaches; plural: Tannaim). This is distinguished from the amoraic period, between 200 CE and about 550 CE (the redaction of the Talmud), and *Amora* (from the Hebrew root "to say"; plural: Amoraim), a rabbi who lived during this later era.

T'chi'at hametim (pronounced t'chee-YAHT hah-may-TEEM): Literally, "the resurrection of the dead," a term for one of the three most common eschatological promises of rabbinic Judaism. The others are *olam haba* (pronounced oh-LAHM hah-BAH or, commonly, OH-lahm hah-BAH), "the world-to-come," and *y'mot hamashi'ach* (pronounced y'MOHT hah-mah-SHEE-ahkh), "messianic days" (that is, the era after the coming of the messiah).

Tosafot (pronounced toh-sah-FOHT or, commonly, TOH-sah-foht): Literally, "additional," referring to "additional" twelfth- to fourteenth-century Franco-German halakhists and commentators, the spiritual (and, to some extent, even familial) descendants of the French commentator *Rashi* (1040–1105).

Tosefta (pronounced toh-SEHF-tah): Tannaitic law code or teaching manual structured along the lines of the Mishnah. A supplement (literally, "addition") to the Mishnah, but perhaps containing a core of pre-Mishnaic (i.e., pre-200 CE) material that was reworked in the Mishnah. It contains a description of the night of Passover that differs from the Mishnah; for example, it lacks the question-and-answer approach to telling the story of the Exodus (see Appendix I, *My People's Passover Haggadah*, Volume 2, pp. 225–234).

Tsitsit (pronounced tsee-TSEET): A Hebrew word meaning "tassels" or "fringes" and used to refer to the tassels affixed to the four corners of the *tallit* (the prayer shawl), as Numbers 15:38 instructs.

Tur (pronounced TOOR): The shorthand title applied to a fourteenth-century code of Jewish law, compiled by Jacob ben Asher in Spain, and the source for much of our knowledge about medieval liturgical practice. *Tur* means "row" or "column." The full name of the code is *Arba'ah Turim* (pronounced ahr-bah-AH too-REEM), "The Four Rows," with each row (or *Tur*) being a separate section of law on a given broad topic.

Vayosha: See **Midrash Vayosha**.

Ya'akov Yosef of Polnoye (died c. 1782): First theoretician of Chasidism and author of *Toledot Ya'akov* (pronounced tohl-DOHT yah-ah-KOHV or, commonly, following Ashkenazi pronunciation, TOHL-dohs YAH-k'v), "The Generations of Jacob," the first Chasidic book ever printed.

Yalkut Shimoni (pronounced YAHL-koot shih-MOH-nee): Vast midrashic anthology on the entire Bible compiled from more than fifty sources, many of which are now lost. Compiled by Shimon Hadarshan (pronounced hah-dahr-SHAHN or, commonly, hah-DAHR-shahn), possibly from Frankfurt, twelfth or thirteenth century.

Judah Aryeh Leib of Ger (1847–1905): Founder of Gerer Chasidic dynasty and known also by the name of his book, the *S'fat Emet* (pronounced si-FAHT EH-meht or, commonly, using Ashkenazi pronunciation, s'-FAHS EH-mehs)—literally, "language of truth" (Prov. 12:19), a commentary on the Torah and festivals.

Yerushalmi: See **Talmud**.

YHVH: The ineffable (so, unpronounceable) four-letter name of God, referred to in English as "the tetragrammaton," and traditionally pronounced *Adonai*.

Zevach Pesach (pronounced ZEH-vakh PEH-sakh): Literally, "The offering of the Passover sacrifice"; Haggadah commentary by Isaac ben Judah Abarbanel (1437–1508, Spain and Italy). Written in 1496, it was widely circulated thereafter.

Zohar (pronounced ZOH-hahr): Classic text of Jewish mysticism (literally, the book of "Splendor") by Spanish Kabbalist Moshe ben Tov de Leon (d. 1305). Traditionally ascribed to Rabbi Shimon bar Yochai, mid-second century.

About the Contributors

DAVID ARNOW

David Arnow, PhD, a psychologist by training, has been writing about the Passover Seder for twenty years. He is widely recognized for his innovative work to make the Seder a truly exciting encounter each year with Judaism's central ideas. He is the author of *Creating Lively Passover Seders: A Sourcebook of Engaging Tales, Texts and Activities* (Jewish Lights Publishing) and the creator of its website, www.livelyseders.com. He lectures widely and writes on a broad variety of topics of Jewish interest.

CAROLE B. BALIN

Carole B. Balin is professor of Jewish history at Hebrew Union College–Jewish Institute of Religion in New York. She was educated at Wellesley College, ordained at HUC-JIR, and earned her PhD at Columbia University. She specializes in modern Jewish history, specifically Eastern European Jewish history. She is the author of *To Reveal Our Hearts: Jewish Women Writers in Tsarist Russia* (HUC Press), co-editor with Wendy Zierler of a forthcoming collection of the Hebrew writings of Hava Shapiro (Resling Press), and co-author with Eugene Borowitz of a forthcoming revision of *Liberal Judaism* (URJ Press).

MARC BRETTLER*

Marc Brettler, PhD, is Dora Golding Professor of Biblical Studies in the Department of Near Eastern and Judaic Studies at Brandeis University. His major areas of research are biblical historical texts, religious metaphors, and gender issues in the Bible. Brettler is author of *God Is King: Understanding an Israelite Metaphor* (Sheffield Academic Press), *The Creation of History in Ancient Israel* (Routledge), *The Book of Judges* (Routledge), *How to Read the Bible* (Jewish Publication Society), and *How to Read the Jewish Bible* (Oxford University Press), as well as a variety of articles on the Bible. He is also associate editor of the new edition of the *Oxford Annotated Bible* and coeditor of the *Jewish Study Bible* (Oxford University Press).

* Contributor to the *My People's Prayer Book: Traditional Prayers, Modern Commentaries* Series, winner of the National Jewish Book Award.

NEIL GILLMAN

Neil Gillman, rabbi and PhD, is professor of Jewish philosophy at The Jewish Theological Seminary in New York, where he has served as chair of the department of Jewish philosophy and dean of the Rabbinical School. He is author of *Sacred Fragments: Recovering Theology for the Modern Jew* (Jewish Publication Society), winner of the National Jewish Book Award; *The Death of Death: Resurrection and Immortality in Jewish Thought* (Jewish Lights), a finalist for the National Jewish Book Award and a *Publishers Weekly* "Best Book of the Year"; *The Way Into Encountering God in Judaism* (Jewish Lights); *Traces of God: Seeing God in Torah, History, and Everyday Life* (Jewish Lights), and *The Jewish Approach to God: A Brief Introduction for Christians* (Jewish Lights).

ALYSSA GRAY*

Alyssa Gray, PhD, JD, is associate professor of codes and responsa literature at Hebrew Union College–Jewish Institute of Religion in New York. She has also taught at The Jewish Theological Seminary in New York. She has written on the topics of martyrdom and sexuality in rabbinic literature, Talmudic redaction, Talmudic *aggadah*, liturgy, and women and *tzedakah* in medieval Jewish law. She is the author of *A Talmud in Exile: The Influence of Yerushalmi Avodah Zarah on the Formation of Bavli Avodah Zarah* (Brown Judaic Studies) and the co-editor (with Bernard Jackson) of *Studies in Mediaeval Halakhah in Honor of Stephen M. Passamaneck* (Deborah Charles). Her current research focuses on wealth and poverty in classical rabbinic literature.

ARTHUR GREEN

Arthur Green is rector of the Hebrew College Rabbinical School and Irving Brudnick Professor of Jewish philosophy and religion. He is also professor emeritus of Jewish thought at Brandeis University. He is former president of the Reconstructionist Rabbinical College. He is a rabbi, a historian of Jewish mysticism, and a theologian. His works include *Tormented Master: The Life and Spiritual Quest of Rabbi Nahman of Bratslav* (Jewish Lights); *Keter: The Crown of God in Early Jewish Mysticism; Seek My Face: A Jewish Mystical Theology* (Jewish Lights); *These Are the Words: A Vocabulary of Jewish Spiritual Life* (Jewish Lights); *Ehyeh: A Kabbalah for Tomorrow* (Jewish Lights), and *A Guide to the Zohar*. His translations and interpretations of Hasidic Thought include *Upright Practices and The Light of the Eyes*, by Rabbi Menahem Nahum of Chernobyl; *Your Word Is Fire: The Hasidic Masters on Contemplative Prayer* (with B. W. Holtz; Jewish Lights), and *The Language of Truth: Teachings from the Sefat Emet*.

JOEL M. HOFFMAN*

Joel M. Hoffman, Ph.D., lectures around the globe on popular and scholarly topics spanning history, Hebrew, prayer, and Jewish continuity. He has served on the faculties of Brandeis University, the Academy for Jewish Religion, and, currently, Hebrew Union

College–Jewish Institute of Religion in New York, where he teaches advanced classes on Hebrew and on translation. Hoffman's research in theoretical linguistics brings him to a new approach to ancient Hebrew, viewing it not merely as a dead language, but as a spoken language of antiquity. Hoffman is the author of *In the Beginning: A Short History of the Hebrew Language* (NYU Press). In addition to his graduate-level teaching, Hoffman serves as scholar-in-residence at Temple Shaaray Tefila in Bedford, New York, and finds time to teach youngsters a few afternoons a week.

LAWRENCE A. HOFFMAN*

Lawrence A. Hoffman, Ph.D., was ordained and received his doctorate from Hebrew Union College–Jewish Institute of Religion. He has served in its New York campus for more than three decades, most recently as the Barbara and Stephen Friedman Professor of Liturgy, Worship and Ritual. Widely recognized for his scholarship and classroom teaching, Hoffman has combined research with a passion for the spiritual renewal of contemporary Judaism. He has written and edited over twenty-five books, including *The Art of Public Prayer, 2nd Edition: Not for Clergy Only* (SkyLight Paths), now used nationally by Jews and Christians as a handbook for liturgical planners in church and synagogue, as well as a revision of *What Is a Jew?*, the best-selling classic that remains the most widely read introduction to Judaism ever written in any language. He is editor of the *My People's Prayer Book: Traditional Prayers, Modern Commentaries* Series, winner of the National Jewish Book Award; and author of *Israel—A Spiritual Travel Guide: A Companion for the Modern Jewish Pilgrim and The Way Into Jewish Prayer* (both Jewish Lights Publishing). Hoffman is a founder of Synagogue 2000 (now renamed Synagogue 3000), a transdenominational project designed to transform synagogues into the moral and spiritual centers of the twenty-first century. His latest book, *Rethinking Synagogues: A New Vocabulary for Congregational Life* (Jewish Lights), an outgrowth of that project, was a finalist for the National Jewish Book Award.

LAWRENCE KUSHNER*

Lawrence Kushner is the Emanu-El scholar at congregation Emanu-El in San Francisco, an adjunct faculty member at Hebrew Union College–Jewish Institute of Religion, and a visiting professor of Jewish spirituality at the Graduate Theological Union in Berkeley, California. He served as spiritual leader of Congregation Beth El in Sudbury, Massachusetts, for twenty-eight years and is widely regarded as one of the most creative religious writers in America. Ordained a rabbi by Hebrew Union College–Jewish Institute of Religion, Kushner led his congregants in publishing their own prayer book, *V'taher Libenu* (Purify Our Hearts), the first gender-neutral liturgy ever written. Through his lectures and many books, including *The Way Into Jewish Mystical Tradition; Invisible Lines of Connection: Sacred Stories of the Ordinary; The Book of Letters: A Mystical Hebrew Alphabet; Honey from the Rock: An Introduction to Jewish Mysticism; God Was in This Place and I, i Did Not Know: Finding Self, Spirituality, and Ultimate*

Meaning; Eyes Remade for Wonder: A Lawrence Kushner Reader; and *Jewish Spirituality: A Brief Introduction for Christians*, all published by Jewish Lights, he has helped shape the Jewish community's present focus on personal and institutional spiritual renewal.

DANIEL LANDES*

Daniel Landes is director and Rosh HaYeshivah of the Pardes Institute of Jewish Studies in Jerusalem and was an adjunct professor of Jewish law at Loyola University Law School in Los Angeles. Ordained a rabbi by Rabbi Isaac Elchanan Theological Seminary, Landes was a founding faculty member of the Simon Wiesenthal Center and the Yeshiva of Los Angeles, and served as a judge in the Los Angeles Orthodox Beith Din. He has lectured and written various popular and scholarly articles on the subjects of Jewish thought, social ethics, and spirituality.

NEHEMIA POLEN*

Nehemia Polen is professor of Jewish thought and director of the Hasidic Text Institute at Boston's Hebrew College. He is the author of *The Holy Fire: The Teachings of Rabbi Kalonymus Shapira, the Rebbe of the Warsaw Ghetto* (Jason Aronson) as well as many academic and popular articles on Chasidism and Jewish spirituality, and coauthor of *Filling Words with Light: Hasidic and Mystical Reflections on Jewish Prayer* (Jewish Lights). He received his Ph.D. from Boston University, where he studied with and served as teaching fellow for Nobel laureate Elie Wiesel. In 1994 he was Daniel Jeremy Silver Fellow at Harvard University, and he has also been a Visiting Scholar at the Hebrew University in Jerusalem. He was ordained a rabbi at the Ner Israel Rabbinical College in Baltimore, Maryland, and served as a congregational rabbi for twenty-three years. In 1998–1999 he was a National Endowment for the Humanities Fellow, working on the writings of Malkah Shapiro (1894–1971), the daughter of a noted Chasidic master, whose Hebrew memoirs focus on the spiritual lives of women in the context of prewar Chasidism in Poland. This work is documented in his book *The Rebbe's Daughter* (Jewish Publication Society), winner of the National Jewish Book Award.

WENDY I. ZIERLER*

Wendy I. Zierler is Associate Professor of Modern Jewish Literature and Feminist Studies at Hebrew Union College–Jewish Institute of Religion. Prior to joining HUC–JIR she was a research fellow in the English Department of Hong Kong University. She holds PhD and MA degrees in comparative literature from Princeton University, and a BA from Yeshiva University, Stern College. She is the author of *And Rachel Stole the Idols: The Emergence of Hebrew Women's Writing* (Wayne State University Press) and co-editor with Carole B. Balin of a forthcoming collection of the Hebrew writings of Hava Shapiro (Resling Press). At HUC she teaches courses dealing with modern Jewish and Hebrew literature, popular culture and theology, and gender and Judaism.

The editors are grateful to the following for permission to reproduce the material listed below. This page constitutes a continuation of the copyright page.

Page 2: (Top right) From *The Kibbutz Haggada: Israeli Pesach in The Kibbutz*, edited by Moki Tsur and Yuval Danieli (Israel: Yad Izhak Ben Zvi, et al, 2004), p. 63. Reprinted with permission. (Top left) From *Haggadah* (Cologne: Renard and Dubyen, 1838), frontispiece. From the collection of David Arnow. (Bottom right) From *Haggadah Shel Pesach* (Chicago, Lazar's Kosher Sausage Factory, undated). From the collection of Stephen P. Durchslag. (Bottom left) From *Union Haggadah: Revised* (New York: Central Conference of American Rabbis, 1923), frontispiece. Reprinted with permission of the Central Conference of American Rabbis (Reform).

Page 20: From *HUC Manuscript 444, The First Cincinnati Haggadah*. Reprinted with permission of Klau Library, Cincinnati, Hebrew Union College–Jewish Institute of Religion.

Page 93: From *Haggadah Shel Pesach: Otsar Perushim V'tsi'urim*, J. D. Eisenstein, ed. (New York, published by the author, 1920), p. 1. Reprinted with permission, © Hebrew Publishing Company.

Page 106: From *Seder Haggadah Shel Pesach*, illustrated by Otto Geismar (Berlin: Yalkut, 1927), p. 3. From the collection of Lawrence A. Hoffman.

Page 133: From *Haggadah Shel Pesach* (Augsburg, 1534). Reprinted with permission of the Library, The Jewish Theological Seminary of America.

Page 146: Cairo Genizah Collection, Halper 211. Reprinted with permission of the University of Pennsylvania Center for Advanced Jewish Studies.

Page 161: From *The Kibbutz Haggada: Israeli Peach in The Kibbutz*, Moki Tsur and Yuval Danieli, eds. (Israel: Yad Izhak Ben Zvi, et al, 2004), p. 91. Reprinted with permission.

Page 179: From *Haggadah Shel Pesach* (Prague: 1526). Reprinted with permission of the Klau Library, Cincinnati, Hebrew Union College–Jewish Institute of Religion.

Page 180: From *Services for the First Two Nights of the Feast of Passover with New Illustrations edited by Hayyim Liberman* (Chicago, 1883). From the collection of Stephen P. Durchslag.

Page 181: From *The Haggadah of Passover* (New York, 1944); a gift of the Labor Zionist Committee for Relief and Rehabilitation, Inc. Nota Koslowsky, illustrator. From the collection of Stephen P. Durchslag.

Page 182: From *Haggadah Shel Pesach*, Zvi Livni, illustrator (Tel Aviv, Yavne Publishing, 1955). © Yavne Publishing, reprinted with permission.

Page 183: From *The Open Door: A Passover Haggadah*, ed. Sue Levi Elwell (New York: Central Conference of American Rabbis, 2002). Reprinted with permission.

Page 212: From *The Union Haggadah, Home Service for the Passover Eve* (New York, The Central Conference of American Rabbis, 1907), frontispiece. Reprinted with permission of the Central Conference of American Rabbis (Reform).

Every effort has been made to trace and acknowledge copyright holders of all images included in this book. The editors apologize for any errors or omissions that may remain, and ask that any omissions be brought to their attention so that they may be corrected in future editions.

Notes

Notes

Bar/Bat Mitzvah

The JGirl's Guide: The Young Jewish Woman's Handbook for Coming of Age
By Penina Adelman, Ali Feldman, and Shulamit Reinharz
This inspirational, interactive guidebook helps pre-teen Jewish girls address the many
issues surrounding coming of age.   6 x 9, 240 pp, Quality PB, 978-1-58023-215-9 **$14.99**
 Also Available: **The JGirl's Teacher's and Parent's Guide**
8½ x 11, 56 pp, PB, 978-1-58023-225-8 **$8.99**

Bar/Bat Mitzvah Basics: A Practical Family Guide to Coming of Age Together
Edited by Cantor Helen Leneman 6 x 9, 240 pp, Quality PB, 978-1-58023-151-0 **$18.95**

The Bar/Bat Mitzvah Memory Book, 2nd Edition: An Album for Treasuring the
Spiritual Celebration *By Rabbi Jeffrey K. Salkin and Nina Salkin*
8 x 10, 48 pp, Deluxe HC, 2-color text, ribbon marker, 978-1-58023-263-0 **$19.99**

For Kids—Putting God on Your Guest List, 2nd Edition: How to Claim the
Spiritual Meaning of Your Bar or Bat Mitzvah *By Rabbi Jeffrey K. Salkin*
6 x 9, 144 pp, Quality PB, 978-1-58023-308-8 **$15.99** *For ages 11–13*

Putting God on the Guest List, 3rd Edition: How to Reclaim the Spiritual
Meaning of Your Child's Bar or Bat Mitzvah *By Rabbi Jeffrey K. Salkin*
6 x 9, 224 pp, Quality PB, 978-1-58023-222-7 **$16.99**; HC, 978-1-58023-260-9 **$24.99**
 Also Available: **Putting God on the Guest List Teacher's Guide**
8½ x 11, 48 pp, PB, 978-1-58023-226-5 **$8.99**

Tough Questions Jews Ask: A Young Adult's Guide to Building a Jewish Life
By Rabbi Edward Feinstein 6 x 9, 160 pp, Quality PB, 978-1-58023-139-8 **$14.99** *For ages 12 & up*
 Also Available: **Tough Questions Jews Ask Teacher's Guide**
8½ x 11, 72 pp, PB, 978-1-58023-187-9 **$8.95**

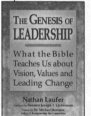

Bible Study/Midrash

**Abraham's Bind & Other Bible Tales of Trickery, Folly, Mercy
and Love** *By Michael J. Caduto*
Re-imagines many biblical characters, retelling their stories.
6 x 9, 224 pp, HC, 978-1-59473-186-0 **$19.99** *(A SkyLight Paths book)*

Ancient Secrets: Using the Stories of the Bible to Improve Our Everyday Lives
By Rabbi Levi Meier, PhD 5½ x 8½, 288 pp, Quality PB, 978-1-58023-064-3 **$16.95**

The Genesis of Leadership: What the Bible Teaches Us about Vision,
Values and Leading Change *By Rabbi Nathan Laufer; Foreword by Senator Joseph I. Lieberman*
Unlike other books on leadership, this one is rooted in the stories of the Bible.
6 x 9, 288 pp, HC, 978-1-58023-241-8 **$24.99**

Hineini in Our Lives: Learning How to Respond to Others through 14 Biblical Texts and
Personal Stories *By Norman J. Cohen* 6 x 9, 240 pp, Quality PB, 978-1-58023-274-6 **$16.99**

Moses and the Journey to Leadership: Timeless Lessons of Effective Management from
the Bible and Today's Leaders *By Dr. Norman J. Cohen* 6 x 9, 250 pp, HC, 978-1-58023-227-2 **$21.99**

Self, Struggle & Change: Family Conflict Stories in Genesis and Their Healing Insights for
Our Lives *By Norman J. Cohen* 6 x 9, 224 pp, Quality PB, 978-1-879045-66-8 **$18.99**

The Triumph of Eve & Other Subversive Bible Tales *By Matt Biers-Ariel*
5½ x 8½, 192 pp, Quality PB, 978-1-59473-176-1 **$14.99**; HC, 978-1-59473-040-5 **$19.99**
(A SkyLight Paths book)

The Wisdom of Judaism: An Introduction to the Values of the Talmud
By Rabbi Dov Peretz Elkins
Explores the essence of Judaism.   6 x 9, 192 pp, Quality PB, 978-1-58023-327-9 **$16.99**
 Also Available: **The Wisdom of Judaism Teacher's Guide**
8½ x 11, 18 pp, PB, 978-1-58023-350-7 **$8.99**

Or phone, fax, mail or e-mail to: **JEWISH LIGHTS Publishing**
Sunset Farm Offices, Route 4 • P.O. Box 237 • Woodstock, Vermont 05091
Tel: (802) 457-4000 • Fax: (802) 457-4004 • www.jewishlights.com
Credit card orders: **(800) 962-4544** (8:30AM–5:30PM ET Monday–Friday)
Generous discounts on quantity orders. SATISFACTION GUARANTEED. Prices subject to change.

Congregation Resources

The Art of Public Prayer, 2nd Edition: Not for Clergy Only *By Lawrence A. Hoffman*
6 x 9, 272 pp, Quality PB, 978-1-893361-06-5 **$19.99** *(A SkyLight Paths book)*

Becoming a Congregation of Learners: Learning as a Key to Revitalizing
Congregational Life *By Isa Aron, PhD; Foreword by Rabbi Lawrence A. Hoffman*
6 x 9, 304 pp, Quality PB, 978-1-58023-089-6 **$19.95**

Finding a Spiritual Home: How a New Generation of Jews Can Transform the
American Synagogue *By Rabbi Sidney Schwarz*
6 x 9, 352 pp, Quality PB, 978-1-58023-185-5 **$19.95**

Jewish Pastoral Care, 2nd Edition: A Practical Handbook from Traditional &
Contemporary Sources *Edited by Rabbi Dayle A. Friedman*
6 x 9, 528 pp, HC, 978-1-58023-221-0 **$40.00**

Jewish Spiritual Direction: An Innovative Guide from Traditional and Contemporary
Sources *Edited by Rabbi Howard A. Addison and Barbara Eve Breitman*
6 x 9, 368 pp, HC, 978-1-58023-230-2 **$30.00**

The Self-Renewing Congregation: Organizational Strategies for Revitalizing
Congregational Life *By Isa Aron, PhD; Foreword by Dr. Ron Wolfson*
6 x 9, 304 pp, Quality PB, 978-1-58023-166-4 **$19.95**

Spiritual Community: The Power to Restore Hope, Commitment and Joy
By Rabbi David A. Teutsch, PhD 5½ x 8½, 144 pp, HC, 978-1-58023-270-8 **$19.99**

The Spirituality of Welcoming: How to Transform Your Congregation into a
Sacred Community *By Dr. Ron Wolfson* 6 x 9, 224 pp, Quality PB, 978-1-58023-244-9 **$19.99**

Rethinking Synagogues: A New Vocabulary for Congregational Life
By Rabbi Lawrence A. Hoffman 6 x 9, 240 pp, Quality PB, 978-1-58023-248-7 **$19.99**

Children's Books

What You Will See Inside a Synagogue
By Rabbi Lawrence A. Hoffman and Dr. Ron Wolfson; Full-color photos by Bill Aron
A colorful, fun-to-read introduction that explains the ways and whys of Jewish
worship and religious life.
8½ x 10½, 32 pp, Full-color photos, HC, 978-1-59473-012-2 **$17.99** *For ages 6 & up (A SkyLight Paths book)*

The Kids' Fun Book of Jewish Time
By Emily Sper 9 x 7½, 24 pp, Full-color illus., HC, 978-1-58023-311-8 **$16.99**

In God's Hands
By Lawrence Kushner and Gary Schmidt 9 x 12, 32 pp, HC, 978-1-58023-224-1 **$16.99**

Because Nothing Looks Like God
By Lawrence and Karen Kushner
Introduces children to the possibilities of spiritual life.
11 x 8½, 32 pp, Full-color illus., HC, 978-1-58023-092-6 **$17.99** *For ages 4 & up*
Also Available: **Because Nothing Looks Like God Teacher's Guide**
8½ x 11, 22 pp, PB, 978-1-58023-140-4 **$6.95** *For ages 5–8*
    Board Book Companions to *Because Nothing Looks Like God*
5 x 5, 24 pp, Full-color illus., SkyLight Paths Board Books *For ages 0–4*

What Does God Look Like? 978-1-893361-23-2 **$7.99**
How Does God Make Things Happen? 978-1-893361-24-9 **$7.95**
Where Is God? 978-1-893361-17-1 **$7.99**

The Book of Miracles: A Young Person's Guide to Jewish Spiritual Awareness
By Lawrence Kushner. All-new illustrations by the author
6 x 9, 96 pp, 2-color illus., HC, 978-1-879045-78-1 **$16.95** *For ages 9 and up*

In Our Image: God's First Creatures
By Nancy Sohn Swartz 9 x 12, 32 pp, Full-color illus., HC, 978-1-879045-99-6 **$16.95** *For ages 4 & up*
Also Available as a Board Book: **How Did the Animals Help God?**
5 x 5, 24 pp, Board, Full-color illus., 978-1-59473-044-3 **$7.99** *For ages 0–4 (A SkyLight Paths book)*

What Makes Someone a Jew?
By Lauren Seidman
Reflects the changing face of American Judaism.
10 x 8½, 32 pp, Full-color photos, Quality PB Original, 978-1-58023-321-7 **$8.99** *For ages 3–6*

Children's Books
by Sandy Eisenberg Sasso

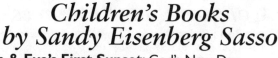

Adam & Eve's First Sunset: God's New Day
Engaging new story explores fear and hope, faith and gratitude in ways that will delight kids and adults—inspiring us to bless each of God's days and nights.
9 x 12, 32 pp, Full-color illus., HC, 978-1-58023-177-0 **$17.95** *For ages 4 & up*

Also Available as a Board Book: **Adam and Eve's New Day**
5 x 5, 24 pp, Full-color illus., Board, 978-1-59473-205-8 **$7.99** *For ages 0–4* *(A SkyLight Paths book)*

But God Remembered
Stories of Women from Creation to the Promised Land
Four different stories of women—Lillith, Serach, Bityah, and the Daughters of Z—teach us important values through their faith and actions.
9 x 12, 32 pp, Full-color illus., HC, 978-1-879045-43-9 **$16.95** *For ages 8 & up*

Cain & Abel: Finding the Fruits of Peace
Shows children that we have the power to deal with anger in positive ways. Provides questions for kids and adults to explore together.
9 x 12, 32 pp, Full-color illus., HC, 978-1-58023-123-7 **$16.95** *For ages 5 & up*

God in Between
If you wanted to find God, where would you look? This magical, mythical tale teaches that God can be found where we are: within all of us and the relationships between us.
9 x 12, 32 pp, Full-color illus., HC, 978-1-879045-86-6 **$16.95** *For ages 4 & up*

God's Paintbrush: Special 10th Anniversary Edition
Wonderfully interactive, invites children of all faiths and backgrounds to encounter God through moments in their own lives. Provides questions adult and child can explore together.
11 x 8½, 32 pp, Full-color illus., HC, 978-1-58023-195-4 **$17.95** *For ages 4 & up*

Also Available: **God's Paintbrush Teacher's Guide**
8½ x 11, 32 pp, PB, 978-1-879045-57-6 **$8.95**

God's Paintbrush Celebration Kit
A Spiritual Activity Kit for Teachers and Students of All Faiths, All Backgrounds
Additional activity sheets available:
8-Student Activity Sheet Pack (40 sheets/5 sessions), 978-1-58023-058-2 **$19.95**
Single-Student Activity Sheet Pack (5 sessions), 978-1-58023-059-9 **$3.95**

In God's Name
Like an ancient myth in its poetic text and vibrant illustrations, this award-winning modern fable about the search for God's name celebrates the diversity and, at the same time, the unity of all people.
9 x 12, 32 pp, Full-color illus., HC, 978-1-879045-26-2 **$16.99** *For ages 4 & up*

Also Available as a Board Book: **What Is God's Name?**
5 x 5, 24 pp, Board, Full-color illus., 978-1-893361-10-2 **$7.99** *For ages 0–4* *(A SkyLight Paths book)*

Also Available: **In God's Name video and study guide**
Computer animation, original music, and children's voices. 18 min. **$29.99**

Also Available in Spanish: **El nombre de Dios**
9 x 12, 32 pp, Full-color illus., HC, 978-1-893361-63-8 **$16.95** *(A SkyLight Paths book)*

Noah's Wife: The Story of Naamah
When God tells Noah to bring the animals of the world onto the ark, God also calls on Naamah, Noah's wife, to save each plant on Earth. Based on an ancient text.
9 x 12, 32 pp, Full-color illus., HC, 978-1-58023-134-3 **$16.95** *For ages 4 & up*

Also Available as a Board Book: **Naamah, Noah's Wife**
5 x 5, 24 pp, Full-color illus., Board, 978-1-893361-56-0 **$7.95** *For ages 0–4* *(A SkyLight Paths book)*

For Heaven's Sake: Finding God in Unexpected Places
9 x 12, 32 pp, Full-color illus., HC, 978-1-58023-054-4 **$16.95** *For ages 4 & up*

God Said Amen: Finding the Answers to Our Prayers
9 x 12, 32 pp, Full-color illus., HC, 978-1-58023-080-3 **$16.95** *For ages 4 & up*

Current Events/History

A Dream of Zion: American Jews Reflect on Why Israel Matters to Them
Edited by Rabbi Jeffrey K. Salkin Explores what Jewish people in America have to say about Israel. 6 x 9, 304 pp, HC, 978-1-58023-340-8 **$24.99**
Also Available: **A Dream of Zion Teacher's Guide** 8½ x 11, 18 pp, PB, 978-1-58023-356-9 **$8.99**

The Jewish Connection to Israel, the Promised Land: A Brief Introduction for Christians *By Rabbi Eugene Korn, PhD* 5½ x 8½, 192 pp, Quality PB, 978-1-58023-318-7 **$14.99**

The Story of the Jews: A 4,000-Year Adventure—A Graphic History Book
Written & illustrated by Stan Mack 6 x 9, 288 pp, illus., Quality PB, 978-1-58023-155-8 **$16.99**

A 4,000-Year Adventure
Stan Mack

Hannah Senesh: Her Life and Diary, the First Complete Edition
By Hannah Senesh; Foreword by Marge Piercy; Preface by Eitan Senesh
6 x 9, 368 pp, Quality PB, 978-1-58023-342-2 **$19.99**; 352 pp, HC, 978-1-58023-212-8 **$24.99**

The Ethiopian Jews of Israel: Personal Stories of Life in the Promised Land *By Len Lyons, PhD; Foreword by Alan Dershowitz; Photographs by Ilan Ossendryver* Recounts, through photographs and words, stories of Ethiopian Jews.
10½ x 10, 240 pp, 100 full-color photos, HC, 978-1-58023-323-1 **$34.99**

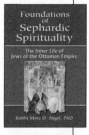
Foundations of Sephardic Spirituality
The Inner Life of Jews of the Ottoman Empire
Rabbi Marc D. Angel, PhD

Foundations of Sephardic Spirituality: The Inner Life of Jews of the Ottoman Empire
By Rabbi Marc D. Angel, PhD 6 x 9, 224 pp, HC, 978-1-58023-243-2 **$24.99**

Judaism and Justice: The Jewish Passion to Repair the World
By Rabbi Sidney Schwarz 6 x 9, 250 pp, HC, 978-1-58023-312-5 **$24.99**

Ecology/Environment

A Wild Faith: Jewish Ways into Wilderness, Wilderness Ways into Judaism
By Rabbi Mike Comins; Foreword by Nigel Savage
Offers ways to enliven and deepen your spiritual life through wilderness experience.
6 x 9, 240 pp, Quality PB, 978-1-58023-316-3 **$16.99**

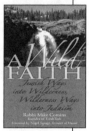
A Wild Faith
Jewish Ways into Wilderness, Wilderness Ways into Judaism
Rabbi Mike Comins

Ecology & the Jewish Spirit: Where Nature & the Sacred Meet
Edited by Ellen Bernstein 6 x 9, 288 pp, Quality PB, 978-1-58023-082-7 **$16.95**

Torah of the Earth: Exploring 4,000 Years of Ecology in Jewish Thought
Vol. 1: Biblical Israel: One Land, One People; Rabbinic Judaism: One People, Many Lands
Vol. 2: Zionism: One Land, Two Peoples; Eco-Judaism: One Earth, Many Peoples
Edited by Arthur Waskow Vol. 1: 6 x 9, 272 pp, Quality PB, 978-1-58023-086-5 **$19.95**
Vol. 2: 6 x 9, 336 pp, Quality PB, 978-1-58023-087-2 **$19.95**

The Way Into Judaism and the Environment
By Jeremy Benstein 6 x 9, 224 pp, HC, 978-1-58023-268-5 **$24.99**

Grief/Healing

Healing and the Jewish Imagination: Spiritual and Practical Perspectives on Judaism and Health *Edited by Rabbi William Cutter, PhD*
Explores Judaism for comfort in times of illness and perspectives on suffering.
6 x 9, 240 pp, HC, 978-1-58023-314-9 **$24.99**

HEALING and the JEWISH IMAGINATION
Spiritual and Practical Perspectives on Judaism and Health
Edited by Rabbi William Cutter, PhD

Grief in Our Seasons: A Mourner's Kaddish Companion *By Rabbi Kerry M. Olitzky*
4½ x 6½, 448 pp, Quality PB, 978-1-879045-55-2 **$15.95**

Healing of Soul, Healing of Body: Spiritual Leaders Unfold the Strength & Solace in Psalms *Edited by Rabbi Simkha Y. Weintraub, CSW*
6 x 9, 128 pp, 2-color illus. text, Quality PB, 978-1-879045-31-6 **$14.99**

2nd Edition
TEARS OF SORROW, SEEDS OF HOPE
A Jewish Spiritual Companion for Infertility and Pregnancy Loss
Rabbi Nina Beth Cardin

Mourning & Mitzvah, 2nd Edition: A Guided Journal for Walking the Mourner's Path through Grief to Healing *By Anne Brener, LCSW*
7½ x 9, 304 pp, Quality PB, 978-1-58023-113-8 **$19.99**

Tears of Sorrow, Seeds of Hope, 2nd Edition: A Jewish Spiritual Companion for Infertility and Pregnancy Loss *By Rabbi Nina Beth Cardin*
6 x 9, 208 pp, Quality PB, 978-1-58023-233-3 **$18.99**

A Time to Mourn, a Time to Comfort, 2nd Edition: A Guide to Jewish Bereavement *By Dr. Ron Wolfson*
7 x 9, 384 pp, Quality PB, 978-1-58023-253-1 **$19.99**

WHEN A Grandparent DIES
A Kid's Own Remembering Workbook for Dealing with Shiva and the Year Beyond
Nechama Liss-Levinson, Ph.D.

When a Grandparent Dies: A Kid's Own Remembering Workbook for Dealing with Shiva and the Year Beyond *By Nechama Liss-Levinson, PhD*
8 x 10, 48 pp, 2-color text, HC, 978-1-879045-44-6 **$15.95** *For ages 7–13*

Spirituality/Women's Interest

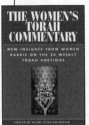

The Quotable Jewish Woman: Wisdom, Inspiration & Humor from the Mind & Heart
Edited and compiled by Elaine Bernstein Partnow
6 x 9, 496 pp, Quality PB, 978-1-58023-236-4 **$19.99**; HC, 978-1-58023-193-0 **$29.99**

The Divine Feminine in Biblical Wisdom Literature: Selections Annotated &
Explained *Translated and Annotated by Rabbi Rami Shapiro*
5½ x 8½, 240 pp, Quality PB, 978-1-59473-109-9 **$16.99** *(A SkyLight Paths book)*

The Women's Haftarah Commentary: New Insights from Women Rabbis on the
54 Weekly Haftarah Portions, the 5 Megillot & Special Shabbatot
Edited by Rabbi Elyse Goldstein 6 x 9, 560 pp, HC, 978-1-58023-133-6 **$39.99**

The Women's Torah Commentary: New Insights from Women Rabbis on the
54 Weekly Torah Portions *Edited by Rabbi Elyse Goldstein*
6 x 9, 496 pp, HC, 978-1-58023-076-6 **$34.95**

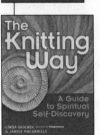

The Year Mom Got Religion: One Woman's Midlife Journey into Judaism
By Lee Meyerhoff Hendler 6 x 9, 208 pp, Quality PB, 978-1-58023-070-4 **$15.95**

See Holidays for *The Women's Passover Companion: Women's Reflections
on the Festival of Freedom* and *The Women's Seder Sourcebook: Rituals &
Readings for Use at the Passover Seder.* Also see Bar/Bat Mitzvah for *The
JGirl's Guide: The Young Jewish Woman's Handbook for Coming of Age.*

Spirituality / Crafts

(from SkyLight Paths, our sister imprint)

The Knitting Way: A Guide to Spiritual Self-Discovery
By Linda Skolnick and Janice MacDaniels
Shows how to use the practice of knitting to strengthen our spiritual selves.
7 x 9, 240 pp, Quality PB, 978-1-59473-079-5 **$16.99**

The Quilting Path: A Guide to Spiritual Self-Discovery through Fabric,
Thread and Kabbalah *By Louise Silk*
Explores how to cultivate personal growth through quilt making.
7 x 9, 192 pp, Quality PB, 978-1-59473-206-5 **$16.99**

The Painting Path: Embodying Spiritual Discovery through Yoga, Brush
and Color *By Linda Novick; Foreword by Richard Segalman*
Explores the divine connection you can experience through art.
7 x 9, 208 pp, 8-page full-color insert, Quality PB, 978-1-59473-226-3 **$18.99**

The Scrapbooking Journey: A Hands-On Guide to Spiritual Discovery
By Cory Richardson-Lauve; Foreword by Stacy Julian
Reveals how this craft can become a practice used to deepen and shape your life.
7 x 9, 176 pp, 8-page full-color insert, b/w photos, Quality PB, 978-1-59473-216-4 **$18.99**

Travel

Israel—A Spiritual Travel Guide, 2nd Edition
A Companion for the Modern Jewish Pilgrim
By Rabbi Lawrence A. Hoffman 4¾ x 10, 256 pp, Quality PB, illus., 978-1-58023-261-6 **$18.99**
Also Available: **The Israel Mission Leader's Guide** 978-1-58023-085-8 **$4.95**

12-Step

100 Blessings Every Day: Daily Twelve Step Recovery Affirmations, Exercises for
Personal Growth & Renewal Reflecting Seasons of the Jewish Year
By Rabbi Kerry M. Olitzky; Foreword by Rabbi Neil Gillman
4½ x 6½, 432 pp, Quality PB, 978-1-879045-30-9 **$16.99**

Recovery from Codependence: A Jewish Twelve Steps Guide to Healing Your Soul
By Rabbi Kerry M. Olitzky 6 x 9, 160 pp, Quality PB, 978-1-879045-32-3 **$13.95**

Twelve Jewish Steps to Recovery: A Personal Guide to Turning from Alcoholism &
Other Addictions—Drugs, Food, Gambling, Sex ...
By Rabbi Kerry M. Olitzky and Stuart A. Copans, MD; Preface by Abraham J. Twerski, MD
6 x 9, 144 pp, Quality PB, 978-1-879045-09-5 **$15.99**

Meditation

The Handbook of Jewish Meditation Practices
A Guide for Enriching the Sabbath and Other Days of Your Life
By Rabbi David A. Cooper Easy-to-learn meditation techniques.
6 x 9, 208 pp, Quality PB, 978-1-58023-102-2 **$16.95**

Discovering Jewish Meditation: Instruction & Guidance for Learning an Ancient
Spiritual Practice *By Nan Fink Gefen*
6 x 9, 208 pp, Quality PB, 978-1-58023-067-4 **$16.95**

A Heart of Stillness: A Complete Guide to Learning the Art of Meditation
By David A. Cooper 5½ x 8½, 272 pp, Quality PB, 978-1-893361-03-4 **$16.95** *(A SkyLight Paths book)*

Meditation from the Heart of Judaism: Today's Teachers Share Their Practices,
Techniques, and Faith *Edited by Avram Davis*
6 x 9, 256 pp, Quality PB, 978-1-58023-049-0 **$16.95**

Silence, Simplicity & Solitude: A Complete Guide to Spiritual Retreat at Home
By David A. Cooper 5½ x 8½, 336 pp, Quality PB, 978-1-893361-04-1 **$16.95**
(A SkyLight Paths book)

Ritual/Sacred Practice

The Jewish Dream Book: The Key to Opening the Inner Meaning of
Your Dreams *By Vanessa L. Ochs with Elizabeth Ochs; Full-color illus. by Kristina Swarner*
Instructions for how modern people can perform ancient Jewish dream practices
and dream interpretations drawn from the Jewish wisdom tradition.
8 x 8, 128 pp, Full-color illus., Deluxe PB w/flaps, 978-1-58023-132-9 **$16.95**

God in Your Body: Kabbalah, Mindfulness and Embodied Spiritual Practice
By Jay Michaelson
The first comprehensive treatment of the body in Jewish spiritual practice and an
essential guide to the sacred.
6 x 9, 288 pp, Quality PB, 978-1-58023-304-0 **$18.99**

The Book of Jewish Sacred Practices: CLAL's Guide to Everyday & Holiday
Rituals & Blessings *Edited by Rabbi Irwin Kula and Vanessa L. Ochs, PhD*
6 x 9, 368 pp, Quality PB, 978-1-58023-152-7 **$18.95**

Jewish Ritual: A Brief Introduction for Christians
By Rabbi Kerry M. Olitzky and Rabbi Daniel Judson
5½ x 8½, 144 pp, Quality PB, 978-1-58023-210-4 **$14.99**

The Rituals & Practices of a Jewish Life: A Handbook for Personal Spiritual
Renewal *Edited by Rabbi Kerry M. Olitzky and Rabbi Daniel Judson*
6 x 9, 272 pp, illus., Quality PB, 978-1-58023-169-5 **$18.95**

The Sacred Art of Lovingkindness: Preparing to Practice
By Rabbi Rami Shapiro 5½ x 8½, 176 pp, Quality PB, 978-1-59473-151-8 **$16.99**
(A SkyLight Paths book)

Science Fiction/Mystery & Detective Fiction

Mystery Midrash: An Anthology of Jewish Mystery & Detective Fiction
Edited by Lawrence W. Raphael; Preface by Joel Siegel
6 x 9, 304 pp, Quality PB, 978-1-58023-055-1 **$16.95**

Criminal Kabbalah: An Intriguing Anthology of Jewish Mystery & Detective Fiction
Edited by Lawrence W. Raphael; Foreword by Laurie R. King
6 x 9, 256 pp, Quality PB, 978-1-58023-109-1 **$16.95**

Wandering Stars: An Anthology of Jewish Fantasy & Science Fiction
Edited by Jack Dann; Introduction by Isaac Asimov
6 x 9, 272 pp, Quality PB, 978-1-58023-005-6 **$18.99**

More Wandering Stars: An Anthology of Outstanding Stories of Jewish Fantasy and
Science Fiction *Edited by Jack Dann; Introduction by Isaac Asimov*
6 x 9, 192 pp, Quality PB, 978-1-58023-063-6 **$16.95**

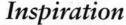

Inspiration

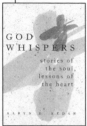

Happiness and the Human Spirit: The Spirituality of Becoming the Best You Can Be *By Abraham J. Twerski, MD*
Shows you that true happiness is attainable once you stop looking outside yourself for the source.   6 x 9, 176 pp, HC, 978-1-58023-343-9 **$19.99**

The Bridge to Forgiveness: Stories and Prayers for Finding God and Restoring Wholeness *By Rabbi Karyn D. Kedar*
Examines how forgiveness can be the bridge that connects us to wholeness and peace.
6 x 9, 176 pp, HC, 978-1-58023-324-8 **$19.99**

God's To-Do List: 103 Ways to Be an Angel and Do God's Work on Earth
By Dr. Ron Wolfson 6 x 9, 150 pp, Quality PB, 978-1-58023-301-9 **$15.99**

God in All Moments: Mystical & Practical Spiritual Wisdom from Hasidic Masters
Edited and translated by Or N. Rose with Ebn D. Leader
5½ x 8½, 192 pp, Quality PB, 978-1-58023-186-2 **$16.95**

Our Dance with God: Finding Prayer, Perspective and Meaning in the Stories of Our Lives *By Karyn D. Kedar* 6 x 9, 176 pp, Quality PB, 978-1-58023-202-9 **$16.99**
Also Available: **The Dance of the Dolphin** (HC edition of *Our Dance with God*)
6 x 9, 176 pp, HC, 978-1-58023-154-1 **$19.95**

The Empty Chair: Finding Hope and Joy—Timeless Wisdom from a Hasidic Master, Rebbe Nachman of Breslov *Adapted by Moshe Mykoff and the Breslov Research Institute*
4 x 6, 128 pp, 2-color text, Deluxe PB w/flaps, 978-1-879045-67-5 **$9.99**

The Gentle Weapon: Prayers for Everyday and Not-So-Everyday Moments—Timeless Wisdom from the Teachings of the Hasidic Master, Rebbe Nachman of Breslov *Adapted by Moshe Mykoff and S. C. Mizrahi, together with the Breslov Research Institute*
4 x 6, 144 pp, 2-color text, Deluxe PB w/flaps, 978-1-58023-022-3 **$9.99**

God Whispers: Stories of the Soul, Lessons of the Heart *By Karyn D. Kedar*
6 x 9, 176 pp, Quality PB, 978-1-58023-088-9 **$15.95**

Restful Reflections: Nighttime Inspiration to Calm the Soul, Based on Jewish Wisdom
By Rabbi Kerry M. Olitzky & Rabbi Lori Forman 4½ x 6½, 448 pp, Quality PB, 978-1-58023-091-9 **$15.95**

Sacred Intentions: Daily Inspiration to Strengthen the Spirit, Based on Jewish Wisdom
By Rabbi Kerry M. Olitzky and Rabbi Lori Forman 4½ x 6½, 448 pp, Quality PB, 978-1-58023-061-2 **$15.95**

Kabbalah/Mysticism/Enneagram

Awakening to Kabbalah: The Guiding Light of Spiritual Fulfillment
By Rav Michael Laitman, PhD 6 x 9, 192 pp, HC, 978-1-58023-264-7 **$21.99**

Seek My Face: A Jewish Mystical Theology *By Arthur Green*
6 x 9, 304 pp, Quality PB, 978-1-58023-130-5 **$19.95**

Zohar: Annotated & Explained
Translation and annotation by Daniel C. Matt; Foreword by Andrew Harvey
5½ x 8½, 176 pp, Quality PB, 978-1-893361-51-5 **$15.99** *(A SkyLight Paths book)*

Ehyeh: A Kabbalah for Tomorrow
By Arthur Green 6 x 9, 224 pp, Quality PB, 978-1-58023-213-5 **$16.99**

The Flame of the Heart: Prayers of a Chasidic Mystic *By Reb Noson of Breslov. Translated by David Sears with the Breslov Research Institute* 5 x 7¼, 160 pp, Quality PB, 978-1-58023-246-3 **$15.99**

The Gift of Kabbalah: Discovering the Secrets of Heaven, Renewing Your Life on Earth
By Tamar Frankiel, PhD 6 x 9, 256 pp, Quality PB, 978-1-58023-141-1 **$16.95;**
HC, 978-1-58023-108-4 **$21.95**

Kabbalah: A Brief Introduction for Christians
By Tamar Frankiel, PhD 5½ x 8½, 208 pp, Quality PB, 978-1-58023-303-3 **$16.99**

The Lost Princess and Other Kabbalistic Tales of Rebbe Nachman of Breslov
The Seven Beggars and Other Kabbalistic Tales of Rebbe Nachman of Breslov
Translated by Rabbi Aryeh Kaplan; Preface by Rabbi Chaim Kramer
Lost Princess: 6 x 9, 400 pp, Quality PB, 978-1-58023-217-3 **$18.99**
Seven Beggars: 6 x 9, 192 pp, Quality PB, 978-1-58023-250-0 **$16.99**

See also *The Way Into Jewish Mystical Tradition* in Spirituality / The Way Into... Series

Holidays/Holy Days

Rosh Hashanah Readings: Inspiration, Information and Contemplation
Yom Kippur Readings: Inspiration, Information and Contemplation
Edited by Rabbi Dov Peretz Elkins with Section Introductions from Arthur Green's These Are the Words
An extraordinary collection of readings, prayers and insights that enable the modern worshiper to enter into the spirit of the High Holy Days in a personal and powerful way, permitting the meaning of the Jewish New Year to enter the heart.
RHR: 6 x 9, 400 pp, HC, 978-1-58023-239-5 **$24.99**
YKR: 6 x 9, 368 pp, HC, 978-1-58023-271-5 **$24.99**

Jewish Holidays: A Brief Introduction for Christians
By Rabbi Kerry M. Olitzky and Rabbi Daniel Judson
5½ x 8½, 144 pp, Quality PB, 978-1-58023-302-6 **$16.99**

Reclaiming Judaism as a Spiritual Practice: Holy Days and Shabbat
By Rabbi Goldie Milgram
7 x 9, 272 pp, Quality PB, 978-1-58023-205-0 **$19.99**

7th Heaven: Celebrating Shabbat with Rebbe Nachman of Breslov
By Moshe Mykoff with the Breslov Research Institute
5⅛ x 8¼, 224 pp, Deluxe PB w/flaps, 978-1-58023-175-6 **$18.95**

Shabbat, 2nd Edition: The Family Guide to Preparing for and Celebrating the Sabbath
By Dr. Ron Wolfson 7 x 9, 320 pp, illus., Quality PB, 978-1-58023-164-0 **$19.99**

Hanukkah, 2nd Edition: The Family Guide to Spiritual Celebration
By Dr. Ron Wolfson. Edited by Joel Lurie Grishaver.
7 x 9, 240 pp, illus., Quality PB, 978-1-58023-122-0 **$18.95**

The Jewish Family Fun Book: Holiday Projects, Everyday Activities, and Travel Ideas
with Jewish Themes *By Danielle Dardashti and Roni Sarig. Illus. by Avi Katz.*
6 x 9, 288 pp, 70+ b/w illus. & diagrams, Quality PB, 978-1-58023-171-8 **$18.95**

The Jewish Lights Book of Fun Classroom Activities: Simple and Seasonal
Projects for Teachers and Students *By Danielle Dardashti and Roni Sarig*
6 x 9, 240 pp, Quality PB, 978-1-58023-206-7 **$19.99**

Passover

My People's Passover Haggadah
Traditional Texts, Modern Commentaries
Edited by Rabbi Lawrence A. Hoffman, PhD, and David Arnow, PhD
A diverse and exciting collection of commentaries on the traditional Passover Haggadah—in two volumes!
Vol. 1: 7 x 10, 304 pp, HC, 978-1-58023-354-5 **$24.99**
Vol. 2: 7 x 10, 320 pp, HC, 978-1-58023-346-0 **$24.99**

Leading the Passover Journey
The Seder's Meaning Revealed, the Haggadah's Story Retold
By Rabbi Nathan Laufer
Uncovers the hidden meaning of the Seder's rituals and customs.
6 x 9, 224 pp, HC, 978-1-58023-211-1 **$24.99**

The Women's Passover Companion: Women's Reflections on the Festival of Freedom
Edited by Rabbi Sharon Cohen Anisfeld, Tara Mohr, and Catherine Spector
6 x 9, 352 pp, Quality PB, 978-1-58023-231-9 **$19.99**

The Women's Seder Sourcebook: Rituals & Readings for Use at the Passover Seder
Edited by Rabbi Sharon Cohen Anisfeld, Tara Mohr, and Catherine Spector
6 x 9, 384 pp, Quality PB, 978-1-58023-232-6 **$19.99**

Creating Lively Passover Seders: A Sourcebook of Engaging Tales, Texts & Activities
By David Arnow, PhD 7 x 9, 416 pp, Quality PB, 978-1-58023-184-8 **$24.99**

Passover, 2nd Edition: The Family Guide to Spiritual Celebration
By Dr. Ron Wolfson with Joel Lurie Grishaver 7 x 9, 352 pp, Quality PB, 978-1-58023-174-9 **$19.95**

Life Cycle
Marriage / Parenting / Family / Aging

The New Jewish Baby Album: Creating and Celebrating the Beginning of a Spiritual Life—A Jewish Lights Companion
By the Editors at Jewish Lights. Foreword by Anita Diamant. Preface by Rabbi Sandy Eisenberg Sasso.
A spiritual keepsake that will be treasured for generations. More than just a memory book, *shows you how—and why it's important*—to create a Jewish home and a Jewish life. 8 x 10, 64 pp, Deluxe Padded HC, Full-color illus., 978-1-58023-138-1 **$19.95**

The Jewish Pregnancy Book: A Resource for the Soul, Body & Mind during Pregnancy, Birth & the First Three Months
By Sandy Falk, MD, and Rabbi Daniel Judson, with Steven A. Rapp
Includes medical information, prayers and rituals for each stage of pregnancy, from a liberal Jewish perspective. 7 x 10, 208 pp, Quality PB, b/w photos, 978-1-58023-178-7 **$16.95**

Celebrating Your New Jewish Daughter: Creating Jewish Ways to Welcome Baby Girls into the Covenant—New and Traditional Ceremonies *By Debra Nussbaum Cohen; Foreword by Rabbi Sandy Eisenberg Sasso* 6 x 9, 272 pp, Quality PB, 978-1-58023-090-2 **$18.95**

The New Jewish Baby Book, 2nd Edition: Names, Ceremonies & Customs—A Guide for Today's Families *By Anita Diamant* 6 x 9, 336 pp, Quality PB, 978-1-58023-251-7 **$19.99**

Parenting As a Spiritual Journey: Deepening Ordinary and Extraordinary Events into Sacred Occasions *By Rabbi Nancy Fuchs-Kreimer*
6 x 9, 224 pp, Quality PB, 978-1-58023-016-2 **$16.95**

Parenting Jewish Teens: A Guide for the Perplexed
By Joanne Doades
Explores the questions and issues that shape the world in which today's Jewish teenagers live.
6 x 9, 200 pp, Quality PB, 978-1-58023-305-7 **$16.99**

Judaism for Two: A Spiritual Guide for Strengthening and Celebrating Your Loving Relationship *By Rabbi Nancy Fuchs-Kreimer and Rabbi Nancy H. Wiener; Foreword by Rabbi Elliot N. Dorff* Addresses the ways Jewish teachings can enhance and strengthen committed relationships. 6 x 9, 224 pp, Quality PB, 978-1-58023-254-8 **$16.99**

Embracing the Covenant: Converts to Judaism Talk About Why & How
By Rabbi Allan Berkowitz and Patti Moskovitz 6 x 9, 192 pp, Quality PB, 978-1-879045-50-7 **$16.95**

The Guide to Jewish Interfaith Family Life: An InterfaithFamily.com Handbook
Edited by Ronnie Friedland and Edmund Case 6 x 9, 384 pp, Quality PB, 978-1-58023-153-4 **$18.95**

Introducing My Faith and My Community
The Jewish Outreach Institute Guide for the Christian in a Jewish Interfaith Relationship
By Rabbi Kerry M. Olitzky 6 x 9, 176 pp, Quality PB, 978-1-58023-192-3 **$16.99**

Making a Successful Jewish Interfaith Marriage: The Jewish Outreach Institute Guide to Opportunities, Challenges and Resources *By Rabbi Kerry M. Olitzky with Joan Peterson Littman*
6 x 9, 176 pp, Quality PB, 978-1-58023-170-1 **$16.95**

The Creative Jewish Wedding Book: A Hands-On Guide to New & Old Traditions, Ceremonies & Celebrations *By Gabrielle Kaplan-Mayer*
9 x 9, 288 pp, b/w photos, Quality PB, 978-1-58023-194-7 **$19.99**

Divorce Is a Mitzvah: A Practical Guide to Finding Wholeness and Holiness When Your Marriage Dies *By Rabbi Perry Netter; Afterword by Rabbi Laura Geller.*
6 x 9, 224 pp, Quality PB, 978-1-58023-172-5 **$16.95**

A Heart of Wisdom: Making the Jewish Journey from Midlife through the Elder Years
Edited by Susan Berrin; Foreword by Harold Kushner
6 x 9, 384 pp, Quality PB, 978-1-58023-051-3 **$18.95**

So That Your Values Live On: Ethical Wills and How to Prepare Them
Edited by Jack Riemer and Nathaniel Stampfer
6 x 9, 272 pp, Quality PB, 978-1-879045-34-7 **$18.99**

Spirituality

Journeys to a Jewish Life: Inspiring Stories from the Spiritual Journeys of American Jews *By Paula Amann*
Examines the soul treks of Jews lost and found. 6 x 9, 208 pp, HC, 978-1-58023-317-0 **$19.99**

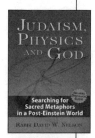

The Adventures of Rabbi Harvey: A Graphic Novel of Jewish Wisdom and Wit in the Wild West *By Steve Sheinkin*
Jewish and American folktales combine in this witty and original graphic novel collection. Creatively retold and set on the western frontier of the 1870s.
6 x 9, 144 pp, Full-color illus., Quality PB, 978-1-58023-310-1 **$16.99**
Also Available: **The Adventures of Rabbi Harvey Teacher's Guide**
8½ x 11, 32 pp, PB, 978-1-58023-326-2 **$8.99**

Ethics of the Sages: Pirke Avot—Annotated & Explained
Translation and Annotation by Rabbi Rami Shapiro
5½ x 8½, 192 pp, Quality PB, 978-1-59473-207-2 **$16.99** *(A SkyLight Paths book)*

A Book of Life: Embracing Judaism as a Spiritual Practice
By Michael Strassfeld 6 x 9, 528 pp, Quality PB, 978-1-58023-247-0 **$19.99**

Meaning and Mitzvah: Daily Practices for Reclaiming Judaism through Prayer, God, Torah, Hebrew, Mitzvot and Peoplehood *By Rabbi Goldie Milgram*
7 x 9, 336 pp, Quality PB, 978-1-58023-256-2 **$19.99** .

The Soul of the Story: Meetings with Remarkable People
By Rabbi David Zeller 6 x 9, 288 pp, HC, 978-1-58023-272-2 **$21.99**

Aleph-Bet Yoga: Embodying the Hebrew Letters for Physical and Spiritual Well-Being
By Steven A. Rapp. Foreword by Tamar Frankiel, PhD and Judy Greenfeld. Preface by Hart Lazer.
7 x 10, 128 pp, b/w photos, Quality PB, Layflat binding, 978-1-58023-162-6 **$16.95**

Does the Soul Survive? A Jewish Journey to Belief in Afterlife, Past Lives & Living with Purpose *By Rabbi Elie Kaplan Spitz; Foreword by Brian L. Weiss, MD*
6 x 9, 288 pp, Quality PB, 978-1-58023-165-7 **$16.99**

First Steps to a New Jewish Spirit: Reb Zalman's Guide to Recapturing the Intimacy & Ecstasy in Your Relationship with God *By Rabbi Zalman M. Schachter-Shalomi with Donald Gropman* 6 x 9, 144 pp, Quality PB, 978-1-58023-182-4 **$16.95**

God in Our Relationships: Spirituality between People from the Teachings of Martin Buber *By Rabbi Dennis S. Ross* 5½ x 8½, 160 pp, Quality PB, 978-1-58023-147-3 **$16.95**

Judaism, Physics and God: Searching for Sacred Metaphors in a Post-Einstein World
By Rabbi David W. Nelson 6 x 9, 368 pp, Quality PB, inc. reader's discussion guide, 978-1-58023-306-4 **$18.99**;
HC, 352 pp, 978-1-58023-252-4 **$24.99**

The Jewish Lights Spirituality Handbook: A Guide to Understanding, Exploring & Living a Spiritual Life *Edited by Stuart M. Matlins*
What exactly is "Jewish" about spirituality? How do I make it a part of my life? Fifty of today's foremost spiritual leaders share their ideas and experience with us.
6 x 9, 456 pp, Quality PB, 978-1-58023-093-3 **$19.99**

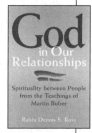

Bringing the Psalms to Life: How to Understand and Use the Book of Psalms
By Daniel F. Polish 6 x 9, 208 pp, Quality PB, 978-1-58023-157-2 **$16.95**;
HC, 978-1-58023-077-3 **$21.95**

God & the Big Bang: Discovering Harmony between Science & Spirituality
By Daniel C. Matt 6 x 9, 216 pp, Quality PB, 978-1-879045-89-7 **$16.99**

Minding the Temple of the Soul: Balancing Body, Mind, and Spirit through Traditional Jewish Prayer, Movement, and Meditation *By Tamar Frankiel, PhD, and Judy Greenfeld*
7 x 10, 184 pp, illus., Quality PB, 978-1-879045-64-4 **$16.95**
Audiotape of the Blessings and Meditations: 60 min. **$9.95**
Videotape of the Movements and Meditations: 46 min. **$20.00**

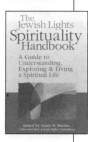

One God Clapping: The Spiritual Path of a Zen Rabbi *By Alan Lew with Sherril Jaffe*
5½ x 8½, 336 pp, Quality PB, 978-1-58023-115-2 **$16.95**

There Is No Messiah ... and You're It: The Stunning Transformation of Judaism's Most Provocative Idea *By Rabbi Robert N. Levine, DD*
6 x 9, 192 pp, Quality PB, 978-1-58023-255-5 **$16.99**

These Are the Words: A Vocabulary of Jewish Spiritual Life
By Arthur Green 6 x 9, 304 pp, Quality PB, 978-1-58023-107-7 **$18.95**

Theology/Philosophy

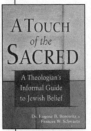

A Touch of the Sacred: A Theologian's Informal Guide to Jewish Belief
By Dr. Eugene B. Borowitz and Frances W. Schwartz Explores the musings from the
leading theologian of liberal Judaism. 6 x 9, 256 pp, HC, 978-1-58023-337-8 **$21.99**

Talking about God: Exploring the Meaning of Religious Life with
Kierkegaard, Buber, Tillich and Heschel *By Daniel F. Polish, PhD*
Examines the meaning of the human religious experience with the greatest theolo-
gians of modern times. 6 x 9, 160 pp, HC, 978-1-59473-230-0 **$21.99** *(A SkyLight Paths book)*

Jews & Judaism in the 21st Century: Human Responsibility, the
Presence of God, and the Future of the Covenant
Edited by Rabbi Edward Feinstein; Foreword by Paula E. Hyman
Five celebrated leaders in Judaism examine contemporary Jewish life.
6 x 9, 192 pp, HC, 978-1-58023-315-6 **$24.99**

Christians and Jews in Dialogue: Learning in the Presence of the Other
By Mary C. Boys and Sara S. Lee; Foreword by Dr. Dorothy Bass
6 x 9, 240 pp, HC, 978-1-59473-144-0 **$21.99** *(A SkyLight Paths book)*

The Death of Death: Resurrection and Immortality in Jewish Thought
By Neil Gillman 6 x 9, 336 pp, Quality PB, 978-1-58023-081-0 **$18.95**

Ethics of the Sages: Pirke Avot—Annotated & Explained
Translation & Annotation by Rabbi Rami Shapiro
5½ x 8½, 208 pp, Quality PB, 978-1-59473-207-2 **$16.99** *(A SkyLight Paths book)*

Hasidic Tales: Annotated & Explained
By Rabbi Rami Shapiro; Foreword by Andrew Harvey
5½ x 8½, 240 pp, Quality PB, 978-1-893361-86-7 **$16.95** *(A SkyLight Paths Book)*

A Heart of Many Rooms: Celebrating the Many Voices within Judaism
By David Hartman 6 x 9, 352 pp, Quality PB, 978-1-58023-156-5 **$19.95**

The Hebrew Prophets: Selections Annotated & Explained
Translation & Annotation by Rabbi Rami Shapiro; Foreword by Zalman M. Schachter-Shalomi
5½ x 8½, 224 pp, Quality PB, 978-1-59473-037-5 **$16.99** *(A SkyLight Paths book)*

A Jewish Understanding of the New Testament
By Rabbi Samuel Sandmel; Preface by Rabbi David Sandmel
5½ x 8½, 368 pp, Quality PB, 978-1-59473-048-1 **$19.99** *(A SkyLight Paths book)*

Keeping Faith with the Psalms: Deepen Your Relationship with God Using the Book
of Psalms *By Daniel F. Polish* 6 x 9, 320 pp, Quality PB, 978-1-58023-300-2 **$18.99**

A Living Covenant: The Innovative Spirit in Traditional Judaism
By David Hartman 6 x 9, 368 pp, Quality PB, 978-1-58023-011-7 **$20.00**

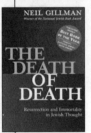

Love and Terror in the God Encounter
The Theological Legacy of Rabbi Joseph B. Soloveitchik
By David Hartman 6 x 9, 240 pp, Quality PB, 978-1-58023-176-3 **$19.95**

The Personhood of God: Biblical Theology, Human Faith and the Divine Image
By Dr. Yochanan Muffs; Foreword by Dr. David Hartman 6 x 9, 240 pp, HC, 978-1-58023-265-4 **$24.99**

Traces of God: Seeing God in Torah, History and Everyday Life
By Neil Gillman 6 x 9, 240 pp, HC, 978-1-58023-249-4 **$21.99**

We Jews and Jesus: Exploring Theological Differences for Mutual Understanding
By Rabbi Samuel Sandmel; Preface by Rabbi David Sandmel
6 x 9, 176 pp, Quality PB, 978-1-59473-208-9 **$16.99** *(A SkyLight Paths book)*

Your Word Is Fire: The Hasidic Masters on Contemplative Prayer
Edited and translated by Arthur Green and Barry W. Holtz
6 x 9, 160 pp, Quality PB, 978-1-879045-25-5 **$15.95**

I Am Jewish
Personal Reflections Inspired by the Last Words of Daniel Pearl
Almost 150 Jews—both famous and not—from all walks of life, from all around
the world, write about many aspects of their Judaism.
Edited by Judea and Ruth Pearl
6 x 9, 304 pp, Deluxe PB w/flaps, 978-1-58023-259-3 **$18.99**
**Download a free copy of the *I Am Jewish Teacher's Guide* at our website:
www.jewishlights.com**

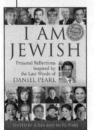

Theology/Philosophy/The Way Into... Series

The Way Into... series offers an accessible and highly usable "guided tour" of the Jewish faith, people, history and beliefs—in total, an introduction to Judaism that will enable you to understand and interact with the sacred texts of the Jewish tradition. Each volume is written by a leading contemporary scholar and teacher, and explores one key aspect of Judaism. *The Way Into...* series enables all readers to achieve a real sense of Jewish cultural literacy through guided study.

The Way Into Encountering God in Judaism
By Neil Gillman
For everyone who wants to understand how Jews have encountered God throughout history and today.
6 x 9, 240 pp, Quality PB, 978-1-58023-199-2 **$18.99**; HC, 978-1-58023-025-4 **$21.95**
Also Available: **The Jewish Approach to God:** A Brief Introduction for Christians
By Neil Gillman
5½ x 8½, 192 pp, Quality PB, 978-1-58023-190-9 **$16.95**

The Way Into Jewish Mystical Tradition
By Lawrence Kushner
Allows readers to interact directly with the sacred mystical text of the Jewish tradition. An accessible introduction to the concepts of Jewish mysticism, their religious and spiritual significance and how they relate to life today.
6 x 9, 224 pp, Quality PB, 978-1-58023-200-5 **$18.99**; HC, 978-1-58023-029-2 **$21.95**

The Way Into Jewish Prayer
By Lawrence A. Hoffman
Opens the door to 3,000 years of Jewish prayer, making available all anyone needs to feel at home in the Jewish way of communicating with God.
6 x 9, 208 pp, Quality PB, 978-1-58023-201-2 **$18.99**

Also Available: **The Way Into Jewish Prayer Teacher's Guide**
By Rabbi Jennifer Ossakow Goldsmith
8½ x 11, 42 pp, PB, 978-1-58023-345-3 **$8.99**
Visit our website to download a free copy.

The Way Into Judaism and the Environment
By Jeremy Benstein
Explores the ways in which Judaism contributes to contemporary social-environmental issues, the extent to which Judaism is part of the problem and how it can be part of the solution.
6 x 9, 288 pp, HC, 978-1-58023-268-5 **$24.99**

The Way Into *Tikkun Olam* (Repairing the World)
By Elliot N. Dorff
An accessible introduction to the Jewish concept of the individual's responsibility to care for others and repair the world.
6 x 9, 320 pp, HC, 978-1-58023-269-2 **$24.99**; 304 pp, Quality PB, 978-1-58023-328-6 **$18.99**

The Way Into Torah
By Norman J. Cohen
Helps guide in the exploration of the origins and development of Torah, explains why it should be studied and how to do it.
6 x 9, 176 pp, Quality PB, 978-1-58023-198-5 **$16.99**

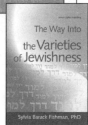

The Way Into the Varieties of Jewishness
By Sylvia Barack Fishman, PhD
Explores the religious and historical understanding of what it has meant to be Jewish from ancient times to the present controversy over "Who is a Jew?"
6 x 9, 288 pp, HC, 978-1-58023-030-8 **$24.99**

Spirituality/Lawrence Kushner

Filling Words with Light: Hasidic and Mystical Reflections on Jewish Prayer
By Lawrence Kushner and Nehemia Polen
5½ x 8½, 176 pp, Quality PB, 978-1-58023-238-8 **$16.99**; HC, 978-1-58023-216-6 **$21.99**

The Book of Letters: A Mystical Hebrew Alphabet
Popular HC Edition, 6 x 9, 80 pp, 2-color text, 978-1-879045-00-2 **$24.95**
Collector's Limited Edition, 9 x 12, 80 pp, gold foil embossed pages, w/limited edition silkscreened print, 978-1-879045-04-0 **$349.00**

The Book of Miracles: A Young Person's Guide to Jewish Spiritual Awareness
6 x 9, 96 pp, 2-color illus., HC, 978-1-879045-78-1 **$16.95** *For ages 9 and up*

The Book of Words: Talking Spiritual Life, Living Spiritual Talk
6 x 9, 160 pp, Quality PB, 978-1-58023-020-9 **$16.95**

Eyes Remade for Wonder: A Lawrence Kushner Reader *Introduction by Thomas Moore*
6 x 9, 240 pp, Quality PB, 978-1-58023-042-1 **$18.95**

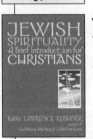

God Was in This Place & I, i Did Not Know: Finding Self, Spirituality and Ultimate Meaning   6 x 9, 192 pp, Quality PB, 978-1-879045-33-0 **$16.95**

Honey from the Rock: An Introduction to Jewish Mysticism
6 x 9, 176 pp, Quality PB, 978-1-58023-073-5 **$16.95**

Invisible Lines of Connection: Sacred Stories of the Ordinary
5½ x 8½, 160 pp, Quality PB, 978-1-879045-98-9 **$15.95**

Jewish Spirituality—A Brief Introduction for Christians
5½ x 8½, 112 pp, Quality PB, 978-1-58023-150-3 **$12.95**

The River of Light: Jewish Mystical Awareness
6 x 9, 192 pp, Quality PB, 978-1-58023-096-4 **$16.95**

The Way Into Jewish Mystical Tradition
6 x 9, 224 pp, Quality PB, 978-1-58023-200-5 **$18.99**; HC, 978-1-58023-029-2 **$21.95**

Spirituality/Prayer

My People's Passover Haggadah: Traditional Texts, Modern Commentaries
Edited by Rabbi Lawrence A. Hoffman, PhD, and David Arnow, PhD Diverse commentaries on the traditional Passover Haggadah—in two volumes! Vol. 1: 7 x 10, 304 pp, HC 978-1-58023-354-5 **$24.99** Vol. 2: 7 x 10, 320 pp, HC, 978-1-58023-346-0 **$24.99**

Witnesses to the One: The Spiritual History of the *Sh'ma* By Rabbi Joseph B. Meszler; Foreword by Rabbi Elyse Goldstein 6 x 9, 176 pp, HC, 978-1-58023-309-5 **$19.99**

My People's Prayer Book Series

Traditional Prayers, Modern Commentaries   *Edited by Rabbi Lawrence A. Hoffman*
Provides diverse and exciting commentary to the traditional liturgy, helping modern men and women find new wisdom in Jewish prayer, and bring liturgy into their lives. Each book includes Hebrew text, modern translation, and commentaries from all perspectives of the Jewish world.

Vol. 1—The *Sh'ma* and Its Blessings
7 x 10, 168 pp, HC, 978-1-879045-79-8 **$24.99**

Vol. 2—The *Amidah*
7 x 10, 240 pp, HC, 978-1-879045-80-4 **$24.95**

Vol. 3—*P'sukei D'zimrah* (Morning Psalms)
7 x 10, 240 pp, HC, 978-1-879045-81-1 **$24.95**

Vol. 4—*Seder K'riat Hatorah* (The Torah Service)
7 x 10, 264 pp, HC, 978-1-879045-82-8 **$23.95**

Vol. 5—*Birkhot Hashachar* (Morning Blessings)
7 x 10, 240 pp, HC, 978-1-879045-83-5 **$24.95**

Vol. 6—*Tachanun* and Concluding Prayers
7 x 10, 240 pp, HC, 978-1-879045-84-2 **$24.95**

Vol. 7—Shabbat at Home
7 x 10, 240 pp, HC, 978-1-879045-85-9 **$24.95**

Vol. 8—*Kabbalat Shabbat* (Welcoming Shabbat in the Synagogue)
7 x 10, 240 pp, HC, 978-1-58023-121-3 **$24.99**

Vol. 9—Welcoming the Night: *Minchah* and *Ma'ariv* (Afternoon and Evening Prayer) 7 x 10, 272 pp, HC, 978-1-58023-262-3 **$24.99**

Vol. 10—Shabbat Morning: *Shacharit* and *Musaf* (Morning and Additional Services) 7 x 10, 240 pp, HC, 978-1-58023-240-1 **$24.99**

Passover Resources

Leading the Passover Journey
The Seder's Meaning Revealed, the Haggadah's Story Retold
By Rabbi Nathan Laufer
Uncovers the hidden meaning of the Seder's rituals and customs

6 x 9, 224 pp, Hardcover
ISBN-13: 978-1-58023-211-1; ISBN-10: 1-58023-211-6 **$24.99**

Passover, 2nd Edition
The Family Guide to Spiritual Celebration
By Dr. Ron Wolfson with Joel Lurie Grishaver
Concepts, ritual and ceremony with step-by-step procedures for observance.

7 x 9, 352 pp, Quality PB Original
ISBN-13: 978-1-58023-174-9; ISBN-10: 1-58023-174-8 **$19.95**

Creating Lively Passover Seders
A Sourcebook of Engaging Tales, Texts and Activities
By David Arnow, PhD
No more boring Seders! Engaging material for creating a truly exciting evening.

7 x 9, 416 pp, Quality PB Original
ISBN-13: 978-1-58023-184-8; ISBN-10: 1-58023-184-5 **$24.99**

Brings together the voices of over 150 Jewish women, providing in *The Women's Passover Companion* a complete exploration of the questions at the heart of this contemporary ritual, and in *The Women's Seder Sourcebook* over 200 texts and ideas for a women's seder and practical guidance for planning the event.
Edited by Rabbi Sharon Cohen Anisfield, Tara Mohr, and Catherine Spector.

The Women's Seder Sourcebook
Rituals and Readings for Use at the Passover Seder

6 x 9, 384 pp, Quality PB
ISBN-13: 978-1-58023-232-6; ISBN-10: 1-58023-232-9 **$19.99**

The Women's Passover Companion
Women's Reflections on the Festival of Freedom

6 x 9, 352 pp, Quality PB
ISBN-13: 978-1-58023-231-9; ISBN-10: 1-58023-231-0 **$19.99**

About Jewish Lights

People of all faiths and backgrounds yearn for books that attract, engage, educate, and spiritually inspire.

Our principal goal is to stimulate thought and help all people learn about who the Jewish People are, where they come from, and what the future can be made to hold. While people of our diverse Jewish heritage are the primary audience, our books speak to people in the Christian world as well and will broaden their understanding of Judaism and the roots of their own faith.

We bring to you authors who are at the forefront of spiritual thought and experience. While each has something different to say, they all say it in a voice that you can hear.

Our books are designed to welcome you and then to engage, stimulate, and inspire. We judge our success not only by whether or not our books are beautiful and commercially successful, but by whether or not they make a difference in your life.

For your information and convenience, at the back of this book we have provided a list of other Jewish Lights books you might find interesting and useful. They cover all the categories of your life:

Bar/Bat Mitzvah	Life Cycle
Bible Study / Midrash	Meditation
Children's Books	Parenting
Congregation Resources	Prayer
Current Events / History	Ritual / Sacred Practice
Ecology/ Environment	Spirituality
Fiction: Mystery, Science Fiction	Theology / Philosophy
Grief / Healing	Travel
Holidays / Holy Days	12-Step
Inspiration	Women's Interest
Kabbalah / Mysticism / Enneagram	

Stuart M. Matlins, Publisher

Or phone, fax, mail or e-mail to: **JEWISH LIGHTS** Publishing
Sunset Farm Offices, Route 4 • P.O. Box 237 • Woodstock, Vermont 05091
Tel: (802) 457-4000 • Fax: (802) 457-4004 • www.jewishlights.com
Credit card orders: (800) 962-4544 (8:30AM–5:30PM ET Monday–Friday)
Generous discounts on quantity orders. SATISFACTION GUARANTEED. Prices subject to change.

For more information about each book, visit our website at www.jewishlights.com